# Good Intentions, Bad Outcomes

# Good Intentions, Bad Outcomes

*Social Policy, Informality, and Economic Growth in Mexico*

Santiago Levy

BROOKINGS INSTITUTION PRESS
*Washington, D.C.*

*Library of Congress Cataloging-in-Publication data*

Levy, Santiago.
  Good intentions, bad outcomes : social policy, informality, and economic growth in
Mexico / Santiago Levy.
      p.      cm.
  Summary: "Argues that incoherent social programs significantly contribute to poverty
and little growth. Proposes converting the existing social security system into universal
social entitlements. Advocates eliminating wage-based social security contributions and
raising consumption taxes on higher-income households to increase the rate of GDP
growth, reduce inequality, and improve benefits for workers"—Provided by publisher.
  Includes bibliographical references and index.
  ISBN 978-0-8157-5219-6 (pbk. : alk. paper)
  1. Mexico—Social policy. 2. Mexico—Social conditions—1970– I. Title.

HN113.5.L49 2008
331.10972—dc22                                                    2008005704

9 8 7 6 5 4 3 2 1

The paper used in this publication meets minimum requirements of the
American National Standard for Information Sciences—Permanence of Paper
for Printed Library Materials: ANSI Z39.48-1992.

Typeset in Adobe Garamond

Composition by Circle Graphics
Columbia, Maryland

Printed by R. R. Donnelley
Harrisonburg, Virginia

# Contents

Foreword     ix
*Strobe Talbott*

Acknowledgments     xv

Introduction     1
    *Main Hypothesis*     6
    *Organization*     9

**1**   Institutions, Workers, and Social Programs     11
    *Salaried and Nonsalaried Labor*     11
    *Labor Status and Social Programs*     16
    *Resources for Social Programs from 1998 to 2007*     26

**2**   Formality and Informality     33
    *Definitions*     33
    *Interpretation and Implications*     40

**3**   Workers' Valuation of Social Programs     47
    *Determinants of Workers' Valuation of Social Security*     47
    *Determinants of Workers' Valuation of Social Protection*     61
    *Wages and Social Benefits*     63
    *An Assessment*     66

**4   Social Programs and Poor Workers**                                                71
*Households and Workers in Progresa-Oportunidades*                                       71
*Poor Workers' Valuation of Social Programs*                                             79

**5   Mobility of Workers in the Labor Market**                                          85
*Labor Force*                                                                            85
*Mobility of Workers: Some Examples*                                                     91
*Evidence of Mobility from Social Security Registries*                                   96
*Evidence of Mobility from Employment Surveys*                                          111
*Mobility and Wage Rates*                                                               114
*Implications of Mobility for Social Policy*                                            129

**6   Social Programs, Welfare, and Productivity**                                      134
*Demand for Salaried and Nonsalaried Labor*                                             136
*The Labor Market with Formal and Informal Sectors*                                     142
*The Static Efficiency Costs of the Formal-Informal Dichotomy*                          155
*Empirical Estimates of Static Efficiency Costs*                                        160
*The Labor Market with Different Valuations for Poor Workers*                           163

**7   Productivity and Illegal Firms**                                                  166
*The Labor Market When Social Security Is Evaded*                                        166
*Illegal and Legal Firms*                                                               177
*Informality and the Size Distribution of Firms*                                        179
*Informality and the Demand for Legal and Illegal Labor*                                193
*Informality and the Composition of Output*                                             199

**8   Investment and Growth under Informality**                                         208
*Investment in the Formal and Informal Sectors*                                         208
*Social Programs and the Allocation of Aggregate Investment*                            211
*Investments in Labor Training and Technology Adoption*                                 214
*Remarks on Saving under Informality*                                                   216
*Growth and Job Creation under Persistent Informality*                                  219
*Static and Dynamic Efficiency Losses under Informality*                                223
*Implications for Poverty Reduction and Progresa-Oportunidades*                         225

**9   Social Programs and the Fiscal Accounts**                                         234
*Government Subsidies for Social Security*                                               234
*Feedback from Social Programs to the Fiscal Accounts*                                   240
*Is Social Policy Redistributive?*                                                      243

**10** Can Social Policy Increase Welfare and Growth?    253

*The Case for Reform*    253

*A Reference Equilibrium: Universal Social Entitlements*    256

*What Should Universal Social Entitlements Be?*    269

*How Much Would Universal Social Entitlements Cost?*    276

*Implications for Noncontributory Pensions*    280

*From Here to There: Isolated Reforms versus Step-by-Step Reform*    283

*A Final Word*    288

Appendixes

**1** Resources for Social Programs    293

**2** Regional Coverage of Social Programs    298

**3** Land Holdings of Progresa-Oportunidades Households    304

**4** Estimation of Mexico's Economically Active Population    306

**5** Mean Wage-Rate Comparisons by Matching Methods    313

**6** Equilibrium in the Labor Market with Differences in Workers' Valuations    317

**7** Equilibrium in the Labor Market with Evasion of Social Security    327

**8** Profit Maximization under Informality    329

**9** Further Remarks on Retirement Pensions as a Social Entitlement    336

References    343

Index    349

# Foreword

For reasons that hardly need belaboring—geographic contiguity, immigration, trade, and the nexus between a healthy economy and political stability—few countries are as important to the United States as Mexico. That is why Mexico looms large in U.S. domestic politics—and why it should loom larger than it does in U.S. foreign policy. Hence the perennial timeliness of this book.

Over the last decade, Mexico has increased the resources that it spends on social programs in order to raise the welfare of its workers and redistribute income toward those in need. In *Good Intentions, Bad Outcomes* Santiago Levy argues that despite those investments, the social policies promoted by the Mexican government are ineffective in accomplishing the government's objectives and that they diminish the country's economic potential.

Two broad features distinguish the social security system in Mexico from the systems in most developed countries. First, it encompasses a broader set of benefits, including health care, housing, day care, and severance pay in addition to various types of pensions. Second, it covers only salaried workers: self-employed individuals and people who are employed by a firm in a nonsalaried capacity are excluded. That institutional design creates a dilemma for the government: it can leave millions of workers without coverage against various risks, or it can provide coverage through a parallel set of programs, here labeled social protection programs, at the expense of lowering productivity and GDP growth. The main thesis of this volume is that Mexico's combination of social security and social protection programs segments the country's labor market into a formal and an informal sector, induces workers and firms to seek employment and to invest in informal activities that impede productivity growth, provides large incentives to workers and firms to violate the laws meant to protect workers, and fails to reduce income inequality effectively. In other words, this book posits that social policy is a cause of informality in Mexico and that informality—apart from thwarting the government's social objectives—in turn reduces labor and capital productivity and the rate of growth of GDP.

To substantiate that thesis, Santiago reviews the country's main health, pension, housing, day care, severance pay, and related programs, distinguishing between the government's objectives in instituting the programs and workers' perceptions of the programs' benefits. He argues that social security contributions act as a tax on formal employment, the effects of which are compounded by the subsidy to informal employment associated with social protection programs. As a result, social policy in Mexico heavily punishes legal salaried labor, an effect that is precisely the opposite of what is required to provide workers, particularly unskilled ones, with stable formal jobs that offer social security coverage.

The pages that follow provide empirical evidence that challenges the view that informal workers are rationed from formal jobs. This volume documents that there is high mobility of individual workers between the formal and the informal sectors and that mobility is, in fact, observed more often among lower-wage than higher-wage workers. It combines that evidence with an analysis of the mechanisms through which social programs affect employment and investment. The key point made is that in an environment characterized on one hand by a combination of a large net tax on formal employment and a large net subsidy to informal employment and, on the other, by labor mobility and wage flexibility, the utility-maximizing choices of workers and the profit-maximizing choices of firms produce socially inefficient outcomes. Finally, considering the fiscal implications of social policy, the volume suggests that program benefits have been financed in part by a combination of higher oil rents and lower public investment. That mix limits the effectiveness of social policy in reducing income inequality and, given the lack of adequate public infrastructure, reduces growth.

A radical change in the incentives presented to firms and workers is required if Mexico is to grow faster and provide better jobs for its workers. *Good Intentions, Bad Outcomes* makes the case that reforming the country's social policy is essential to changing those incentives. It calls for eliminating the current combination of social security and social protection programs for formal and informal workers and instituting universal social entitlements instead—actions that are imperative if the government is to provide similar benefits to similar workers in a context of greater equity and broader social inclusion. To finance that proposal, the book makes a case for fiscal reform to replace the existing taxes on formal labor and subsidies to informal labor with a system of taxes on and subsidies to consumption. The proposed changes would align the incentives of workers and firms in the direction of increasing productivity and would permit effective and fiscally sustainable redistribution of income in favor of low-wage workers; moreover, those changes are necessary to foster greater compliance among workers and firms with the country's social security and labor laws. Mexican firms need an environment of greater legality in order to access commercial credit, exploit economies of scale, and adopt newer technologies. They need to be able to devote more time to training their workers and less time to hiding from and bribing government inspectors while depriving their workers of their social rights.

At Brookings, we believe in sound, fact-based analysis that leads to pragmatic but imaginative suggestions for solving problems. This book rises to that standard of quality. Moreover, the proposal presented here is relevant to other Latin American countries characterized by an informal labor market and limited social security coverage. The transition to democracy in the region is associated with increasing efforts to reduce income inequality. Governments are facing political pressures to provide pensions and health services, among other social benefits, to workers without social security, and those pressures will intensify in the years ahead as the region experiences rapid population aging and health care issues become more complex. This volume does not suggest that governments ignore such pressures, least of all in what is one of the more unequal regions of the world; it does, however, assert that not any combination of social programs is an appropriate response to those pressures and that some combinations are harmful. As programs to deliver social benefits to informal workers expand, Latin American countries run the risk of reducing their growth potential relative to that of developing countries in other regions of the world. The general welfare of workers will be higher, but their productivity will not; the question is whether such a state of affairs is sustainable.

This book also is pertinent to our understanding of and response to a regional and global challenge—the reduction of poverty. A decade ago, Mexico pioneered Progresa-Oportunidades, a program based on cash transfers to poor people contingent on their investment in their own health and education. Brazil and Colombia, among other countries in the region, have implemented programs very similar in spirit and design to Mexico's. These programs seek to break the intergenerational transmission of poverty by improving the health and education of children: healthier and more educated youngsters are expected to find jobs that offer them higher wages and social security coverage once they enter the labor market, eventually making Progresa-type transfers unnecessary. A stable formal job provides the exit from the program.

Santiago argues that Mexico's social protection programs are blocking that exit. Despite the best of intentions, the recent proliferation of social protection programs for informal workers traps poor workers in informal jobs that offer few prospects for increased productivity and higher real wages. There is a risk that instead of breaking the intergenerational transmission of poverty, income transfer programs may become permanent because, under the current combination of social security and social protection programs, the incentives presented to poor youngsters once they enter the labor market and to the firms that eventually hire them are not aligned in the direction of increasing productivity. The radical change in incentives required to implement universal social entitlements will raise Mexico's growth rate; equally important, it will doubly benefit the poor by both improving their access to social benefits and creating conditions under which they can find more productive jobs.

A final word: we at Brookings are proud to be publishing a work that, in addition to its other merits, underscores the institution's heightened long-term commitment to strengthening our capacity for work in—and on—the western hemisphere. Brookings's new Latin America Initiative will raise the profile of Latin America among U.S. political and opinion leaders and foster policies that contribute to the region's stability and prosperity. The initiative will provide fresh ideas to public and political leaders alike, enabling them to break out of the lassitude, stereotyping, and mutual misunderstanding that contribute to interstate frictions. It will also, we hope, help cure the United States of its attention deficit syndrome with regard to its own neighborhood—a lamentable and seemingly chronic condition from which we "North Americans" have suffered in the past.

While the primary objective of the initiative is to affect the U.S. policy debate, real U.S. engagement with Latin America must be built on a deep understanding of the region's economies and societies. That requires Latin American participation in the initiative's research and events. The Brookings Latin America Initiative will seek to engage policymakers, academics, civil society, and business leaders from the region in developing organic solutions to regional problems rather than "importing" solutions conceived in and of Washington.

Santiago's distinction as an author is indicative of the quality of talent we are bringing to bear on the initiative. He undertook this project as part of the global research program on effective and sustainable development policies at the Wolfensohn Center for Development at Brookings. He was a public official in Mexico for many years. As deputy finance minister in the administration of President Ernesto Zedillo, he was the chief architect of Progresa-Oportunidades; as director general of Mexico's Social Security Institute in the administration of President Vicente Fox, he promoted various reforms to improve the functioning and extend the coverage of the social security system. He currently is a nonresident senior fellow at Brookings and chief economist at the Inter-American Development Bank.

This volume confronts a central challenge for Mexico and Latin America: how to promote effective and sustainable policies to simultaneously reduce inequality

and enhance growth. It is demonstrative of the Latin America Initiative's objective—
to increase the accessibility of Latin American policy issues for U.S. political and
opinion leaders in order to strengthen the partnerships between the United States
and its southern neighbors.

STROBE TALBOTT
*President*
*Brookings Institution*
*Washington, D.C.*
*January 2008*

# Acknowledgments

I would like to express my gratitude to the Wolfensohn Center for Development at the Brookings Institution for its generous support. In particular, I want to thank James D. Wolfensohn for inviting me to work with the center and Johannes Linn, executive director, for his continuing confidence, support, encouragement, and suggestions.

I also thank Gary Fields, Homi Karas, Eduardo Lora, William Maloney, and Michael Walton for valuable discussions over the months that I worked on this volume. I am grateful to Ravi Kanbur for reading the entire text and making very useful observations and recommendations. I also express my gratitude to Angel Calderón for his guidance and advice regarding some econometric results that I could not have produced without him. In addition, I want to mention David Razú, who, more than a research assistant, was an extremely effective and responsible research collaborator; *mil gracias* David. Finally, I want to thank Eileen Hughes for her excellent editing. As usual, responsibility for the views expressed is mine.

I wrote this book at home in Mexico City, where I often was interrupted by two *chiquitas* who wanted me to help them with their homework, buy them ice cream, go bicycling, or simply join them for lunch—diversions that were not only long overdue but also a delight. I dedicate this work to Natania and Ariela, and to Anthea for making it all possible.

# Introduction

Three features of Mexico's development over the period from 1997 to 2006 stand out. One, per capita GDP and productivity growth was slow by international standards, despite the fact that Mexico experienced a decade of macroeconomic stability and implemented some reforms to increase efficiency.[1] Two, growth in formal employment was equally slow.[2] And three, there was a large expansion of health, housing, day care, and pension programs for households lacking social security coverage.[3]

The first two features generally are not associated with the third, at least not in the sense of there being a causal relationship between the increase in social programs for workers in the informal sector and diminished growth in GDP, productivity, and formal employment. If anything, the greater opportunities associated with

1. Average annual GDP growth was 3.4 percent and per capita growth 2.2 percent from 1997 to 2006. In the same period, output per worker grew at an average rate of 1.3 percent (see table 5-3 in chapter 5 and table 8-3 in chapter 8).

2. From 1997 to 2006, workers registered with the Instituto Mexicano del Seguro Social (IMSS) (Mexican Institute of Social Security), the social security institute for non–public sector workers, increased at an average rate of 3 percent. As a result, the share of workers registered with IMSS in the total labor force increased only from 28.4 to 31.6 percent. At that rate it would take approximately five more decades to achieve universal coverage (see table 8-3).

3. Resources for such programs were expected to increase by 110 percent in real terms from 1998 to 2007 (see table 1-5).

expanded social programs are assumed to contribute to economic growth by help-ing to improve the health and education of the labor force and, more generally, to improve the political environment in which policies are made by reducing inequality. The reduction of inequality is assumed to result from expanded social spending.

Many would attribute Mexico's lackluster growth in formal employment and productivity not to the increase in social programs for informal workers but to other factors, such as the high cost and uncertain supply of energy associated with public monopolies in the energy sector; the high cost of telecommunications, derived in turn from the monopolistic features of the telecom industry; generally infrequent lending to firms because of the uncertainty of property rights and the oligopolistic behavior of private banks; rigidities in the labor market derived from costly and cumbersome regulations; deficient education, associated in turn with the monopolistic position of the union of public school teachers; and an abnormally low tax base, resulting in insufficient public investment in growth-promoting infrastructure.

Those are substantive factors that would reduce the growth rate of any economy, even more if they occurred in some combination or if all of them existed at the same time. My objective here is not to argue the merits of each or to weigh their relative importance. It is to argue that there is yet another factor that contributes to low growth in GDP, formal employment, and productivity in Mexico: an incoherent social policy that gives workers incentives to seek low-productivity jobs and firms incentives to invest in privately profitable but socially suboptimal projects. More generally, *I argue that the incentive structure implicit in social programs leads workers and firms to behave in ways that are contrary to enhancing long-term productivity growth.*

Economic development usually is associated with a process whereby workers gradually shift from low- to high-productivity activities because of changes in the composition of output (generally reduced employment in agriculture and increased employment in manufacturing and services) or because of the adoption of more capital- or technology-intensive production processes. Either way, the result is an increase in labor productivity, which is the basis for an increase in real wages. The arguments made here, if correct, imply that *social policy in Mexico acts as a drag on that process* because it slows down the reduction of low-productivity agricultural employment; subsidizes inefficient self-employment and other forms of nonsalaried employment as well as illegal salaried employment; and interferes on one hand with the process by which workers seek more productive jobs and on the other hand with the way firms invest, grow, adopt new technologies, train workers, and, more generally, take measures to increase productivity.

I must state at the outset that I am not arguing against social programs. On the contrary, I believe that they are an indispensable part of any government effort to protect households from various risks, increase equality of opportunity, and combat poverty—especially so in Mexico, given the country's deep inequalities. My argument is different. It is, first, that the specific mechanisms by which social programs operate de facto generate incentives for workers to seek employment and firms to invest in low-productivity activities; second, that those mechanisms are an obstacle to achieving the very objectives of the programs; and third, that the sources of funds used to pay for the programs imply that the programs have a weak redistributive impact. The point therefore is not to eliminate social programs but to improve them; it is a question of means, not ends.

For the purposes of this book I define social policy as the set of programs through which the government offers health services, housing loans, day care services, and various types of pensions to workers of any income level, type of employment, or labor status. Those programs take the form of *social security* when they deal with workers in the formal sector, in which case they also include firing and severance pay regulations;[4] they take the form of *social protection* when dealing with workers in the informal sector. I exclude from social policy any policies dealing with education and other policies to increase households' welfare, such as infrastructure projects to improve the supply and quality of potable water and measures to protect households from natural disasters, terms-of-trade shocks, and the like.

I emphasize here that social protection programs are *not* equivalent to poverty reduction programs; they are programs that provide benefits to all workers who are not covered by social security, regardless of their income level. The common denominator of the social security and social protection programs considered here is that they bear on the labor market and, as detailed below, are contingent on the employment status—formal or informal—of workers.

In this volume, my first aim is to analyze the effects on workers and firms of the incentives offered by social security and social protection programs. The analysis focuses on two dimensions: one, a *social dimension,* by asking to what extent the two programs in combination protect workers from various risks and redistribute income in their favor; two, an *economic dimension,* by determining the effects of this combination of programs on workers' and firms' behavior along various dimensions that affect productivity growth. My second aim is to convince the reader that *Mexico's current combination of social programs is detrimental in both social and economic terms.*

This is not a monograph on poverty. Nevertheless, the framework developed here extends to consider the impact of social programs on poor workers; as a result, the analysis focuses on workers in general and poor workers in particular. In that context I pay special attention to the Progresa-Oportunidades program, which, because it targets households on the basis of income level, is a poverty reduction

---

4. Those regulations usually are catalogued under the rubric of labor policy, but their effect on the incentives of firms and workers is similar to that of the social programs analyzed here, so I treat them as analogous.

program, *not* a social protection program. My third aim is to analyze the incentive compatibility between the Progresa-Oportunidades program and the social security and social protection programs, which target workers on the basis of labor status, regardless of income level.

The focus on poor workers is important given the importance of poverty itself but also because I try to show that *the incentives of social protection and social security programs in Mexico are especially detrimental to poor workers* and may offset the positive effects of a direct income transfer program like Progresa-Oportunidades.[5] I argue in particular that under current conditions, poor youth who enter the labor force in the coming years after having benefited from Progresa-Oportunidades will be very unlikely to find jobs in the formal sector, which offer social security coverage, and that few firms will be willing to invest in training them and gradually raising their productivity. Those youngsters, while healthier and more educated than their elder peers, will end up in low-productivity jobs in the informal sector. Under current conditions, Progresa-Oportunidades is unlikely to break the intergenerational transmission of poverty, even if the program continues to deliver its benefits to poor households. That will not be because of the program itself but because the incentives to poor workers and the firms that hire them generated by the interplay of social security and social protection programs in the labor market are not aligned in the direction of raising productivity and increasing real wages. The human capital of poor workers may be raised by Progresa-Oportunidades, but their productivity in the labor market will not increase.

It is my view that much of the attention given to formality and informality in employment—certainly in Mexico and probably in Latin America in general—has focused on barriers to entry in formal employment, on one hand, and on the inequities created by the lack of social benefits for informal workers, on the other. My fourth aim is to argue that those views are flawed. I show that even with full mobility of workers, the labor market is segmented and that in fact that segmentation is *caused* by social programs. My view of informality differs from other views in two substantive aspects. First, I provide evidence indicating that workers in the informal sector are not unprotected from risks. Second, I argue that the relevant segmentation caused by the formal-informal dichotomy is in the productivity of workers across sectors, not in their standard of living. More pointedly, *I argue that by lowering productivity, informality hurts both formal and informal workers and also lowers the productivity of capital, with negative implications for GDP growth. I also argue that informality will persist; it will not fade away automatically as a result of economic growth.*

5. The ratio of poor households to total households increased from 23 to 37 percent as a result of the 1994–95 peso crisis and then fell steadily to 18 percent by 2004 (World Bank, 2005a, vol. 2, p. 153). Evidence shows that the income transfers from Progresa-Oportunidades have contributed to that reduction; see Levy (2006a, chap. 3).

My fifth and final aim is to explore policy alternatives. To do that, I discuss in a simple but I hope useful way the budgetary constraints under which social policy is carried out in Mexico. I try to separate two aspects of the government's social goals that are at times confused: those associated with protecting workers from risk, on one hand, and those associated with redistributing income, on the other. Having shown (I hope!) that at present both aims have been only very partially achieved, that labor and capital productivity have been lowered by the government's social policies, and that poor workers have been the ones who have lost the most from the current policy stance, I sketch the basic profile of an alternative policy—one that is better in social and economic terms in general and better for poverty reduction in particular.

*My core proposal is to redefine social security—in terms of both its scope and the way in which it is financed—and to provide universal social entitlements to all Mexican workers, financed out of consumption taxes. The negative income effects of increased consumption taxes on poor and low-wage workers would be offset through direct income transfers.* This proposal is feasible, it can be gradually implemented over the course of the next several years, it is fiscally sound, it suits the needs of Mexico's workers better than current policies, it is more effective at redistributing income toward low-wage workers, and it will make GDP grow faster. But it can be carried out only if the strategic interactions between social and economic policy are recognized and fully integrated into policy design. Policymakers must cease to view informality and the illegalities associated with it as a transitory nuisance that will fade away as GDP grows; they also must abandon the notion that simply maximizing social spending subject to the fiscal constraint from a growing and increasingly disjointed set of programs contributes to Mexico's long-term development. The proposal made here requires changes in the way policies are thought of, discussed, and implemented in Mexico; it requires the explicit recognition that social programs have a large impact on the relative price of the single most important non-traded input, labor; and it requires a focus on the adoption of policies that promote legality, social cohesion, and productivity *at the same time.*

This core proposal is complemented by a plea for Progresa-Oportunidades to keep a sharp focus on its human capital formation objectives and for policymakers to resist the temptation to use the program to solve all poverty-related problems. To bring about more rapid, permanent poverty reduction in Mexico, Progresa-Oportunidades has to be complemented by a radical change in incentives in the nation's labor market. Providing continuous increases in income transfers to the poor cannot substitute for making that change.

In sum, in this book I argue that the design of social policy in Mexico is flawed and that many of the programs introduced over the last few years have aggravated the problem. I argue that if present policies persist, the country will continue to experience low productivity growth, large-scale violation of the laws meant to protect workers, and reduced international competitiveness. I argue that while preserving the country's hard-won macroeconomic stability, it is high time to address the substantive distortions that are limiting Mexico's growth and that social policy reform needs to be at the center of that effort. I argue that it is feasible to design a new social policy that is fiscally sustainable, that is more effective at reducing Mexico's income inequality and protecting workers against risks, and that contributes to higher productivity and faster growth. And I argue that a social policy with those characteristics is indispensable to Mexico's development strategy.

The analysis and discussion in this volume may be relevant to other countries that have a dual system of social provisioning in an economy characterized by both a formal and an informal sector, which is the case in many Latin American countries at least. Its relevance is greater if informality in those countries, as in Mexico, is a cause of low productivity and results in part from the incentive structure implicit in their social programs. Despite the best intentions, in some countries, social security and social protection programs are a source of social exclusion and seg- mentation. As a result, it may be as indispensable in those countries as it is in Mexico to drastically reform those programs to move toward social inclusion and universal social entitlements and at the same time toward increased productivity and faster growth. Such countries face a great challenge and an equally great opportunity, as does Mexico.

This analysis also may be relevant to policymaking in other countries that have income transfer programs like Progresa-Oportunidades, of which there currently are more than twenty. In my view, an insufficiently studied aspect of such programs relates to their eventual phase-out, in particular their inter- face with other social programs that affect opportunities and outcomes for the poor in the labor market. If that interface is not given the attention it requires, the medium-term objectives of the programs will be more difficult to reach. I argue that poverty policy, after raising current consumption and ensuring that poor workers do not enter the labor market at a disadvantage vis-à-vis other workers (which a program like Progresa-Oportunidades can do), needs to focus on the impediments faced by poor workers to obtaining formal sector jobs with prospects for increasing productivity (which a program like Progresa-Oportunidades cannot do).

## Main Hypothesis

My central hypothesis consists of three parts. First, social policy takes the form of social security programs for salaried workers and social protection programs for nonsalaried workers, who consist of self-employed workers and workers having nonsalaried contractual relationships with firms. Differences in the nature of the benefits and in the financing of social security and social protection programs result in *a tax on salaried labor and a subsidy to nonsalaried labor*. The labor force is segmented into a formal sector, which has social security coverage, and an informal sector, which has social protection coverage. But because social security and social protection programs are not the same, workers of similar characteristics and abilities receive unequal social benefits—in one case being forced to purchase a bundled set of benefits and in the other being given the option to choose any of the benefits in an unbundled set or none of them. If the government's social objective is to provide similar benefits to similar workers, that objective is not being achieved. Further, if the government's social objective is to ensure that all workers have health insurance and save for retirement at the same time (or have any other joint set of benefits), the combination of social security and social protection programs leads the government further away from accomplishing that objective.

Second, the tax on salaried labor reduces salaried employment and the subsidy to nonsalaried labor increases nonsalaried employment. *Larger than optimal informal employment lowers aggregate labor productivity.* In addition, some firms hiring salaried workers evade social security laws, giving rise to illegal salaried employment in the informal sector. The labor costs of formal firms hiring salaried workers are higher than those of informal firms hiring nonsalaried workers and those of informal, illegal firms hiring salaried workers. The cost difference occurs because the supply of labor to the formal sector is reduced and because formal firms have to cover all the costs associated with the governance mechanisms that apply to salaried labor while other firms do not. In turn, differences in the cost of labor produce differences in the returns to capital across firms. Given the cost of credit, investment is distorted in favor of the informal sector, where the productivity of labor is lower and the additional GDP obtained from a given investment effort is less. In other words, the formal-informal dichotomy increases the economy's incremental capital-output ratio. *Distortions in the allocation of investment reduce the productivity of capital and cause dynamic productivity losses and a lower rate of growth in GDP.*

Third, because of differences in the quality and regional availability of health care facilities and other infrastructure to deliver social security and social protection benefits, poor workers value social security benefits less and social protection benefits more than other workers do. On one hand, poor workers self-select into the informal sector; on the other, because there are larger rents to share between firms and poor workers when social security is evaded than between firms and non-poor workers, evasion is more common with poor workers.

The net effect of social programs is that poor workers account for a disproportionate share of informal employment. Whether they are hired as salaried workers by illegal informal firms, are employed by legal firms in nonsalaried positions, or are self-employed, their productivity is lower than it could be if they were employed in the formal sector. Aside from being less productive, poor workers receive benefits through various unbundled social protection programs, not through a bundled social security program; that implies that they may or may not save for retirement, save for a house, or have health insurance. *Social policy therefore fails where it is needed most and, despite Progresa-Oportunidades, contributes to trapping the poor in poverty.*

I present two subsidiary hypotheses, not necessary to the main argument but relevant for Mexico. Because there is large-scale mobility of workers in Mexico's labor market, the incidence of wage-based social security contributions falls mostly on workers, formal and informal. In fact, given labor mobility, those adjectives are misleading. Rather than just formal and informal workers, in Mexico there are workers who work part-time in the formal and part-time in the informal sector. In that context, the potential redistribution of income that can occur through social security and social protection programs is limited to the share of the programs' costs paid with government subsidies. But the extent to which that potential redistribution is realized depends in turn on the nature of the fiscal adjustments made to pay for the subsidies. In other words, even if social security and social protection programs are subsidized, income is not necessarily being redistributed from high-income to low-income households.

The first subsidiary hypothesis is that in the 1997–2006 period, an important share of the subsidies to social security and social protection programs has been paid for with oil rents and not with additional taxes on higher-income households, limiting the effectiveness of the programs in reducing Mexico's income inequality. The second subsidiary hypothesis is that another share of subsidies to the programs has been paid for by reducing public investment in infrastructure, contributing to lower GDP growth.

The central hypothesis is consistent with the literature that points to micro-economic distortions in factor markets as an important determinant of aggregate productivity growth.[6] The novelty here lies in three areas: first, in identifying social programs as another source of microeconomic distortion; second, in showing that *these programs can segment the labor market into a formal and an informal sector even when there are no barriers to workers' mobility, such as binding minimum wages or others;* and third, in pointing out that the illegal nature of some informal economic activity affects productivity growth. Informality is not innocuous.

This volume hopes to contribute to answering four questions: one, how can social programs affect productivity and growth? Two, why do firms producing very similar or identical products do so at very different levels of productivity? Three, when wages are fully flexible, why do similar workers have different levels of productivity and different social benefits? And four, why is informal employment concentrated among poor workers? Those questions, aside from being interesting in their own right, are important for development policy in Mexico for two simple

---

6. See, for example, Banerjee and Duflo (2004) for an analytical discussion and Hsieh and Klenow (2006) for some empirical measurements.

but powerful reasons: *the majority of firms and workers are informal, and almost one of every four workers is poor.*

## Organization

This book has ten chapters, divided conceptually in three parts. The first part deals with the *setting* of the problem and consists of five chapters. Chapter 1 describes Mexico's social security and social protection programs and presents data on the budgetary resources channeled to each over the 1998–2007 period. Chapter 2 introduces the concepts of formality and informality and discusses the differences between previous treatments of informality and the one proposed here. Chapter 3 discusses the factors affecting workers' valuation of the benefits of social programs in Mexico. Chapter 4 provides information on patterns of land ownership and labor market participation among poor workers and explains why their valuation of social programs differs from that of non-poor workers. Chapter 5 presents stylized facts on the labor market, provides evidence on worker mobility, and discusses the implications of mobility for social policy.

The second part, which consists of three chapters, deals with the *behavior* of the main actors. Chapter 6 develops a framework to identify how workers and firms react to the incentives implicit in social policy, which determine the productivity of labor and the composition of employment, which in turn determine the coverage of social security and social protection programs. The chapter also focuses on the static efficiency costs of those programs. Chapter 7 focuses on the illegal dimensions of informality, analyzing why there is illegal salaried labor in Mexico and how the behavior of illegal firms—those hiring salaried workers without social security coverage—affects the size distribution of firms and the composition of output. Chapter 8 assesses how informality affects the composition of investment and explores other dimensions of firms' behavior that affect the productivity of capital and the rate of growth of GDP. It also discusses the incentive compatibility between the social security and social protection programs, on one hand, and between those programs and Progresa-Oportunidades, on the other.

The third part of the book, which consists of two chapters, deals with *policy*. Chapter 9 discusses the fiscal implications of social policy and elaborates on the centrality of the fiscal constraint in determining the current combination of policies; it also discusses the extent to which social programs in Mexico serve to redistribute income toward workers. Chapter 10 presents a fiscally and administratively feasible proposal to reach the government's social objectives more effectively with all workers while increasing productivity and GDP growth.

Given the scope and complexity of the issues involved, I try to find a middle ground between a general discussion and a detailed analysis of each issue. The risk of the former is that I will fail to convince more academically minded readers that the propositions made have some merit; the risk of the latter is that more policy-minded readers might find the paper too technical or far removed to be of practical value. Each of the issues discussed deserves a more detailed analytical and empirical exploration than the one presented here.

My methodological approach is eclectic. I avoid mathematical arguments, relying instead on graphs, which I hope make it possible for the nontechnical reader to follow the main points. Various appendices elaborate on the technical aspects of some arguments. I also try to present empirical examples of the various propositions to convey a sense of the order of magnitude of the points made in the text. In chapter 5, I do present a more systematic empirical and econometric analysis of wage rates and worker mobility in the labor market, which plays an important role in the overall argument. However, this volume does not present a rigorous mathematical or econometric analysis, nor is its emphasis on the technical complexities of such an analysis.

My approach is based on the belief that there is much to be gained by taking a broad view of the issues and, further, that only if policymakers have an understanding of the *interactions* between different social programs can sensible reforms be carried out. An analysis of the details of individual social programs is necessary but not sufficient for understanding the net effects of social policy. That requires considering how the various pieces of the puzzle fit together rather than only a careful analysis of each piece in isolation. But focusing on the interactions among the social programs in Mexico as opposed to the detailed workings of a single program necessarily involves trade-offs, and the ones that I have made inevitably are biased by my own abilities and interests, tilted as they are in the direction of policy. If this volume has merit, it is in contributing to the elaboration of a framework for understanding and reforming social policy in Mexico *and in pointing out that such understanding and reform are crucial for economic policy.* I hope that the more academically minded readers find the discussion thought provoking, while the more policy-minded readers consider the analysis relevant to their tasks.

# 1

## Institutions, Workers, and Social Programs

M exico's social policy makes a critical distinction between social security programs, which target salaried workers, and social protection programs, which target nonsalaried workers—in both cases regardless of income level— and between those programs and poverty reduction programs, which target poor people regardless of their salaried or nonsalaried status. Understanding those distinctions is essential to identifying the mechanism through which social programs influence workers in general and poor workers in particular. The distinctions serve in turn to identify the nature of the monetary resources channeled to social spending and to measure the relative magnitude of the efforts made to provide benefits to workers of different types of labor status and income levels. This chapter describes the institutional framework of Mexico's social policy.

### Salaried and Nonsalaried Labor

Mexico's legal framework makes a distinction between salaried and nonsalaried employment that has fundamental implications for the nation's social policies. Articles 20 and 21 of the Federal Labor Law define salaried workers as those performing work for someone else ("subordinated work") in exchange for a wage. Those two conditions—performance of work for someone else and payment of a wage—are necessary and sufficient to establish the existence of a "relationship between a worker and a boss."[1] An important consideration is that the law does not require a written contract or set a minimum number of workers who have to be subordinated to a boss in order to establish that relationship, nor does it distinguish between sectors (agriculture, service, or industry), wage levels, or genders in doing so. The provisions of the law are very broad; the key elements are the existence of a subordinated relationship, so that there is a boss from whom the worker takes orders, and payments that take the form of "wages." Salaried workers can be employed in industry (maintenance personnel in a factory), construction (brick-layers), agriculture (field laborers or employees of a produce packaging plant), or services (dishwashers in restaurants, maids in hotels). As shown in chapter 5, salaried employment is the most common form of employment in Mexico but far from the only one. In fact, it is noteworthy that salaried employment accounts for only 57 percent of the total labor force (see figure 5-1).

Nonsalaried workers are defined by exclusion. They represent various categories, the most important being the self-employed (*trabajadores por cuenta propia*) and workers who have a nonsubordinated relationship with a firm and for whom payment does not take the form of a wage but of a profit-sharing agreement or a commission.

Self-employed workers can be employed in rural areas (agricultural producers) or in urban areas (fruit juice vendors on city streets).[2] They may or may not own a productive asset, such as land in the case of a farmer or a blender and a stand in the case of a fruit juice vendor. Workers who make handicrafts (*artesanos*) with a few simple tools (a drill, a hammer, and some paints) also fall into this category, as do those who shine shoes using shoe polish, a brush, and a box; seamstresses and tailors who use a sewing machine to make clothes at home for sale in a *tianguis* ("market" in Nahuatl); and gardeners who go from one home to another with their lawnmower and hedge trimmer.[3]

---

1. Chen (2006, p. 80) writes: "Historically the 'employment relationship' has represented the cornerstone—the central legal concept—around which labour law and collective bargaining agreements have sought to recognize and protect the rights of workers. Whatever its precise def-inition in different national contexts, it has represented a universal notion that links a person, called employee (frequently referred to as a worker), with another person, called the employer, to whom she or he provides labour or services under certain conditions in return for remuneration." In Mexico the "employment relationship" is defined in the Federal Labor Law as the worker-boss relation-ship (in Spanish, *la relación obrero-patronal*). That relationship is the central legal concept because its existence implies legally enforceable obligations for both the worker and the boss. Among the obligations of the boss, who can be an individual person or a firm, is to enroll workers in social security.

2. Lawyers, doctors, accountants, and others who work independently also are self-employed workers, but the discussion here centers on unskilled labor.

3. Note that for most of these self-employed workers there is a salaried equivalent: artisans working in a large shop making standardized handicrafts for export; full-time shoeshine men hired by a hotel; a seamstress working at a small enterprise making bridal gowns; and staff gardeners hired by hotels, golf courses, and local governments.

Individuals who wash and park cars on the street also are self-employed. One might think that they own no productive assets, but they may own or have access to intangible capital in the form of special or exclusive rights to the street where they perform their tasks. Washing car windshields on a busy avenue in Mexico City is not the same as doing so on a quiet street in a small city. Since spots on busy avenues are scarce, car washers and parkers with access to those spots have access to intangible capital, which may or may not be theirs, depending on the system for allocating property rights for such valuable working locations. In any case, their gross earnings reflect the implicit quasi-rent on the intangible capital (see figure 6-1).[4]

Of course, many self-employed people own no productive assets: the men who carry heavy loads of produce delivered by various rural producers to various individually operated stands in the city food markets; a woman who serves as a cook at a number of different residences; the men in rural areas who today look after sheep on a nearby farm and tomorrow drive a tractor at a different farm.[5]

Other nonsalaried workers may have a nonsubordinated relationship with a firm based on various contractual arrangements that may be devised to solve information problems, diversify risk, or elicit effort. Many workers in Mexico sell all sorts of products in the streets that they do not own or produce (newspapers, food, contraband, lottery tickets). The products are advanced to them as working capital by a larger distributor, and the workers receive a fee or commission for every newspaper, lottery ticket, or other item sold. Their effort cannot be monitored because they peddle their wares in the streets at times of their own choosing. These workers usually sell different products from different suppliers—for example, newspapers in the morning, candy at mid-day, contraband in the afternoon (umbrellas if it is raining), and the late-edition newspaper at dusk. Such workers are sometimes thought of as self-employed and are so classified in the labor statistics, but they are not. They are workers who earn commissions (*comisionistas*). They are conceptually different from the self-employed to the extent that their earnings come mostly from commissions, which are the payment for their labor; the self-employed usually own some productive assets, in which case their earnings consist of the implicit payment for their labor and the quasi-rent on their assets. Furthermore, *comisionistas* work for a firm that they do not own; the self-employed have no contractual relationship with anyone.

Nonsalaried contractual relationships between workers and firms also are established to diversify risk. Share-cropping agreements in rural areas are a typical example; contracts between owners of fishing boats and fishermen are another. In such cases workers' earnings reflect their labor but also contain an element of

4. Note again that if the person washes cars for a car wash business, then he or she is salaried, as is the person who parks cars for a hotel or a commercial parking lot.

5. These self-employed individuals also have their equivalent in salaried labor. A man who unloads produce from trucks for a single supermarket or supermarket chain is a salaried worker, as is a cook who works for a restaurant and a man who performs various tasks for the same large farm all the time.

reward for risk. These are not academic differences; they matter in interpreting earnings and productivity differentials between workers (see chapters 5 and 6).

*A sharp distinction cannot always be made between subordinated work in exchange for a wage and nonsubordinated work in exchange for a commission.* In Mexico hundreds of thousands of workers are engaged in door-to-door sales of the products of only one firm. Cosmetic products and health foods are two examples; another is cell phone cards, commonly sold by street vendors. Such workers cannot sell products from any other firm, and their merchandise must be offered at the prices set by the firm. One could call them sales agents. But because the firm cannot monitor how hard they work, it does not pay them a wage. In these cases it is unclear whether there exists a boss and a subordinate worker. In practice, ambiguity with respect to salaried and nonsalaried employment is resolved by the courts.[6]

*At times, the distinction between self-employment and salaried employment also is tenuous.* A self-employed vendor who owns a stand at which he makes fruit juices for sale at a city corner is a firm: a combination of capital (a mixer, a stand) and labor, which together with intermediate inputs like fruit, water, and electricity (perhaps stolen from the grid) produces output. He is a one-man firm. The same is true of an agricultural producer who owns a half-hectare of rain-fed land. But the owner of the fruit juice stand might also have one or two helpers; in that case, he becomes a boss with two salaried employees. However, if the two employees receive no monetary remuneration, there is no salaried employment involved because there is no wage (if, for example, the helpers are his relatives and implicitly get paid in kind). In the labor statistics such helpers appear as "workers without remuneration" (*trabajadores sin remuneración*); nevertheless, they are working. Again, the same holds in rural areas for plots of two to three hectares of rain-fed land exploited by a family. Thus, two-to-three person firms can exist without creating the conditions for salaried employment.

Unrelated workers also can work together without there being salaried labor. They may be partners in a cooperative venture in which there is no boss and no wage, sharing, for example, a small fishing boat and the proceeds of the catch. There is monetary remuneration for all partners but no salaried employment of any.

---

6. That ambiguity is greatly appreciated by lawyers, who can charge fees while they argue endlessly about how many angels fit on the head of a pin. Ambiguity also matters when illegal behavior occurs as a result of attempts by firms and workers to evade social security contributions by disguising salaried employment as nonsalaried employment and wages as commissions. However, I postpone the discussion of illegal behavior until chapter 7 and assume here that behavior is fully legal and that a clear difference exists between salaried and nonsalaried employment. In general, if there is a fixed place of work and the relationship between the worker and the firm has endured for some time, the courts resolve in favor of salaried employment. A relevant case is that of waiters, who receive a wage and a commission (tip), the latter based on effort. If waiters work in a fixed place, a restaurant, they are salaried workers; if they do not—like those who walk the beaches, bringing drinks to tourists, or walk the streets, bringing soft drinks to drivers—they are not salaried. See also Chen (2006, pp. 86–87) for a discussion.

Such nonsalaried working arrangements—lacking a hierarchy and entailing implicit payments in kind or some form of profit sharing—have one critical feature in common: *inefficiencies increase as the number of participants increases.* Problems of shirking and monitoring soon appear, and the division of tasks cannot become too specialized. Historically salaried labor has been associated with increasing size of an enterprise and a growing division of labor. In the absence of distortions, the micro- or small enterprise without salaried labor eventually gives way to the not-so-small firm with salaried labor.

Many one to two- or three-person firms or joint ventures face very low entry and exit costs and have intermittent lives. A self-employed taco vendor who works at her stand on the streets might, depending on wages and benefits, put her stand away and join a taco chain as an employee. Her abilities remain the same, but her labor status does not: she is now a salaried worker. Or her taco-stand business may grow into a larger enterprise as she moves from the street to a space in a commercial building and gets some help; she then turns into a boss with a couple of salaried assistants. Taco makers may be self-employed workers, salaried employees, or bosses, and the number of taco-producing firms can change rapidly in tandem with the status of taco makers.

In a similar vein, the owner of a half-hectare of rain-fed land working on his own to produce corn might, depending on wages and benefits, let his land lay fallow and work as a salaried agricultural laborer for a large firm exporting tomatoes. Chapter 5 presents a discussion of mobility, but the point I want to make here is that the boundary between self-employment and salaried employment—and between being truly self-employed, being a boss, and being a partner—must be thought of as permeable.

To summarize, the law in Mexico divides labor into two mutually exclusive categories: salaried and nonsalaried employment. The first corresponds to arrangements in which a worker's performance can de directly observed and monitored, the worker usually has a fixed place of work, a boss gives the worker orders, and the worker receives fixed compensation in the form of a wage for work performed. The second responds to arrangements in which work performance cannot be observed, some risks may be shared, the place of work may be variable, and compensation takes various non-wage forms: commissions, payments in kind, profit sharing, and so forth. The second category is very broad but can be aggregated into two large subcategories: self-employed workers and *comisionistas.*

A precise division between salaried workers, self-employed workers, and *comisionistas* cannot always be made. For the purposes of this volume, however, the division is conceptually necessary; *the law makes it necessary.* These three categories of workers, together with a fourth to be discussed below—illegal salaried workers—are required to capture the phenomenon under study, because from the standpoint of social policy in Mexico they are the categories that matter. At times I refer to rural or urban workers, but that classification is driven more by the availability of data than by underlying categories needed for the analysis. The urban-rural distinction is not central; the salaried-nonsalaried dichotomy is.

Before turning to social policy, I want to make four remarks. First, I refer to firms in the economic sense of the term, as a combination of capital and labor or land and labor that produces output. Second, firms can have salaried or nonsalaried contractual relationships with workers, and some firms might consist of one person—the self-employed owner. Third, the various forms of employment—self-, salaried, and commission-based employment—are influenced but not fully determined by the ownership of productive assets. As elaborated on in chapter 6, even workers who own productive assets might change from salaried to nonsalaried labor and vice versa. Finally, note that depending on the form of employment, earnings may take the form of a pure wage; a wage plus commission; or the wage equivalent of a commission only; they also may reflect a component of quasi-rent to a productive asset or some compensation for risk.[7]

## Labor Status and Social Programs

The legal distinction between salaried and nonsalaried employment is fundamental to Mexico's social policy because articles 12 and 13 of the Social Security Law state that social security is a right of salaried workers only and an obligation of bosses or firms only with regard to their salaried workers. The law refers to the Federal Labor Law for the definition of "salaried worker." There are deep historical reasons behind this institutional construct and some practical ones as well (see chapter 9). *But whatever the motivation, it has permeated and decisively influenced the attitudes and behavior of workers and firms since the first Social Security Law was promulgated in Mexico in 1943, and it has large implications for productivity and welfare.*

Nonsalaried workers in Mexico, however, are not left without social benefits. Over the years the government has introduced various social programs for them that are imperfect substitutes for the benefits provided by social security. In this volume I group all those programs—apart from social security for salaried workers—under the label of social protection programs, but I exclude Progresa-Oportunidades. As a result, *social benefits in Mexico are inextricably linked to labor status,* with salaried workers having a right, or an entitlement, to social security benefits and nonsalaried workers having various degrees of entitlement to social protection benefits. It is crucial to note that the distinction is not a function of income, age, gender, education, rural-urban location, type of work, or wage level: in principle, all salaried and nonsalaried workers receive social security or social

---

7. The point here is that the distribution of workers' earnings reflects not only education and inherent ability but also these other characteristics of employment. In the discussion above I have referred to cases of workers with similar education and abilities who are at times salaried and at times nonsalaried. I show in chapter 7 that the wages of salaried workers depend on their legal status.

Table 1-1. *Social Benefits, Income Level, and Salaried and Nonsalaried Status*

| Income level | Salaried workers | Nonsalaried workers (self-employed and comisionistas) |
|---|---|---|
| Non-poor | I. Social security | II. Social protection |
| Poor | III. Social security and Progresa-Oportunidades | IV. Social protection and Progresa-Oportunidades |

Source: Author's illustration.

protection benefits. And all firms hiring salaried workers are obliged to enroll all their salaried workers in social security, while firms having a relationship with non-salaried workers are not.

Progresa-Oportunidades is another source of social benefits for some workers. Unlike the social security and social protection programs, it targets beneficiaries on the basis of income. As elaborated below, Progresa-Oportunidades does not provide direct benefits to poor workers individually. Nevertheless, workers who are members of households enrolled in Progresa-Oportunidades receive the benefits of the program regardless of whether they are salaried or nonsalaried, in addition to receiving benefits from participating in the labor market under one form of contract or another.

Table 1-1 depicts the combinations of income level and labor status of Mexican workers and the corresponding social benefits. Four combinations, labeled I through IV, are possible. Two observations are relevant to the discussion that follows. First, note that poor workers can receive benefits from the Progresa-Oportunidades program in addition to those from the social security and social protection programs, regardless of the labor status of the working-age members of the program's beneficiary households. Second, as a result, *within Mexico's institutional framework it is wrong to associate social security with non-poor workers and social protection with poor workers.*

In chapter 5, I show that in Mexico poor and non-poor workers are distributed throughout all four combinations. *This volume is concerned with how the incentives of social programs affect the distribution of workers among the four combinations and with the implications of various distributions for welfare and productivity growth.*

### Characteristics of Social Security

Mexico's social security program offers eight legally grouped, or *bundled*, benefits:
—health insurance
—disability insurance
—work-risk insurance
—life insurance
—day care for workers' children

—sports and cultural facilities
—retirement pensions
—housing loans.

Four points should be noted. First, for the most part, benefits are paid for with wage-based contributions from workers and firms; government subsidies account for less than 15 percent of the total non-wage costs of labor (see table 9-1). (The effects of those subsidies are analyzed in chapter 9.)[8] Second, workers and firms must pay for all services in the bundle, regardless of whether they want only some or none of them. It is an all-or-nothing deal.

Third, each worker covered by social security has an individual account that includes two sub-accounts. The first sub-account is for the worker's retirement savings. It is funded from the share of the worker's and the firm's social security contributions allocated to the worker's retirement pension, combined with a government subsidy for the same purpose, which is called the social contribution for retirement (*cuota social para el retiro*). The second is for housing, and it is completely funded from the share of the worker's and the firm's social security contributions allocated to that purpose because there is no government subsidy for housing. The worker's individual account is managed by a private financial firm known as an *administradora de fondos de retiro* (administrator of retirement funds), or Afore. Each worker can freely choose his or her Afore.

Fourth, benefits are provided or regulated by three federal agencies: the Instituto Mexicano del Seguro Social (IMSS) (Mexican Institute of Social Security), the Instituto del Fondo Nacional de la Vivienda para los Trabajadores (Infonavit) (Institute of the National Fund for Workers' Housing), and the Comisión Nacional del Sistema del Ahorro para el Retiro (Consar) (National Commission of the System of Retirement Saving). The first agency is in charge of collecting all social security contributions and, by and large, directly providing the first six of the eight benefits previously listed.[9] The second administers the resources in a worker's housing sub-account: on one hand, it invests those resources, paying the worker a rate of return; on the other, it provides the worker with a housing loan. The third agency regulates the Afore pricing and investment regime. (Note that even though an Afore manages the worker's account, it invests only the funds in the retirement

8. The 2007 federal budget includes a new program, Programa de Primer Empleo (First Job program), which offers a subsidy to firms that hire salaried workers and enroll them in IMSS for the first time. The new subsidy is in addition to the social security subsidy (see chapter 9).

9. Not all services are directly provided by IMSS. In some cases, day care services are outsourced to private providers and benefits from permanent disability insurance, life insurance, and work-risk insurance are offered through annuities that IMSS purchases from private insurance companies. However, whether someone qualifies for day care services or a pension is determined by IMSS. Most important, with very few exceptions health services are directly provided by IMSS. As a result, IMSS has more than 360,000 employees and is one of the largest vertically integrated providers of health services worldwide (offering services to around 40 million people), apart from being the second-largest collector of fiscal revenues in Mexico, after the Ministry of Finance.

Table 1-2. *Wages and Social Security Contributions*

| Wage and contributions (monthly) | Pesos (2007) |
|---|---|
| Wage | 2,931.60 |
| Social security contributions | 864.30 |
|   Health insurance | 358.61 |
|   Work-risks insurance | 76.20 |
|   Disability and life insurance | 69.60 |
|   Retirement pension | 184.00 |
|   Day care centers and sports facilities | 29.31 |
|   Housing fund | 146.60 |
|     Total | 864.30 |
| Wage plus social security contributions | 3,795.90 |

Source: Author's calculations based on current legislation.

sub-account.) Funds for the retirement and housing sub-accounts are collected by IMSS and deposited in each sub-account in the Afore chosen by the worker.

Mexico's pension system is a defined-contribution system. When a worker retires, the funds accumulated in his or her retirement account are used to purchase an annuity with a private insurance company. Since a worker's enrollment with IMSS automatically implies enrollment with Infonavit and an Afore, being covered by social security is equivalent to being enrolled or registered with IMSS. The same holds with respect to firms: a firm that registers or enrolls its workers in social security is registered with IMSS.

Table 1-2 gives the monetary value in 2007 pesos of both worker and firm contributions to social security for a worker who earns twice the minimum wage, which is the wage earned by the lower-third of all workers enrolled in IMSS.[10] Note that social security contributions are almost 30 percent of the wage.

*Characteristics of Social Protection*

Social protection consists of various benefits for nonsalaried workers:
    —health services provided by federal and state organizations distinct from IMSS[11]
    —subsidies for housing through federal and state programs and agencies distinct from Infonavit

10. Unless otherwise specified, all peso figures in this volume refer to 2007 pesos. As a reference, the average exchange rate for the first four months of 2007 was 11.01 pesos per U.S. dollar.

11. Provision of public health services is delegated to state governments, which provide them through their ministries or specialized agencies. However, the federal government also provides health services to workers and their families not covered by social security through specialized hospitals operated directly by the Ministry of Health and, confusingly, through a federally funded program that is operated by IMSS, although it is not part of IMSS. The latter program, labeled IMSS-Oportunidades, operates in seventeen of Mexico's thirty-two states.

—access to saving for retirement pensions in the same type of individual accounts operated by Afores for salaried workers and to various noncontributory pension programs

—access to day care centers provided through federal and state programs distinct from IMSS

—access to life insurance associated with some health services.

Four comments are worth making. First, these benefits are *unbundled* and *voluntary*. As a result, workers can decide to enroll in a health program but not to save for retirement in an individual account, or they can decide to do the opposite. They can access a housing loan through a federal or state program without either saving for retirement or participating in a health program.

Second, the services provided are almost fully funded from public monies. At times private contributions are required from the worker, depending on the nature of the benefit, but the amount paid varies erratically because very large differences exist between formal charges and actual payments. Further, charges are low and usually decrease along with a worker's wage or income; for workers specifically classified as poor, charges are nonexistent. *By and large, from the perspective of nonsalaried workers and the firms that they may be associated with, social protection benefits are free.*

Third, social protection benefits generally are not an entitlement.[12] However, in 2003 the president proposed and Congress approved legal reforms to create a voluntary health insurance program for workers not covered by social security, commonly known as Seguro Popular (Popular Insurance). Services are offered in the same public facilities that tend to nonsalaried workers who are not enrolled in this program, although special efforts are made to provide beneficiaries with a reliable supply of medicines and better services than those provided to workers who are not enrolled. Program regulations specify that households in the first two deciles of the income distribution—which correspond to households in Progresa-Oportunidades—pay no fees at all.[13] As a result, workers from Progresa-Oportunidades households have free access to health insurance for themselves and their family if they are nonsalaried, but if they are salaried they and the firm that hires them must pay for health insurance and the other benefits bundled

12. In Mexico, an entitlement must be established by law. Most social protection programs are not; instead they must receive annual congressional approval in the budget decree. In principle, the president could exclude the programs from the annual budget proposal or Congress could refuse to approve resources for them in the budget. When social programs are enacted in law (like social security), the president must include the corresponding resources in the annual budget proposal and Congress must approve them in the budget decree; until the law is changed, workers have a right, or an entitlement, to the programs.

13. See articles 122 and 127 of the Reglamento de la Ley General de Salud en Materia de Protección Social en Salud (Regulations of the General Health Law on Social Protection with Respect to Health). Article 127 in particular states that households in the first two deciles of the income distribution are exempt from any contributory fees and, in addition, that the exemption may apply also to households that are beneficiaries of any federal poverty alleviation program; see *Diario Oficial de la Federación* (Official Journal of the Federation), April 5, 2004.

in social security, for a total of 864 pesos a month (table 1-2). Positive fees have been formally established for higher-income workers, but so far collections have been practically nil.[14] Fourth, some programs specifically state that benefits are lost if workers enroll in social security.[15]

The number of social protection programs has increased over the last few years, although some health and housing programs have been in place for many decades. Various new housing programs and Seguro Popular started between 2001 and 2006. Seguro Universal de Primera Generación (Universal Insurance for the First Generation), a new program to provide health insurance to all infants born after December 1, 2006, began in 2007. A new federal program to provide day care services for children of working women without social security coverage also started in early 2007.[16] In addition, in 2007 a new federal program, Programa de Atención a Adultos Mayores de Setenta Años (Adults over Seventy program), was introduced to provide a noncontributory pension to all persons over seventy years of age living in communities of 2,500 inhabitants or fewer. This program provides a monthly pension of 500 pesos to each eligible person, approximately 0.35 times the monthly minimum wage in 2007.[17]

The proliferation of social protection programs has been accompanied by efforts to strengthen the institutional framework under which they operate. In

14. It is very unlikely that substantial fees could be recovered because fees are collected by state governments, so thirty-two agencies would be needed for that purpose; fees are low relative to collection costs, so incentives to collect are weak; fees do not have the legal status of social security contributions, which are akin to taxes, implying that the legal instruments to enforce beneficiaries' obligations are weak. As shown in table A1-6 in appendix 1, in 2006 federal subsidies for Seguro Popular totaled 17,738 million pesos while private fees amounted to 145 million pesos (or 0.8 percent of the program's total budget). Even in the unlikely event that any beneficiaries were to lose access to Seguro Popular for lack of payment, they could still access health services provided by the state health ministries where they live, which are offered in the same facilities where they received services under Seguro Popular, or they could access facilities at IMSS-Oportunidades, if they live in a state where facilities are available.

15. Two examples: First, the newly created federal day care program for working mothers states that only poor households can benefit from the program and establishes as a condition for participation "lack of access to a day care center or a child care service through a public social security institution or other means" (my translation of clause 4.3.1 of the Acuerdo por el que se Emiten y Publican las Reglas de Operación del Programa de Guarderías y Estancias Infantiles para Apoyar a las Madres Trabajadoras para el Ejercicio Fiscal 2007 (Rules of Operation of the Nursery School and Day Care Program for Working Mothers for Fiscal Year 2007); see *Diario Oficial de la Federación,* January 9, 2007. Second, article 77-bis-7 of the General Health Law states that "households whose members comply with the following prerequisites will enjoy the benefits of the Health Social Protection System (Seguro Popular): . . . II. Not being beneficiaries of social security." Further, article 77-bis-39 states that the benefits of the Health Social Protection System will be suspended "when the principal income earner of a beneficiary household joins a federal or state social security institution" (my translation).

16. Day care services for workers without social security are erratically provided by state governments through a state-level agency called Desarrollo Integral de la Familia (DIF) (Comprehensive Family Development). The new day care program started in 2007 is operated directly by the federal Ministry of Social Development.

17. A household with two elders gets two pensions. One million people are expected to be eligible, and 6,550 million pesos for that purpose were budgeted in 2007; see Secretaría de Desarrollo Social (Ministry of Social Development), *Diario Oficial de la Federación,* February 28, 2007.

2006 the National Council for Social Protection was created by presidential decree with, among others, the following purpose: "To guarantee the observance of social protection policy, ensuring the functional integration of benefits in health, housing, and savings for retirement, among others, that the Federal Government offers to the population lacking social security coverage."[18] Thus, *while not yet enacted by Congress in law, an integrated system of social benefits parallel to social security—as opposed to a collection of individual programs—is now part of the institutional context in which federal ministries and agencies operate social programs for informal workers.* These institutional efforts are reflected in budgetary allocations. Before discussing them, I briefly describe Mexico's income transfer program for the poor.

### Characteristics of Progresa-Oportunidades

Progresa-Oportunidades makes cash income transfers to poor households, contingent on their compliance with requirements to enhance their human capital. In particular, the demand for health services is subsidized with a transfer based on compliance by household members with an age- and gender-specific health protocol, while the demand for educational services for children and youth is subsidized with an additional transfer based on the gender and grade level of the individual attending school.[19]

Progresa-Oportunidades seeks to postpone the age at which young people enter the labor market by providing scholarships through the end of high school, at approximately eighteen or nineteen years of age. One purpose of the program is to increase the capabilities of poor youth so that after they enter the labor market their productivity will be higher than that of the current generation of poor workers. Income transfers, investments in the human capital of all household members, and improved productivity potential for those entering the labor market are the program's key contribution to combating current poverty today and at the same time breaking the intergenerational transmission of poverty. Put differently, by augmenting future workers' capabilities, Progresa-Oportunidades differs from Mexico's previous income transfer programs for the poor (in cash or in kind); instead of "income transfers today and income transfers tomorrow," it offers "income transfers today, contingent on investments in human capital contributing to higher earned income tomorrow."

As with other non–social security programs, benefits under Progresa-Oportunidades have increased recently. I mention three. First, in 2006 the government announced the addition of a saving-for-retirement component to the program, whereby working-age members of Progresa-Oportunidades households would get a special subsidy—contingent on not having a job with social security

18. My translation of article 4 of the decree, published in the *Diario Oficial de la Federación*, February 27, 2006.
19. See Levy (2006a) for a fuller description.

coverage—if they voluntarily opened an individual retirement account with an Afore.[20] However, as of 2007 that effort was discontinued. Second, in 2006 the government added another component, Apoyo a Adultos Mayores (Support for Older Adults), in the form of a cash subsidy of 250 pesos a month for all adults seventy years of age or older. Third, in January 2007, through a new component called Oportunidades Energético (Energy Oportunidades), the government increased transfers by 50 pesos a month to all beneficiary households to help pay for their energy expenses.[21] The net result is that as of 2006, income transfers to Progresa-Oportunidades households increased in real terms by 15 percent on average.

My purpose is not to assess the impact of these additional income transfers. But it is critical to note that Progresa-Oportunidades does not offer any individually targeted benefits conditioned on the labor status of the working-age members of the household (particularly after the suspension in 2007 of the saving-for-retirement component of the program introduced in 2006). As a result, in principle Progresa-Oportunidades has no impact on the labor status preferences of poor workers once they enter the labor market.[22] Progresa-Oportunidades cannot ensure that progressively healthier and better-educated workers will end up in more productive jobs, so that "higher earned income tomorrow" will in fact be the outcome. That is not the program's job; the outcome depends on the incentives of poor workers once they enter the labor market and on the incentives of the firms that hire them.

It is from that perspective that it is critical to note that *the influence of social security and social protection programs on the choice between salaried and nonsalaried employment for Progresa-Oportunidades workers differs from the programs' influence on the choice for non-poor workers.* In particular, because programs like Seguro Popular and others condition benefits on being poor *and* on not being covered by social security, the incentives faced by poor and non-poor workers are different. That effect is strengthened to the extent that actual, as opposed to statutory, social security and social protection benefits differ for poor and non-poor workers (chapter 4). It is further strengthened because, as I show in chapter 7, the incentives to evade social security are stronger for poor than for non-poor workers. As a result, despite the neutrality of Progresa-Oportunidades with respect to the labor choices of its

20. This was the Mecanismo de Ahorro para el Retiro de Oportunidades (Oportunidades Mechanism of Saving for Retirement); see the presidential decree, published in the *Diario Oficial de la Federación,* March 27, 2006.

21. The new energy component was introduced despite the fact that there had been no changes in the relative price of electricity or of gas for domestic consumption, so that the measure was de facto a pure increase in income transfers. There also is no substantive meaning to the concept of a transfer for energy expenses; because the additional transfer is in cash, households can dispose of it freely, on energy consumption or something else.

22. Impact evaluations show that so far the program has had no effect on workers' labor-leisure choices, although it has changed the study-work allocation of children's time; see Levy (2006a) for a general review of the impact of Progresa on the allocation of household members' time and Skoufias and di Maro (2006) for the finding that Progresa has had no effect on adult labor force participation.

working members, *the incentives associated with social security and social protection programs encourage poor workers to seek low-productivity informal jobs.*

### Regulations on Firing and Severance Pay as Social Policy

Mexico's Federal Labor Law contains detailed regulations for firing workers that share with social security the same general objective of protecting workers from various risks. In the case of labor law, the risk comes from loss of income associated with output and employment shocks and in the case of social security law from ill health, disability, and low income after retirement.[23] The fact that the regulations are found in separate laws should not distract from the fact that they form part of an integrated social policy for workers; more important for my purposes, they both have a direct bearing on the labor market.[24] In my view, labor regulations concerning firing and severance pay should be thought of as another social program, as they are in many countries where unemployment insurance is considered a component of social security.

There is a second reason why these regulations matter: *as with entitlement to social security, they apply only to salaried workers.* The self-employed, by definition, are not hired by anybody and therefore cannot be fired, while *comisionistas* are not formally the employees of the firms that they are associated with.

Firing and severance pay regulations impose a contingent cost on firms hiring workers; if the contingency materializes they provide a benefit to the worker in the form of severance pay.[25] In that sense they are no different from, say, disability or work-risk insurance regulations, which as shown in table 1-2 are part of social security. The only difference is that the Federal Labor Law does not obligate firms to pay ex ante for that contingency and deposit the necessary funding in some account, as with other components of social security that are paid upfront (and with unemployment insurance in countries where that forms part of social security). That does not mean that firms do not have to include contingent costs as part of their labor costs. Workers also know that severance pay is one of the contingent benefits of being a salaried employee, paid when they are fired as their firm adjusts output downward as a result of lack of demand; it is similar in nature to a work-risk

23. See Dávila (1994) and Calderón (2000). There is no unemployment insurance in Mexico; to some extent severance pay and restrictions on firing act as an imperfect substitute. As IDB (2004, p. 38) notes: "Most countries in the region [Latin America] do not have unemployment insurance mechanisms that cover workers against the risk of job loss. Instead, the mechanism of choice to insure against these risks has been mandatory severance pay and indemnities for dismissal."

24. That is in fact reflected in Mexico's legal structure. Article 123 of the Constitution is the principal statement of workers' rights and responsibilities and is the constitutional basis of the Federal Labor Law, which regulates firing and severance payments; the Social Security Law; the Infonavit Law; and others.

25. Severance pay is equivalent to three months and twenty days of salary for every year of service; in addition, for workers with fifteen years of service or more there is a seniority premium of twelve days per year of service.

pension (received, for example, because a worker loses a limb at work) or a disability pension (received, for example, if a worker acquires a disease that prevents him or her from working). Finally, firms and workers understand that being registered with social security also implies being legally covered by severance pay regulations. In other words, *firing and severance pay regulations are bundled with the rest of social security benefits and must be observed jointly by firms and workers.*

Insurance costs depend on the risks of the activity in which the firm is engaged. In the case of mining companies and miners, for instance, the costs of work-risk insurance are higher than for restaurants and waiters. The same is true of the implicit costs of severance pay regulations. Firms facing relatively stable demand and small variance in output will have low costs relative to firms facing unstable demand and high output variance. Heckman and Pagés (2004) estimates the equivalent monetary costs of firing and severance pay regulations, which can be added to the explicitly legislated and ex ante covered costs of social security. For Mexico it estimates them to be, on average, 3.2 percent of wages.[26]

A salaried labor relationship between a firm and a worker also involves other costs that are absent in a nonsalaried relationship, most notably labor taxes. These taxes are conceptually different from social security and severance pay regulations because in principle the worker does not receive a direct benefit in return for the cost. Alternatively, one can suppose that the benefit associated with labor taxes is considered by firms and workers to be irrelevant or to be valued at zero. I mention these taxes because they are quantitatively important and because, again, *they apply only to salaried workers.*

In sum, social security, firing and severance pay, and labor taxes constitute the total non-wage costs of salaried labor. For future reference, they are summarized in table 1-3.

There are other costs associated with hiring workers that apply only to salaried labor, such as profit sharing by firms. I ignore them because hardly any data exist to quantify them.[27] In any event, table 1-3 conveys the basic message: *the bundled*

26. See Heckman and Pagés (2004, table 3, p. 30). Unfortunately the variance is not reported, so one can only speculate how much higher the costs are in sectors like construction and agriculture, which traditionally have faced very erratic demand and higher labor turnover, than in sectors like electricity, where demand is relatively more stable. That is important because, as seen in chapter 4, a large share of poor salaried workers are employed in agriculture and construction and therefore probably face higher implicit costs of firing and severance pay regulations than non-poor workers. It also is worth noting that these calculations include only the monetary costs of the benefits and do not capture the procedural requirements, which suggests that 3.2 percent might be an underestimate of the true cost. Calderón (2000, p. 21) notes that in some sectors these payments can represent up to 7 percent of the wage bill, although he notes that the average for the manufacturing industry is below 4 percent, consistent with the estimates of Heckman and Pagés.

27. Informal conversations with accounting firm executives and individual entrepreneurs indicate a 40 percent difference between wages and labor costs in Mexico as a result of profit-sharing and other regulations. But since I cannot document that figure, I use the 35 percent shown in table 1-3.

Table 1-3. *Non-Wage Costs of Salaried Labor*

| Cost | Percent of wage |
|---|---|
| Social security contributions | 29.5 |
| Firing and severance pay regulations | 3.2 |
| Labor taxes[a] | 2.0 |
| Total | 34.7 |

Sources: Table 1-2; Heckman and Pagés (2004, table 3, p. 30); tax legislation.

a. State taxes only, as federal labor taxes apply only to workers earning four times the minimum wage or more, who are ignored in this study, which focuses on low-wage workers.

and unavoidable non-wage costs of salaried workers are at least 35 percent of wages; as a result, the productivity of salaried workers needs to be 35 percent higher than their wage for firms to hire them. Of course, in principle the costs should translate into direct benefits to workers; if so, they should be fully considered by workers and the firms hiring them, so that what the firm pays is equivalent to what the worker gets.[28] The extent to which that occurs is discussed in chapter 3.

## Resources for Social Programs from 1998 to 2007

Social security is financed with wage-based social security contributions paid by firms and workers together with subsidies from the federal government for retirement and disability pensions and the health components of social security. (Subnational governments do not contribute to social security.)[29] Therefore I refer to both private and public resources for social security. On the other hand, social protection programs are financed by federal and subnational governments (public resources) and by beneficiaries (private resources). Progresa-Oportunidades, finally, is fully funded by the federal government.

Data on public resources for social programs refer only to those channeled to workers currently in the labor force. The data exclude federal government funds for the pensions of already retired workers, who are covered under the pay-as-you-go system of the old (1973) Social Security Law; the current (1997) law provides for a defined-contribution system. Resources used by IMSS to

28. That is not the case with labor taxes, but that is well known. In the discussion that follows I ignore these taxes, although it is useful to keep them in mind when numerical issues are discussed.

29. The Social Security Law currently in place came into effect on July 1, 1997. I present information from 1998 onward because that was the first full year of the law and the rest of the budgetary information is available only on an annual basis. Social security and social protection programs existed before 1997, but they cannot be compared with the current ones because the 1997 law substantially changed the nature of some programs and their sources of financing (particularly for health and pensions). The point here is to note that the coexistence of social security and social protection programs for salaried and nonsalaried workers has been observed for many years, although as documented below there has recently been a notable change in resource flows.

Table 1-4. *Resources for Social Security Programs, 1998–2007*
2007 pesos (billions)

| Program | 1998 | 1999 | 2000 | 2001 | 2002 | 2003 | 2004 | 2005 | 2006 | 2007 |
|---|---|---|---|---|---|---|---|---|---|---|
| Health | 84.9 | 93.5 | 103.8 | 105.1 | 104.7 | 104.6 | 110.4 | 113.6 | 101.6 | 112.1 |
| Housing | 30.6 | 34.6 | 39.1 | 41.9 | 42.9 | 43.8 | 45.9 | 48.3 | 48.9 | 48.6 |
| Day care | 5.8 | 6.6 | 7.4 | 7.9 | 8.0 | 8.2 | 8.5 | 8.9 | 8.9 | 8.8 |
| Pensions | 74.0 | 80.9 | 91.0 | 98.0 | 98.8 | 99.5 | 105.9 | 111.1 | 115.1 | 117.5 |
| First Job program[a] | ... | ... | ... | ... | ... | ... | ... | ... | ... | 3.0 |
| Total | 195.3 | 215.5 | 241.3 | 252.9 | 254.3 | 256.1 | 270.7 | 281.8 | 274.5 | 290.1 |

Source: Appendix 1.
a. Program began in 2007.

cover the additional costs of the special pensions of its own retired workers are netted out of its budget.[30] Finally, federal and subnational resources for the social security institutes of public sector workers covered by these institutes are not included. Put differently, the *resources described refer only to those that provide present or future benefits for workers currently in the labor market but not employed by the national or subnational governments* and that affect a worker's choice between salaried and nonsalaried employment.

Appendix 1 presents details of the calculations described above. Table 1-4 shows net available resources for social security programs; table 1-5, for social protection programs; and table 1-6, for Progresa-Oportunidades. Table 1-7 expresses those numbers as shares of GDP. I emphasize two points here, however. One, I was unable to obtain complete data for social protection programs provided by subnational governments, particularly for housing and day care.[31] Two, table 1-5 *excludes* resources for noncontributory pension programs: the federal Adults over Seventy program (with 6,550 million pesos) and various state-level programs. Noncontributory pensions arguably are part of social protection benefits because nonsalaried workers expect to benefit from them when they retire. But I decided to exclude them because there is some uncertainty regarding their permanence, as opposed to that of retirement pensions, to which salaried workers are entitled. *For those two reasons, total public resources for social protection programs are clearly underestimated.*

Various observations are relevant to the discussion. First, as shown in figure 1-1, over the period 1998–2007 total resources for social security and social protection

30. That is because the additional pensions are paid from the contributions of the workers and firms currently enrolled in social security and therefore cannot be used to provide health and other services to them. See IMSS (2004, 2005) and the discussion in chapter 3 for a description of this special pension regime.

31. The incomplete data that I was able to gather show that between 1998 and 2005 states allocated a total of 17,546 million pesos to housing subsidies; those figures are not in table 1-5. For day care, data are scarcer.

Table 1-5. *Resources for Social Protection Programs, 1998–2007*
2007 pesos (billions)

| Program | 1998 | 1999 | 2000 | 2001 | 2002 | 2003 | 2004 | 2005 | 2006 | 2007 |
|---|---|---|---|---|---|---|---|---|---|---|
| Health | 75.4 | 82.8 | 89.2 | 99.0 | 102.6 | 109.8 | 118.1 | 128.3 | 140.3 | 153.2 |
| Housing | 1.8 | 1.1 | 1.3 | 1.1 | 2.1 | 3.4 | 3.8 | 4.5 | 10.5 | 8.2 |
| Day care[a] | ... | ... | ... | ... | ... | ... | ... | ... | ... | 1.0 |
| Total | 77.2 | 83.8 | 90.5 | 100.2 | 104.7 | 113.2 | 121.8 | 132.8 | 150.8 | 162.4 |

Source: Appendix 1.
a. Program began in 2007.

Table 1-6. *Resources for Progresa-Oportunidades, 1998–2007*
2007 pesos (billions)

| Resources | 1998 | 1999 | 2000 | 2001 | 2002 | 2003 | 2004 | 2005 | 2006 | 2007 |
|---|---|---|---|---|---|---|---|---|---|---|
| Total | 6.5 | 11.5 | 14.2 | 17.4 | 22.3 | 27.0 | 28.9 | 33.2 | 36.1 | 39.5 |

Source: Appendix 1.

Figure 1-1. *Resources for Social Programs, 1998–2007*[a]

2007 pesos (millions)

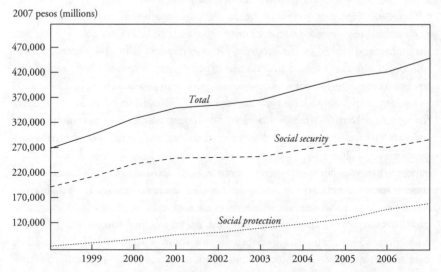

Source: Tables 1-4 and 1-5.
a. Variation from 1998 to 2007: 66.1 percent (total); 48.6 percent (social security); 110.4 percent (social protection).

Figure 1-2. *Resources for Health Programs, 1998–2007*[a]

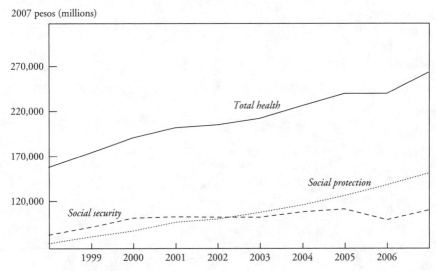

2007 pesos (millions)

Source: Tables 1-4 and 1-5.

a. Variation from 1998 to 2007: 65.7 percent (total); 32.3 percent (social security); 103.3 percent (social protection).

programs, excluding Progresa-Oportunidades, were projected to increase by 66 percent. That results from the weighted average of a 48.6 percent increase for social security programs and a 110.4 percent increase for social protection programs. *In other words, over the decade resources for social protection programs were projected to increase by a factor of 2.1 and for social security by a factor of 1.5.*

Second, figure 1-2 shows that resources for health services provided through social security programs were projected to increase by 32.3 percent and those for services provided through social protection programs by 103.3 percent. In other words, over that decade the additional resources allocated to health services for informal workers were expected to exceed by a factor of three those for formal workers. Note that *as of 2003 there were more resources for health services for informal workers than for formal workers. That difference was expected to exceed more than 36 percent in 2007: 153.1 billion pesos for the former and 112.2 billion for the latter.*

Third, with regard to housing, I note that resources for Infonavit were projected to increase by 60 percent over the decade and resources for housing programs for informal workers by 353 percent. In the case of housing, the absolute amount of resources is still 5.9 times larger for formal than for informal workers (48.6 versus 8.2 billion pesos in 2007), although the difference has narrowed since 1998, when it was 16.9 times larger (30.5 versus 1.8 billion pesos). Recall that subnational resources are excluded, so that the difference is lower but hard to pin down. With

Figure 1-3. *Public Resources for Social Programs, 1998–2007*[a]

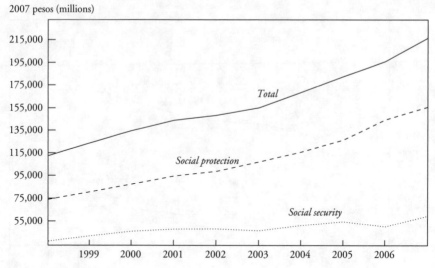

2007 pesos (millions)

Source: Tables 1-4 and 1-5.

a. Variation from 1998 to 2007: 90.1 percent (total); 57.7 percent (social security); 108.0 percent (social protection.).

day care the situation is similar: there are 7 billion pesos for formal workers versus 1 billion for informal workers as a result of the new program created for the latter in 2007.[32] It remains to be seen how that program will grow in the next few years.

Fourth, figure 1-3 shows the behavior of total *public* resources for social security and social protection programs. The results are similar: over the decade subsidies to the former were projected to increase by 57.7 percent and to the latter by 108 percent. Another measure of the difference in the budgetary effort is obtained by simply accumulating subsidies over the period: 497.7 billion pesos for social security versus 1,102.8 for social protection.

Fifth, public resources for Progresa-Oportunidades also have grown significantly, in tandem with the increased coverage of the program from 300,000 families in 1997 to 5 million families as of 2005; expansion of educational scholarships to include high school as of 2001; the Support for Older Adults Program, added in 2006; and the new energy component introduced in 2007.

Table 1-7 shows real GDP in 1998–2007 and compares it with total and public resources for social programs. Over the decade there was a notable increase in

32. As shown in table 1-4, funds for day care centers and recreational and cultural facilities for formal workers amounted to 8.87 billion pesos in 2007, but the Social Security Law states that 80 percent of those are for day care centers and the rest for recreational and cultural facilities, so the difference is one to seven. (As an aside, IMSS is the largest single operator of performing arts theaters in Mexico.)

Table 1-7. GDP and Resources for Social Programs, 1998–2007

| GDP and resources | 1998 | 1999 | 2000 | 2001 | 2002 | 2003 | 2004 | 2005 | 2006 | 2007 |
|---|---|---|---|---|---|---|---|---|---|---|
| GDP[a] | 6,982 | 7,357 | 7,704 | 7,599 | 7,750 | 7,914 | 8,298 | 8,504 | 8,867 | 9,186 |
| *Total resources*[b] | | | | | | | | | | |
| Social security | 2.88 | 3.03 | 3.24 | 3.47 | 3.44 | 3.39 | 3.43 | 3.50 | 3.32 | 3.38 |
| Social protection | 1.10 | 1.14 | 1.18 | 1.32 | 1.35 | 1.43 | 1.47 | 1.57 | 1.71 | 1.77 |
| Progresa-Oportunidades | 0.09 | 0.15 | 0.18 | 0.22 | 0.28 | 0.34 | 0.35 | 0.39 | 0.40 | 0.43 |
| Social security plus social protection | 3.98 | 4.17 | 4.42 | 4.79 | 4.79 | 4.82 | 4.90 | 5.07 | 5.03 | 5.15 |
| Social security plus social protection plus Progresa-Oportunidades | 4.07 | 4.32 | 4.60 | 5.01 | 5.07 | 5.16 | 5.25 | 5.46 | 5.43 | 5.58 |
| *Public resources*[b] | | | | | | | | | | |
| Social security | 0.55 | 0.59 | 0.61 | 0.65 | 0.64 | 0.61 | 0.63 | 0.66 | 0.58 | 0.66 |
| Social protection | 1.08 | 1.12 | 1.16 | 1.26 | 1.30 | 1.38 | 1.42 | 1.51 | 1.65 | 1.71 |
| Social security plus social protection | 1.63 | 1.71 | 1.77 | 1.91 | 1.94 | 1.99 | 2.05 | 2.17 | 2.23 | 2.37 |
| Social security plus social protection plus Progresa-Oportunidades | 1.72 | 1.86 | 1.95 | 2.13 | 2.28 | 2.33 | 2.40 | 2.56 | 2.63 | 2.80 |

Source: Appendix 1.
a. 2007 pesos (trillions). GDP for 2007 is based on the official estimate of real growth (3.6 percent) contained in the federal budget.
b. Percent of GDP.

resources for all three programs (social security, social protection, and Progresa-Oportunidades). While real GDP increased 31.5 percent, total resources for all three programs did so by 76.5 percent. As a result, the share of the three programs in GDP increased from 4.07 to 5.58 percent.

It is worth pointing out, finally, that if one focuses on public resources only, over this period the effort made for all three programs represents an increase in expenditures of 113.5 percent, in contrast to the GDP increase of 31.5 percent. Note that in 2007, public subsidies for social protection programs as a share of GDP were 2.6 times public subsidies for social security; that compares with a difference of 1.9 times in 1998.

# 2

## Formality and Informality

As discussed in chapter 1, workers in Mexico are divided according to their employment status, salaried or nonsalaried. Salaried workers are covered by social security, firing and severance pay regulations, and labor taxes, and nonsalaried workers are covered by social protection programs. However, the Social Security Law is massively violated in Mexico, ruling out a one-to-one correspondence between salaried and nonsalaried status and coverage of social security and social protection programs, respectively.

### Definitions

This chapter elaborates on the concept of *formal* and *informal workers*. Formal workers are defined as salaried workers employed by a firm that registers them with IMSS; given the bundled nature of obligations pertaining to salaried labor, they also are covered by firing and severance pay regulations and labor taxes. Informal workers are defined as self-employed individuals and *comisionistas* working on their own or in a legal nonsalaried capacity with a firm, along with salaried workers who are hired by a firm and paid a wage but, in violation of the law, not registered with IMSS. In turn, *formal firms* are those that hire salaried workers and register at least some of them with IMSS; *informal firms* consist of both firms that have a legal nonsalaried labor relationship with *comisionistas* and firms that hire salaried workers but register neither themselves nor any of their workers with

IMSS.[1] Last, the *formal sector* is composed of formal firms and formal workers and the *informal sector* by informal firms and informal workers. Four worthwhile observations can be made about these definitions.

First, *the informal sector is not defined by the size of a firm.* That is a very important consideration because, as elaborated on in chapter 7, firm size is endogenous to the incentive structure of social policy; further, as shown in table 7-2, many small firms are registered with IMSS. Second, *the informal sector is not defined by economic sector or activity;* formality and informality can and do coexist in agriculture, industry, and services; see tables 7-3 and 7-4. That also is very important because, as I argue in chapter 7, the distribution of firms and workers across activities also is endogenous to the incentive structure of social policy. Third, *informality is not synonymous with illegality.* Under the definitions above, some economic activity in the informal sector is fully legal; in fact, the only illegal component of informality is the existence of a salaried labor relationship between firms and workers not registered with IMSS.[2] Fourth, *illegality is defined as the violation of laws regarding social security, firing and severance pay, and labor taxes (which occur jointly).* At this point I do not consider laws regarding payment of income taxes, registration with municipal authorities, and other dimensions of illegal behavior that also are associated with informality.[3] I do that deliberately because my objective here is to focus sharply on the incentives of social programs. (In chapters 7 and 8, however, I discuss income taxes and registration costs in reference to illegal firms when relevant.)

I do not argue that those definitions are the correct ones. Guha-Khasnobis, Kanbur, and Ostrom point out that there is no uniform definition of informality.[4] They note that "instead, it turns out that formal and informal are better thought of as a metaphor that conjures up a mental picture of whatever the user has in mind at that particular time." But I do argue that they are the *relevant* ones for Mexico, in the sense of being driven by the country's laws and institutions pertaining to the labor market.

Guha-Khasnobis and colleagues note that two elements usually are present in informality: first, activity that occurs outside the reach of different levels and mechanisms of official governance; second, activity that "lacks structure" or is

1. There is some ambiguity about whether the self-employed constitute a firm. From the standpoint of being a combination of capital (or land) and labor that produces output, they are. That interpretation is especially relevant in terms of the demand for their own labor (see chapter 6). But they are not a firm from the standpoint of there being a salaried labor relationship and the associated obligations with regard to social security. The law does not impose legal obligations on bosses when they are only their own boss.

2. I ignore here illegal trade in goods like drugs and firearms or services like prostitution and child labor. All goods and services produced and consumed here are legal; the focus is on the status of the firms and workers of legal working age who at times might violate social security laws.

3. I also ignore minimum wage laws because the evidence shows that they are not binding in Mexico; see chapter 5.

4. Guha-Khasnobis, Kanbur, and Ostrom (2006a, p. 3).

"simple" or at times even "disorganized." Of the two elements, one is clearly present in my definitions: the informal sector in Mexico is outside the reach of the official governance mechanisms that apply to salaried labor, namely social security obligations, regulations on firing and severance pay, and labor taxes. That might be the result of deliberate legal design (the exclusion of nonsalaried labor from those governance mechanisms) or of an illegal act (firms evading the mechanisms).

On the other hand, when associating informality with lack of structure or with being simple or disorganized, it is crucial not to overlook the fact that *economic structures are endogenous to the incentives of the governance mechanisms that bear on them.* As a result, one should not associate simplicity or the (apparent) absence of structure with the absence of maximizing behavior. Agents in the informal sector are as rational as agents in the formal sector, and the simplicity of their form of economic production or distribution needs to be understood as a maximizing response to the constraints and incentives that they encounter. In other words, simplicity needs to be seen at least in part as a response to the governance mechanisms that apply to salaried labor. Of course, that simplicity might be suboptimal from the point of view of aggregate labor and capital productivity; in fact, in chapters 7 and 8 I argue that at times that is true. As noted, at some point economic processes might become so complex that they unavoidably require salaried labor and some minimum scale. The same is true with "disorganization," which on second thought might be seen as an organized response to the same governance mechanisms; see chapter 7.

My definition of informality is not equivalent to illegality. Bosch and Maloney note that "there is broad consensus in the literature on the definition of an informal worker. Generally speaking, formal workers are those working in firms licensed with the government and conforming to tax and labor laws, including minimum wage directives, pension and health insurance benefits for employees, workplace standards of safety, etc. The informal workers, on the contrary, are those *owners* of firms that are largely de-linked from state institutions and obligations and their employees who are not covered by formal labor protections." That definition refers mostly to illegal salaried workers. But the self-employed and *comisionistas* are not illegal; as a result, legality and illegality coexist in informality.[5]

More generally, the composition of the informal sector is not homogeneous in terms of the legality of employment, the type of firms involved, or the areas of economic activity. As shown in chapter 7, that heterogeneity matters greatly in terms of productivity and the response of employment in each sector to exogenous shocks. As shown in chapter 8, it also affects the economy's growth rate. Further, while part of informality refers only to self-employed workers, with no firm

5. Bosch and Maloney (2006, p. 7). See also IDB (2004, box 1.3, p. 23) for a discussion of informality in the context of labor markets in Latin America. Guha-Khasnobis, Kanbur, and Ostrom (2006a, 2006b) contains an excellent collection of recent essays on informality covering issues beyond the labor market.

Table 2-1. *Economic Dimensions of Formality and Informality*

| Type of employment | Legal | Firm involved | Registration costs[a] | Access to bank credit/training[b] |
|---|---|---|---|---|
| *Formal* | | | | |
| Salaried | Yes | Yes | Yes | Yes |
| *Informal* | | | | |
| Salaried | No | Yes | No | No |
| Self-employed | Yes | ? | No | ? |
| *Comisionista* | Yes[c] | Yes | Yes | Yes |

Source: Author's illustration.

a. Refers to registration and operation costs of various legal requirements.

b. Refers to access to commercial bank credit, government-sponsored job-training programs, and the like.

c. Refers to firms having genuine nonsalaried relationships with workers, which do not use nonsalaried contracts to evade the law (see chapter 7).

involved, another part—*comisionistas* and illegal salaried employees—involves both a worker and a firm and thereby the interaction of two separate agents with different objective functions. Moreover, that interaction is legal in the first case and illegal in the second. In other words, the definition of informality also involves firms, who like workers may be formal or informal depending on incentives and the outcome of the simultaneous decisions of all parties involved.

Table 2-1 highlights key economic dimensions that I believe need to be incorporated in the analysis of formality and informality. Consider the first and last rows. As shown, the only difference between formal and informal firms lies in their labor costs, because formal firms must incorporate the costs of the official governance mechanisms that apply to salaried labor. Otherwise, however, firms in the two categories face the same constraints and opportunities in terms of the key factors that determine their productivity: the possibility of achieving economies of scale or scope, optimal level of vertical integration, access to commercial bank credit, access to officially sponsored job-training programs, and other benefits of legality. *They face no constraints on growth inherent in their formal or informal status.* Indeed, in Mexico there are very large firms associated with tens of thousands of *comisionistas,* and, of course, one also finds large formal firms with tens of thousands of salaried workers.[6] In fact, from the economic point of view, those two rows in table 2-1 could be merged; indeed, in most analyses of informality the distinction made

6. A firm based in Guadalajara, in the state of Jalisco, is reputed to employ more than 250,000 workers in door-to-door sales of health products. Two large firms in Mexico City (one of them subsidiary of a foreign corporation) jointly employ more than 150,000 workers selling beauty products. There also are firms employing workers selling kitchen utensils (plastic containers and the like). A large cell phone company in Mexico has thousands of *comisionistas* in the city streets selling calling cards. These are all legally established firms.

here is ignored. *But from the social point of view that cannot be done,* as the social benefits that workers receive in each case are different.

Consider next the first and second rows. Clearly, aside from facing different labor costs, *firms and workers face different constraints and possibilities in terms of the factors that affect their productivity:* the ability to achieve economies of scale and optimal vertical integration while remaining informal, access to commercial bank credit, and so on. The difference arises from illegality, which offers some advantages but also entails some disadvantages. That difference matters greatly for the firm, for the social benefits that workers can receive, and for the government's social objectives.

Consider finally the contrast between the third and all other rows in table 2-1. A self-employed worker might become more productive over time as he or she acquires new abilities or access to improved complementary inputs, but one cannot properly think of growth in a one-person firm in a quantitative sense (unless, as discussed in chapter 1, the worker becomes a boss, legal or illegal, or forms a joint venture or a cooperative with other workers). The determinants of productivity are different in a one-person firm and so are the implications for the social programs to which the worker has access.

I show in chapter 6 that the formal-informal dichotomy lowers aggregate labor productivity even with fully legal behavior. However, I attach great importance to the impact of illegality on productivity. De Soto states that "because they are not incorporated, extralegal entrepreneurs cannot lure investors by selling shares; they cannot secure low-interest formal credit because they do not even have legal addresses. They cannot reduce risk by declaring limited liability or obtaining insurance coverage. The only 'insurance' available to them is that provided by their neighbors and the protection that local bullies or mafias are willing to sell them. Moreover, because extralegal entrepreneurs live in constant fear of government detection and extortion from corrupt officials, they are forced to split and compartmentalize their production facilities between many locations, thereby rarely achieving important economies of scale. . . . With one eye always on the lookout for the police, underground entrepreneurs cannot openly advertise to build up their clientele or make less costly bulk deliveries to customers."[7]

In chapters 6 to 8, I develop a framework within which some of those effects can be quantified and argue that they result in both static and dynamic productivity losses. Although it may not be feasible to quantify other effects of informality on productivity, they still may exist. Informality probably increases transactions costs in the sense argued long ago by Coase in his analysis of the nature of the firm. In particular, he points out that "outside the firm, price movements direct production, which is coordinated through a series of exchange transactions on the

---

7. De Soto (2000, p. 155)

market. Within a firm these market transactions are eliminated, and in place of the complicated market structure with exchange transactions is substituted the entrepreneur-coordinator, who directs production."[8] As a result, up to a point the costs of some transactions can be reduced if carried out inside the firm by increased vertical integration as opposed to arm's-length market-based operations. "This coordination of the various factors of production is, however, normally carried out without the intervention of the price mechanism. As is evident, the amount of vertical integration, involving as it does the supersession of the price mechanism, varies greatly from industry to industry and from firm to firm."[9]

The point here is that the optimal amount of vertical integration is reduced if a firm has to take into account the effects of larger size and broader scope on its illegal status, particularly when, as shown in chapter 7, illegality may lower the firm's labor costs but only if it is "small" (in a sense that I try to make precise in that chapter). The result is that in the case of informal firms, the balance between economic transactions internalized by a firm and those carried out through the price mechanism in the market tilts in the direction of the latter, generating smaller firms that have lower-than-optimal vertical integration and higher transaction costs than formal firms. That is not an academic point: as shown in table 7-2, in Mexico there are almost 2.7 million firms with up to five workers, *excluding* firms that carry out their activities in an ambulatory fashion or in portable premises on the street. *In that context the "simplicity" of informal firms (in the sense of having very little vertical integration) is an optimal response to an incentive structure that offers an implicit trade-off between labor costs and transaction costs—a trade-off that in the absence of the formal-informal dichotomy would not occur.*[10]

On the other hand, it is useful to recall from chapter 1 that the distinction between the different categories of employment and firm participation in economic activity cannot be made with full precision. Legal ambiguities and borderline cases aside, I show in chapter 5 that in Mexico, workers—particularly low-wage workers— cannot be unambiguously classified as formal or informal because during their working lives they are engaged at times in formal employment and at other times in informal employment. And I show in chapter 7 that firms cannot be sharply divided between formal and informal because some register only a share of their workers with IMSS; *as a result, in some formal firms there are formal and informal workers.* For those reasons it is best to think of a continuum of firms and workers, with some firms at one end fully complying with all the official governance mech-

---

8. Coase (1988, pp. 35–36).

9. (Coase, 1988, p. 36). "The main reason why it is profitable to establish a firm would seem to be that there is a cost of using the price mechanism. . . . The costs of negotiating and concluding a separate contract for each exchange transaction which takes place on a market must also be taken into account. . . . It is true that contracts are not eliminated when there is a firm, but they are greatly reduced" (Coase, 1988, pp. 38–39).

10. Chapter 7 discusses an example based on the experience of the garment industry in Mexico in which vertical integration appears to be socially suboptimal.

anisms that apply to salaried labor and some firms at the other end evading them altogether. Likewise, some workers spend their entire working life in formal employment and others in informal employment. But the fact that the border between formality and informality cannot be drawn with precision should not distract from the more important fact that *that border is not exogenous;* it responds to changes in the incentives presented to firms and workers, in particular the structure of labor taxes and subsidies implicit in Mexico's social programs.

Three more remarks. First, it is necessary to separate the issue of labor mobility from the issue of informality even though they are sometimes discussed together. Under the definitions given above, there will always be an informal sector, even with full labor mobility, because there is an efficient level of nonsalaried employment (chapter 6 makes that concept precise). Some production is best performed through cooperative or joint ventures, through a *comisionista* relationship between a firm and its workers, or even by workers on their own. In other words, some economic processes do not require salaried labor and are carried out more efficiently under other contractual arrangements. *Informality does not result only from the existence of barriers to entering the formal sector, and even with full labor mobility there is substantial informality.*

Second, at times the notion of informality carries the negative connotations of low-quality jobs and low earnings. But that need not always be the case. Under the definitions given above, a self-employed doctor visiting a patient at home is informal in the sense that he operates outside the reach of the official governance mechanisms that apply to salaried labor, but he can have high earnings, register with the Health Ministry, and pay income taxes. He is not, however, being forced to save in an Afore for his retirement, purchase health insurance from IMSS, and save for a future housing loan with Infonavit, nor will he receive any severance pay if he loses all his patients. The same is true of a farmer who devotes all his time to working his own land. As I show in chapter 5, not all informal workers have low earnings and not all formal workers have high earnings (see table 5-1).

Third, the view of informal firms varies. At times they are treated in the literature as disorganized or unstructured and at other times they are described as the more dynamic, job-generating segment of the economy.[11] I think it is best to think of informal firms in the same terms as formal ones: as a combination of capital (or land) and labor that maximizes profit. *The decision to be informal or to comply in part or in full with the official governance mechanisms that apply to salaried labor is the result of the incentives presented to the firm, on one hand, and of the technology available, on the other.* As noted, that decision has implications in terms of the firm's access to credit and insurance, transaction costs, and the like. But the point to emphasize is that the formality or informality of a firm is *endogenous* and that an informal firm's dynamism or lack of it is a response to incentives. Formality or informality

---

11. Chen (2006, p. 81, table 5-1) provides a useful summary of the various views of informal firms.

is not a permanent or exogenously given characteristic of firms. Moreover, as elaborated on below, I do not assume that entrepreneurs in the formal sector are better than those in the informal sector. My assumption is that, on average, from the private point of view firms and entrepreneurs are equally efficient in both sectors. *The problem is that the labor costs faced by firms depend on the sector that they are in and that the difference in labor costs results in a loss of efficiency because labor and capital are misallocated.*

## Interpretation and Implications

There are three broad views of informality in Latin America. One has intellectual roots that go back to the celebrated two-sector model in Harris and Todaro (1970), in which there is a binding minimum wage or a restriction on entry to the formal sector. That view also is associated with International Labor Office (1972) and other studies that argue that there are barriers to entry to formal jobs and that the informal sector plays the role of a "residual" in which workers have lower utility than their formal counterparts while they queue for a formal job; see also Tokman (1978).

The second view, perhaps more recent, is associated with the work of Dávila (1994), Maloney (1999, 2004), IDB (2004), Heckman and Pagés (2004), World Bank (2007), and others. It claims that there are no barriers to mobility and that informality consists of a dynamic sector of small firms and self-employed individuals escaping from rigid labor regulations and high transaction costs. As Bosch and Maloney state, "Given the size of the [informal] sector, the stakes in terms of policy formulation are very high indeed. If most of the informal sector is in fact rationed out of good jobs, then the implicit labor distortions in the formal sector are very large and the need for regulatory reform compelling. Further, social policy becomes a fairly straightforward question of offsetting one distortion with transfers to the disadvantaged sector. If, however, the informal sector is best seen as offering jobs with differing packages of characteristics—more flexibility, no boss, evasion of restrictive and inefficient regulation (including costly and badly designed labor protections), ease of free riding on publicly provided goods—and which are equally desirable for the worker at the margin, then the incidence of segmenting labor legislation is in all probability less acute, and the design of social policy requires considering all the incentives and disincentives to participate in one sector or the other."[12]

12. Bosch and Maloney (2006, pp. 7–8). In a similar vein, Gong, Soest, and Villagomez (2004, p. 1) observes that "the traditional staging hypothesis . . . is that formal sector employment is rationed. Those who cannot obtain a formal job either search from unemployment or, if they cannot afford to be unemployed, work in the informal sector. The other view sees the two as symmetric and competitive. The formal and informal sectors have different production functions, and heterogeneity among workers implies that some are more productive in one sector while others have larger productivity in the other sector."

The third view, which is associated with de Soto (2000), emphasizes cumbersome and obsolete laws and procedures with regard to titling and validation of property rights, which in turn result in paralegal arrangements in which property cannot be fully collateralized or securitized because ownership is uncertain and the property is therefore undervalued. Informality is a parallel way of doing business that hinders the process of capital accumulation. In reference to rural migrants who squat in places like Jakarta, Mexico City, and São Paulo, among others, de Soto notes that "the failure of the legal order to keep pace with this astonishing economic and social upheaval has forced the new migrants to invent extralegal substitutes for established law. Whereas all manners of anonymous business transactions are widespread in advanced countries, the migrants in the developing world can deal only with people they know and trust. Such informal, ad hoc business arrangements do not work very well. The wider the market, as Adam Smith pointed out, the more minute the division of labor can be. And as labor grows more specialized, the economy grows more efficient, and wages and capital values rise. A legal failure that prevents enterprising people from negotiating with strangers defeats the division of labor and fastens would-be entrepreneurs to smaller circles of specialization and low productivity."[13]

I want to put forth a fourth alternative view of informality that I argue is more useful for Mexico. My view partly coincides with some elements of the previous views, but it is substantively different in the following respects. First, I focus on a definition of the formal-informal dichotomy that is relevant to social policy in that it refers to workers of similar characteristics, abilities, and income levels who receive different social benefits. In that respect my view is similar to the one expressed by Bosch and Maloney, except that I emphasize that, first, despite the absence of barriers to workers' mobility, there are important differences in productivity across sectors and, second, that under informality it is impossible to reach the government's social objectives. I contend, in fact, that some social programs make those objectives even harder to reach.

Second, I do not associate all informality of workers with self-employed individuals and microenterprises. As discussed, informal workers can also be in medium-size and large firms—sometimes legally, as in the case of *comisionistas,* and sometimes illegally, as a result of evasion of regulations by firms that hire salaried workers. Third, I directly associate the existence of illegal salaried labor with social policies. That association is crucial because, on one hand, it highlights the problems with social policies that discriminate between workers, and, on the other, because illegal salaried labor has fiscal and productivity implications that by and large have been ignored. Fourth, I do not associate formality with good jobs and informality with bad ones. Instead, I emphasize the implications of the formal-informal dichotomy for productivity and economic growth. Fifth, I emphasize

13. De Soto (2000, p. 71).

that informality is a characteristic of both workers and firms and that it is jointly determined as a result of their simultaneous actions. Sixth, I do not assume that large or small informal firms are more efficient or inefficient than large or small formal firms.

In chapter 5, I present evidence showing that *the labor market is characterized by substantial mobility of workers between the formal and the informal sectors and that in fact mobility is higher for lower-wage workers than for higher-wage workers.* Low-wage workers can and do enter the formal sector; in fact, they enter more often than high-wage workers (and exit more often). Further, there is hardly any evidence of segmentation produced by minimum wages. That does not imply that there are no barriers to entry to some jobs, but they are within formal sector jobs. An example is the case of IMSS employees themselves. Because the IMSS union controls entry and because the labor contract specifies above-average pensions, vacations, and so on, there is a long line of workers trying to enter IMSS, even for simple jobs like cleaning hospitals and offices or mowing the lawn in recreational centers.[14] The same occurs in some large private firms, some of which might share part of their monopoly profits with their workers. But that is because there are pure rents in such jobs. That fact is well known; the point I want to make here is that *those barriers to entry apply to a subset of formal jobs, not to all formal jobs,* and moreover that the subset is small.[15]

Ignoring the exceptional cases of union or firm monopoly power, in Mexico workers move from one sector to the other, and it is clear that from that standpoint the distribution of the labor force must be such that utility is equalized across sectors. *That means that from the point of view of workers, there are good and bad jobs in both sectors, not only in the informal sector;* see the evidence on wage rates in tables 5-10 to 5-13. However, it does not mean that the formal-informal dichotomy is irrelevant to workers; on the contrary, it matters greatly, because the fact that there is full mobility does not imply that the allocation of labor is efficient. Despite the existence of mobility and the associated implication that workers in both sectors have the same utility (though not necessarily the same wage), *the labor market is segmented in the sense that workers with similar abilities and characteristics have different productivities.* That segmentation produces an outcome that lowers the productivity and the utility of all workers. In other words, informality affects productivity in both sectors. As a result, the argument needs to be restated, from "informality is bad because informal workers are worse off than formal workers" to "the formal-informal dichotomy is bad because it hurts all workers." And attention needs to be shifted from wage differentials to productivity differentials.

14. Levy (2006d).

15. There also are barriers to entry to some jobs in the public sector because of large and powerful unions in fields like education and health; those union-created barriers also provide rents for public workers. These are all "good" formal jobs, *but most formal jobs in Mexico do not have rents associated with them.*

I also argue in chapter 6 that segmentation in the labor market is *provoked* by social policy, particularly by the coexistence of social security and social protection programs. Segmentation would persist, moreover, even if there were no labor regulations regarding firing and severance pay, even if there were no taxes on salaried labor, and even if all property was fully registered and titled. And I argue in chapters 7 and 8 that segmentation distorts the size distribution of firms and the composition of output, lowers the productivity of capital and, by raising the incremental capital/output ratio, lowers the rate of growth of GDP. Thus, aside from the asymmetric protection of workers from risks, the formal-informal divide creates substantive problems for aggregate productivity and growth that need to be given equal weight and attention.

I argue in chapter 7 that firms divide endogenously into formal and informal. As a result, one cannot make any ex ante assumptions about differences in the efficiency of firms. In this book I assume that all firms—formal and informal, large and small—maximize profits. In other words, all firms hire labor up to the point where the value of the marginal product of labor *to the firm* is equal to the expected cost of labor *to the firm,* and all firms invest on the basis of the comparison of the cost of capital to the expected rate of return on investments. There is no basis on those grounds to argue that there are systematic differences between firms in the private efficiency with which they operate. Nevertheless, because the formal-informal dichotomy implies that the expected cost of labor to firms varies across firms, there are systematic differences in labor productivity between formal and informal firms and, when investments are considered, systematic differences in the productivity of capital. There is a difference between the private efficiency with which firms exploit capital and labor and the social productivity of capital and labor. I do not speak about inefficiency at the level of the individual firm; I speak about privately efficient firms whose actions, when aggregated, result in outcomes that fail to maximize the aggregate productivity of labor and capital. *Informality is inefficient from a social point of view, not a private one.*

The foregoing remarks can be put differently. Much of the literature on labor markets and informality makes two implicit assumptions: one, that social security contributions are fully valued by formal workers; two, that social protection programs either do not exist or are not valued at all by informal workers. If that were so, any differences in productivity between formal and informal workers would be independent of social programs and would have to be associated with binding minimum wages or other barriers to mobility. But if, as substantiated in chapter 3, those two assumptions are incorrect in the case of Mexico, then social programs are a source of segmentation even with full mobility of workers and in the absence of minimum wages and other barriers—*understanding by segmentation not the difference in workers' utility but the difference in workers' productivity.*

As a result, the policy problem created by the formal-informal dichotomy does not lie only in designing social programs to extend to workers in the informal sector the same protections that workers in the formal sector have; it is more complicated than that. In extending protection, policymakers first must consider the implications of the mix of social interventions on labor and capital productivity and second must ensure that the protection offered is equally effective for all workers along all the essential dimensions of the government's social objectives.

My view of informality complements de Soto's view. As shown in chapters 6 to 8, informality exists and would persist even if there were full property rights and no registration costs. Informality is *created* by social programs, regardless of property laws and registration costs. I show in chapter 8 that even if all firms had the same access to credit and their property could be fully collateralized, variations in the marginal product of labor and capital across workers and firms would still be present and productivity thereby hindered. Further, one component of informal employment—*comisionistas* and illegal salaried workers—is associated with formal firms, in which the issues of property rights and undervalued collateral are not relevant. However, if the property rights problem stressed by de Soto is present, the forces generating informality are doubly strong. More important, in both "property rights induced" and "social programs induced" informality, the result is that the economic activity that occurs is less than the potential activity given the economy's underlying technology and endowment of productive assets.

In this volume I emphasize social programs–induced informality for three reasons:

—First, because although it works directly through the labor market, it spills over into the composition of output, the allocation of investment, and possibly the volume of savings, as opposed to property rights–induced informality, which works through asset markets.

—Second, because social programs–induced informality is expressly subsidized by the government with fiscal resources (in increasing amounts, as shown in chapter 1). Chapter 9 argues that by doing so, the government creates fiscal problems that are relevant in their own right and makes costly trade-offs to maintain fiscal balance.

—Third, because, as shown in chapters 5 and 7, there is a quantitatively important component of informal employment associated with firms that are fully registered and have full property rights but nevertheless hire salaried workers without social security coverage.

By stressing the implications of informality on workers' and firms' behavior jointly I show the paradoxical result that *the best of government social intentions— as reflected in the programs and budgetary allocations described in chapter 1— unfortunately contribute to undermining essential elements of Mexico's social contract and future wealth: the entitlement of workers to social security, on one hand, and the productivity of the economy, on the other.*

A methodological consideration needs to be highlighted at this point: in the analysis that follows, the division of the economy into a formal and an informal sector is not exogenous; it results from the interaction of institutions and behavior. Legal institutions give substance to the analytical distinction between salaried and nonsalaried labor relationships between firms and workers (including self-employment); the institutions are, so to speak, the primary raison d'etre of the distinction. But the response of firms and workers to those institutions also gives substance to that analytical distinction between legal and illegal salaried labor relationships, which also is an essential component of the formal-informal division of the economy. In what follows I try to derive a framework wherein the equilibrium level of firms and workers in legal salaried and nonsalaried labor relationships, on one hand, and the equilibrium level of firms and workers in illegal salaried labor relations, on the other, are both endogenous to the legal institutions and to the profit- and utility-maximizing responses of firms and workers, respectively, to the functioning of those institutions.

*Understanding the nature and causes of the formal-informal dichotomy and its implications for welfare and productivity is essential for policy in Mexico, for five reasons.* First, from the quantitative standpoint, social programs are more important as a cause of informality than regulations on firing and severance pay and labor taxes. Table 1-3 is useful in assessing the relevant magnitudes involved. Even if labor regulations on firing and severance pay were not valued at all by workers, the equivalent associated tax on salaried labor would be less than 4 percent of wages. Contrast that with social security contributions, which, even if valued at, say, two-thirds of their cost, would be equivalent to an associated tax on salaried labor of 10 percent. Moreover, an insufficiently noticed aspect of social protection programs is that they are equivalent to a subsidy to nonsalaried labor (see chapter 6). The point is that in Mexico the distortion in the labor market coming from the tax-cum-subsidy associated with social security and social protection programs is much larger than the distortion coming from labor taxes and firing and severance pay regulations. As shown in chapter 7, the differences in the costs of salaried and nonsalaried labor to firms can be on the order of 50 percent.

Second, *the formal-informal dichotomy has created a dilemma for the government:* on one hand, it wants to provide informal workers with the same protection against various risks that formal workers have; on the other, as it does so it increases the size of the informal sector and deepens the distortions that lower everyone's productivity (see table 10-1). To compete successfully in the world and raise workers' living standard through increased productivity and higher wages—not through increased transfers from social programs—Mexico needs to escape that dilemma.

Third, the formal-informal dichotomy matters because, from the perspective of equity, it is very worrisome that workers with similar abilities performing similar tasks have unequal entitlements to social benefits and, from the perspective of efficacy, that the government's social objectives are partly nullified as workers arbitrage between formal and informal status.

Fourth, the formal-informal dichotomy matters because there are important fiscal implications of the divide that are relevant for public investment, for redistributive reasons, and for the medium-term sustainability of social interventions. Firing and severance pay regulations also are a source of informality, but they, unlike other social programs, have no fiscal costs.

The fifth reason is of a different nature. The informal sector does not contribute the largest share of Mexico's GDP (or measured GDP) or the largest share of exports, nor is it the largest user of commercial bank credit. By those measures it could be seen as secondary. But the informal sector does account for the largest number of workers and the largest number of firms in Mexico (see table 5-1 and table 7-2). From that perspective, *informality is not a secondary issue; it is the arena in which the majority of Mexico's workers and firms deploy their efforts and skills every day, and it is the mechanism by which the government's social objectives are continuously thwarted. Understanding informality is a crucial issue for Mexico.*

In this volume I highlight six intimately associated dimensions of the formal-informal dichotomy that, from a policy standpoint, need to be identified separately but analyzed jointly: one, its impact on wages and workers' utility; two, its impact on firms' profits; three, its impact on the government's social objectives; four, its impact on labor and capital productivity; five, its impact on fiscal accounts; and six, its impact on poverty, given that the dichotomy is especially harmful to poor workers.

# 3

## Workers' Valuation of Social Programs

Social programs exist because the government has social goals. It is essential to identify those goals clearly in order to ensure that the programs implemented to realize them are the most appropriate. A program may, for example, confuse the government's redistributive goal with its goal of protecting households against risks and ultimately accomplish neither effectively. It also is essential to decide whether social goals apply—or should apply—to all salaried and nonsalaried workers or to only a subset of them, in the latter case identifying clearly the reasons for any discrimination. Are social security and social protection programs instruments for protecting workers against risks, redistributing income, or both? Can the programs accomplish those goals?

On the other hand, workers' perceptions of the government's social interventions through various social programs may differ from those of the government, creating a gap between the costs of the programs and workers' valuation of them. Depending on whether the gap applies to all workers and all social programs or only to some workers and a subset of programs, it can have important effects on firms and workers, which in turn affect the extent to which the government's social goals can be realized.

### Determinants of Workers' Valuation of Social Security

In Mexico, salaried workers receive as compensation for their labor a monetary wage that they can dispose of as desired and a claim to a set of different present and future goods and services. Consider the worker exemplified in table 1-2 in

47

chapter 1. He receives a monthly wage of 2,931 pesos in cash and a claim to goods and services worth 864 pesos. In exchange for 358 of those 864 pesos, he and his family can receive health services from IMSS as needed. IMSS also deposits 184 pesos in the retirement sub-account of his Afore account, managed by the Afore of his choice, so that twenty or thirty years hence he will have income after retirement. IMSS deposits 146 pesos in the housing sub-account of his Afore account so that at some point he can get a housing loan from Infonavit.[1] In exchange for 29 pesos, he can send his child to a day care center from the age of two months to four years, and so on.

In an idealized setting in which the worker wanted to consume the same combination of goods and services as listed in table 1-2 and in which the mechanisms to do so were available, social security would be irrelevant in the sense that, with or without it, present and future consumption would be the same. He could receive 2,931 pesos in cash and social security benefits worth 864 pesos, or he could receive 3,795 pesos (2,931 + 864) in cash and use 864 pesos to buy the same present and future goods and services provided by social security. In the second case, two conditions would have to be met: first, the worker must be able to find an insurance company willing to sell him a health insurance policy covering himself and his family for 358 pesos, he must be able to find a financial firm willing to invest his 184 pesos in a long-term savings instrument with the same risk-return combination that an Afore offers, and so on. Second, he must be willing to do so—that is, out of his wage of 3,795 pesos, he has to be willing to use 864 pesos to purchase those services in the amounts shown in table 1-2.

Social security exists for two reasons: one, because failures in insurance markets imply that in some cases the possibility of private contracting does not exist; two, because even if workers could contract for services, they might not want to do so.[2] The first reason calls for intervention in the markets for health insurance, day care services, housing loans, long-term savings, and so on, in order to open up contracting possibilities or reduce their cost. But it is important to note that there would be no need to force workers to buy services or to tie services in a single bundle. If the only problem were that insurance markets failed to work well, in principle the problem would be solved by improving market functioning.[3] The situa-

---

1. If the worker never gets a housing loan, the funds deposited in the housing sub-account are returned to him on retirement and, together with those accumulated in his retirement sub-account, are used to purchase an annuity. Ex post, the worker saved 330 pesos a month (184+146) for retirement, not 184 pesos.

2. There is a third reason: that a worker's wage is insufficient for him to purchase insurance instruments even if they are available and he wants to purchase them. That is the redistributive reason. But a moment's thought reveals that the issue could be solved by a simple income transfer (say, Progresa-style but without conditions). Social security involves some element of failure in insurance markets and, in my view, some equally important element of the government imposing its preferences on workers.

3. That is, of course, no easy matter. Under some circumstances the solution might be to provide insurance through a public entity and, to spread the risk, obligate all workers to buy insurance through that entity.

tion with respect to the second reason is different. Even if a worker could buy services from a private or a public insurance firm, she might not want to, or she might not want to buy all of them at the same time, or she might not want to buy them in the proportions offered. Perhaps the worker wants to spend a little less on health insurance and more on day care services, or perhaps she is not interested in a housing loan but wants to buy more life insurance, and so on. The second reason is associated with the government's desire to ensure that various goods be consumed at the same time and in the amounts set by the government.

The Mexican government addresses the two reasons for social security through the combination of IMSS, Infonavit, the Afores, and regulations on severance pay. By obligating workers to enroll, the government both tackles the market problems associated with contracting for insurance and obtains the benefits of pooling risks from a large universe; at the same time, it makes sure that workers actually purchase a claim to all the goods and services offered even if they do not want to. In other words, it imposes its own preferences on workers.

The government may or may not be right, but it is not relevant here to argue for or against its position. Substantive reasons associated with risk pooling, moral hazard, free riding, or myopic behavior may justify what the government does. But substantive or not, the key point for my purposes is that social security in Mexico is a mechanism *to force workers to purchase a claim to certain present and future goods and services even if they do not want to.*[4]

In this volume I define "the government's social objectives" as the government's insistence that workers *simultaneously* have access to health, life, disability, and work-risk insurance; a housing loan; retirement income; day care services; cultural and sports facilities; and severance pay when fired. That is what the Constitution and various laws require.

But workers' objectives may be quite different. Myopic or not, free riders or not, and moral hazard notwithstanding, workers want to maximize their own utility. That need not imply purchasing a claim to all of the goods and services that the government requires or even to any of them. Further, from the perspective of the worker, if he is going to receive a subsidy because the government wants to redistribute income in his favor, he wants to allocate it as he deems best.

*It is essential to make a sharp distinction between the worker's point of view and the government's point of view.* It is not that one viewpoint is right and the other wrong; it is just that they are different. The government and workers might assign a different value to social security benefits; in particular, *the value to the worker of those benefits may be different from their monetary costs.* In other words, the worker probably would prefer 864 pesos in cash to 864 pesos in a claim to

4. The government might also think that social security serves to redistribute income from firms to workers by making the former pay for the greater part of the benefits, but that is not so (see chapter 6). Only when social security is subsidized by the government does it have the *potential* to be redistributive (see chapter 9).

various services, so that his take-home pay was 3,795 pesos, not 2,931. He might not value the services offered at the equivalent of 864 pesos.

That scenario need not apply to all workers. For some, the value of a single social security benefit might exceed 864 pesos. Think of a single mother who has no family members who can look after her two-year-old child; access to a day care center might make all the difference in her ability to take a job as a seamstress at a maquiladora. Think of a worker in his early fifties suffering from high blood pressure, for whom the medicines that he gets free from IMSS are worth more than 864 pesos as well. In short, for some workers social security benefits can be worth more than their cost.

However, I argue that in Mexico that is the exception, not the rule, and that the available evidence indicates that workers value social security at less than its cost. I believe that that is true for two reasons: design problems, on one hand, and performance problems that create a gap between statutory and actual benefits, on the other. The following discussion reviews the main problems in each area, providing a sense of the factors underlying workers' valuation of social security. The review provides an understanding of the factors that drive the results presented in later chapters; because it points out where reforms are needed, it also is critical for policy. However, the reader can go directly to table 3-7 for a summary of the arguments.

### Design Problems

Bundling benefits lowers the utility that workers derive from social security.[5] Furthermore, the bigger the bundle, the higher the cost, because buying all the services costs more than buying some or none and because the match between workers' individual needs and the set of benefits provided is increasingly imperfect. It is worth pointing out that valuing social security requires workers to make a judgment about a large number of offered goods and services: future consumption (retirement pensions), fixed assets (a house), current services (day care), certain contingencies (becoming disabled, having an accident at work, being fired), and complex services (health care), among others. Bundling requires workers to make a judgment about all those components at the same time.

Consider next household composition. While all benefits must be paid by each worker enrolled in social security, some benefits extend to all members of the household. For example, a husband's health insurance covers his wife and their children. However, if the wife is a salaried employee, she and her employer also have to pay for health insurance for her, her husband, and their children, even though the family already has it. In other words, the wife of a salaried worker who gets a salaried job derives no additional benefit at all from the extra 358 pesos paid

5. This is a standard revealed preference argument: workers could always acquire each benefit separately and then consume them jointly if they wanted to.

for health insurance. A second example is working couples without children of day care age, who derive no direct personal benefit from the 29 pesos paid for day care services but have to pay for them anyway. Yet a third example is a wife who is forced to save for a housing loan even though her husband already has one; because she will not need it, she ends up being forced to save 146 pesos more than her husband.

Consider, finally, migration patterns. Assume a young worker is planning to immigrate to the United States, as do approximately 400,000 workers (slightly less than 1 percent of the labor force) each year. What is the value to him of saving 184 pesos a month for a retirement pension while he works in Mexico if he is not planning to retire in Mexico? And why should he save another 146 pesos for a housing loan that he is never going to request? Most likely that worker would prefer 330 pesos (184 + 146) today to save for his immigration costs. Although he may be willing to pay 358 pesos for health insurance alone while he is in Mexico, he may not be if that implies "wasting" 330 pesos on something that he does not need, which, de facto, is the same as paying 688 pesos (358 + 330) for health insurance.

### Statutory versus Actual Benefits

Bundling, mixing individual and collective benefits for individual workers regardless of household composition, and international migration (which in Mexico is large) all contribute to lowering workers' valuation of social security benefits. But equally important reasons reside in the gap between statutory and actual benefits or, in other words, in problems associated with the quality of performance of IMSS, the Afores, Infonavit, and the labor tribunals that administer firing and severance pay regulations.

#### IMSS SERVICES

IMSS provides its 360,000 workers with its own pension regime, in addition to the one that all salaried workers have a right to under the Social Security Law. This regime, labeled the Regimen de Jubilaciones y Pensiones (RJP) (Retirement and Pension Regime), has resulted in unfunded pension liabilities of approximately 10 percent of GDP.[6] As a result, over the years IMSS has used an increasing share of social security contributions paid by affiliated workers to service those liabilities, reducing the share channeled to provide health, day care, and other services to beneficiaries. Table A1-1 in appendix 1 shows that in 1998, five centavos of every peso of worker and firm contributions paid to IMSS were used to pay for RJP; the amount increased to fifteen centavos in 2006. The implications of that behavior can be illustrated by two facts. First, over the 1994–2004 period, IMSS contributions to RJP amounted to 122,256 million pesos; in the same period,

6. See Levy (2006d).

Table 3-1. *IMSS Investment and Beneficiary Population, 1981–2005*
2007 pesos (thousands)

| Period | Total investment | Number of beneficiaries | Investment per beneficiary |
|--------|------------------|-------------------------|----------------------------|
| 1981–1985 | 20,574,000 | 28,339 | 725 |
| 1986–1990 | 19,285,000 | 35,250 | 547 |
| 1991–1995 | 17,435,000 | 36,806 | 473 |
| 1996–2000 | 19,089,000 | 41,951 | 454 |
| 2001–2005 | 19,265,000 | 44,103 | 436 |

Source: IMSS (2005, table IX-35).

accumulated investment by IMSS in hospitals, clinics, medical equipment, and the like to provide medical and other services amounted to 32,110 million pesos—a ratio of 3.8 to 1. Second, in 2005 IMSS allocated 19,898 million pesos to approximately 120,000 RJP beneficiaries but only 45,432 million pesos for medicines, materials, medical equipment, day care services, and operating expenses to provide services to almost 40 million beneficiaries (affiliated workers and their families).

Table 3-1 shows the decline in investment by IMSS over the last quarter-century. As a result, the number of hospital beds per 1,000 beneficiaries fell from 1.85 in 1980 to 0.83 in 2005 and the number of doctor's offices at first-level health clinics fell from 0.60 to 0.42.[7]

What does that imply for a salaried worker? Every month he and the firm that employs him channel 358 pesos to the IMSS health fund. In return, he expects that he and his family will receive health care when needed. But if the medical facilities are of very low quality, the lines are long, the equipment is old, some medicines are unavailable (so that he has to purchase them out of his own pocket), or—more to the point—facilities simply are not there, then the value he attaches to his 358 pesos diminishes.[8] A recent editorial in one of Mexico's leading newspapers provides another view: "The number of IMSS beneficiaries who prefer to

7. See IMSS (2006, graphs X-8 and X-9). It is important to note that most of the costs of RJP have yet to be borne. Over the next decade the number of IMSS employees reaching retirement age will double the existing stock of retired workers and expenditures in RJP will increase faster than any reasonable increases in IMSS revenues given growth in employment of workers enrolled in social security. IMSS estimates that in less than a decade it will channel 34 cents of every peso of social security contributions to RJP.

8. In his sociological studies of informal workers in Guadalajara, Roberts notes that "the absence of welfare coverage is a drawback, but, on the other hand, many informants cited the deductions made for welfare as a disadvantage of formal employment, particularly since the services they received were poor" (Roberts 1991, p. 50). Note that his survey was conducted more than fifteen years ago, when IMSS medical infrastructure was better than it is today. Furthermore, it was conducted in Mexico's second-largest city, where IMSS infrastructure is relatively more abundant than in the country as a whole. I thank William Maloney for calling my attention to this study.

Table 3-2. *Regional Distribution of IMSS Health Infrastructure*

| Ratio | National | Locality of less than 20,000 inhabitants | Locality of more than 20,000 inhabitants |
|---|---|---|---|
| *Beneficiaries per first-level doctor's office* | | | |
| Mean | 7,476 | 14,724 | 6,645 |
| Standard deviation | 1,125 | 12,329 | 1,440 |
| *Beneficiaries per hospital bed* | | | |
| Mean | 2,076 | 16,333 | 1,542 |
| Standard deviation | 689 | 15,802 | 545 |

Source: Appendix 2.

go to health clinics for the poor operated by the Health Ministry is amazing. These clinics were created for those without IMSS coverage and without resources for private medical care. Yet a third or more of the clinics' patients are IMSS beneficiaries. They prefer to go there and pay symbolic fees because they lose less time. The in-kind fees charged by IMSS are very high for the worker, the firm, and the country. The lost productivity in waiting, . . . the bureaucratic treatment, . . . are frankly destructive costs. They convince many that seeking treatment through IMSS is worse than having the disease."[9]

Deficiencies in health services also affect the worker's valuation of the 76 pesos paid for work-risk insurance and the 69 pesos for disability insurance, because the assessment of whether a work accident or a disease merits an interim or a permanent work-risk or disability pension must be done at IMSS facilities by IMSS doctors. If facilities are overflowing with patients or are far away, it is more difficult to claim those benefits.

These problems are not homogeneous across Mexico because the distribution of IMSS health facilities is uneven across regions. Table 3-2 shows the mean and the standard deviation of two summary measures of health infrastructure measured at the state level: the number of IMSS beneficiaries per doctor's office where first-level care is provided and the number of IMSS beneficiaries per hospital bed.[10] I also present the mean and the standard deviation within states between areas with more or less than 20,000 inhabitants, which I take here as a proxy for IMSS's rural and urban coverage areas; more details are presented in appendix 2.

9. Gabriel Zaid, "Universitarios Desempleados," *Reforma,* March 25, 2007 (my translation).

10. The expression "first-level medical care" is used in Mexico to denote primary care, the level at which diagnostics and simple tests and procedures are carried out and doctors issue prescriptions. The distinguishing feature is that there is no hospitalization. Medical treatment involving hospitalization is called second-level treatment and, when it involves more sophisticated procedures, third-level treatment (cancer treatment, organ transplants, and the like). Table 3-2 does not distinguish between the second and third levels, but IMSS has third-level hospitals only in Mexico's six largest cities.

Problems are more acute when it comes to day care services for affiliated workers' children. In 2006 there was demand for 918,968 spaces at day care centers for children who qualified (those from forty-five days to four years of age), but only 227,365 children were cared for at IMSS-operated or subrogated centers. The probability that a beneficiary parent finds a space at a day care center is approximately 0.25, so that for three of every four parents who request a space, services are denied.[11]

AFORES

Any system of forced saving imposes costs on workers to the extent that it alters the composition of their present and future consumption in a way that does not reflect their preferences. But in the absence of cross-subsidies between workers, forced saving that occurs in an individual account has a potentially lower cost for workers because their savings are fully reflected in their future pension. Contributions and benefits are in principle brought together. The value of that mechanism to the worker is enhanced if the government adds a subsidy to the account, as it does in Mexico; that subsidy is part of the public resources devoted to social security, commonly labeled social contribution for retirement (*cuota social para el retiro*). The judgment that saving for retirement in an individual account is less costly to the worker than other options for saving for retirement, however, needs to take into account the net risk-adjusted rate of return on a worker's individual account, which is the result of the interplay between the gross rate of return in the portfolio invested on his or her behalf by an Afore and the commission charged for managing the portfolio.

The law regulating the Afores relies on competition to bring commissions in line with their marginal costs and to maximize benefits to workers.[12] Over the first nine years, however, net rates of return to workers were low because of very high

11. See IMSS (2005, table I-23).
12. There are difficult regulatory issues and competition problems in the market for retirement saving because the information that workers have to assess to make their choices as consumers of investment services is complex. There also are issues of trust associated with the fact that in the previous pay-as-you-go system, the real value of pensions was drastically eroded by the inflationary episodes related to Mexico's various macroeconomic crises. Many of those problems have been resolved in the last few years or are in the process of being resolved, although some do not admit easy solutions. Most recently, in March 2007 the law was modified to simplify the structure of commissions and to improve the quality of information provided to workers. There has been a significant reduction in commissions since 2005, and that will increase real rates of return in the future, particularly for workers who will join the system as of 2008. It also will benefit workers who have been in the system since 1997 but who will not retire for, say, another decade. It is difficult to answer the question of how the mix of past experience, information problems, cost of forced saving, and oligopolistic behavior on the part of the Afores, at least until recently, affects workers' valuation of the system; see Madero and Mora (2006) and Levy (2006d). Moreover, *given the bundled nature of benefits, workers cannot value their Afore account on its own; they have to value all social security benefits together.*

Table 3-3. *Afore's Income from Commissions and Pension Subsidies, 1998–2006*
Millions of pesos of year noted

| Year | Commissions | Pension subsidies[a] |
|------|-------------|----------------------|
| 1998 | 4,778 | 5,297 |
| 1999 | 6,958 | 7,201 |
| 2000 | 8,779 | 8,343 |
| 2001 | 10,390 | 9,798 · |
| 2002 | 10,960 | 9,984 |
| 2003 | 12,173 | 8,778 |
| 2004 | 13,119 | 11,081 |
| 2005 | 13,726 | 11,947 |
| 2006 | 13,604 | 14,550 |
| Total | 94,487 | 86,979 |

Source: Pension subsidy figures are from the Cuenta de la Hacienda Pública Federal of the corresponding year, published by the Secretaría de Hacienda y Crédito Público. Afore's commissions are from Consar (www.consar.gob.mx/estadisticas/index.shtml).

a. *Cuota social para el retiro.*

commissions. Table 3-3 compares Afore income from commissions with government subsidies to workers' retirement accounts.

For the period as a whole, Afore commissions were 1.08 times the *cuota social para el retiro.* The implication is simple but powerful: *from the time the current Social Security Law went into effect up to 2006 the full amount of government subsidies to workers' retirement savings was absorbed by Afore commissions.* In fact, the latter have exceeded government subsidies by 8 percent, meaning that the Afores also have absorbed part of workers' and firms' contributions to the system.

Table 3-4 presents the annualized real rates of return to workers' savings net of commissions over the 1997–2006 period for five Afores that jointly managed more than 60 percent of all resources in 2006. The table is based on results for an individual worker who has been in the Afore system since the current Social Security Law went into effect, and it uses a methodology comparable to that used by

Table 3-4. *Real Annualized Net Rates of Return on Savings in Afores, 1997–2006*

| Afore | Wage level[a] | | | |
|-------|----|----|----|----|
|       | 2  | 3  | 5  | 7  |
| Santander | 2.7 | 2.2 | 1.7 | 1.5 |
| BBVA | 2.9 | 2.4 | 1.9 | 1.6 |
| GNP | 3.6 | 3.1 | 2.6 | 2.4 |
| ING | 3.4 | 2.9 | 2.4 | 2.1 |
| Banamex | 3.9 | 3.4 | 2.9 | 2.6 |

Source: Author's calculations based on Consar data (www.consar.gob.mx).
a. Wage level is measured in multiples of the minimum wage.

Consar (Comisión Nacional del Sistema del Ahorro para el Retiro) (National Commission of the System of Retirement Saving). The simple average over the period is 2.6 percent. These rates were paid on an account from which there can be no withdrawals until retirement and that cannot serve as collateral for a loan.[13]

There are two alternative ways in which those results can be used to measure the costs that workers incur because they are forced to save in an Afore. The first alternative is to compare returns on different savings instruments. That is difficult to do to the extent that workers in Mexico face obstacles to saving in formal financial institutions—for example, because of minimum deposit requirements.[14] To make a reasonable comparison, I approximated workers' returns to savings in formal financial institutions, assuming that they were paid 1.5 percentage points *less* than the real rate of interest paid by the government on its bonds, *certificados de depósito de la tesorería* (Cetes) (treasury deposit certificates). Under those assumptions, a worker saving in a financial institution would have received an annual average real rate of return of 3.2 percent;[15] if he or she saved in an Afore, the rate would have been 2.6 percent. The comparison is inexact because the accounts have different characteristics (use as collateral, liquidity, and so on). Nonetheless, it provides some indication not of the cost of saving, because in both cases there is postponement of current consumption, but of the cost of doing so in an Afore.

The second alternative is to compare Afore returns with the opportunity cost of investment options. That also is difficult to do because the range of alternatives is very broad and the risk and time profiles of investments are very different. Nonetheless, an example can be found in McKenzie and Woodruff (2003), which gives the rates of return on investment projects in Mexican microenterprises of one to two people. Those rates were on the order of 3 percent *per month* for investments of around 11,000 pesos and up to 15 percent *per month* for investments of less than 2,200 pesos. A worker earning twice the minimum wage saves 2,208 pesos a year in his or her Afore, so the difference between an *annual* return of 2.6 percent and a *monthly* return of 3 to 15 percent is very high indeed. Of course, over a period of twenty to thirty years, savings accumulated in an Afore

---

13. Withdrawals from Afore accounts can occur after sixty years of age if a worker loses his or her job or at sixty-five following retirement.

14. Most private banks in Mexico require large balances to allow savers to purchase instruments like investment funds or simple diversified portfolios of bonds and stocks; at times they also require that savers also have a checking account or use other bank services. That limits workers' access to financial products, particularly for low-wage workers. There are other mechanisms through which workers save, such as informal credit markets and rotating accounts (*tandas*) established by a small group of households in which periodically everyone makes a contribution and the accumulated funds are progressively allocated to households through a lottery. It is not possible to obtain reliable information on the risk-return characteristics of those instruments.

15. This rate is the simple average of the real rates paid on Cetes over the 1997–2006 period, less 1.5 percentage points in each year.

account would be higher; workers would not have the option of obtaining such high rates on much larger investments in what might no longer be microenterprises. But even if rates on the alternatives fell to, say, 0.5 percent a month, they would still dominate the return on savings in an Afore. The comparison ignores issues of risk and security and the fact that investment options in microenterprises might not be open to all workers (and that not all have the same entrepreneurial talent); as a result, a direct comparison of rates would be erroneous. Nevertheless, the orders of magnitude do provide an indication that forced saving in an Afore can be costly.

Retirement pensions also depend on the length of time that workers contribute to social security. In principle, in a defined-contribution system the longer a worker is enrolled, the higher his or her pension. But in Mexico the law introduces a discontinuity relevant for low-wage workers. In particular, it states that if a worker is enrolled with IMSS for at least 1,250 weeks (approximately twenty-five years), he or she is guaranteed a minimum pension equivalent to the minimum wage even if the resources accumulated in his or her individual account are insufficient to finance such a pension. Chapter 5 presents data on the proportion of a worker's working life spent contributing to social security, given shifts between the formal and the informal sector. Current data show that less than half of low-wage workers will accumulate 1,250 weeks;[16] that is corroborated by direct data from Consar (see table A9-1 in appendix 9). Workers with similar wages therefore will retire with different pensions. Those who qualified for a minimum pension will be better off than those who did not, with perhaps only two or three months' difference in time enrolled in IMSS over their working life. Some will value their retirement pension more, some less.

Complementary information, which can be thought of as revealed preference, provides indirect evidence of workers' valuation of their Afore account. The law permits workers enrolled in IMSS to complement their obligatory savings for retirement in their Afore accounts with voluntary contributions. During the 1997–2006 period, forced savings in the Afores amounted to 1 trillion pesos; in the same period, voluntary savings in the accounts amounted to 2.2 billion pesos, or 0.2 percent of the total. For all practical purposes, voluntary savings in the accounts were nonexistent.

INFONAVIT

Workers' valuations of the housing component of social security contributions depend on the performance of Infonavit along two dimensions: access to housing loans for purchase, renovation, or construction of a home; and the rate of return

---

16. See Casal and Hoyo (2007).

Table 3-5. *Real Rates of Return on Savings Paid by Infonavit, 1997–2006*
Year

| | 1997 | 1998 | 1999 | 2000 | 2001 | 2002 | 2002 | 2004 | 2005 | 2006 |
|---|---|---|---|---|---|---|---|---|---|---|
| Rate | (2.71) | (2.12) | 1.69 | 1.79 | 2.26 | 2.26 | 3.06 | 1.50 | 3.39 | 3.55 |

Source: Author's calculations based on information from Consar (www.consar.gob.mx).

paid by Infonavit on workers' housing sub-accounts. Regarding the former, Infonavit operational rules allocate housing loans by means of a point system based on total and *continuous* time in formal employment.[17] Many workers enter and exit formal employment over time. High-wage workers have a higher average stay and lower frequency of entry and exit, implying that they accumulate more continuous time in formal employment than low-wage workers.

Loan size is a function of a worker's wage level. Because high-wage workers have a greater probability of getting a loan than low-wage workers and also get bigger loans, a larger share of Infonavit's portfolio is allocated to them. (Recall that there are no government subsidies for Infonavit.) The net result is that Infonavit serves as a housing agency for about half of all formal workers and, de facto, serves as an investment agency for retirement savings for the other half, who probably will not receive a housing loan and instead will get the resources deposited in their Infonavit account at the end of their working lives at the rate of return paid by Infonavit.

I was unable to find an official publication of the real rates of return paid by Infonavit on workers' housing sub-accounts since implementation of the current Social Security Law in 1997. Those rates are set by Infonavit's board of trustees as a function of the performance of the institution's loan portfolio; there appears to be no clear mechanism to link them to the rates in capital markets, as is the case with the rates paid by Afores on retirement sub-accounts. That implies that workers face uncertainty about the return on their contributions to the housing fund. Table 3-5 shows the implicit rates paid since 1997 on the accounts of workers who obtained a retirement pension under the 1997 law. The average annual rate of return on their housing sub-accounts was approximately 1.7 percent (versus 2.6 percent on their retirement sub-accounts).

What does that mean for workers? Consider a worker earning twice the minimum wage who does not obtain a housing loan and for whom, de facto, the Infonavit component of social security is just another mechanism of saving for

---

17. See rule 10 in Infonavit (2007). Loans can be requested directly by the workers or by their union or the firm that hires them (rule 11); that might give more access to unionized workers hired by larger firms. The Federal Labor Law stipulates that at least twenty workers are required to form a union, so that access route is not open to all workers in Mexico hired by small firms; see table 7-2.

retirement. Over the last decade, she channeled 11.2 percent of her wage to retirement savings: 184 pesos a month into her retirement sub-account, on which she earned an annual rate of 2.6 percent, and 146 pesos a month into her housing sub-account, on which she earned an annual rate of 1.7 percent. In other words, she channeled 55 percent of her savings $(184/(184 + 146))$ into an account with one rate of return and 45 percent $(146/(184 + 146))$ into another account with another rate of return. The average rate of return on her savings was 2.2 percent.

Of course, if a worker does obtain a housing loan the calculation is different. In that case the benefit is equal to the difference between the rate paid on loans with private financial intermediaries and the implicit rate paid on the Infonavit loan (controlling for amount and maturity). However, that calculation cannot be performed because until recently workers had hardly any access to housing loans from private financial intermediaries, so one could say that the alternative rate was infinity. So if a worker gets an Infonavit loan, the benefit can be very large.

Table 4-7 in chapter 4 presents information on the distribution of Infonavit housing loans by wage levels. It shows that over the 2000–06 period, 0.61 percent of workers earning twice the minimum wage or less received a loan; in contrast, 4.3 percent of workers earning five times the minimum wage or more did so. To the extent that Infonavit's loans reach only a small subset of low-wage workers—while the rate of return paid on the housing sub-accounts of the large subset that does not get a loan is below the Afore average—*this component of social security acts as a mechanism to redistribute income from low- to high-wage workers.*

Finally, as with IMSS benefits, there are important variations in the regional allocation of housing loans. Table 3-6 shows that most Infonavit loans and resources are allocated to workers who live in localities of 20,000 inhabitants or more. In other words, salaried workers living in small urban or in rural areas receive hardly any benefits from Infonavit.

LABOR REGULATIONS

What about labor regulations or, more precisely, the 93 pesos of implicit costs associated with firing and severance pay regulations? In principle, they constitute a benefit for workers. However, the transaction costs associated with claiming the benefits are large, given that the law makes a distinction between "justified" and "unjustified" dismissals and severance payments are made only in the second case.[18] That results in uncertainty and in litigation between workers and firms, which is carried out in labor tribunals created to mediate or arbitrate between them (*juntas de conciliación y arbitraje*). In some cases, workers and firms settle without litigation; in others, the process can be very long. As a result, it is estimated that between

18. See Calderón (2000).

Table 3-6. *Distribution of Infonavit's Housing Loans by Size of Locality, 1998–2006*
(thousands of loans and billions of pesos of 2007)

| Loans and resources | 1998 | 1999 | 2000 | 2001 | 2002 | 2003 | 2004 | 2005 | 2006 | Total |
|---|---|---|---|---|---|---|---|---|---|---|
| *Number of loans*[a] | 106.1 | 198.3 | 250.1 | 205.3 | 275.0 | 300.0 | 306.0 | 376.4 | 421.7 | 2,439.0 |
| Localities with more than 20,000 inhabitants | 104.8 | 196.4 | 231.2 | 203.1 | 273.0 | 297.2 | 304.1 | 371.6 | 411.4 | 2,392.8 |
| Localities with less than 20,000 inhabitants | 1.2 | 1.9 | 18.9 | 2.3 | 2.0 | 2.8 | 1.9 | 4.9 | 10.4 | 46.2 |
| *Resources allocated*[b] | 20.1 | 38.1 | 48.7 | 47.6 | 60.6 | 66.7 | 69.1 | 81.3 | 92.2 | 524.5 |
| Localities with more than 20,000 inhabitants | 20.0 | 37.9 | 45.4 | 47.1 | 60.3 | 66.2 | 68.7 | 80.4 | 90.0 | 516.0 |
| Localities with less than 20,000 inhabitants | 0.2 | 0.2 | 3.3 | 0.5 | 0.3 | 0.5 | 0.4 | 0.9 | 2.1 | 8.4 |

Source: Infonavit registries, various years.
a. Thousands.
b. 2007 pesos (billions)

lawyers' fees, delays, and "facilitating fees," workers receive only approximately sixty centavos of every peso that they should receive.[19]

VOLUNTARY AFFILIATION

The law offers a voluntary incorporation scheme to nonsalaried workers that bundles retirement, health, life, and disability insurance as for salaried workers, but it excludes day care services, housing, and work-risk insurance. Workers obtain the same government subsidies as those in the obligatory scheme and pay the lowest possible fees, equal to those paid by registered workers who earn the minimum wage. Tellingly, in June 2006, only 498,891 workers in a potential universe of 25 million were enrolled. In other words, *less than 2 percent of informal workers who could voluntarily opt for a system of benefits similar to that obtained by formal workers have actually done so.*

Table 3-7 summarizes the discussion so far. It presents substantive reasons why workers in Mexico prefer to receive the benefits of social security in cash rather than as a claim to a set of goods and services.

## Determinants of Workers' Valuation of Social Protection

Aside from design and quality issues, workers' valuations of social security are influenced by the alternatives that they have, by the cost and quality of those alternatives, and by the possibility of unbundling a package of benefits that they do not want to consume in its entirety so that the alternatives can be accessed separately and voluntarily. In Mexico, those alternatives are provided by social protection programs.

The voluntary, unbundled, and by and large free nature of social protection programs implies that valuation issues are substantially less complex than in the case of social security. However, these programs also have problems regarding the quality of benefits, rationing of some services, and regional disparities in service provision; as a result, again, actual benefits may be lower than statutory benefits. But as seen in chapter 1, public resources for the programs have increased rapidly in the last years; in principle, workers' valuation of their benefits also should increase.

The most important programs are the various health programs offered: the new Seguro Universal de Primera Generación, programs offered by states to those not covered by social security, Seguro Popular, and the IMSS-Oportunidades Program. For the most part, all services are provided within the health infrastructure of state governments and IMSS-Oportunidades. Table 3-8 presents summary statistics on the distribution of infrastructure by size of locality; see appendix 2 for more details. When the distribution of social protection infrastructure is compared with the corresponding distribution for IMSS, three patterns emerge. One, where IMSS infrastructure is relatively less abundant, social protection infrastructure is relatively more abundant, and vice versa. Two, social security infrastructure

19. Dávila (1994).

Table 3-7. *Factors Affecting Workers' Valuation of Social Security*

| Problem | Cost (pesos) | Factor |
|---|---|---|
| *Design* | ? | Forced to buy all benefits simultaneously |
| | | Household characteristics ignored |
| | | Patterns of international migration ignored |
| *Quality* | | |
| Health care | 358 | Fifteen centavos of every peso diverted to RJP |
| | | Uneven regional distribution of infrastructure |
| | | Substantial underinvestment in facilities |
| | | Service provided under monopoly conditions |
| Disability and work-risk benefits | 69 | Fifteen centavos of every peso diverted to RJP |
| | | Uneven regional distribution of access |
| Day care | 29 | Fifteen centavos of every peso diverted to RJP |
| | | Uneven regional access |
| | | Twenty-five percent probability of finding a space |
| Retirement pension | 184 | Ex post net rates of return of 2.6 percent so far |
| | | Patterns of mobility affect minimum pension guarantee |
| | | Other investment options with higher returns |
| Housing | 146 | Access to loans based on continuous time in formality; lower access for workers with higher mobility |
| | | Uneven regional distribution of loans |
| | | Ex post rates of return of 1.7 percent so far |
| | | Uncertainty about rates of return |
| Labor regulations | 93 | Uncertainty about "just cause" |
| | | Approximately 40 percent of benefits lost in transaction costs |
| Labor taxes | 58 | No direct benefit at all |
| Total | 937 + ? | Monetary costs associated with social security coverage are at least 35 percent of wages |

Source: Author's analysis. See discussion in text.

Table 3-8. *Distribution of Social Protection Health Infrastructure*

| Ratio | National | Locality of less than 20,000 inhabitants | Locality of more than 20,000 inhabitants |
|---|---|---|---|
| *Beneficiaries per first-level doctor's office* | | | |
| Mean | 1,951 | 2,355 | 2,368 |
| Standard deviation | 1,196 | 1,889 | 1,528 |
| *Beneficiaries per hospital bed* | | | |
| Mean | 1,865 | 2,378 | 2,336 |
| Standard deviation | 906 | 2,161 | 1,408 |

Source: Appendix 2.

is relatively more abundant in richer states and social protection infrastructure in poorer states. Three, social security infrastructure is relatively more abundant in urban areas and social protection infrastructure in rural areas.

I was unable to find similar information for the distribution of social protection housing projects, which also have received increasing resources in the last few years. But my hypothesis is that it is biased toward smaller urban and rural areas, in contrast to the distribution observed for Infonavit. The same holds for the distribution of day care services.

Social protection programs also offer workers the possibility to save for retirement. Since 2005, workers without social security have been able to open an individual retirement account with an Afore voluntarily. However, only 4,469 workers of a total of more than 25 million (0.002 percent) have opened an account since then, providing direct evidence of the insignificant value that informal workers so far have attached to saving for retirement through the Afore system.

Finally, as noted before, noncontributory pension programs have recently been introduced. It remains to be seen whether those programs will become permanent, as has been the case with pretty much all other social protection programs introduced in the past, or whether they will provide income transfers only for those who currently are elderly. That distinction is of the essence because it determines whether workers currently in the labor force who lack social security coverage can reasonably expect to have access to some pension when they retire; it also may influence their saving behavior.

## Wages and Social Benefits

This section synthesizes the previous discussion, presenting a simple representation of the difference between the costs of social security and of social protection programs, on one hand, and the value attached to them by workers, on the other. $T_f$ and $T_i$ are the total monetary cost per worker of social security and social protection programs respectively, regardless of who pays for them.[20] These costs include the cost of the following components:

$$T_f = [\text{health insurance} \oplus \text{retirement pensions} \oplus \text{disability pensions}$$
$$\oplus \text{housing loans} \oplus \text{work-risk pensions} \oplus \text{day care services}$$
$$\oplus \text{sports and cultural facilities} \oplus \text{life insurance}$$
$$\oplus \text{firing and severance pay} \oplus \text{labor taxes}]$$

(3-1)
$$T_i = [\text{health insurance} + \text{life insurance} + \text{housing loans}$$
$$+ \text{retirement pensions} + \text{day care services}]$$

20. The subscripts $f$ and $i$ are used to denote that social security pertains to workers in the formal sector and social protection to workers in the informal sector, respectively.

Table 3-9. *Costs of Social Security and Social Protection Benefits, 2006*
2007 pesos (millions)

| Cost Cost | | Total | Percent of GDP | Total pesos per worker |
|---|---|---|---|---|
| $T_f$ | | | | |
| | IMSS, Infonavit, and Afores | 294,375 | ... | ... |
| | Firing and severance pay | 31,301 | ... | ... |
| | Labor taxes | 19,564 | ... | ... |
| | Total | 345,240 | 3.9 | 24,519 |
| $T_i$ | | | | |
| | Total | 146,351 | 1.7 | 5,670 |

Source: Author's calculations based on tables 1-3, 1-4, 5-1 and tables A1-1 and A1-6 in Appendix 1.

The circles around the plus signs in the $T_f$ equation indicate that the benefits in the package are *bundled,* while the absence of a circle in the $T_i$ equation means that they are *unbundled.* Note that $T_f$ generally is expressed as a proportion of the wage (at least 35 percent, according to table 1-3), but to make it comparable to $T_i$ I express it as a monetary cost. Note also that $T_f$ includes all the nonwage costs of a salaried worker, not only social security; in other words, it captures the costs of the official governance mechanisms that apply to salaried labor.

Table 3-9 estimates $T_f$ and $T_i$ for 2006.[21] The average annual cost of the official governance mechanisms that apply to salaried labor was equivalent to 24,519 pesos per worker, while the average annual cost of social benefits provided to nonsalaried workers was 5,670 pesos per worker.

The costs of social programs are different from their benefits, however. The arguments previously made in this chapter suggest that from the point of view of a Mexican worker, the value of the official governance mechanisms that apply to salaried labor is less than 24,519 pesos a year and the value of social protection benefits is less than 5,670 pesos a year. To capture the difference between costs and benefits, I introduce two coefficients, $\beta_f$ and $\beta_i$, which are less than or equal to unity and measure workers' valuation of social security and social protection programs, respectively.[22] On that basis,

21. Following the arguments in chapter 1 about noncontributory pensions for informal workers, I exclude resources for social protection programs like Adults over Seventy and others from the figures in table 3-9, so $T_i$ is underestimated.

22. In principle, $\beta_f$ and $\beta_i \in [0, \infty]$, as some individuals might value benefits for more than their cost. As discussed previously, however, the relevant analysis for Mexico centers on the case in which $\beta_i, \beta_f \leq 1$.

$T_f$ = cost per worker of the official governance mechanisms that apply to salaried labor

(3-2)

$\beta_f T_f$ = value to the worker of social security programs

$T_i$ = cost per worker of social protection programs for nonsalaried labor

$\beta_i T_i$ = value to the worker of social protection programs.

Note that in the case of $\beta_f$, I speak of workers' valuation of social security programs interchangeably with workers' valuation of the official governance mechanisms that apply to salaried labor. That is because firms and workers in salaried labor relationships must pay for all the components of $T_f$ simultaneously, even if some components have no value for workers.

Workers receive wages in addition to the social benefits associated with being formally or informally employed. Let $w_f$ and $w_i$ be the wage rates (or take-home pay) in each sector. Assume that the only components of worker's utility, $U$, are take-home pay and the value of the social benefits associated with each job.[23] Then the total utility that workers obtain from working in each sector is the sum of wages and the value of social benefits:

(3-3)

$$U_f = \text{formal wages} + \text{value of social security benefits} = \left(w_f + \beta_f T_f\right)$$

$$U_i = \text{informal wages} + \text{value of social protection benefits} = \left(w_i + \beta_i T_i\right).$$

On the other hand, firms hiring salaried workers must pay the full costs of the official governance mechanisms that apply to salaried workers, $T_f$. In contrast, self-employed workers and firms having nonsalaried relationships with workers do not have to pay for social protection programs, given that those programs are funded from general government revenues. The difference in the costs to firms of formal and informal labor caused by social programs, on one hand, and the difference between the costs of social programs and the value to workers, on the other, are central to the analysis in the chapters that follow. Table 3-10 highlights those differences.

I argue in chapter 2 that much of the literature on labor markets and informality makes two implicit assumptions: one, that social security contributions are fully valued by formal workers; two, that social protection programs either do

---

23. I ignore here the value that workers attach to hierarchy, flexibility, and other characteristics of salaried and nonsalaried jobs.

Table 3-10. *Total Costs and Benefits of Salaried and Nonsalaried Labor*

| Cost and benefits | Salaried labor | Nonsalaried labor |
|---|---|---|
| Cost to firms | $w_f + T_f$ | $w_i$ |
| Benefits to workers | $w_f + \beta_f T_f$ | $w_i + \beta_i T_i$ |

Source: Author's analysis.

not exist or are not valued at all by informal workers. Those two assumptions are critical because they indicate that social security and social protection programs have no impact on the labor market or on productivity. Table 3-10 helps to make the two assumptions more precise. First, the assumption that social security is fully valued by workers is equivalent to the statement that $\beta_f = 1$, so that the total cost to firms of hiring a salaried worker and the utility to a worker of being salaried coincide. Second, the assumption that informal workers receive no social benefits is equivalent to the statement that $T_i = 0$ (alternatively, the assumption that the benefits are not valued at all by workers implies that $\beta_i = 0$), so that the cost to firms of nonsalaried workers coincides with the utility to a worker of being employed in the informal sector.

*The discussion in this chapter shows that in the case of Mexico, those two assumptions are flawed.* On one hand, the arguments summarized in table 3-7 indicate why workers value the official governance mechanisms that apply to salaried labor at a fraction of their cost or, in the terminology introduced above, why $\beta_f$ is less than 1. As a result, *the amount that firms in the formal sector pay for labor is more than the amount that workers get.* On the other hand, table 3-9 shows that informal workers do receive social benefits (equivalent to at least 1.7 percent of GDP, or 5,670 pesos per worker) or, in the terminology introduced, that $T_i$ is greater than zero. As a result, *firms in the informal sector pay less for labor than workers get.*

Chapter 5 complements the qualitative discussion of workers' valuation of social programs with econometric estimates obtained from Mexico's employment surveys. However, two important points can be made at this stage, highlighted by table 3-10: first, social programs introduce *two* wedges between the cost of labor to firms and the utility that workers receive from work, one in the formal sector and another in the informal. And second, those wedges operate in *opposite* directions, increasing the utility of working in the informal sector relative to informal firms' costs and decreasing the utility of working in the formal sector relative to formal firms' costs. In other words, *the interaction between social security and social protection introduces two distortions in the labor market. As shown in the next chapters, those distortions are quantitatively significant and together operate to increase informality and reduce productivity.*

## An Assessment

The discussion in this chapter should *not* be read as a call to abolish IMSS, Infonavit, and the Afores and the various social protection programs described. On the contrary, all those institutions and programs play an important role in Mexico, and some are at the core of the social contract between the state and workers. In particular, the Federal Labor Law and the Social Security Law need to be understood as emerging from the circumstances following the consolidation of the country in the decades after the Mexican Revolution, in 1910. The institutions and programs resulting from those laws—and other institutions and programs created over the course of more than seven decades of effort by various administrations—are today the main mechanisms available to the government to redistribute income to workers and protect them from various risks.

For substantive historical and political reasons, the Federal Labor Law and the Social Security Law were born with a particular and then prevailing view of the world and of the role of government in protecting workers from risks and redistributing income *through interventions in the labor market.* That some or most of those risks were independent of the labor market and of the labor status of workers was not the primary concern. The Mexican government was not the only one to associate health, life, and retirement insurance and regulations on firing and severance pay with salaried labor and to finance them with wage-based contributions.[24] Moreover, like other governments, at the time the social security and labor laws were first issued and associated institutions created, the Mexican government expected that the evolution of the economy would lead to growth in salaried employment, accompanied by increasing social security coverage.

However, as GDP growth and salaried employment began to stagnate in the mid-1970s, its expectations were not fulfilled. Successive macroeconomic crises, on one hand, and rapid population growth, on the other, combined to generate a growing population of workers without social security coverage; at the same time, rapid rural to urban migration began to occur. As a result, the government over the years has reacted caringly and pragmatically—but at times also opportunistically—with successive programs to provide at least some social benefits to workers without social security. In addition, the government also created a large number of programs to subsidize consumption, particularly of food.[25] *The result has been an increasing plethora*

24. Mexico is perhaps more uncommon in including housing, day care services, and access to sports and cultural facilities as part of social security.

25. Through the mid-1990s the government relied on various food programs to attempt to redistribute income toward low-income families, but those programs were organically disconnected from the labor status–based social security and social protection programs described here, although all are generally grouped under the rubric of social policy. Progresa-Oportunidades was introduced as a more effective alternative that could replace both targeted and generalized food subsidy programs and some isolated health and educational interventions with an integrated incentive-based approach. However, the incentives of Progresa-Oportunidades and those of the social security and social protection programs described here have yet to be organically integrated; see chapter 8 of this volume and Levy (2006a, chapter 5).

*of social programs, some channeling benefits to workers because they are poor; some because they lack social security coverage, regardless of income level; and some because of both.*

This chapter tries to point out that nevertheless—and despite the best of intentions—the institutions and programs constructed over many decades to deliver social benefits to Mexican workers have inherent design flaws that limit their impact. In addition, over the years a combination of macroeconomic crises, budget cuts, and rent-seeking activities of various groups has affected the operation of those institutions and programs, limiting their ability to deliver quality services to workers. One result of that complex interaction of motives and circumstances is the current concatenation of social security and social protection programs, along with the valuation problems that I have tried to identify.

Of course, the fact that workers might not fully value the benefits of social programs does not mean that the programs are unimportant, and it means even less that they should be abolished. *It is critical to reiterate here the difference between workers' valuation of the programs and the government's social objectives.* Institutions and programs can be very well designed and perform very well in terms of quality and yet be insufficiently valued by workers.[26] Regardless of whether workers want to save for retirement or a housing loan or to purchase disability or health insurance, *the government has its own objectives and those are what matter for policy.*

But this chapter also points out that the government's social objectives are unclear, not to say contradictory. Because, de facto if not de jure, the distinction between formal and informal employment implies that workers with very similar characteristics performing very similar tasks are subject to different social interventions. Worse still, because workers often move between the formal and the informal sectors, the *same* worker is subject to different social interventions. That is why *it is important to understand whether the current combination of social security and social protection programs is what the government wants or whether it is the best that the government can do given the constraints under which social policy is designed and implemented in Mexico.* In the first case, it is necessary to understand, for example, why the government forces a worker to save if he is salaried—regardless of wage or income level—but gives him the option to do so if he is not. And it also is necessary to understand why in one case the government obliges the worker to simultaneously consume a large set of bundled benefits and in the other case gives him the option to voluntarily and separately consume any or none of various unbundled benefits.

One could argue that it is because salaried workers are myopic (or because they are free riders) and nonsalaried workers are not—or perhaps because there are failures in the market for insurance services for salaried workers that do not occur in

---

26. In other words, there are two separate reasons why workers would undervalue the costs of the official governance mechanisms that apply to salaried labor, that is, why $\beta_f$ is less than 1: because workers are being forced to consume something that they do not want and because the quality of the services that they are forced to consume is low.

the case of nonsalaried workers. However, it is difficult to construct a theoretical argument or to find empirical evidence supporting such claims. Moreover, in light of the results regarding worker mobility presented in chapter 5, it would be absurd to argue that the *same* worker is myopic while he holds a salaried job and not myopic while he holds a nonsalaried job.

If explanations based on asymmetries in behavior or in the markets for insurance are ruled out, then the explanation for the government's discriminatory treatment of salaried and unsalaried workers must rest on the fact that the current policy is, *though clearly undesirable from the social point of view,* the best that the government can do given the constraints that it faces. And that may be so. But if that is the case, it is essential that policymakers understand the nature of the constraints and understand also whether government policy in the face of those constraints is in fact the best possible, or whether—recognizing the second-best context in which policy is designed and implemented—they can find better options for realizing the government's social objectives.

I do not argue that the problem is that the government imposes its preferences on workers, nor do I argue that insurance markets work well. On the contrary, I take it as given that the government needs to solve the contracting problems that workers face in insurance markets *and* impose its preferences on them. My point is this: the problem is with the discriminatory nature of the government's policy, which introduces a qualifying condition on workers—to be salaried—before they are subject to social interventions. In other words, *the problem is that the government does not solve the contracting problems in insurance markets and does not impose its preferences on all workers at the same time.*

Those considerations are central for workers and firms and raise the stakes associated with the government's social interventions because their impacts spill over from the social to the economic domain. That occurs because workers and firms do not remain passive in the face of the discriminatory nature of the interventions. *Workers and firms have choices.* Being salaried or nonsalaried is not a fixed natural characteristic; it is something that a worker can change. Workers see a large set of social programs "out there," offering different benefits in exchange for different prerequisites—some costly and some free, some of good quality and some of poorer quality. Workers try to do the best that they can for themselves given the opportunities in the labor market and the portfolio of social programs available; they do not care whether or not the government's social objectives are fulfilled as a result. The same is true of firms. They are competing with other firms in Mexico and, in most cases, with firms in China, India, and the rest of the world. In order to maximize profits, firms will choose between paying salaried workers a wage and paying nonsalaried workers a commission without considering whether their choices fulfill the government's social objectives.

Such responses, of course, have a limit, as the discussion in chapter 1 points out. Nonsalaried labor is not a perfect substitute for salaried labor. In some cases salaried labor may be unavoidable, even if more costly, because it is the only way to control quality given the sequential nature of the production process, because the scale of operations requires it to prevent free riding, or because a hierarchy is needed to ensure the timely delivery of output, to manage inventory, and so on. But workers and firms have yet another option: to break the law by engaging in salaried labor relationships while evading the official governance mechanisms that apply to salaried labor. As shown in chapter 7, however, even that option has a limit. All such social policy–induced changes from salaried to nonsalaried employment, from one type of labor contract to another, and from legal to illegal behavior have implications for labor productivity, for firms' investments and size, for the composition of aggregate output, for asset prices, and for training and adoption of technology—in short, for productivity growth.

# 4

## Social Programs and Poor Workers

Poor workers in Mexico, rural or urban, own few productive assets, including land. The expectation therefore would be that most of them are salaried, employed in the formal sector. But as shown in chapter 5, the opposite is observed: less than 7 percent of all poor workers are formally employed. Furthermore, poor workers account for a disproportionate share of workers who evade social security: while they constitute only 23 percent of all workers, they represent almost 58 percent of evading workers. Understanding the role played by social programs in contributing to those outcomes is central in designing effective poverty reduction policies. This chapter focuses on the differences in the programs' effects on poor and non-poor workers. However, the reader interested in the general argument and not in how it applies to poverty can go directly to chapter 5.

### Households and Workers in Progresa-Oportunidades

At the end of 2005, Progresa-Oportunidades covered 5 million households, slightly more than the entire population estimated to be living in poverty. Inclusion and exclusion errors create a difference between the covered population and the population living in poverty; however, those errors are not large.[1] Because the errors are small and the program's databases provide very detailed information on beneficiary households, the characteristics of the population in the program can be

---

1. See Levy (2006a).

Table 4-1. *National and Progresa-Oportunidades Population, 2005*[a]

| | Total | | National | | Progresa-Oportunidades | |
|---|---|---|---|---|---|---|
| Age range | National | P-O | Urban | Rural | Urban | Rural |
| 0–16 | 35,839 | 9,648 | 25,949 | 9,890 | 3,268 | 6,380 |
| 17–65 | 58,564 | 12,910 | 46,118 | 12,446 | 3,641 | 9,269 |
| 66 + | 8,859 | 1,521 | 6,919 | 1,940 | 465 | 1,056 |
| Total | 103,262 | 24,079 | 78,986 | 24,276 | 7,374 | 16,075 |

Source: National Institute of Statistics, Geography, and Information Sciences and National Coordination of Progresa-Oportunidades.

a. Thousands of persons.

considered equivalent to those of the poor population. I refer to poor workers as the working members of program households or, in short, as Progresa workers.

Table 4-1 combines data from the National Population Count for 2005 with census data from Progresa-Oportunidades beneficiaries for the same year. Note that approximately 23.3 percent of Mexico's total population lives in poverty; that while 76.4 percent of the total population lives in urban areas, only 30 percent of the poor do;[2] and that 22 percent of the total working-age population is poor.

*Land Ownership*

The fact that 70 percent of all poor households live in rural areas does not imply that they are landowners or primarily employed in agricultural activities. On one hand, land ownership by poor households is infrequent; on the other, both the urban and rural working poor migrate within Mexico and at times to other countries.[3]

Mexico's laws distinguish between full ownership of land and possession of land with the right to exploit it. That distinction is associated with the *ejido* tenure system, and it affects the use of land as collateral and the functioning of the land market. For my purposes, however, the distinction is less relevant because in both cases households appropriate land rents. Therefore, in my analysis I added households that fully own land to those who exploit it in *ejidos,* although some could argue that doing so overestimates land ownership. I also differentiate between rainfed and irrigated land because yields are higher with the latter and possibilities for using fertilizers, diversifying crops, and so on, which affect productivity, are

2. The rural population is defined as that living in localities of 2,500 inhabitants or less and the urban population as that living in localities of 2,500 inhabitants or more. The rural poor live in more than 80,000 localities spread throughout the country.

3. Angelucci (2005) analyzed migration patterns of poor rural households and found that 95 percent of all migrants in those households were between fourteen and forty-five years of age and that 13 percent of the households had at least one member who migrated for work reasons, within Mexico or to the United States. There are no studies that I am aware of that deal with urban households.

Table 4-2. *Land Ownership by Progresa-Oportunidades Households*[a]

| Ownership | Rural | Urban | Total |
|---|---|---|---|
| With land | 1,345 | 172 | 1,517 |
| Without land | 2,153 | 1,326 | 3,479 |
| Total | 3,500 | 1,500 | 5,000 |

Source: Author's tabulations from Progresa-Oportunidades household surveys; see appendix 3.
a. Thousands of families.

better. That does not mean that all rain-fed land is of equal quality, but available data do not allow for drawing distinctions. In any event, because ownership is so small, correcting for the quality of rain-fed land would not make much difference. If anything, I overestimate its value to the poor because much of their rain-fed land is of low quality; for example, it may have steep slopes that are more useful for grazing than cultivation.

I used Progresa-Oportunidades surveys to estimate land ownership by the poor. Data and estimating assumptions are discussed in appendix 3; here I present summary results. Table 4-2 divides poor urban and rural households between those that owned land of any type and those that did not. (Urban households also may own land, particularly in smaller urban areas.) It is striking that only 30 percent of all poor households owned any land. Dividing ownership by place of residence reveals that 88 percent of all urban and 61.6 percent of all rural households owned no land. *The majority of the poor people in Mexico, urban or rural, are landless.*

I next focused on the subset of rural households that owned land. Table 4-3 classifies the 38.4 percent of rural households in that category by the number of their working-age members and the number of hectares of land that they owned,

Table 4-3. *Poor Rural Families Owning Land: Type, Amount, and Distribution*

| Hectares | | Total families (percent) | Families by number of working-age members (percent) | | | |
|---|---|---|---|---|---|---|
| Rain-fed | Irrigated | | 0 | 1–2 | 3–4 | 5+ |
| 1 | | 44.9 | 5.2 | 34.3 | 31.2 | 29.3 |
| 2 | | 22.7 | 5.9 | 31.6 | 30.5 | 31.9 |
| 3 | 0 | 8.9 | 6.7 | 30.1 | 28.9 | 34.3 |
| 4 | | 5.0 | 7.0 | 29.5 | 28.7 | 34.8 |
| 4+ | | 11.7 | 8.8 | 27.6 | 29.6 | 33.9 |
| 0 | 1 | 2.3 | 8.0 | 32.0 | 31.0 | 29.0 |
| 0+ | | 0.5 | 11.6 | 33.4 | 28.2 | 26.7 |
| 0 | 2 | 1.1 | 8.0 | 31.0 | 29.0 | 32.0 |
| 0+ | | 0.3 | 10.1 | 29.2 | 27.4 | 33.2 |
| Remainder | | 2.3 | 10.3 | 29.5 | 30.2 | 30.0 |

Source: Appendix 3.

dividing the latter between rain-fed and irrigated land. The first column captures families with no irrigated land and one or more hectares of rain-fed land; with one hectare of irrigated land and some or no rain-fed land; with two hectares of irrigated land and some or no rain-fed land; and with three or more hectares of irrigated land and any or no rain-fed land. The second column shows the share of rural families owning land in each case, and the last four columns classify them by number of working-age members.

Various results are noteworthy. Of the 38.4 percent of all rural households that owned some land, 93.2 percent owned only rain-fed land; 44.9 percent owned only one hectare of rain-fed land; and 67.6 percent owned two hectares or less of rain-fed land. Only 6.5 percent owned any irrigated land.

Tables 4-2 and 4-3 lead to one conclusion: few poor households own land and those that do have small holdings, particularly if measured on the basis of the household's working-age members. Figure 4-1 summarizes the results. To avoid presenting a three-dimensional figure, I converted irrigated land into rain-fed land, assuming that one hectare of the former is equivalent to five of the latter. I also did the analysis assuming a conversion of one to ten, with very similar results. The figure shows the distribution density of land per working-age member of all poor rural households for two time periods. For 2005, observed values are shown; for 2012, a projection is shown that was made holding land ownership constant while

Figure 4-1. *Hectares per Working-Age Member of Poor Rural Households*

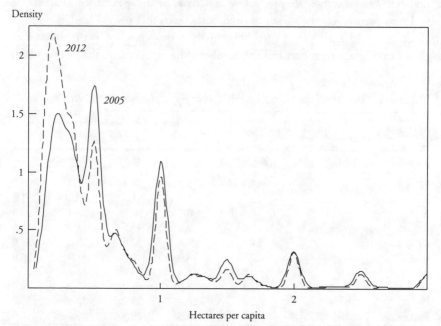

Source: Appendix 3.

allowing for the net effect of demographic change (household members entering working age minus those leaving after sixty-five years of age). The highest frequency of the distribution is 0.45 hectares in 2005; that declines by more than half in less than six years to 0.18 in 2012. For both years most of the distribution is concentrated in one hectare or less. *Not only are the per capita land holdings of the rural poor very small today, but population growth will reduce them by more than half in six years. That will occur independently of the erosion and depletion of their land as a result of slash-and-burn farming and other agricultural practices.*[4]

Two implications of those results should be noted. First, as elaborated on in Gertler, Martinez, and Rubio (2005), land ownership plays a central role in poor people's access to investment projects and the projects' profitability. The authors show that Progresa-Oportunidades households are credit constrained and that the liquidity associated with the program's transfers allows them to invest in productive projects with real annual rates of return of around 5 percent. The projects contribute to households' ability to attain "higher earned income tomorrow" by allowing them to permanently increase their consumption without program transfers. But it is crucial to note that the results hold only for households owning three hectares of land or more. The profitability of investing in productive projects diminishes rapidly with decreasing land holdings; for households with less than three hectares, the rate of return is close to zero. Because very few of the rural poor who do own land have more than three hectares, it follows that *profitable investment projects in agriculture or other activities associated with land are very scarce among the rural poor and practically nonexistent for the urban poor.*

Second, the 88 percent of the urban poor and the 62 percent of the rural poor who own no land cannot derive rents from investing in productive projects associated with land. But as seen, that is also the case with the majority of those who own land. That does not imply that a subset of the rural poor cannot earn sufficient income (imputed rent and wages) as agricultural producers to pull out of poverty; with better access to credit, improved education and health, and appropriate technical assistance, some poor rural households may be able to do so. However, the results imply that the subset is small. While it is difficult to estimate its size, it is extremely unlikely that more than 15 percent of all Progresa-Oportunidades households would be able to escape poverty as agricultural producers.[5] Of course,

4. The Progresa-Oportunidades surveys also contain information on other productive assets, such as draft animals (bullocks, donkeys) and production animals (poultry, sheep). I do not present that information here, but note that it is strongly correlated with land ownership. The poor also own other types of productive assets, like tools for handicrafts, fishing boats, and so on, but there is little direct information on them.

5. This is a mechanical estimate for illustrative purposes only. It results from assuming that at least two hectares of rain-fed land are required for a household to devote itself full-time to agricultural production. The estimate follows from noting that poor rural households make up two-thirds of total poor households, that 38 percent of them own land, and that only 55 percent of that 38 percent own two hectares or more.

many poor households combine agricultural activities with other forms of work to earn additional income and to diversify risk. But that is precisely the point. Because the rent derived from exploiting their own land is small and tends to fall, the fundamental determinant of poor workers' ability to generate "higher earned income tomorrow" is the income that they earn in the labor market. *Aside from the social benefits that they may have access to given their salaried or nonsalaried status, the wages, commissions, or other forms of income earned by the poor as laborers are the single most important determinant of their chances of escaping from poverty. Those wages and commissions are a direct reflection of their productivity. Without more productive jobs, poor workers will need Progresa-type transfers permanently.*

## Characteristics of the Labor Force

Table 4-4 classifies poor workers by age, occupation, and labor status based on data from the Progresa-Oportunidades surveys, which indicate that almost 80 percent of all poor workers are salaried (see appendix 4 for details). Those surveys, however, overestimate salaried labor because agricultural workers (*jornaleros agrícolas*) are not separated from agricultural laborers (*peónes agrícolas*). The former clearly are salaried employees, while the latter may not be if they work under a share-cropping agreement with a landowner. In chapter 5, I use the employment survey for 2006 as an alternative source of information, but that underestimates salaried labor in the rural areas, treating all workers who are employed in agriculture as nonsalaried (see appendix 4 for details). According to the employment survey,

Table 4-4. *Occupational Distribution of Poor Workers*[a]

| Occupation | Age range | | | | | Distribution by occupation |
|---|---|---|---|---|---|---|
| | 16–24 | 25–35 | 36–45 | 46–55 | 56–65 | |
| *Salaried* | | | | | | |
| Agricultural worker/laborer | 39.3 | 41.1 | 43.6 | 48.4 | 51.6 | 47.7 |
| Construction worker/ | | | | | | |
| factory worker/employee | 43.8 | 40.2 | 37.2 | 31.1 | 24.9 | 32.1 |
| *Nonsalaried* | | | | | | |
| Boss/business owner | 1.7 | 1.3 | 0.9 | 0.6 | 0.6 | 1.2 |
| Self-employed | 4.7 | 7.8 | 8.5 | 9.2 | 10.7 | 8.7 |
| Domestic worker | 1.3 | 2.1 | 1.9 | 2.0 | 2.4 | 1.3 |
| Member of cooperative | 1.7 | 2.2 | 2.6 | 2.4 | 2.3 | 1.7 |
| Worker without | | | | | | |
| remuneration | 3.8 | 1.4 | 1.1 | 1.3 | 1.6 | 2.2 |
| *Ejidatario* or communal | | | | | | |
| worker | 0.5 | 1.1 | 1.7 | 2.7 | 3.6 | 2.0 |
| Other | 3.1 | 2.7 | 2.3 | 2.0 | 2.2 | 2.9 |
| Distribution by age | 21.6 | 30.2 | 25.1 | 14.6 | 8.3 | 100.0 |

Source: Appendix 3.
a. Percent.

Table 4-5. *Social Security Coverage of Poor Workers*[a]

| Occupation | With | Without | Total |
|---|---|---|---|
| *Salaried* | | | |
| Agricultural worker/laborer | 2.4 | 97.6 | 100 |
| Construction worker/factory worker/employee | 14.0 | 86.0 | 100 |
| *Nonsalaried* | | | |
| Boss/business owner | 13.4 | 86.6 | 100 |
| Self-employed | 3.5 | 96.5 | 100 |
| Domestic worker | 1.7 | 98.3 | 100 |
| Member of cooperative | 6.1 | 93.9 | 100 |
| Worker without remuneration | 2.8 | 97.2 | 100 |
| *Ejidatario* or communal worker | 3.1 | 96.9 | 100 |
| Other | 5.7 | 94.3 | 100 |

Source: Appendix 3.
a. Percent.

only 49.6 percent of poor workers are salaried (see appendix 4). Without other data, it can be said that *between 50 and 80 percent of all poor workers are salaried.*[6]

Table 4-5 shows social security coverage of poor workers using the same classification as table 4-4 and the same Progresa-Oportunidades surveys.

The contrast between tables 4-4 and 4-5 is sharp. According to table 4-4, approximately 80 percent of all poor workers are salaried and should be covered by social security, but as table 4-5 shows, less than 6 percent ($0.024 \times 0.47 + 0.14 \times 0.32$) are actually covered. Even if the employment survey's 50 percent estimate for poor salaried labor is used, the gap is still very large. The explanation is simple and very important for later results: *in the case of poor workers, the Social Security Law is massively violated.* In fact, as shown in the next chapter, it is violated substantially more than in the case of non-poor workers.

On the other hand, even if compliance with the law were universal, between 20 and 50 percent of all poor workers would be without social security coverage because, as seen in table 4-4, they are nonsalaried. The absence of social security for poor workers has two separate causes:

—Design problems, which result in the exclusion of some workers because they are not subordinated to a boss and do not receive a wage.

—Performance problems, which lead a large subset of poor salaried workers and their employers to evade the law.

Table 4-5 shows that evasion takes place in occupations that could be considered more urban, like construction and manufacturing, as well as those that are

6. World Bank (2005a, vol. 2, table 2-6, p. 166) used the income-expenditure surveys to classify poor workers by labor status and found that in 2002, 36 percent of all salaried workers were poor. Given the estimate of 25 million salaried workers provided in table 5-1, that implies that 9 million poor workers are salaried, almost the entire universe of poor workers. Clearly, the estimate that at least 50 percent of poor workers are salaried is very conservative.

Table 4-6. *Age and Schooling of Poor Workers*[a]

|  | Years of schooling | | | | | |
| Age range | 0 | 1–5 | 6–8 | 9 | 10 or more | Total |
|---|---|---|---|---|---|---|
| 16–24 | 10.3 | 4.3 | 8.6 | 6.4 | 4.0 | 33.7 |
| 25–35 | 5.7 | 7.2 | 8.7 | 4.5 | 2.7 | 27.2 |
| 36–45 | 5.0 | 7.5 | 4.8 | 1.7 | 0.5 | 19.6 |
| 46–55 | 4.9 | 4.9 | 1.5 | 0.3 | 0.1 | 11.7 |
| 56–65 | 4.4 | 2.7 | 0.4 | 0.0 | 0.0 | 7.6 |
| Total | 30.3 | 26.6 | 24.0 | 12.9 | 7.3 | 100.0 |

Source: Appendix 3.
a. Percent.

clearly rural, like agriculture. *Evasion of social security, then, is not only a rural phenomenon.* Note too that category 3 (boss/business owner), despite being non-salaried, has high social security coverage by the standards of poor workers. That reflects a phenomenon wherein small enterprises register only a few of their workers (perhaps one or two), including in some cases the owner, as part of their strategy to evade the law (see chapter 7). Table 4-6 classifies poor workers by age and years of schooling.

Three points should be noted. First, 80 percent of all poor workers were forty-five years of age or younger in 2005; 60 percent were less than thirty-five years old. Second, educational levels as measured by years of schooling are quite low. Thirty percent of all poor workers have no years of schooling and an additional 26.6 percent did not finish primary school (repetition rates are ignored here). On the other hand, 12.9 percent had completed secondary school (nine years of schooling), and an additional 7.3 percent had moved beyond that level.

Progresa-Oportunidades so far has had almost no impact on those numbers because most of the beneficiaries of the program's educational component have yet to enter the labor force. If the program continues and is successful, over time the share of poor workers in the labor force with more than ten years of schooling will increase. But that will be a gradual process. For the large majority of poor workers currently in the labor force, the program's benefits come, for the most part, from the health and food components.[7] For those workers, on-the-job training is the best option for acquiring new and improving old skills and so getting a chance to increase their productivity and generate higher earned income in the future. As discussed, extremely few will find productive employment as agricultural producers. *That is why it is so important that they find jobs that offer them train-*

7. The program's evaluations do show a reduction in the number of sick days taken by adults and better health indicators in general, which should translate into improved performance at work; see Levy (2006a, chap. 3) for a summary of the results.

*ing and opportunities to engage in activities that can raise their productivity.* Finding such jobs depends on wages and on poor workers' valuation of social security and social protection programs, which determines whether they choose to look for formal or informal jobs; it also depends on whether firms offer them formal or informal jobs.

## Poor Workers' Valuation of Social Programs

Many factors can account for the differences in worker valuations of social programs. Worker preferences might differ: some people may have higher discount rates, some may be more risk averse, some more prone to disease. Valuations also are affected by age, gender, household composition, and migration patterns. Differences in worker preferences, then, are a factor that, given all other characteristics of work (earnings, hierarchy, flexibility), leads to a process of self-selection whereby those who value relatively more social security seek jobs with such coverage.

But it is useful to put all these relatively well-known characteristics aside momentarily and focus on a different set. Assume that all workers have *identical preferences,* and ignore the complications arising from household composition. Even in that case, two workers might have *different valuations* of social security and social protection programs. For example, if worker A lives in a region (state, municipality) where there are good IMSS health and day care facilities and there is access to Infonavit housing and worker B lives in a region where that is not the case, worker A will value social security more than worker B. This is obvious: *even though workers are identical, in their daily life social security will mean more to one worker than to the other.* The same is true of social protection programs. If workers C and D live in two regions in which the availability and quality of program services are different, they will have different valuations even if, as assumed, they are identical in all other respects.

The analysis in chapters 6, 7, and 8 *does not require one to assume that valuations of social programs across workers are heterogeneous or that there are systematic differences between poor and non-poor workers' valuations.* In fact, for the most part I assume that all workers value social security equally and do the same with respect to social protection. But it is illustrative—and in practice highly relevant—to consider the case in which their valuations differ not because of systematic differences in preferences but because of systematic differences between statutory and actual benefits across groups of workers. This analysis is important for poverty because I argue that *statutory and actual benefits differ for poor and non-poor workers.*

### Savings for Retirement and Housing Loans

Assume that all workers have the same discount rate and that all think that being forced to save for retirement in an Afore is costly—that is, if they were not forced to do so, they would save less. If poor workers are forced to save more than non-poor workers, their costs will be higher than those for the non-poor. Why are poor workers forced to save more? Recall that a worker covered by social security in Mexico must contribute to his retirement and housing sub-accounts. If he does not obtain a housing loan from Infonavit during his working life, the funds accumulated in the housing sub-account are added to those accumulated in the retirement sub-account, increasing the size of the worker's pension. In other words, a worker who never gets an Infonavit loan saves more than a worker who does, in fact, up to 44 percent more (146/(146 + 184)) (see table 1-2). *One worker saves 11.3 percent of his wage while the other saves only 6.3 percent.*

Table 4-7 shows the yearly average number of Infonavit housing loans made from 2000 to 2006 by wage level and contrasts that with the distribution of workers enrolled in social security. Clearly, the probability of obtaining a housing loan is greater for higher- than for lower-wage workers. Although IMSS registries do not directly identify Progresa workers, it stands to reason that, being the poorest of all, they are the ones with the lowest wage levels. For them the probability of obtaining a housing loan is four times lower than the average for all workers enrolled in IMSS (0.6 versus 2.4) and seven times lower than for workers earning five times the minimum wage (0.6 versus 4.3). The implication is as straightforward as it is important: *poor workers are forced, de facto though not de jure, to save more than non-poor workers.* Furthermore, the rate of return paid by Infonavit on the housing sub-account has so far been lower than the rate paid by Afores on the retirement sub-account, and, as discussed, there is no legal mechanism to link the rates paid by Infonavit to rates of return in the capital markets. *Poor workers therefore receive a lower average rate of return on their total forced savings and face more uncertainty than non-poor workers with regard to those rates.*

There is another factor that may increase poor workers' cost of saving relative to that of non-poor workers. As mentioned, Gertler, Martinez, and Rubio (2005) shows that as a result of the additional liquidity provided by Progresa-Oportunidades transfers, some households invested in productive projects with

Table 4-7. *Average Number of Infonavit Housing Loans by Wage Level, 2000–06*

| Wage level[a] | Number of workers in social security | Number of housing loans | Percent of workers receiving a loan |
|---|---|---|---|
| Under 2 | 4,131,126 | 24,999 | 0.61 |
| 2 to 2.9 | 2,863,817 | 72,336 | 2.53 |
| 3 to 3.9 | 1,986,871 | 61,925 | 3.12 |
| 4 to 4.9 | 1,155,081 | 38,685 | 3.35 |
| 5 or more | 2,323,428 | 99,457 | 4.28 |

Source: IMSS and Infonavit registries.
a. Wage level is measured in multiples of the minimum wage.

real annual rates of return of approximately 5 percent. Because those households could not borrow, the investments could not have occurred without the transfers. Progresa-Oportunidades households that include a member who has social security coverage may find themselves saving 11.3 percent of the worker's wage in the Afore-cum-Infonavit instrument at a real rate of return of 2.2 percent, while they are unable to find credit for investment projects with a real rate of return of 5 percent. The same could be true, of course, for non-poor workers; there is little direct evidence concerning their investment alternatives and access to credit.[8] But if credit constraints are in fact more acute for the poor, their opportunity cost of saving will be higher.

*Health and Day Care Infrastructure*

Appendix 2 shows that the infrastructure to provide health and day care services is unevenly distributed across states and regions. But there are certain broad patterns that influence how poor and non-poor workers value the two services. Consider health. First, the Progresa-Oportunidades surveys indicate that about two-thirds of all poor workers live in rural or small urban areas of up to 20,000 inhabitants.[9] Second, between 50 and 80 percent of all Progresa-Oportunidades workers are salaried, so in principle at least half of all poor workers have the right to receive health services from IMSS. Third, as shown in table 3-2, the regional distribution of IMSS health infrastructure implies that there are 2.2 more beneficiaries per doctor's office and 10.6 more beneficiaries per hospital bed in areas of less than 20,000 inhabitants than in areas of more than 20,000. In other words, while in general salaried workers face problems of access and quality with IMSS health services, *those problems are on average more substantial for poor than for non-poor workers, particularly with regard to hospitalization and second- and third-level care, because less medical infrastructure exists in the areas where the former live.* In fact, in many of those areas there is no IMSS health infrastructure at all.

Next consider day care services. In 2006, the average probability of accessing a space was 0.25, but that probability is a weighted average of urban and rural areas. In 2006 only forty-seven of a total of 1,433 (3.3 percent) IMSS-operated or subrogated day care centers were in rural or urban areas with fewer than 20,000 inhabitants. That means that for the vast majority of rural workers, IMSS-provided day care services are nonexistent.

8. McKenzie and Woodruff (2003) provides some indirect evidence from rates of return to microenterprises, which initially are large but rapidly decline. It is reasonable to assume that those enterprises are an investment option for some of the not-so-poor workers who transit from salaried to self-employment.

9. As table 4-1 shows, two-thirds of Progresa-Oportunidades households live in communities of 2,500 or fewer inhabitants. I identified communities of up to 20,000 inhabitants with adequate health infrastructure as places that rural inhabitants of smaller nearby communities could go to in order to receive medical care.

*The factors that make poor workers value social security less than the non-poor operate in the opposite direction when it comes to social protection.* Access is better for the poor to the extent that the differences in the urban-rural distribution of health infrastructure are smaller. In the case of IMSS-Oportunidades, facilities are, by design, located in the poorer rural areas of Mexico. In the case of facilities owned and operated by state governments, the facilities are more evenly spread across urban and rural areas.

Day care centers operated by social protection programs are scarce altogether, although the scope of the federal day care program for mothers without social security coverage that began in 2007 remains to be seen. So while there is insufficient evidence to define what happens with social protection day care services, it is clear that non-poor salaried workers have better access to social security day care centers than poor salaried workers have. The same is true with housing programs, as those provided by agencies and programs other than Infonavit concentrate in smaller urban and rural areas.

That is no coincidence. *It is the result of decades of government program design and service provision policies that have proceeded, de facto, under the assumption that nonsalaried workers are poor and salaried workers are non-poor. Those program design and service provision policies contribute to trapping the poor in poverty and are inconsistent with Mexico's legal framework because, as argued in chapter 1, social security is a right of all salaried workers, poor and non-poor.* And while, as discussed, at least 50 percent of all poor workers are salaried, that assumption results in their having substantially lower social security coverage than the non-poor. It is difficult to believe that poor workers' underlying preferences for social programs are systematically different from those of the non-poor. Government policy makes them develop different valuations, which in turn make them behave as if they had different preferences. The key point, however, is that *the difference arises because the poor are responding rationally to the fact that social programs for them and the non-poor differ and provide them with different incentives.*

### Time in Formal Employment

On average, low-wage workers move between formal and informal jobs more often than high-wage workers and they spend less time in formal employment (see chapter 5). That affects their valuation of social security benefits to the extent that some benefits depend on *accumulated* time of enrollment in IMSS. In the case of Infonavit, for example, the probability of obtaining a loan depends on the number of months a worker has contributed to the system. Moreover, a worker who spends the first ten years of his working life in the formal sector and the next ten in the informal sector will be able to buy a house ten years earlier than a worker who does the opposite. A similar situation occurs with retirement pensions: a few months more or less of formal or informal employment during his working life might qualify or disqualify him for the

Table 4-8. *Poor Workers' Valuation of Social Security and Social Protection Programs*

**Social Security**

*Preferences*
Poor workers are forced to save more than other workers.
Poor workers may face more binding credit constraints.

*Design and operation*
Poor workers have less access to Infonavit housing loans.
Poor workers have reduced access to IMSS medical services.
Poor workers have almost no access to IMSS day care services.

*Financing*
The worker and the firm pay for all statutory benefits.
The worker and the firm pay for firing and severance pay and for labor taxes.

**Social Protection**

*Preferences*
Poor workers are not forced to save at all.

*Design and operation*
Poor workers have better access to health services.
Poor workers have easier access to housing programs.
Poor workers may have access to day care services if current programs grow.
Poor workers may have access to a pension in the future without saving if current noncontributory pension programs continue.

*Financing*
Free.

Source: See discussion in text.

minimum pension guarantee.[10] The point is this: *workers' valuation of social security and social protection programs is not independent of their pattern of formal and informal employment.* But, in turn, their search for formal and informal jobs is affected by their valuation of the social benefits attached to each job.

Table 4-8 summarizes the discussion in this section. Even if all workers have equal preferences, poor workers value social security less and social protection programs more than non-poor workers. All else being equal, that leads poor workers

10. The minimum pension guarantee applies only if a worker is registered with IMSS for twenty-five years. A forty-five-year-old Progresa worker who has worked in the informal sector all his working life would need to work permanently in the formal sector until he is seventy to qualify for the minimum pension. Even a forty-year-old worker would find it difficult to qualify given the patterns of formal-informal mobility (see chapter 5). All other things being equal, workers who for the most part have been in informal employment in the past will value social security less than workers who have had longer spells of formal employment. To the extent that the minimum pension guarantee is more relevant for poor workers, their labor history will influence their current valuation of social security. If they have been mostly in the informal sector in the past (particularly rural workers), that will lead them to continue being informal, all other things being equal.

to value jobs that entail enrollment in social security less than non-poor workers. But it is critical to note that that occurs because *despite the equality of statutory benefits for all workers, in practice the interplay of social security and social protection programs discriminates against poor workers having social security coverage* and not because of Progresa-Oportunidades.

In chapter 3, I represent the fact that workers value the benefits of social security and social protection programs at a fraction of their cost through two valuation coefficients, $\beta_f$ and $\beta_i$, respectively. The discussion here suggests the need to make a distinction between poor and non-poor workers; therefore I use superscripts P and NP to refer to each respectively:

(4-1)
$$\beta_f^P < \beta_f^{NP} \quad \text{poor workers value social security less than non-poor workers}$$
$$\beta_i^P > \beta_i^{NP} \quad \text{poor workers value social protection more than non-poor workers}$$

On the other hand, because the costs of the official governance mechanisms that apply to salaried labor are the same for all workers, regardless of income level, the differences in valuation translate, de facto, into a larger wedge between the costs and benefits of social security for poor than for non-poor workers and a larger wedge between the benefits and costs of social protection for the poor than for the non-poor (see table 3-10). In the next chapters I show that *those differences trap poor workers proportionately more than non-poor workers in low-productivity informal jobs and that that fact contributes to the persistence of poverty.*

# 5

## Mobility of Workers in the Labor Market

This chapter serves as a bridge between the description of Mexico's social programs and workers' valuation of their benefits presented in the first four chapters and the analysis of the behavioral response of workers and firms to those programs presented in chapters 6 through 8. After salaried and nonsalaried workers in Mexico's labor force are identified and classified by wage level, a heuristic discussion of workers' movements between sectors based on ethnographic case studies is presented. The registries of IMSS and Consar are analyzed to allow for a more systematic assessment of the patterns of worker mobility over the 1997–2006 period, and work based on Mexico's employment surveys to measure worker mobility across labor status and test for barriers to mobility is reviewed. The results of an econometric analysis that takes advantage of worker mobility to compare wage rates between sectors also are presented. The chapter ends with a discussion of the implications of worker mobility for social policy.

### Labor Force

Table 5-1 shows Mexico's labor force in 2006, divided into groups of formal, informal, and unemployed workers. In this table and hereafter I refer to high-wage workers as those earning three times the minimum wage or more and low-wage workers as those earning less than three times the minimum wage. In the case of nonsalaried workers, the reference is to equivalent earnings.[1] The table is based on

1. Three times the minimum wage is close to the mode of the distribution of the wages of workers enrolled in IMSS.

Table 5-1. *Economically Active Population (EAP), 2006*[a]

| Type of employment | EAP | Share in group | Share in EAP |
|---|---|---|---|
| Formal | 17,069,018 | 100.0 | 38.4 |
| ISSSTE and others | 2,988,651 | 17.5 | 6.7 |
| F1 (IMSS high-wage) | 5,986,441 | 15.0 | 13.5 |
| F2 (IMSS low-wage) | 7,457,138 | 17.8 | 16.8 |
| F3 (IMSS Progresa) | 636,788 | 1.7 | 1.4 |
| Informal | 25,777,123 | 100.0 | 58.0 |
| Illegal salaried | 8,092,111 | 31.4 | 18.2 |
| I1 (High-wage) | 2,922,849 | 11.3 | 6.6 |
| I2 (Low-wage) | 442,955 | 1.7 | 1.0 |
| I3 (Progresa) | 4,726,307 | 18.3 | 10.6 |
| Self-employed workers and *comisionistas* | 17,685,012 | 68.6 | 39.8 |
| I4 (High-wage) | 5,818,369 | 22.6 | 13.1 |
| I5 (Low-wage) | 7,175,133 | 27.8 | 16.1 |
| I6 (Progresa) | 4,691,510 | 18.2 | 10.6 |
| Open unemployment | 1,600,891 | 100.0 | 3.6 |
| Total | 44,447,032 | . . . | 100.0 |
| Total without ISSSTE | 41,458,381 | 100.0 | 93.3 |

Source: Appendix 4.
a. Number of workers.

data from the Encuesta Nacional de Ocupación y Empleo (ENOE) (National Occupation and Employment Survey) for 2006 (see appendix 4). Because the ENOE does not identify workers in Progresa-Oportunidades, I complement it with information from the program's household surveys (see appendix 3). As usual when different data sources are combined, results should be interpreted as an indication of the relative magnitudes of each category and not as precise estimates. In addition, the data are too weak to separate nonsalaried workers between *comisionistas* and self-employed individuals. Appendix 4 provides details on assumptions and methodology, but three points need to be made here: one, *comisionistas* are underreported in the employment statistics, making self-employment appear larger than it actually is. Two, because in some cases firms use the legal category of *comisionista* to mask a salaried labor relationship, the number of illegal salaried workers is underestimated. Three, regardless, none of the substantive points made in this or in the next chapters hinge on a precise quantitative distinction between the self-employed and *comisionistas* or between them and illegal salaried workers; the numbers as they stand suffice to indicate the problem at hand.

For completeness, table 5-1 includes formal public sector workers, who have their own social security institute, Instituto de Seguridad y Servicios Sociales de los Trabajadores del Estado (ISSSTE) (Institute of Social Security and Social Services for State Workers), as well as members of the armed forces, who also have

Figure 5-1. *Composition of the Labor Force, 2006*

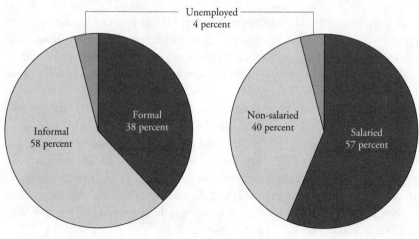

Source: Appendix 4.

their own social security institute. Those workers, however, are not considered here as the demand for their labor is based not on the profit motive but on services provided by national and subnational ministries and agencies for the national welfare.[2] Note that the total labor force in 2006, 44.4 million workers, includes 1.6 million openly unemployed individuals, implying an unemployment rate of 3.6 percent.

Two observations on the composition of the labor force need to be made up front. One, formal employment is 38.4 percent of the total labor force. Therefore, measured by employment, *the informal sector is larger than the formal sector,* and the same holds if it is measured by number of firms (see chapter 7). Two, total salaried employment (legal and illegal) is only 56.6 percent of the total labor force. Of course, to the extent that there is some illegal salaried employment hidden in the figure for *comisionistas,* the total is higher, although it is difficult to quantify. Nevertheless, the observation stands: *in Mexico, a large share of the labor force is nonsalaried.* Figure 5-1 depicts the two results.

Five observations can be drawn from table 5-1. First, even if there were no illegal salaried employment, social security would cover only 57 percent of the labor force, which highlights the limitations of associating social security with salaried

2. However, not all public sector employees are enrolled in ISSSTE. Workers of the public electricity companies and IMSS workers at the federal level are enrolled in IMSS. At the state and municipal level, public workers at some educational institutions, water treatment plants, and other public agencies are enrolled with IMSS. On the other hand, no private workers are enrolled in ISSSTE. As a result, the total number of workers registered in IMSS exceeds the number of formal workers employed by private firms.

labor. Second, *illegal salaried labor is substantial:* 36.5 percent of total nonpublic salaried labor.[3] In other words, in the absence of evasion, IMSS coverage would be at least 58 percent higher than it is today![4] Those figures raise fundamental questions about the efficacy of social security in Mexico, particularly if we recall that the first Social Security Law was promulgated more than sixty years ago.

Third, legal informal employment (I4 through I6) is more than double illegal informal employment (I1 through I3). That fact reinforces the notion that informality and illegality are not the same. The large level of legal informal employment also is the other side of the coin of the low level of salaried employment. To state that the proportion of legal informal employment in total employment is 40 percent ((I4 to I6)/EAP) begs the question of why there are so many self-employed workers and *comisionistas* in Mexico. Even assuming that the *comisionista* disguise hides a lot of salaried labor, the question remains: why are so many workers self-employed, particularly low-wage and poor workers (I5 + I6)? Why aren't they working for a firm and earning a wage?

Fourth, poor workers (F3 + I3 + I6) account for 23 percent of the labor force; in other words, almost one of every four workers in Mexico belongs to a Progresa-Oportunidades household. Finally, note that some poor workers are affiliated with IMSS (F3 > 0), although coverage is low, because 88 percent (I3/(I3 + F3)) of poor salaried workers are illegal. The other side of that is that evasion of social security is most common with poor workers. Although, as noted, poor workers make up only 23 percent of the labor force, they account for 58 percent of evasion. Why is evasion concentrated in the poor?

*International Comparisons of Employment Status*

Mexico's formal-informal dichotomy results in a tax on salaried labor and a subsidy to informal labor, thereby leading to the underdevelopment of salaried labor (see chapter 6). Because it is impossible to measure what the composition of Mexico's labor force would be in the absence of that dichotomy, I compared it with that of other countries to provide an indication of the orders of magnitude of the phenomenon.

International comparisons of labor statistics are problematic. As the International Labor Office notes, "There are often differences in definitions, as well as in coverage, across countries and for different years, resulting from variations in information sources and methodologies that make comparisons difficult."[5]

3. As discussed in appendix 4, this is a lower-bound estimate given that the assumptions made to estimate evasion are deliberately conservative. Using data from the International Labor Office yields a higher estimate of evasion; see table 5-2.

4. However, it is not correct to state that the sum of the observed levels of legal and illegal salaried workers is the equilibrium level of salaried employment without evasion, because in the absence of evasion, the equilibrium structure of wages would change, affecting the composition of all employment. In fact, salaried employment would be higher (see chapter 7).

5. ILO (2005, chap. 3, p. 3).

Table 5-2. *Percent of Salaried Labor in Total Employment for Selected Countries*

| Country | Year | GDP[a] | Percent |
|---------|------|--------|---------|
| Spain | 2004 | 14,691 | 81.9 |
| Portugal | 2003 | 10,283 | 73.1 |
| Hungary | 2005 | 5,103 | 86.3 |
| Poland | 2004 | 4,634 | 73.3 |
| Mexico | 2005 | 5,792 | 64.2 |
| Argentina | 2003 | 7,165 | 71.8 |
| Chile | 2005 | 5,195 | 70.2 |
| Brazil | 2003 | 3,510 | 62.1 |

Source: ILO (2005), Key Indicators of the Labor Market, Indicator 3: Status in Employment, tables 3 and A.1.

a. Per capita GDP in 2000 U.S. dollars.

On the other hand, ignoring measurement issues, the composition of employment in one country should not be identical to that of another country with a similar GDP. The share of agriculture in total GDP, the distribution of land ownership, and many other factors also have an effect. It would be better from that perspective to compare changes in the composition of employment across countries over long periods of time rather than the level of employment at any one point in time.[6] Below I provide some data for Mexico, although not for other countries, given the difficulty of putting together long series on the composition of employment.

With those caveats in mind, see table 5-2, which shows the share of salaried employment in total employment for four countries in Latin America and four in Europe as computed by the ILO. I tried to find countries with roughly similar per capita GDP, although that was not fully possible given the higher average level of GDP in Europe. It is critical to note that the numbers refer to salaried employment, not formal employment; in other words, they include legal and illegal salaried workers. Thus, the figure of 64 percent for Mexico is higher than the 57 percent shown in figure 5-1 above, probably because the ILO classifies some *comisionistas* as salaried employees, who, as noted above, may be underrepresented in the ENOE used to construct table 5-1. In any case, if the ILO data are closer to the true figure, the implication is that illegal salaried employment in Mexico exceeds the 8.1 million workers noted above. According to the ILO, there would be approximately 11.4 million illegal salaried workers, or 80 percent of employees registered in IMSS (since the measurement

6. The ILO notes that "a high proportion of wage and salaried workers in a country can signify advanced economic development" and that "countries that show falling proportions of either the share of own-account workers or contributing family members, and a complementary rise in the share of employees, accompany the move from a low-income situation with a large informal or rural sector to a higher-income situation with high job growth" (ILO 2005, chap. 3, pp. 2–3).

of legal salaried workers is based on fairly accurate registries from ISSSTE and IMSS).

The comparison of Mexico with Poland and Hungary is illustrative. The share of salaried employment in the two latter countries, which have similar per capita GDP, is approximately 11 percent higher than in Mexico. Chile also has a higher share of salaried employment than Mexico, although its per capita GDP is lower. The country whose share is most similar to Mexico's is Brazil, although its per capita GDP is almost 50 percent lower. *Using the countries listed in table 5-2 as comparators, Mexico's share of salaried employment in total employment is low.*

## Evolution of the Labor Force, 1991–2006

Table 5-3 and figure 5-2 show the composition of the labor force over the 1991–2006 period in Mexico, dividing it among formal, informal, and open unemployment. (Appendix 4 provides details on data sources and methodology.) As expected, there were fluctuations associated with various short-run shocks, particularly the fall in formal employment in 1995. *But the basic result is that over the last decade and a half, informal employment has accounted for more than half of the labor force despite positive economic growth in most of those years—and that in absolute terms, it has increased.*

Table 5-3. *Size and Composition of the Labor Force, 1991–2006*[a]

| | Formal | | | | |
| Year | ISSSTE[b] | IMSS | Informal | Unemployed | Total |
|---|---|---|---|---|---|
| 1991 | 2,527 | 10,290 | 17,321 | 706 | 30,844 |
| 1992 | 2,534 | 10,182 | 18,554 | 769 | 32,040 |
| 1993 | 2,586 | 10,000 | 19,818 | 832 | 33,236 |
| 1994 | 2,655 | 10,137 | 20,118 | 1,268 | 34,178 |
| 1995 | 2,702 | 9,322 | 21,391 | 1,704 | 35,120 |
| 1996 | 2,728 | 10,142 | 21,882 | 1,376 | 36,129 |
| 1997 | 2,771 | 10,753 | 23,346 | 1,001 | 37,871 |
| 1998 | 2,824 | 11,507 | 23,480 | 904 | 38,715 |
| 1999 | 2,853 | 12,207 | 23,038 | 693 | 38,792 |
| 2000 | 2,890 | 12,732 | 22,839 | 918 | 39,379 |
| 2001 | 2,923 | 12,374 | 23,443 | 1,120 | 39,860 |
| 2002 | 2,936 | 12,425 | 23,868 | 1,084 | 40,313 |
| 2003 | 2,935 | 12,334 | 24,917 | 1,483 | 41,670 |
| 2004 | 2,947 | 12,595 | 25,343 | 1,589 | 42,473 |
| 2005 | 2,966 | 13,185 | 25,728 | 1,353 | 43,232 |
| 2006 | 2,989 | 14,080 | 25,778 | 1,600 | 44,447 |

Source: Appendix 4.
a. Thousands of workers.
b. ISSSTE includes other public workers covered under special social security regimes.

Figure 5-2. *Formal and Informal Employment and Total Labor Force,*
*1991–2006* [a]

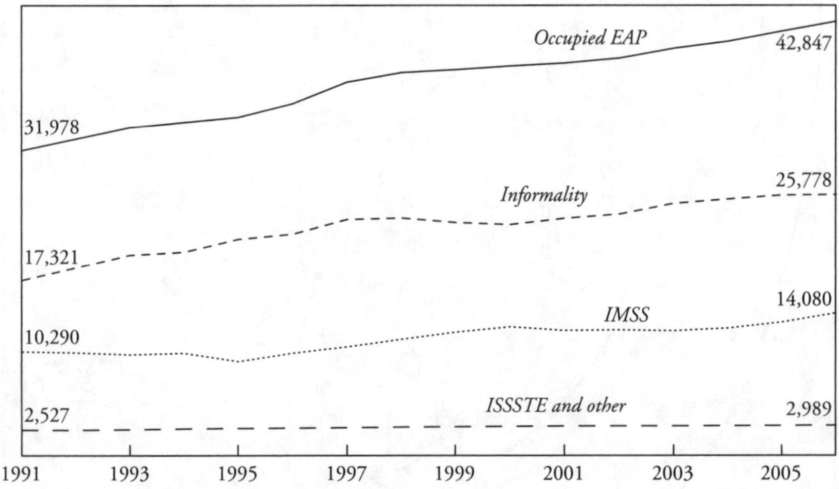

Source: Author's analysis.

a. Unemployment is not shown in the graph to avoid clutter, but it is equal to the difference between the economically active population (EAP) and the sum of IMSS plus ISSSTE and others plus informality; see table 5-3. Variation from 1991 to 2006: 42.2 percent (occupied EAP); 36.8 percent (IMSS); 18.3 percent (ISSSTE and others ); 48.8 percent (informality).

## Mobility of Workers: Some Examples

To demonstrate the very large number of possible variations in a worker's employment history that occur in Mexico's labor market, a heuristic discussion of worker mobility and its implications for the coverage of social programs is presented here.[7] Systematic data to complement and quantify the discussion follow.

Worker A lives in a small rural community near Tlacolula in the state of Oaxaca. (Figure 5-3 presents a map of Mexico identifying the various states referred to here.) During the first half of the year he is self-employed, producing handicrafts for sale at the weekly market in the state capital (also called Oaxaca); while self-employed, he has access to social protection benefits (henceforth, "SP benefits"). However, in July he migrates to Sinaloa to work as a salaried agricultural employee for a large farm exporting tomatoes to California. The farm complies with the labor laws; therefore he is enrolled in IMSS and receives social security benefits (henceforth,

7. The cases discussed below are inspired by ethnographic studies of Mexican women and men whose work trajectories have been followed for some time. The actual case studies relate much more mobility between jobs and locations for each worker than the cases discussed in the text. I created composite cases to capture the aspects relevant to this discussion. See González de la Rocha (2006).

Figure 5-3. *Workers' Migration between Formal and Informal Employment*[a]

Source: Author's illustration.

a. In place names, uppercase letters refer to states and lowercase letters to cities. Two-way arrows denote circular migration; one-way arrows denote one-way migration. The circled capital letters refer to the examples in the text (worker A, B, and so forth).

"SS benefits"). However, in December, at the end of the agricultural season, he returns to Tlacolula, where he resumes his occupation as an artisan, loses his SS benefits, and regains his access to SP benefits. In July of the following year, he migrates to Sinaloa again and becomes a formal worker with SS benefits.

Worker B is a *comisionista* who sells newspapers in the streets of Jalapa, the capital of the state of Veracruz. As an informal worker, he receives SP benefits. He then migrates to work as a custodial worker in a new maquiladora in Ciudad Juárez, Chihuahua, where he spends the next two and a half years. During that time he is a formal worker and so receives SS benefits. A slowdown in the United States forces the management of the maquiladora to cut costs; if he is to remain employed, he has to accept a lower wage. He decides not to accept and returns to Jalapa, where he works as a self-employed car washer in the city center. During that period, he receives SP benefits.

Worker C is a woman in Mérida, the capital of Yucatán, working in a clothing factory as a seamstress. She is a formal worker, registered with IMSS and receiving SS benefits. As a result of competition from abroad, the owners of the firm decide to close the plant and import clothing from China instead. They offer her a job as a *comisionista* selling imported Chinese clothing door-to-door in Mérida. She accepts, losing her SS benefits and gaining SP benefits as an informal worker.

Worker D lives in the capital of San Luis Potosí, where he has been a bricklayer working in the formal sector on a housing project. During that time, he has been receiving SS benefits. The project ends, and while he is waiting for the next one to begin, he migrates to help his relatives at the nearby family ranch in a rural community near Tamuín, where he is paid in kind and receives SP benefits. During that time he is classified as a worker without remuneration. A few months later another housing project starts, in the state capital, and he is offered a job as a bricklayer, but without being enrolled with IMSS. He is willing to go without SS benefits because he heard on the radio that the government was launching a new health insurance program for workers without social security coverage and because by avoiding IMSS he can get a higher wage. He therefore remains in the informal sector, although he is a salaried worker (illegally employed).

In Acapulco, Guerrero, worker E is a woman employed as a dishwasher in the restaurant of a large hotel. She is a formal worker, enrolled in IMSS and receiving SS benefits. She saves some money and starts a small business selling food on the beaches; as a self-employed informal worker, she now gets SP benefits. The business fails, but instead of returning to work at the hotel, she migrates to Los Angeles, California, where a cousin of hers who migrated five years earlier has found her a job as a dishwasher in a restaurant chain there. She drops out of Mexico's labor force.

Worker F owns two hectares of land near Turicato, a semi-urban community in the state of Michoacán, where he grows some corn. As a self-employed informal worker, he has access to SP benefits. The world price of corn falls, so he decides to work in the nearby capital city of Morelia as a truck driver for a soft-drink bottling plant. His new boss offers him a higher wage if he agrees not to be enrolled in IMSS, but he wants SS benefits because his wife is pregnant and he knows that IMSS has just renovated its hospital in the city. He also plans to sell his land and save for a house; therefore he accepts a lower wage, but as a formal salaried worker.

Finally, worker G is formally employed by a dairy farm in Cerralvo, in the state of Nuevo León, that sells milk for a state-sponsored school breakfast program. As a result of budget cuts, the state government suspends the program. To remain in business, the dairy farm offers worker G the option of remaining employed but without SS benefits. The worker accepts and so turns into an informal worker receiving SP benefits.

Ten observations are relevant. First, *all workers are employed.* In Mexico, the open unemployment rate is low and unemployment spells are very short.[8] For low-wage workers, the labor market is best described as being in full employment, including in the definition of "employment" self-employment, work as a *comisionista,* and work without monetary remuneration, like that of the worker from San Luis Potosí.[9] Of course, *the statement that the labor market is in full employment does not mean that workers are efficiently allocated,* and it means even less that outcomes in the labor market are optimal in any social welfare sense.

Second, none of the workers' moves between formal and informal employment were impeded by barriers to mobility or entry into formal employment. The evidence indicates that the minimum wage in Mexico is not binding.[10] Of course, some workers might not accept a wage reduction in order to remain in formality when there is a negative shock, like the worker from Veracruz who migrated to Ciudad Juárez. But it is not that the maquiladora could not lower wages in response to the slowdown in product demand. There is a difference between barriers to mobility and undesirable job characteristics. There also is a difference between entering formality at any salary and getting a high-wage formal job.[11]

8. There is no unemployment insurance in Mexico. The Inter-American Development Bank (IDB) notes that unemployment spells in Mexico are very short: of the sixteen countries for which IDB gathers data on unemployment periods of one year or more, Mexico's periods have the second-shortest duration, after Guatemala's. The mean share of workers who are unemployed for more than one year for all countries is 11.2 percent; the value for Mexico is 0.78 (IDB 2004, table 1-2, p. 19). IDB also notes that "many workers, specially the poorest, cannot afford periods of job search and therefore are forced to accept the first job that comes their way, even if waiting would have meant finding a job in which they were more productive and would earn higher wages" (p. 7).

9. Hart, who originally coined the term "informality," notes that the main message of his paper was "that Accra's poor were generally not unemployed. They worked, often casually, for erratic and generally low returns; but they were definitely working" (Hart 2006, p. 25). At times the expressions "hidden unemployment" or "underemployment" are used in that context, but I fail to find those expressions useful. I think that it is more precise and useful from the policy standpoint to state that the workers are employed but that they have low productivity and then to focus on the causes of low labor productivity.

10. Both Bell (1997) and Maloney and Nuñez (2004) find that the minimum wage in Mexico is not binding. According to IMSS registries, in 2006 less than 4 percent of all enrolled workers were registered as earning a minimum wage; further, a large majority of those cases were waiters and the like, who are paid with a combination of wages and commissions or tips. The latter are not counted as part of the wage for the purposes of social security. Comparing Mexico to Brazil, Chile, and Colombia, the IDB finds that "in contrast with the previous three cases, in Mexico the minimum wage is set low in comparison with average wages and there is little concentration of wages around the minimum, suggesting that it is not very effective" (IDB 2004, p. 228). Table 5-11 in this chapter uses data from ENOE to show that less than 1 percent of formal workers and less than 6 percent of informal workers earn less than the minimum wage.

11. As anecdotal evidence, it is not unusual to see at construction sites or restaurants in the cities of Mexico signs saying "*Se buscan trabajadores*" ("We are looking for workers") in what are formal jobs, while two or three blocks down the road informal workers are peddling goods in the streets. The formal jobs in construction or restaurants (carrying cement or bricks, cleaning floors, and so forth) require few prior skills and little schooling, but given the low wages and the nature of the social security benefits offered in those jobs, some prefer to continue earning wages or commissions in their informal jobs, along with whatever social protection benefits they can access.

Third, in some cases movement between formal and informal employment derives from the cyclical nature of agricultural production and is associated with interstate migration, as with the worker from Oaxaca. In those cases the pattern of movement is fairly predictable. In other cases, formal-informal movement also involves interstate migration, but without any clear pattern of duration. That is the case with the worker from Veracruz.

Fourth, in some cases the shift between formal and informal employment involves no migration at all. In fact, the shift may occur within the same firm, which may, for example, require *comisionista*s rather than salaried workers as it adapts its business plan to international competition, as with the worker from Mérida. Or the pattern of formal-informal transit might involve only intrastate migration, as with the worker from San Luis Potosí. Alternatively, formal-informal shifts may be associated with rural-urban migration, as with the worker from Michoacán; rural-rural migration, as with the worker from Oaxaca; or urban-urban migration, as with the worker from Veracruz.

Fifth, formal-informal transit can occur as a response to government budget cuts, as in the case of the worker in Nuevo León, whose change of labor status resulted from a switch from legal to illegal salaried employment in the same firm—that is, without any job change.

Sixth, the case of the worker from Acapulco illustrates the high failure rate for small businesses and microenterprises. In that example, failure ends in international migration, and neither the IMSS registries nor the employment surveys would record what happens to the worker after she leaves her self-employed job unless she returns to Mexico at some future date.

Seventh, while some shifts from formality to informality are perfectly legal, some are not. The workers from Veracruz and Oaxaca always have legal forms of employment. But the case of the worker from Yucatán is ambiguous—is she an employee of the firm importing clothes from China? In the cases of the bricklayer from San Luis Potosí and the worker at the dairy farm in Nuevo León, the jobs are clearly illegal.

Eighth, patterns of formal-informal mobility are influenced by workers' ownership of productive assets and by their preferences. The workers from Veracruz and Yucatán own no assets other than their labor, and so they always work for a firm, as *comisionistas* or salaried workers; the worker from Oaxaca owns some tools with which he can make handicrafts, and so sometimes he is self-employed; the worker from Michoacán owns some land, but because the price of his output fell and his wife is expecting a baby, he values employment with access to IMSS health services; and the worker from Guerrero saved some financial capital but lost it in an unsuccessful business venture, and so she is forced to become a salaried worker. The worker from San Luis Potosí does not value social security coverage as much as the worker from Michoacán, and so he accepts a salaried job without being registered with IMSS.

Ninth, labor relations and work categories shift with patterns of formal-informal mobility. At one point a worker may be a salaried employee, then he may be self-employed, then he may be an illegally salaried employee, and then he may become a *comisionista*. Later on, he may drop out of Mexico's labor force altogether to go to work in Los Angeles, like the woman from Guerrero. A worker may shift between being a bricklayer and an unpaid ranch hand (San Luis Potosí); an artisan and an agricultural laborer (Oaxaca); an agricultural producer and a truck driver (Michoacán); a custodian and a newspaper salesman (Veracruz); a seamstress and a salesperson (Yucatán); and a dishwasher and small entrepreneur (Guerrero). However, legal status can shift without any change in firm or even in work performed (Nuevo León).

Tenth, despite the different forms of labor relationships and work categories, all the workers are trying to do the best that they can for themselves in whatever country, state, sector, or occupation that suits them best, regardless of legal status. And they all have access to social benefits, either from IMSS, Infonavit, and the Afores or from whatever social protection program happens to be available in the state where they live or to which they migrate. All those labor outcomes are partly a result of their choices and partly a result of the choices of the firms with which they are related. Perhaps the maquiladora in Ciudad Juárez does not offer its workers illegal salaried employment during lean times because, as a large firm, it is afraid of being caught cheating by IMSS and so offers its workers only a lower salary instead. However, the construction company in San Luis Potosí does offer its workers the option of illegal employment, as does the dairy farm in Nuevo León. The firm in Yucatán changes the nature of the offer made to its workers because it changed its business plan from being a producer to being a distributor, and so on.

Outcomes in the labor market thus are the result of the interaction of the choices made by both workers and firms, *not the result of the individual choices of workers or firms*. Outcomes are driven by workers maximizing their utility and firms maximizing their profits, in response to international competition, shifts in demand for products, changes in government expenditures, variations in world prices, and so on. A critical point for the purposes of this volume is that outcomes also are influenced by social programs because those programs strongly affect workers' utility, on one hand, and firms' labor costs and profits, on the other.

## Evidence of Mobility from Social Security Registries

The analysis presented below was carried out by combining IMSS and Consar registries to follow workers' formal and nonformal status.[12] I first used only IMSS reg-

---

12. I refer to formal and nonformal status because social security registries do not capture what happens to workers when they are not enrolled in IMSS; they could have migrated abroad, dropped out of the labor force, or moved to the informal sector. To remedy that situation, I also used the ENEO surveys, which register what happens to workers when they leave formal employment, as discussed later in the chapter.

istries to follow all workers enrolled in IMSS in 1997 for a period of ten years; I then used information from IMSS and Consar registries between 1997 and 2006.

### Workers from the 1997 Generation: IMSS Registries Only

On July 1, 1997, the current Social Security Law went into effect. At that point, 9,279,273 workers were enrolled in IMSS.[13] The analysis given here identifies the formal or nonformal status of each of those workers up to July 1, 2006, and determines whether a worker who was enrolled in IMSS on July 1, 1997, was also enrolled on July 1 of 1998, on July 1 of 1999, and so on, up to July 1, 2006. That allows for measuring the number of each worker's exits and reentries into formal employment. I highlight two facts implicit in the design of the study in the results that follow: first, all the workers entered the formal sector at least once in their working lives. Second, only one cohort of workers was followed; those who entered IMSS after 1997 are not included here.

Before presenting the results, I want to make a few observations. First, the data do not pick up moves that occurred during the year—for example, when a worker left a formal sector job in November 1998 and returned to a formal job in March 1999. Such changes are not recorded because the worker appears in the formal sector on both July 1, 1998, and July 1, 1999. Second, the data do not include workers who change from one formal firm to another; only moves out of and into formality are recorded. Third, the data refer to urban workers only; they do not register formal-informal mobility in agriculture.[14] That matters because most agricultural workers are poor and because, as in the case of the Oaxaca worker previously described, agricultural workers exhibit a lot of cyclical movement between the formal and informal sectors. For those reasons, the results presented here underestimate the magnitude of formal-informal transit, although it is nonetheless quite substantial.

The number of possible combinations of entries into and exits from formal employment is very large.[15] To facilitate interpretation of results, I first recorded average stays in formality and then created an index of frequency of mobility. In other words, the analysis refers to *average length of stay in formal employment*, on one hand, and *frequency of entry and exit*, on the other.

13. Of that total, 2,918,788 were thirty-six years of age or older and 6,630,485 were thirty-six years of age or younger; they were divided into "old" and "young" workers respectively. In 1997 the mean age of the former was forty-six years and of the latter, twenty-seven years. Of "old" workers, only 318,054 were more than fifty-six at the time, and that is the maximum number of workers who could have left the formal sector as a result of retirement, given that Mexico's retirement age is sixty-five.

14. A total of 230,978 agricultural workers are excluded from this database because IMSS registries of those workers are kept separate from the rest and it is technically impossible to merge them.

15. The database is a matrix with 9,279,273 rows and ten columns, from 1997 to 2006. Each cell admits three values: 1 if the ith worker was enrolled in IMSS in the jth year and earned more than three times the minimum wage in that year; 0 if he or she was enrolled but earned less than three times the minimum wage; and −1 if he or she was not enrolled.

Figure 5-4. *Years of Formal Employment by Wage Level, 1997–2006*

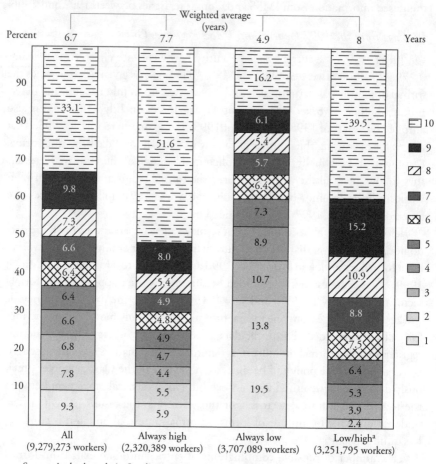

Source: Author's analysis. See discussion in text.

a. The percentage is zero in the low/high wage category for one year of employment because a worker must be employed at least two years to register one year of high and one year of low wages.

AVERAGE STAY IN FORMAL EMPLOYMENT

Figure 5-4 divides the 9.2 million workers enrolled in IMSS into three mutually exclusive groups: those who had high wages every time that they were registered in IMSS, those who had low wages, and those who had low wages at times and high wages at other times. Consider first high-wage workers. Of the 2.32 million workers in that group, 51.6 percent were enrolled for ten continuous years; at the other extreme, 5.9 percent were enrolled for only one year. All in all, the average high-wage worker in Mexico who was enrolled in IMSS in 1997 was in the formal sector 7.7 years of the ten-year period, or 77 percent of his working time, and had another labor status during the remaining 23 percent of the time.[16]

The contrast with low-wage workers is striking. Of the 3.7 million workers in this group, only 16.2 percent were employed in the formal sector for ten continuous years; at the other end, 19.5 percent were formal employees for only one year. The average low-wage worker who was in the formal sector in 1997 had a formal job for 4.9 years of the ten-year period; in other words, he or she was employed in the formal sector for 49 percent of his or her working time and had a different labor status 51 percent of the time.

Workers with mixed wages had longer stays in formality, 80 percent of their time on average.[17] When the figures for all three groups are averaged, the result is that over the ten-year period a worker who was enrolled in IMSS in 1997 spent 67 percent of the time in formal employment and 33 percent of the time in a different labor status. Two conclusions emerge from the above results:

—Most workers who were formally employed in 1997 did not spend the next decade in continuous formal employment.

—Low-wage workers spent less time in formal employment than all other workers.

I explored the consistency of the results from two angles: age and gender differences. First, the 9.2 million workers were divided between those who were thirty-six years of age or less in 1997 (labeled young), and those who were thirty-six years of age or more (labeled old). Figure 5-5 shows the results for the first group and figure 5-6 for the second. In each case, workers were classified by wage: high, low, or mixed. The number of cases in each category is shown at the bottom of each column and the average number of years in formal employment at the top.

Two facts emerge from the results: differences in the average stay in formality of high- and low-wage workers persisted, and for any wage level, older workers stayed in formal employment longer than younger ones. It is nonetheless notable that old low-wage workers had an average stay in formality over the ten-year period of 56 percent, lower than the average stay of young high-wage workers (78 percent).

Second, women and men were contrasted. Figure 5-7 shows that the difference in average stay in formality for high- and low-wage women was actually higher than the difference for high- and low-wage men. It also emerges that regardless of wage level, women had a lower average stay in formal employment than men. But the finding that low-wage workers had a shorter average stay than high-wage workers holds regardless of gender.

16. Of course, some of the workers could have passed away. I do not make any corrections for mortality. However, using data from Inegi and the National Population Council, which is Mexico's official agency for conducting population studies, the mortality rate for persons aged fifteen to sixty-four years is estimated to be 2.9 per thousand for the period 1990–2005, so that factor would not significantly affect the results.

17. Note that by design, no worker in the mixed category could have been enrolled in IMSS only one year, because in that case he or she would be either a high- or a low-wage worker. To be in the mixed category, a worker must be enrolled in IMSS at least two years to allow recording of a high- and a low-wage event. That increases the average stay in formality of those workers vis-à-vis high- or low-wage workers, who can leave IMSS after only one year.

Figure 5-5. *Years of Formal Employment for Young Workers, 1997–2006*

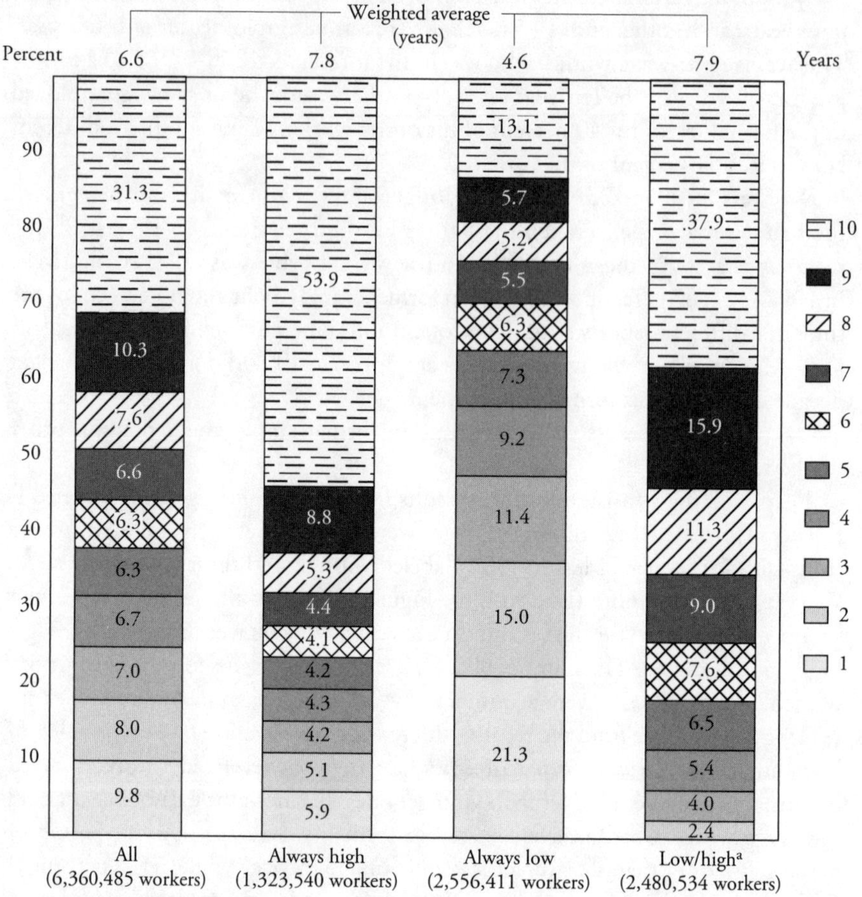

Source: Author's analysis. See discussion in text.

a. The percentage is zero in the low/high wage category for one year of employment because a worker must be employed at least two years to register one year of high and one year of low wages.


FREQUENCY OF ENTRY AND EXIT

A worker's average stay in formal employment can be characterized by many exits and entries or only a few.[18] Because the possible number of combinations is very large, I created an index of frequency of mobility, FM, given by

$$(5\text{-}1) \qquad FM = 100 * \left[ \sum_{k=1}^{t} \left( f(k).k \right) \right] \Big/ t,$$


18. Consider, for example, a worker who over the ten-year period spent six years enrolled in IMSS. That could be because he worked six continuous years in the formal sector and then left for

Figure 5-6. *Years of Formal Employment for Old Workers, 1997–2006*

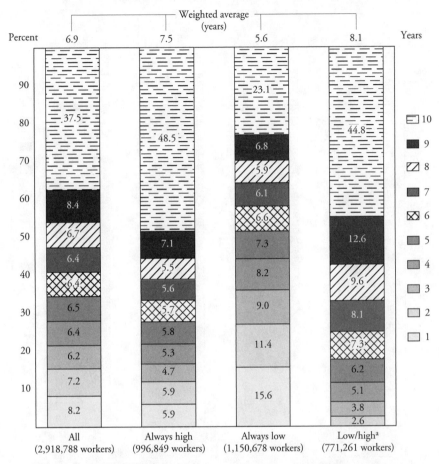

Source: Author's analysis. See discussion in text.

a. The percentage is zero in the low/high wage category for one year of employment because a worker must be employed at least two years to register one year of high and one year of low wages.

where $t$ is the number of years over which workers were followed (in this case, ten), $N$ is the total number of workers in formal employment at the beginning of the period (9.2 million), $F(k)$ is the number of workers who entered or exited IMSS $k$ times, and $f(k)=F(k)/N$.

the next four; because he worked three continuous years, then left for four years, and then returned for the last three; or because he was formal for the first two years, then not the next, then formal again the next year, then not, and so on. In all cases he spent 60 percent of the decade as a formal worker, but at one extreme he only had one entry and one exit, while at the other extreme he had nine entries and exits (including his entry in 1997).

Figure 5-7. *Years of Formal Employment, Women and Men, 1997–2006*

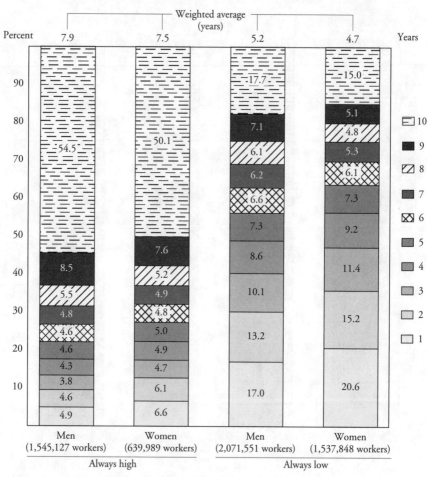

Source: Author's analysis. See discussion in text.

To provide some insight on equation 5-1, I note that if a worker was registered in IMSS for ten years, then $k = 1$ because the worker entered only once. $F(1)$ represents the total number of workers in that category. At the other extreme, if a worker was registered in IMSS in 1997, left at some point during the next ten years, and did not reenter, then $k = 2$. The total number of workers who had one entry and one exit is represented by $F(2)$. Similarly, $F(3)$ is the number of workers who entered, left, and reentered during the decade. A moment's thought shows that $k = 10$ is the maximum number of entries and exits that a worker could have had during the decade: entered in 1997, exited in 1998; entered in 1999, exited in 2000; entered in 2001, exited in 2002; and so forth. $F(10)$ is the number of workers who made ten moves during the decade.

FM has a value of 100 when all workers had the maximum number of entries and exits, which I interpret here as the maximum possible mobility, and a value of $(1/t)$ when all workers who entered IMSS in 1997 stayed continuously for the full decade (because they all had to enter at least once to be registered in IMSS), which I interpret here as the minimum mobility. The index is useful for comparing the relative mobility of different groups of workers. Table 5-4 presents the results.

Three features are worth noting. First, whether young or old, low-wage workers had more mobility than all other workers. Second, younger workers had higher mobility than older workers, but old low-wage workers had more mobility than young high-wage workers. In that case, the condition of wage dominated the condition of age. Third, workers with mixed and low wages had very similar patterns of mobility.

To gain further insight, it is useful to disaggregate FM, because the same average stay in formality is consistent with different patterns of entry and exit. Consider, for example, two workers, both of whom had a five-year stay during the period 1997–2006. Both entered IMSS in 1997, but one stayed for five continuous years through 2001 and then left without returning, at least through 2006; the other had a pattern of entry and exit year after year over the decade. Both had the same average stay of 50 percent, but one had two changes of labor status in ten years and the other had ten. Tables 5-5 and 5-6 reveal the information behind table 5-4 to compare the frequency of entry and exit of high-wage workers with that of low-wage workers.

Note first that the last column of both tables coincides with the corresponding bars of figure 5-4; they show the distribution of workers by average years in formal employment. It follows that those in the last row of each table, who had been in formal jobs for ten continuous years, must be in column $f(1)$, with only one entry into IMSS, necessarily in 1997 (a total of 51.6 percent of high- and 16.2 percent of low-wage workers). It also follows that those who were in IMSS for only one year, in the first row of each table, must be in $f(2)$, having entered in 1997 and necessarily exited in 1998 (5.9 percent of high-wage and 19.5 percent of low-wage workers).

The more revealing cases pertain to workers between those extremes. Compare high- and low-wage workers with a five-year average stay in formal jobs, or

Table 5-4. *Frequency of Mobility by Age and Wage, 1997–2006*

| Workers | All workers | Young workers | Old workers |
|---|---|---|---|
| All workers | 22.6 | 23.8 | 20.0 |
| High-wage | 17.0 | 17.3 | 16.5 |
| Low-wage | 24.8 | 26.1 | 21.9 |
| High-/low-wage | 24.0 | 24.8 | 21.6 |

Source: Author's analysis. See discussion in text.

Table 5-5. *Relative Frequency of Entry and Exit, High-Wage Workers*[a]

| Years in formal employment | f(1) | f(2) | f(3) | f(4) | f(5) | f(6) | f(7) | f(8) | f(9) | f(10) | Total |
|---|---|---|---|---|---|---|---|---|---|---|---|
| 1 | ... | 5.918 | ... | ... | ... | ... | ... | ... | ... | ... | 5.918 |
| 2 | ... | 4.921 | 0.088 | ... | ... | ... | ... | ... | ... | ... | 5.454 |
| 3 | ... | 3.581 | 0.155 | 0.577 | 0.025 | 0.043 | ... | ... | ... | ... | 4.380 |
| 4 | ... | 3.771 | 0.210 | 0.577 | 0.065 | 0.076 | 0.007 | 0.004 | ... | ... | 4.711 |
| 5 | ... | 3.764 | 0.325 | 0.570 | 0.111 | 0.089 | 0.019 | 0.007 | 0.001 | 0.000 | 4.887 |
| 6 | ... | 3.398 | 0.488 | 0.548 | 0.190 | 0.088 | 0.035 | 0.006 | 0.002 | ... | 4.754 |
| 7 | ... | 3.137 | 0.795 | 0.510 | 0.326 | 0.063 | 0.048 | ... | ... | ... | 4.879 |
| 8 | ... | 2.872 | 1.513 | 0.438 | 0.554 | ... | ... | ... | ... | ... | 5.376 |
| 9 | ... | 3.340 | 4.705 | ... | ... | ... | ... | ... | ... | ... | 8.046 |
| 10 | 51.596 | ... | ... | ... | ... | ... | ... | ... | ... | ... | 51.596 |
| Weighted average | 5.160 | 6.940 | 2.484 | 1.466 | 0.635 | 0.215 | 0.076 | 0.013 | 0.003 | 0.000 | 16.993/100.00 |

Source: Author's analysis. See discussion in text.
a. By years in formal employment, 1997–2006.

Table 5-6. Relative Frequency of Entry and Exit, Low-Wage Workers[a]

| Years in formal employment | f(1) | f(2) | f(3) | f(4) | f(5) | f(6) | f(7) | f(8) | f(9) | f(10) | Total |
|---|---|---|---|---|---|---|---|---|---|---|---|
| 1 | ... | 19.510 | ... | ... | ... | ... | ... | ... | ... | ... | 19.510 |
| 2 | ... | 9.782 | 0.499 | 3.567 | ... | ... | ... | ... | ... | ... | 13.848 |
| 3 | ... | 6.203 | 0.575 | 3.004 | 0.273 | 0.612 | ... | ... | ... | ... | 10.667 |
| 4 | ... | 4.710 | 0.618 | 2.288 | 0.421 | 0.697 | 0.085 | 0.073 | ... | ... | 8.893 |
| 5 | ... | 3.421 | 0.694 | 1.801 | 0.541 | 0.578 | 0.158 | 0.082 | 0.012 | 0.002 | 7.290 |
| 6 | ... | 2.780 | 0.825 | 1.373 | 0.677 | 0.444 | 0.204 | 0.050 | 0.016 | ... | 6.369 |
| 7 | ... | 2.234 | 1.102 | 1.070 | 0.858 | 0.258 | 0.192 | ... | ... | ... | 5.715 |
| 8 | ... | 1.880 | 1.736 | 0.757 | 1.071 | ... | ... | ... | ... | ... | 5.443 |
| 9 | ... | 1.887 | 4.167 | ... | ... | ... | ... | ... | ... | ... | 6.054 |
| 10 | 16.211 | ... | ... | ... | ... | ... | ... | ... | ... | ... | 16.211 |
| Weighted average | 1.621 | 10.482 | 3.065 | 5.544 | 1.921 | 1.554 | 0.447 | 0.164 | 0.026 | 0.002 | 24.825/100.00 |

Source: Author's analysis. See discussion in text.
a. By years in formal employment, 1997–2006.

4.88 percent of all high- and 7.29 percent of all low-wage workers respectively. Consider first those with high wages. Table 5-5 shows that 77 percent of those workers (3.76/4.88) were in $f(2)$, with one entry and one exit; 6.6 percent (0.32/4.88) were in $f(3)$, with one entry, one exit, and one reentry; 11.7 percent (0.57/4.88) were in $f(4)$, with one entry, one exit, one reentry, and another exit. In fact, 0.2 percent of all high-wage workers with an average stay of five years were in $f(9)$, for all practical purposes entering and exiting year after year.

Consider now low-wage workers with the same five-year average stay in formal employment. Table 5-6 shows that 46.9 percent (3.42/7.29) were in $f(2)$, with one entry and one exit; 9.4 percent were in $f(3)$; 24.7 percent were in $f(4)$, and so on. In fact, 0.16 percent were in $f(9)$ and 0.03 percent in $f(10)$. The last figure implies that 7,414 low-wage workers (3,707,089 * 0.002) entered and exited IMSS year after year over the ten-year period. Those are extreme cases, but note that 43.5 percent of all low-wage workers with a five-year average stay had four or more entries or exits in the course of ten years—a change of labor status at least every two and a half years! Contrast that with the 16.3 percent of high-wage workers who were in that category.

Tables 5-5 and 5-6 show that that pattern repeats for workers with anywhere between two and nine years on average in formal jobs.[19] That leads to the conclusion that for any given average stay in formality, low-wage workers had greater frequency of entry and exit than high-wage workers. That conclusion must be considered with the one already mentioned above: that low-wage workers had lower average stays in formal jobs than high-wage workers. An immediate implication of the results is that low-wage workers enter formal employment more often than high-wage workers; in other words, *the problem for low-wage workers is not entering a formal job, it is staying in a formal job.*

Those results hold, strictly speaking, only for the 3.7 million low-wage workers followed here who were in IMSS in 1997, and it could be argued that they need not extend to all low-wage workers. But as table 5-3 and figure 5-2 show, during that decade there was not a large contraction of aggregate formal employment, except for the short-lived recession of 1995. If those 3.7 million individuals were formal employees only 49 percent of the time during the decade under study, then someone must have replaced them in the formal sector so that aggregate formal employment was maintained. Other low-wage workers or, paradoxically, they themselves, must have entered formal employment!

The last possibility is not a contradiction. The worker from Nuevo León mentioned earlier in this chapter provides an illustration. As elaborated on in chapter 7, in determining how many workers to hire, firms may decide on certain proportions of registered and nonregistered workers in order to minimize their labor

---

19. The frequency of mobility of workers with mixed wages is very similar to that of low-wage workers.

costs. As a result, it may be that some of the 3.7 million low-wage workers never left their jobs over the decade; instead, some exogenous shock may have forced the firm to change their labor status from salaried and registered with IMSS to salaried but not registered with IMSS. In other words, *it is necessary to distinguish between entering and exiting formal employment, on one hand, and entering and exiting a job with a firm, on the other.* The same individual may be a formal or an informal employee while performing the same job with the same firm if the firm decides, for whatever reason, to register the worker with IMSS sometimes and not to at other times—in other words, to break the law at times.

From the standpoint of the government's social objectives, such behavior by firms and workers represents a major problem. The same worker working in the same firm saves for his retirement pension sometimes and sometimes does not, saves for his housing loan sometimes and sometimes does not, and so on. Of course, low-wage workers could have left formal employment because they became self-employed or went to work as *comisionistas,* either voluntarily or because they were fired from the firm as opposed to being kept on as an unregistered salaried worker. Unfortunately, the IMSS registries used here do not allow for distinguishing between the two alternatives. That is why the results here given need to be complemented with the ones presented below, which are based on the employment surveys—which, however, have other limitations.

Table 5-1 shows that evasion of the Social Security Law is very common, involving more than 8 million workers—or more than 11 million workers according to the International Labor Office statistics used in table 5-2. *The analysis of frequency of mobility highlights why understanding the reasons behind evasion is central to understanding the movement between formal and informal employment.* Some of the moves are a reflection of changes in IMSS registration within the same firm, and such moves are different from moves from salaried to nonsalaried status. Both have the same negative implications for the government's social objectives—workers are left without social security coverage. However, as shown in chapter 7, they do not have the same implications for productivity. A move from formal to informal status within the same firm has a different effect on workers' productivity than a move from formal to informal employment in a different job or a move from salaried employment to self-employment or employment as a *comisionista.*

What does that mean for the existence of barriers to entry into formal jobs? The answer is that for the 3.7 million low-wage workers analyzed here, those barriers did not exist during the decade studied. As shown, low-wage workers entered and exited formal jobs more often than high-wage workers, although as seen, high-wage workers also entered and exited formal jobs. What the data show is that the problem for low-wage workers is the short duration of formal employment. Two important questions, then, are why firms and workers do not comply with the law all the time, and why that phenomenon is more pronounced for low-wage workers.

*Total Entries in the IMSS and Consar Registries, 1997–2006*

To provide another angle on the issue of entry into and exit from formal employ-ment, results using IMSS and Consar registries of all workers who entered IMSS between July 1, 1997, and July 1, 2006, are presented, beginning with the IMSS registries. Table 5-7 follows formal employment between 1997 and 2006. The main diagonal shows the number of workers enrolled in IMSS on July 1 of each year; the rows record the number of workers who entered in a given year and remained *continuously* in formal employment in subsequent years. Consider, for instance, the first row, which shows the 9.27 million workers who were in IMSS on July 1, 1997, who necessarily coincide with the formal labor force on that day. The row identifies those individuals who continued without interruption in for-mal employment in 1998, 1999, and so on, up to July 1, 2006, for a total of 3.08 million individuals. That figure coincides with the one shown in the first bar of figure 5-4 (9.279 * 0.332).[20] Note that an individual worker may appear more than once in this table; for example, a worker who entered formality in, say, 1999 and left in 2001 appears as one of the individuals accounting for the reduction from 7.27 to 6.26 million workers between 2001 and 2002. But if the worker reentered formality in 2003 and stayed through 2006, he or she also appears in the 2003 row up to 2006.

The numbers in this table can be analyzed in various ways. Here I highlight that the number of worker flows exceeds the number of job flows. Consider the change from 1997 to 1998. Formal employment increased by 1.19 million workers (10.47 − 9.27), but 1.83 million of the individuals who were enrolled in IMSS in 1997 left formal employment between those two years (9.27 − 7.44). That means that 3 million new individuals entered IMSS in 1998—1.8 million to replace the ones who left and 1.19 million to account for the net growth in formal employment.

Next, IMSS is combined with Consar information. I note first that the Social Security Law states that when a worker is registered in IMSS for the first time, an individual retirement account is opened in his name in the Afore of his choice. If the worker leaves formal employment, the account is kept in his name, and although no deposits are made while he remains out, the account continues to earn interest for the worker. When the worker reenters formality, the account is reactivated and additional contributions are channeled to it. Thus, accounts are portable, and past contributions to the worker's retirement accounts are not lost during spells of unemployment or informal employment. Table 5-8 shows in the first column the *accumulated* number of individual retirement accounts registered

---

20. The word "continuously" means only that the worker was registered in IMSS on July 1 of each year, so some workers could have left formality and returned within the year. Although table 5-7 shows that they were in continuous formal employment, such an interruption would not be captured in this data set.

Table 5-7. *Evolution of Total IMSS-Registered Employment, 1997–2006*[a]
Millions of workers

| Year | 1997 | 1998 | 1999 | 2000 | 2001 | 2002 | 2003 | 2004 | 2005 | 2006 |
|---|---|---|---|---|---|---|---|---|---|---|
| 1997 | 9.279 | 7.445 | 6.347 | 5.607 | 4.956 | 4.421 | 3.977 | 3.622 | 3.331 | 3.084 |
| 1998 | ... | 10.473 | 8.171 | 6.961 | 6.011 | 5.279 | 4.698 | 4.246 | 3.882 | 3.579 |
| 1999 | ... | ... | 11.104 | 8.726 | 7.278 | 6.264 | 5.503 | 4.930 | 4.478 | 4.110 |
| 2000 | ... | ... | ... | 11.863 | 9.059 | 7.529 | 6.488 | 5.742 | 5.171 | 4.716 |
| 2001 | ... | ... | ... | ... | 11.928 | 9.162 | 7.659 | 6.666 | 5.938 | 5.375 |
| 2002 | ... | ... | ... | ... | ... | 11.846 | 9.207 | 7.794 | 6.833 | 6.125 |
| 2003 | ... | ... | ... | ... | ... | ... | 11.852 | 9.356 | 7.986 | 7.055 |
| 2004 | ... | ... | ... | ... | ... | ... | ... | 12.102 | 9.629 | 8.286 |
| 2005 | ... | ... | ... | ... | ... | ... | ... | ... | 12.409 | 9.992 |
| 2006 | ... | ... | ... | ... | ... | ... | ... | ... | ... | 13.048 |

Source: Author's analysis. See discussion in text.

a. The table excludes agricultural workers and reflects figures at mid-year. Figures shown in table 5-1 refer to the end of the year and include agricultural workers. The rows refer to the year in which workers entered into formal employment, beginning in 1997; the columns register the number of workers who entered in any given year and remained in formal employment for the following years.

Table 5-8. *IMSS and Consar Registries, 1997–2006*

| Year | Consar accumulated accounts | IMSS employment |
|------|------|------|
| 1997 | 11,188,114 | 10,753,442 |
| 1998 | 13,827,674 | 11,506,801 |
| 1999 | 15,594,503 | 12,207,351 |
| 2000 | 17,844,956 | 12,732,430 |
| 2001 | 26,518,534 | 12,373,843 |
| 2002 | 29,421,202 | 12,424,861 |
| 2003 | 31,398,282 | 12,334,430 |
| 2004 | 33,316,492 | 12,594,832 |
| 2005 | 35,276,277 | 13,184,863 |
| 2006 | 37,408,828 | 14,080,367 |

Source: IMSS and Consar registries, various years.

by Consar since July 1, 1997. The second column shows the number of workers registered each year with IMSS.[21]

The contrast is striking. From the second column it follows that over the course of the decade, an average of 369,658 net formal jobs were created each year, but from the first column it follows that an average of 2,913,412 new individual retirement accounts were opened. Assuming a one-to-one correspondence between individual workers and individual retirement accounts implies that 2.9 million *new* workers entered formal employment every year, although only 0.369 million jobs were created.[22] *The number of individuals who were formally employed at least once during the ten-year period is more than double the number of formal jobs available in the same period.*

Many factors account for that result. Over the decade some workers retired; others left the labor force altogether (for example, migrants who went abroad). Those events, however, account for a small part of the phenomenon. The main cause is the existence of the informal sector, to which workers move. But regardless of the reason, the table shows that entry into IMSS of new workers—or reentry of workers who previously were in formal employment but left—was very large over the ten-year period. And because so many more workers entered than net jobs were created, exit from IMSS also was very large.

21. This column does not coincide with the main diagonal of table 5-7 because it records end-of-year numbers in order to be comparable with Consar data in the first column; table 5-7 records numbers on July 1 of each year.

22. Consar figures exaggerate entry of *new* workers to the extent that there may be some duplication of registries—that is, the same worker may have two or more retirement accounts. But note that a duplication of a retirement account occurs when a worker leaves formality and upon reentry is captured with a different name or social security number; it does not occur if a worker remains continuously in formal employment. So the point about entry and exit stands. In any event, unofficial estimates place the number of duplicated accounts at around 10 percent of the total, so it does not affect the conclusions in the text.

I end this section reiterating that labor mobility is underestimated by the IMSS registries. Table A9-1 in appendix 9 presents data from Consar for all workers enrolled in IMSS in the period from July 1997 to February 2007 (the latest data available at the time this volume was written). As opposed to the IMSS registries used before to follow the 1997 generation, these data encompass all generations · since the current Social Security Law went into effect, including rural workers, and captures *within-year entries and exits*. The table implies that for the 37.8 million workers who were enrolled in IMSS at least once over the period, the average length of time that they contributed to their Afore accounts amounted to only 45 percent of the time that they could have contributed. That implies that the average time in formality for all workers who were subject to the current Social Security Law was 45 percent. That figure contrasts with the average of 67 percent shown in figure 5-4 for the 1997 generation, which excluded within-year transits and rural workers. In other words, when considering all workers and within-year entries and exits, mobility of workers in and out of formality is greater.[23]

## Evidence of Mobility from Employment Surveys

The Encuesta Nacional de Empleo Urbano (ENEU) (National Survey of Urban Employment) was a yearly survey of workers in the form of a panel data set that permits following individual workers through four contiguous trimesters and through four types of labor status: formal and informal (including illegal salaried) employment, open unemployment, and nonparticipation in the labor force (drop-outs).[24] In contrast to the IMSS registries, this data set identifies what happens to workers when they leave formal jobs, unless they migrate abroad. On the other hand, it has two shortcomings: individual workers can be followed for only one year, and until 2005 coverage excluded rural areas. As before, therefore, moves between types of labor status probably are underestimated. Nevertheless, it is hoped that results presented here and in the previous discussion give a more rounded view of the issue under discussion.

I used the ENEUs for 1998 and 2001 and the ENOE for 2006 and, as before, divided workers between men and women and high- and low-wage earners, defining high-wage earners as those earning three times the minimum wage or more. Note that 1998 was a year of *high* GDP growth (5 percent), 2001 a year of *negative* GDP growth (−1.3 percent), and 2006 a year of *modest to high* GDP growth (4.3 percent). Table 5-9 presents the results of following 26,500 men between the

23. The observation that there is substantial within-year mobility coincides with the results of the econometric studies quoted below, in particular Calderón (2000). On the other hand, note that table A9-1 shows lower average stays in formality for lower-wage workers than for higher-wage workers, a fact that has large implications for the size of retirement pensions, as discussed in chapter 10.

24. In 2005 the ENEU changed its name to ENOE (Encuesta Nacional de Ocupación y Empleo) because the survey was enhanced to include more information and data from rural areas.

Table 5-9. *Formal-Informal-Unemployed Transit, 1998, 2001, and 2006*[a]

| Number of workers (first trimester) | Percent of labor force (last trimester) |
|---|---|
| *1998* | *1998* |
| Formal < 3 mw[b] (6,173) | 80.8 (formal) |
| | 17.7 (informal) |
| | 1.5 (unemployed) |
| Formal > 3 mw (7,619) | 88.0 (formal) |
| | 11.1 (informal) |
| | 1.0 (unemployed) |
| Informal < 3 mw (7,299) | 18.6 (formal) |
| | 79.3 (informal) |
| | 2.1 (unemployed) |
| Informal > 3 mw (5,409) | 18.3 (formal) |
| | 80.6 (informal) |
| | 1.1 (unemployed) |
| | |
| *2001* | *2001* |
| Formal < 3 mw (5,328) | 78.4 (formal) |
| | 19.2 (informal) |
| | 2.3 (unemployed) |
| Formal > 3 mw (12,674) | 84.5 (formal) |
| | 14.0 (informal) |
| | 1.5 (unemployed) |
| Informal < 3 mw (6,744) | 17.8 (formal) |
| | 80.3 (informal) |
| | 1.9 (unemployed) |
| Informal > 3 mw (8,965) | 18.6 (formal) |
| | 80.1 (informal) |
| | 1.2 (unemployed) |
| | |
| *2006* | *2006* |
| Formal < 3 mw (5,034) | 81.4 (formal) |
| | 15.8 (informal) |
| | 2.7 (unemployed) |
| Formal > 3 mw (8,101) | 86.0 (formal) |
| | 12.1 (informal) |
| | 1.8 (unemployed) |
| Informal < 3 mw (9,538) | 10.9 (formal) |
| | 84.1 (informal) |
| | 5.0 (unemployed) |
| Informal > 3 mw (9,458) | 11.7 (formal) |
| | 84.7 (informal) |
| | 3.5 (unemployed) |

Source: Author's analysis based on data from the Encuesta Nacional de Empleo Urbano for 1998 and 2001 and from the Encuesta Nacional de Ocupación y Empleo for 2006 (www.inegi.gob.mx).

a. GDP growth: 5.0 percent (1998); −1.3 percent (2001); 4.3 percent (2006).

b. mw = minimum wage.

ages of sixteen and sixty-five in 1998; 33,711 men in 2001; and 32,131 men in 2006. The first column shows the number of workers and their labor status in the first trimester of each year; the second column shows the share of those workers in each labor status in the last trimester of the year. I excluded workers who were in the labor force in the first trimester but dropped out by the last trimester. The analysis focuses only on transit of workers who remained in the labor force for the full year.

Three features should be highlighted. The first is that formal-informal transits were qualitatively similar over those three years. Of course, there are quantitative variations reflecting the short-run impact of variations in the rate of growth of GDP. But the important point is that *transits occur all the time and therefore are not driven by the economic cycle; they reflect a different phenomenon.* The second feature is that in any one year, between 10 and 20 percent of workers change labor status. The third feature is that the large majority of the changes are from formal to informal employment and vice versa, not to open unemployment. I conclude that the results obtained using IMSS registries and those obtained using the employment surveys are consistent.

*Econometric Studies*

Various researchers have analyzed formal-informal movements and tested for the existence of barriers to entry into formal employment in Mexico. Most if not all of the studies are based on the ENEU and therefore exclude mobility in rural areas. The results of some of the studies are briefly summarized below to complement the previous discussion.

Maloney (1999) was probably the first systematic analysis of mobility in Mexico using the ENEU and questioning the traditional dualistic view of the labor market, which held that informal workers had to get in line for a chance at getting a formal sector job. Maloney found that "the labor market for relatively unskilled workers may well be integrated with both formal and informal sectors, offering desirable jobs with distinct characteristics from which workers may choose, with little queuing."[25] That was followed by Maloney (2004) and Bosch and Maloney (2006). The results in all three papers are consistent with the results in this chapter, pointing to substantial flow across sectors.

Gong, Soest, and Villagomez (2004) used the ENEU for 1992–93 (mild GDP growth of 2.2 percent), 1995 (a period of economic crisis, with GDP growth of −7.0 percent), and 1999–2000 (high GDP growth of 4.7 percent) to calculate transition matrices for three types of labor status: formal, informal, and outside the labor force. Their analysis also used the panel characteristics of the data to follow individual workers through four trimesters, comparing labor status between the first and the last trimester and for women and men separately. Their results,

25. Maloney (1999, p. 276).

which found movement from one status to the other among 10 to 15 percent of workers, are consistent with the results presented above. They noted, among other findings, that "in the 1999–2000 panel, more than 15 percent of men in the formal sector no longer had a formal sector job one year later, and more than 25 percent of all men in the informal sector had left that sector a year later."[26]

Navarro and Schrimpf (2004) used the ENEU for 1997–98 to test the hypothesis that there were barriers to mobility between the formal and the informal sectors and expressly rejected it. Budar-Mejía and García-Verdú (2003) also estimated the probability that a worker would move from the informal to the formal sector and vice versa and found that in both cases the probability had been increasing over time—that is, transitions in both directions were becoming more common.

The results of Calderón (2000, 2006) are particularly valuable in this context. Applying duration models and semi-Markov processes to various ENEUs for the 1990s, Calderón (2000) found "a) that the time spent in a job and the so-called four- and six-year retention rates are short relative to OECD countries; b) that between 15 and 20 percent of wage earners in the formal sector move out to another job status *in only one quarter* [emphasis added] and that the figures for other job status (informal workers, self-employment, unpaid jobs, etc.) are much higher; and c) that the shares that each job status represented within the total population did not vary significantly, in spite of substantial movements of persons among job statuses."[27]

Finally, Calderón (2006) used the ENEU to estimate transition matrices between formal, informal, and unemployment status, distinguishing between workers earning more or less than three times the minimum wage. The author's findings—for 1997, 2001, and 2005—also are consistent with the two main hypotheses presented here: that there is a great deal of mobility between types of labor status and that mobility is greater for low-wage than for high-wage workers. His results also indicate that mobility is similar in years with different rates of GDP growth.

## Mobility and Wage Rates

The discussion so far has centered on changes in workers' labor status without any reference to wage rates. Comparing wage rates across workers presents significant methodological difficulties. I highlight two that are relevant here. First, it is difficult to identify whether differences in wage rates between formal and informal *salaried* workers result from differences in labor status or from unobserved variables, even after controlling for age, gender, and years of schooling. It is all the more dif-

26. Gong, Soest, and Villagomez (2004, p. 2)
27. Calderón (2000, p. 43).

ficult because some of the unobserved variables refer to workers' abilities or valuation of job characteristics like flexibility, hierarchy, safety, the possibility that a job might offer future training, and so on.[28] Second, in the case of *self-employed* workers it is difficult to separate earnings into imputed wages and returns to productive assets, and in the case of *comisionistas* it is difficult to separate imputed wages from compensation for risk or entrepreneurial ability.

In the next two chapters I develop a simple framework for tracing the impact of social programs on wage rates. The analysis shows that explicit or imputed wage rates and returns to productive assets are interlinked and influenced by firm and worker reactions to the programs; it also shows that the resulting wage rates cannot be interpreted as measures of productivity differences between workers.

In this section I present comparisons of the wage rates of formal and informal *salaried* workers only, exploiting the panel characteristic of the ENOE. I restrict the analysis to salaried workers because the ENOE data are, in my view, insufficient to allow proper separation of the earnings of *comisionistas* and self-employed persons between imputed wages for their labor and returns to productive assets or risk. Because the universe is restricted to salaried workers, the comparison is between formal and informal and, simultaneously, legal and illegal status.

The exercise has two purposes: first, to identify what happens to the wage rates of salaried workers who move between formal and informal status and vice versa; second, to complement the discussion in chapter 3 by providing evidence on how workers value social programs.

The analysis compares wage rates for 8,974 workers interviewed for the ENOE by Inegi (Instituto Nacional de Estadística, Geografía, e Informática) (National Institute of Statistics, Geography, and Information Sciences) in the second trimester of 2005 and again in the second trimester of 2006. The distinguishing characteristics of those workers were that they were continuously employed in the interim; that they answered the questions concerning wages; and that they stayed in the same place.[29]

---

28. See the discussion in World Bank (2007, chap. 3). The important point is that two observationally equivalent workers (that is, having the same age, gender, and years of schooling; living in the same place; and working for the same size of firm) might earn different wages. One, for example, may be willing to take lower pay in exchange for stability while the other wants higher pay because stability is not that important to him; one may be willing to take lower pay because if he stays, the firm eventually will train him, while the other plans to migrate, so earning more today matters more to him than being trained in the future. These *compensating differentials* imply that wage rates may differ between observationally equivalent workers even in the absence of barriers to mobility, minimum wages, or discrimination, and they make wage comparisons across workers extremely difficult.

29. Inegi carries out interviews for the ENOE at workers' homes. The sample refers to individuals who did not change homes during the year and excludes workers who left their homes (because of national or international migration); to that extent it provides a biased picture of the labor market. That disadvantage needs to be weighed against the advantage of observing a subset of individuals at two points in time and at times in different types of labor status.

Workers were separated into those with high and low wages (as before, three times the minimum wage was the cut-off); 4,637 individuals were in the first group and 4,337 in the second. High- and low-wage workers were classified into formal-formal, informal-informal, informal-formal, and formal-informal according to their labor status in the second trimesters of 2005 and 2006, respectively, generating eight groups of workers, four high and four low wage. Workers in each group were classified by gender, age, educational level, rural-urban location, and size of employing firm (measured by the number of workers in the firm in which they worked). Of all workers analyzed,

—39.6 percent were women and 60.4 percent were men

—80.3 percent lived in urban areas and 19.7 percent in rural areas (the latter defined in the ENOE as localities of less than 15,000 inhabitants)

—22.4 percent had at most completed elementary school, 26.7 percent had completed junior high, and 50.9 percent had at least completed high school

—62.1 percent were young and 39.3 percent old (with forty years of age as the cut-off point)

—27.7 percent worked in firms of up to ten workers, 24.7 percent in firms of between eleven and fifty workers, and 45.9 percent in firms of more than fifty workers; 1.7 percent did not specify firm size. Because workers moved and some of those characteristics changed between 2005 and 2006 (particularly age and firm size), workers were classified on the basis of the values observed in 2005.

*Simple Comparisons of Mean Wage Rates*

Table 5-10 presents the results of a simple exercise whereby workers' hourly wages were recorded for the second trimesters of 2005 and 2006 (in 2007 pesos), beginning with high-wage workers. The first row indicates that 191 workers changed from informal to formal status during the period. For 105 of those workers, the change was associated with a lower wage; for eighty-six workers, it was associated with a higher wage. The second row indicates that 159 workers transited from formal to informal status; for 101 of the workers the change was associated with a lower wage and for fifty-eight workers with a higher one. The third row indicates that 3,886 workers remained formal, but despite the absence of change in labor status, 2,176 workers suffered a wage drop while 1,710 workers experienced a wage gain. The fourth row, finally, indicates that 401 workers remained informal but that 278 experienced a wage loss and 123 a wage gain. In all cases, differences in mean wage rates are statistically significant. That implies that for high-wage workers, the transit from formality to informality did not necessarily imply a wage fall, nor did the transit from informality to formality imply a wage gain.

The lower part of table 5-10 shows similar results for low-wage workers. Some moved from formal to informal employment, some moved in the opposite direction, and some did not move at all. But in all four cases, wage rates between 2005 and 2006 changed in both directions, and the result found for high-wage workers obtains here: the transit from formality to informality did not necessarily imply a drop in wages for low-wage workers and the transit from informality to formality did not imply a wage gain.

The columns for gender, firm size, location, education, and age show that there is no clear pattern of association between wage *changes* (not levels) and those variables. There were, for instance, 61 (28 + 33) high-wage informal workers in firms of fifty-one workers or more in 2005 who were then hired formally in 2006. The change in legal status did not imply a uniform change in wages; twenty-eight earned less as a result and thirty-three earned more. Or consider the 215 (79 + 136) low-wage workers informally hired in 2005 in firms of ten workers or fewer who were then hired formally in 2006. For seventy-nine of them, the shift to formal employment implied a wage drop and for 136 of them, a wage increase. Note also that workers of all educational levels moved between formal and informal jobs. For instance, 95 (57 + 38) high-wage workers with a high school education transited from formal to informal status; fifty-seven received a lower wage and thirty-eight received a higher one as a result. Rural-urban location was not systematically associated with the direction of wage changes either. In the case of low-wage rural workers who changed labor status, of the 89 (32 + 57) who transited from informal to formal jobs, thirty-two experienced a wage loss and fifty-seven a wage gain, and of the 79 (33 + 46) who transited in the opposite direction, thirty-three experienced a wage drop and forty-six a wage gain.

The bottom row of table 5-10 shows that the mean wage of all workers in the first trimester of 2005 was 32.2 pesos an hour and that the mean changed to 32.9 pesos an hour in 2006. The change is statistically significant, indicating that for the 8,974 workers there was a 2.2 percent average wage increase. But clearly the mean hides large changes in both directions that, prima facie, do not seem to be correlated with labor status.

What if one compares average wages in the formal and the informal sector? The mean wage of all informally employed workers in 2005 was 20.52 pesos an hour, and in 2006 it was 21.34 pesos; the mean wage of formally employed workers was 36.03 pesos and 36.33 pesos in 2005 and 2006 respectively. One is tempted to conclude from those data that formal workers earn more than informal workers. *But that temptation needs to be resisted, for two reasons:* one, as highlighted earlier in this chapter, it is difficult to define the concept of a "formal" and an "informal" worker; two, workers with different characteristics are being compared. The conclusion that could be drawn from the above data is that wages in the formal sector are on average higher than wages in the informal sector, although as argued below, that statement is not very meaningful.

In any event, the claim that wages in the formal sector are higher on average than wages in the informal sector is different from the claim that a given worker earns more when he or she is formally employed than when informally employed. As table 5-10 shows, the fact that mean wages in the formal sector exceed mean wages

Table 5-10. *Wage Rates and Formal-Informal Transit for Salaried Workers, 2005–06*[a]

| Labor transition | Wage | Mean wage | | | | Gender | |
|---|---|---|---|---|---|---|---|
| | | $w_t$ | $w_{t+1}$ | Percent | Sig | Male | Female |
| **High wage** | | | | | | | |
| Informal to formal | $w_t > w_{t+1}$ | 45.2 | 26.5 | −70.9 | *** | 67 | 38 |
| 191[b] | 105 | (35.2) | (18.3) | (22.3) | | | |
| 2.20[c] | $w_t < w_{t+1}$ | 36.5 | 53.3 | 31.6 | *** | 58 | 28 |
| | 86 | (20.5) | (35.1) | (67.9) | | | |
| Formal to informal | $w_t > w_{t+1}$ | 40.5 | 28.6 | −41.5 | *** | 69 | 32 |
| 159[b] | 101 | (30.2) | (22.3) | (20.0) | | | |
| 2.30[c] | $w_t < w_{t+1}$ | 37.4 | 61.4 | 39.0 | *** | 31 | 27 |
| | 58 | (18.7) | (44.2) | (71.9) | | | |
| Always formal | $w_t > w_{t+1}$ | 55.3 | 38.0 | −45.6 | *** | 1,289 | 887 |
| 3,886[b] | 2,176 | (36.6) | (24.8) | (19.9) | | | |
| 23.50[c] | $w_t < w_{t+1}$ | 43.8 | 61.1 | 28.3 | *** | 1,003 | 707 |
| | 1,710 | (25.1) | (38.1) | (57.5) | | | |
| Always informal | $w_t > w_{t+1}$ | 39.1 | 24.7 | −58.6 | *** | 160 | 118 |
| 401[b] | 278 | (29.9) | (16.9) | (21.0) | | | |
| 12.60[c] | $w_t < w_{t+1}$ | 37.8 | 50.7 | 25.5 | *** | 70 | 53 |
| | 123 | (25.2) | (33.3) | (41.5) | | | |
| **Low wage** | | | | | | | |
| Informal to formal | $w_t > w_{t+1}$ | 16.3 | 13.0 | −25.3 | *** | 79 | 43 |
| 372[b] | 122 | (3.5) | (3.6) | (17.1) | | | |
| 4.70[c] | $w_t < w_{t+1}$ | 13.3 | 22.4 | 40.8 | *** | 172 | 78 |
| | 250 | (4.2) | (13.3) | (88.5) | | | |
| Formal to informal | $w_t > w_{t+1}$ | 16.1 | 12.3 | −31.1 | *** | 49 | 31 |
| 234[b] | 80 | (3.7) | (4.0) | (17.4) | | | |
| 3.60[c] | $w_t < w_{t+1}$ | 13.4 | 21.8 | 38.4 | *** | 103 | 51 |
| | 154 | (4.1) | (11.8) | (153.6) | | | |
| Always formal | $w_t > w_{t+1}$ | 17.0 | 13.9 | −21.6 | *** | 511 | 342 |
| 2,485[b] | 853 | (3.2) | (3.5) | (14.8) | | | |
| 17.50[c] | $w_t < w_{t+1}$ | 15.0 | 23.5 | 36.3 | *** | 1,046 | 586 |
| | 1,632 | (4.0) | (12.7) | (119.6) | | | |
| Always informal | $w_t > w_{t+1}$ | 14.9 | 11.8 | −26.5 | *** | 307 | 206 |
| 1,246[b] | 513 | (3.9) | (3.9) | (16.2) | | | |
| 33.60[c] | $w_t < w_{t+1}$ | 12.3 | 18.6 | 33.9 | *** | 406 | 327 |
| | 733 | (4.5) | (11.0) | (121.4) | | | |
| Total workers | 8,974 | 32.2 | 32.9 | 2.2 | *** | 5,420 | 3,554 |

Source: Author's analysis. See discussion in text.

a. Hourly wages measured in 2007 pesos; standard deviations in parentheses.

b. Number of workers.

c. Percentage of labor force.

**Significant at a 95 percent confidence level; ***Significant at a 99 percent confidence level

| Firm size (number of workers) | | | | Location | | Education Level | | | Age | |
|---|---|---|---|---|---|---|---|---|---|---|
| 0–10 | 11–50 | 51+ | Not available | Rural | Urban | Primary or less | Junior high | High school and above | Young (under 40) | Old (40 or over) |
| 41 | 35 | 28 | 1 | 23 | 82 | 19 | 31 | 55 | 73 | 32 |
| 27 | 25 | 33 | 1 | 12 | 74 | 16 | 12 | 58 | 54 | 32 |
| 28 | 32 | 39 | 2 | 17 | 84 | 18 | 26 | 57 | 70 | 31 |
| 14 | 14 | 29 | 1 | 5 | 53 | 9 | 11 | 38 | 31 | 27 |
| 241 | 616 | 1,292 | 27 | 256 | 1,920 | 209 | 341 | 1,626 | 1,165 | 1,011 |
| 184 | 483 | 1,022 | 21 | 226 | 1,484 | 103 | 275 | 1,332 | 885 | 825 |
| 170 | 45 | 62 | 1 | 78 | 200 | 103 | 80 | 95 | 180 | 98 |
| 64 | 22 | 35 | 2 | 25 | 98 | 32 | 24 | 67 | 76 | 47 |
| 79 | 29 | 14 | 0 | 32 | 90 | 44 | 45 | 33 | 81 | 41 |
| 136 | 52 | 55 | 7 | 57 | 193 | 73 | 97 | 80 | 198 | 52 |
| 23 | 24 | 31 | 2 | 33 | 47 | 36 | 29 | 15 | 54 | 26 |
| 38 | 51 | 59 | 6 | 46 | 108 | 48 | 60 | 46 | 118 | 36 |
| 147 | 221 | 455 | 30 | 184 | 669 | 250 | 355 | 248 | 571 | 282 |
| 269 | 444 | 880 | 39 | 287 | 1,345 | 389 | 617 | 626 | 1145 | 487 |
| 423 | 47 | 36 | 7 | 194 | 319 | 283 | 157 | 73 | 361 | 152 |
| 600 | 75 | 50 | 8 | 293 | 440 | 378 | 233 | 122 | 508 | 225 |
| 2,484 | 2,215 | 4,120 | 155 | 1,768 | 7,206 | 2,010 | 2,393 | 4,571 | 5,570 | 3,404 |

in the informal sector does not imply that when workers move from the formal to the informal sector their wages always fall or that when they change from informal to formal status their wages always increase. For any individual worker, the change in wage after shifting from one labor status to another can go in either direction.

The point is that the information contained in table 5-10—and similar information that is at times used in discussions of informality in the Mexican labor market—does not serve to pin down what happens to wage rates of individual workers who at one point are formal and at another point are informal. That is because the specific characteristics of individual workers are not associated with their personal wages; instead, as in table 5-10, the characteristics and wage rates of many heterogeneous workers are averaged. The simple comparison of mean wage rates in the formal and informal sectors provides little information on what happens when individual workers move from one sector to the other.

Indeed, based on the simple comparison of mean wage rates across sectors, one would be tempted to argue that all informal workers would like to be formal and that no formal workers would like to be informal. But as argued in chapter 3 and elaborated on in chapter 6, that argument is wrong. Workers move across sectors on the basis of the utility derived from wages and other benefits of work in each sector, not of wages only. Furthermore, even if one assumes that social security and social protection programs are valued equally by workers, such large differences in mean wages between the formal and the informal sectors would put downward pressure on formal wages. But that is not observed: the average formal wage in 2007, 36.33 pesos an hour, exceeded by a large margin the minimum wage. Even the average informal wage in 2007, 21.34 pesos an hour, was higher than the minimum wage.[30]

To shed more light on this discussion it is useful to distinguish two separate questions that at times are confused: one, why are mean wages in the formal sector higher than in the informal sector? Two, what happens to the wage rates of individual workers who move from one sector to the other?

Table 5-11 helps in considering the first question. It shows the distribution of hourly wage rates in the formal and the informal sectors in 2006 for the same 8,984 workers considered in table 5-10. Notice that 42.9 percent of workers in the formal sector had wages of four times the minimum wage or more, while only 14.5 percent of informal workers were in that range, for a difference of 28.4 percent. As a result, more informal workers than formal workers earned up to three times the minimum wage: 73.4 percent versus 39.5 percent, for a difference of 33.9 percent. That difference in the distribution is what makes mean wages in the formal sector exceed mean wages in the informal sector.

Why are there not more informal workers in the upper range of the distribution? My hypothesis, developed more fully in chapter 7, is that many capital- or

___

30. The daily minimum wage in 2007 was 48.88 pesos, or 6.11 pesos an hour.

Table 5-11. *Wage Distribution in the Formal and Informal Sector, 2006*

| Hourly wage rate[a] | All | | Formal | | Informal | |
|---|---|---|---|---|---|---|
| | Number of workers | Percent | Number of workers | Percent | Number of workers | Percent |
| 1 or less | 171 | 1.9 | 56 | 0.8 | 115 | 5.6 |
| 1 to 2 | 1,675 | 18.6 | 938 | 13.5 | 737 | 36.1 |
| 2 to 3 | 2,393 | 26.6 | 1,746 | 25.2 | 647 | 31.7 |
| 3 to 4 | 1,457 | 16.2 | 1,209 | 17.4 | 248 | 12.2 |
| 4 to 5 | 863 | 9.6 | 751 | 10.8 | 112 | 5.5 |
| 5 to 6 | 571 | 6.4 | 525 | 7.6 | 46 | 2.3 |
| 6 to 7 | 462 | 5.1 | 426 | 6.1 | 36 | 1.8 |
| 7 to 8 | 238 | 2.6 | 218 | 3.1 | 20 | 1.0 |
| 8 to 9 | 280 | 3.1 | 262 | 3.8 | 18 | 0.9 |
| 9 to 10 | 185 | 2.1 | 167 | 2.4 | 18 | 0.9 |
| 10 to 15 | 477 | 5.3 | 453 | 6.5 | 24 | 1.2 |
| > 15 | 212 | 2.4 | 183 | 2.6 | 19 | 0.9 |
| Total | 8,984 | 100 | 6,934 | 100 | 2,040 | 100 |

Source: Author's analysis. See discussion in text.
a. Measured in multiples of the minimum wage.

technology-intensive activities requiring salaried labor are subject to indivisibilities and a minimum scale, making informal operation prohibitively costly (because given the probability of being detected and fined by IMSS and other authorities, it is not profitable for the firms to hire illegal workers). One does observe informal salaried work in activities like light manufacturing, services, transportation, and commerce; one does not observe informality in activities such as car or steel manufacturing. *Comparison of the mean wage rates of all workers in the formal and all workers in the informal sector is not very meaningful because it mixes a comparison of labor status with a comparison of production activities and workers' abilities and fails to take into account that, as discussed in chapter 7, not all activities can profitably be carried out informally.*

The statement that wages in the formal sector are on average higher than wages in the informal is factually correct, according to the data contained in the ENOE, but it is not very relevant. In countries without the formal-informal dichotomy, the statement would take the form of "Wages in the steel industry are on average higher than wages in the laundry and cleaning industry," yet few would argue on the weight of that evidence that in those countries there are barriers that impede workers in the laundry and cleaning industry from getting jobs in the steel industry. Attention would center on issues such as job training, firms' specific assets, and education and other characteristics of workers that result in some workers being employed in the steel industry and some in the cleaning and laundry industry.

Now consider the second question: what happens to the wage rates of individual workers who move from the formal to the informal sector or vice versa? The main point here is that a proper comparison of wage rates of individual workers across types of labor status requires an analysis that controls for workers' individual characteristics. The question is this: how would the wage of an individual worker if he or she had remained in the same labor status compare with the wage earned by changing labor status?

## Comparison of Mean Wage Rates with ATT

The question just posed is a standard problem in the evaluation of social programs. Assume that a particular person is subject to a given policy intervention and that one wants to determine what would have happened to that person in the absence of the intervention. Ideally one would simultaneously observe the person as he or she would be with and without the intervention. But since that is not possible, the best that can be done is to find a person who is as similar as possible to the person subject to the intervention but who did not receive it (the "control") and then compare that person with the "treatment" person—the one subject to the intervention.

The issue faced here is, mutatis mutandis, the same. Assume that the treatment is a change in labor status. Ideally one would like to know whether for a given individual worker the change in labor status implied a higher or lower wage—in other words, whether a worker who changed from the formal to the informal sector (or vice versa) would have earned a higher or lower wage if he or she had not done so. To make that comparison it is necessary to observe the same worker at the same point in time under two types of labor status, a feat that is impossible because the same worker cannot be simultaneously formal and informal.

The average treatment effect on the treated (ATT) is an econometric technique that helps to solve the problem just described. Here I provide what I hope is an intuitive explanation of the technique; appendix 5 gives the technical details. Consider all the workers who were in formal employment in 2005, and divide them in two groups in 2006: group A, made up of those who were formally employed in 2006 as well as in 2005, and group B, made up of those who changed to informal employment in 2006. Group B is the treatment group. What would have been the wages of the workers in group B if they had not been treated—that is, if they had stayed in the formal sector?

To answer that question, the ATT technique proceeds as follows. First, it matches each worker in group B with a worker in group A whose particular characteristics are as similar as possible to those of the worker in B. The new group is called A*, which is a subset of group A and by design has the same number of workers as group B. Second, it computes the mean wage rate of workers in group B and compares it with the mean wage rate in group A*. An average effect of the treatment on the treated is present to the extent that the mean wage rate of work-ers in A* is different from that of workers in B.[31]

The technique also is used for all workers who were in informal employment in 2005 by dividing them between those who moved to the formal sector in 2006 and those who did not. It provides an answer to two separate but related questions: one, what would have happened to the wages of workers who moved from the formal to the informal sector if they had not moved? Two, what would have happened to the wages of workers who moved from the informal to the formal sector if they had not moved? The symmetry in the questions is important because it helps to deal with the issue of whether movement from one sector to the other was voluntary or involuntary. Workers could have moved from one sector to the other because they were fired (recall that all are salaried workers) but also because they wanted to. As elaborated on below, from the standpoint of social policy, the distinction is not too relevant; nonetheless, looking at movement in both directions gives a fuller picture that encompasses both voluntary and involuntary moves.

Tables 5-12 and 5-13 present the results of applying the ATT technique on the same sample of workers used in table 5-10, divided between men and women. Moves from formal to informal employment are in the upper panel of each table and moves from informal to formal employment in the lower panel. Results are shown for high- and low-wage workers separately. The comparison is between the wage rates of the treatment group and the "counterfactual" wage rates of the con-trol group; both tables identify mean wage rates and the mean wage differences. The last column contains the $t$ statistic, which measures whether differences in mean wage rates are statistically significant.

In interpreting the results, it is useful to recall equation 3-3, for the utility of employment in each sector, which for convenience is reproduced here as equa-tion 5-2:

$$(5\text{-}2) \quad \begin{aligned} U_f &= \text{formal wages} + \text{value of social security benefits} = (w_f + \beta_f T_f) \\ U_i &= \text{informal wages} + \text{value of social protection benefits} = (w_i + \beta_i T_i). \end{aligned}$$

On the other hand, this chapter presents evidence that workers move contin-uously between the formal and the informal sectors. It is natural to assume that

31. The individual worker characteristics that define "similar" are based on the information avail-able in the ENOE and measured with a propensity score derived from a probit regression. The results of the regressions for male and female workers are in tables A5-1 and A5-2 in appendix 5. The method used to match workers in group A* with those in group B is the Kernel method, which matches work-ers on the basis of the weighted average of their propensity score. To control for unobservable char-acteristics of workers, a difference-in-difference approach is used.

Table 5-12. Wage Rate Means in Formal-Informal Transits for Male Kernel-Matched Salaried Workers, 2005–06[a]

| | Workers | | | Mean wage rate | | | Mean wage difference (change in treated minus change in counterfactual) | Standard error | t statistic |
| | Treated (moved) | Control (did not move) | Total | Treated (moved) | Control (did not move) | Counterfactual (similar to treated but did not move)[b] | | | |
|---|---|---|---|---|---|---|---|---|---|
| Wage | | | | | | | | | |
| Formal to informal | | | | | | | | | |
| Low wage | 154 | 1,280 | 1,434 | 15.85 | 16.22 | 15.97 | 0.02 | 0.892 | 0.024 |
| High wage | 98 | 2,178 | 2,276 | 44.61 | 49.91 | 43.43 | 6.33 | 2.884 | 2.196** |
| Informal to formal | | | | | | | | | |
| Low wage | 234 | 605 | 839 | 15.79 | 13.84 | 14.16 | 1.04 | 0.218 | 0.858 |
| High wage | 142 | 143 | 285 | 41.58 | 40.16 | 45.26 | 4.03 | 1.295 | 1.295 |

Source: Author's analysis. See discussion in text.

a. Number of workers and hourly wage rates in 2007 pesos.

b. Mean wage rates of workers from the control group who were as "econometrically similar as possible" to workers who moved—that is, who belonged to the treated group.

**Significant at 95 percent confidence level.

Table 5-13. *Wage Rate Means in Formal-Informal Transits for Female Kernel-Matched Salaried Workers, 2005–06* [a]

| Wage | Workers | | | Mean wage rate | | | Mean wage difference (change in treated minus change in counterfactual) | Standard error | t statistic |
|---|---|---|---|---|---|---|---|---|---|
| | Treated (moved) | Control (did not move) | Total | Treated (moved) | Control (did not move) | Counterfactual (similar to treated but did not move) [b] | | | |
| *Formal to informal* | | | | | | | | | |
| Low wage | 87 | 834 | 921 | 13.92 | 16.24 | 15.74 | −0.67 | 1.044 | −0.646 |
| High wage | 54 | 1,497 | 1,551 | 51.59 | 51.32 | 46.58 | 8.94 | 4.702 | 1.902* |
| *Informal to formal* | | | | | | | | | |
| Low wage | 122 | 449 | 571 | 15.05 | 13.85 | 14.66 | −0.74 | 1.402 | −0.527 |
| High wage | 64 | 129 | 193 | 49.95 | 37.63 | 45.58 | 9.75 | 5.254 | 1.855* |

Source: Author's analysis. See discussion in text.

a. Number of workers and hourly wage rates in 2007 pesos.

b. Mean wage rates of workers from the control group who were as "econometrically similar as possible" to workers who moved—that is, who belonged to the treated group.

*Significant at 90 percent confidence level.

under those conditions the distribution of the labor force equalizes utilities across sectors, or that

$$(w_f + \beta_f T_f) \quad = \quad (w_i + \beta_i T_i)$$

(5-3)      utility of formal    utility of informal

employment      employment.

Tables 5-12 and 5-13 allow comparison of wage rates for formal and informal employment. Consider first the case of low-wage male workers. The results indicate that there is no statistically significant difference between the wage rates that workers earn in the formal sector and the wage rates that they would earn if they were employed in the informal sector instead, and vice versa.

Under the assumption that utilities are equalized across sectors, the results provide indirect evidence of the value attached by low-wage workers to social security and social protection programs. In particular, rearranging equation 5-3 implies that

(5-4)                 $w_f \approx w_i$ such that $\beta_f T_f \approx \beta_i T_i$,

that is, that for low-wage male workers, the value of social security programs is similar to the value of social protection programs.

Consider now high-wage male workers. For workers who move from the formal to the informal sector, there is a statistically significant difference in wage rates, which are higher in the informal than in the formal sector. In terms of equation 5-3, that implies that

(5-5)                 $w_f < w_i$ such that $\beta_f T_f > \beta_i T_i$,

that is, for high-wage workers, social security programs are worth more than social protection programs; consequently, they must earn a higher wage in the informal sector to compensate for the difference in social benefits.[32] Those results, however, do not hold for high-wage male workers who move from the informal to the formal sector, where there is no statistically significant difference in wage rates. In that case, the result is the same as for low-wage male workers, with the interpretation being expression 5-4.

Results for low-wage female workers are the same as for low-wage male workers, and expression 5-4 holds regardless of the direction of transit. Similarly, for high-wage female workers who transit from the formal to the infor-

---

32. The wage difference between the informal and the formal sector is sometimes called the wage premium.

mal sector results are the same as for males, with expression 5-5 holding as well. The only case that does not fit this pattern is that of high-wage female workers who move from the informal to the formal sector: the inequalities in expression 5-5 are in the opposite direction, implying that those workers value the benefits of social protection programs more than those of social security programs.

*On balance, the results suggest that low-wage workers who change labor status value the social security and social protection benefits of each labor status similarly, unlike high-wage workers, who on average tend to assign a higher value to social security benefits than to social protection benefits.* That finding is consistent with the discussion in chapters 3 and 4, where I argue that

—as a result of design problems and large discrepancies between actual and statutory benefits of social security programs, $\beta_f$ is less than one

—these problems and discrepancies are larger for low- than for high-wage workers

—social protection programs offer larger benefits to low- than to high-wage workers.

One is tempted to use the results of tables 5-12 and 5-13 to obtain the individual values of $\beta_f$ and $\beta_i$ directly; unfortunately, those values cannot be recovered from those tables. However, one can use the assumption that utilities between the formal and the informal sector are equalized as in equation 5-3 to calculate the ratio of those coefficients, which provides illustrative information nonetheless. To do that I combined the estimated values of $w_f$ and $w_i$ in tables 5-12 and 5-13 with the values for $T_f$ and $T_i$ calculated in table 3-9. The last two values were estimated to be, respectively, 24,519 and 5,670 pesos per worker annually, or 11.76 and 2.70 pesos per worker hourly.

Using those values for the case of low-wage male workers in equation 5-3 yields $\beta_f/\beta_i = 0.23$. To interpret that, assume that every peso of costs of social protection programs is considered by workers as a peso of benefits, so that $\beta_i = 1$. That implies that low-wage male workers consider each peso of costs of the official governance mechanism that applies to salaried labor (that is, of $T_f$) to be worth only 23 cents—in other words, that there is a gap of 77 cents between the non-wage costs of salaried labor to firms and the value to workers (see table 3-10). Of course, workers may not fully value social protection programs. If, for instance, workers considered each peso spent in these programs to be worth 75 cents to them, then $\beta_f = 0.30$. But even if workers valued every peso of social protection programs at 50 percent, the associated value for $\beta_f$ would be 0.46. More generally, rather than pinpointing the exact value of $\beta_f$, the discussion suggests that for a large range of valuations of social protection programs, the combined results of tables 3-9, on one hand, and tables 5-12 and 5-13, on the other, show that *there is a large gap indeed between the non-wage costs of low-wage formal salaried workers paid by firms in Mexico and the value that workers attach to the non-wage benefits that they receive, a gap that is at least equal to 50 percent and more likely closer to 75 percent.*[33]

## An Assessment

I conclude this section by combining these results with the evidence of worker mobility presented in the previous sections of this chapter, in particular with the finding that mobility is lower for higher-wage workers. I do not attempt to provide an overall assessment of the workings of Mexico's labor market but to put together a picture of those elements that are relevant to the hypothesis advanced in this volume. In particular, I believe that the results presented in this chapter are consistent with the existence of a subset of workers in Mexico who are permanently or almost permanently engaged in formal employment, earning the highest wages of all workers; they are, say, the 20 to 25 percent of all workers in the formal sector at the top of the distribution in table 5-11 earning, say, six times the minimum wage or more. Those are the workers who value social security more because they have access to an Infonavit housing loan and to IMSS medical facilities and contribute continuously to their Afore account for their retirement pension. These workers do not move to informal jobs because, for reasons explained in chapter 7, equivalent occupations are not available in the "informal mode." They are employed in activities in which indivisibilities of capital are significant and the capital-labor ratio is higher than average or in which technology-intensive processes or special operational requirements imply that operating illegally is not profitable.

When reference is made to "good jobs," the jobs at the top of the distribution in table 5-11 probably are what the speaker has in mind: formal jobs with high wages and low rotation. And when reference is made to formal firms, most likely the firms employing high-wage formal workers are meant. But as tables 5-1 and 5-11 show, *such workers are far from the majority of formal workers in Mexico,* and as table 7-2 shows, *such firms are far from the majority of formal firms in Mexico.*

Many formal jobs offered by formal firms are not too different from informal jobs offered by informal firms. As table 5-11 shows, 47 percent of all workers in the formal and 73 percent of all workers in the informal sector earn three times the minimum wage or less; as shown in tables 7-2, 7-3, and 7-4, those workers overlap in activities and sometimes within the same firm. They are the workers who account for the greatest mobility between sectors. Tables 5-12 and 5-13 imply that for them, the value of social security and social protection ben-

---

33. For high-wage male workers, the ratio $\beta_f/\beta_i$ is approximately 0.34, so that for any given value of $\beta_i$ the associated value of $\beta_f$ is higher. For the reference case, when the former is unity, the latter is 0.34, as opposed to 0.23, for low-wage workers, which is another way of saying that high-wage workers value social security programs more than low-wage workers and that the gap between firms' non-wage costs and workers' valuation of non-wage benefits is smaller than for low-wage workers, although still large in absolute terms.

efits is similar, and, as a result, it is not surprising that they earn similar wages. *From the point of view of these workers—the majority in Mexico—the difference between a formal and an informal job is not significant. Both jobs are equally "good" or "bad."*

On the other hand, recall that the analysis excluded *comisionistas* and self-employed workers. But mobility also occurs between those types of workers and salaried workers, as Maloney (1999), Bosch and Maloney (2006), and Calderón (2000) document. It is difficult to imagine that no barriers to mobility exist between legal/formal and illegal/informal salaried workers but that they do exist between salaried and nonsalaried workers. And if that is so, it also is difficult to imagine that, after controlling for individual worker characteristics, imputed wages (not earnings) of nonsalaried workers would be different from the wage rates that they would earn if they chose salaried employment. Computing tables like 5-12 and 5-13 including nonsalaried workers is left for the future, but nevertheless the presumption is that they also compare the wage and social benefits of salaried employment (legal or illegal), on one hand, and the earnings and social benefits of nonsalaried employment, on the other, and make occupational decisions on the basis of that comparison.

The analysis of the impact of social programs on productivity and welfare presented in the next chapters is based on the results of workers' valuations of social programs presented in chapters 3 and 4 and the results on wage rates and labor mobility presented in this chapter. My view is that from the perspective of workers, the labor market is not segmented: when jobs are available in the formal and the informal mode for workers of similar characteristics and abilities, the utility of being employed in one sector is similar to the utility of being employed in the other. But from the perspective of firms, the labor market is segmented: the costs of formal and of informal workers of similar characteristics and abilities are not the same. That segmentation is a central concern for firms and has fundamental implications for labor productivity; for the accomplishment of the government's social objectives; for the incidence of social security contributions; for the productivity of capital; and for the redistributive impact of fiscal subsidies to social protection and social security programs.

## Implications of Mobility for Social Policy

In assessing the results presented in this chapter, it is useful to recall that most are based on either IMSS and Consar registries or on employment surveys that do not always include rural areas. That is an unavoidable shortcoming due to lack of data, but an important shortcoming nonetheless. Given the cyclical nature of agricultural production and patterns of rural to urban migration, it stands to reason that in the context of the whole labor market, not only its urban component, formal-informal mobility would be larger than the figures shown, although that is difficult to quantify.[34] It also is useful to keep in mind that neither the IMSS and Consar registries nor the employment surveys appropriately reflect international migration, which might also be a factor in formal-informal mobility to the extent that the labor status of Mexican workers who return to work in Mexico after a stay in the United States might be different from the one they had when they left. In any event, six results stand out:

—The labor market in Mexico is characterized by high mobility of workers between formal and informal status.[35]

—Mobility occurs in periods of low, medium, and high GDP growth.

—Mobility is greater for lower-wage workers.

—When workers move from one sector to another, they may experience a wage increase or decrease.

—Wages of low-wage workers who move between the formal and the informal sector are on average the same.

—With one exception, wages of high-wage workers who move between sectors are higher in the informal than in the formal sector.

*These results directly contradict the hypothesis that there are barriers to entry into the formal sector.* That does not mean that formal-informal mobility is always smooth and frictionless. Different kinds of shocks occur, and they affect the labor market. Some, like the 1994–95 crisis, are of a macroeconomic nature and affect the whole country and all sectors. Some, like the North American Free Trade Agreement (NAFTA), result from trade changes and have more of an effect on the sector producing goods that are traded in the international markets. Some, like the fall in maquiladora exports in the north of Mexico in 2001–02, result from slowdowns in the United States and affect a particular region of the country more than others. And some, like the entry of China into the World Trade Organization, result from changes in the international environment and impact specific sectors like the textile industry or light manufacturing. Quite naturally, such shocks matter, and depending on their magnitude and nature, in the short run they may have more of an effect on sectors where formal employment is the only form of employment (for example, car exports to the United States) or on sectors where informal and formal employment coexist (for example, the textile industry com-

34. It is also relevant to point out that the analysis has focused on formal-informal transit. But as noted, workers also change from one formal job to another. Kaplan, Martinez, and Robertson (2005) examines that issue, also by using the IMSS registries. The results are important because the study finds that there is a great deal of *formal-to-formal mobility* and that it has responded differently to various shocks over the last fifteen years. I do not pursue this issue given my focus on the implications of formal-informal mobility for coverage of workers by social security and social protection programs. Clearly the social implications of formal-to-formal mobility are different from those of formal-to-informal mobility.

35. In fact, by international standards Mexico appears to be a country with very high labor mobility: Duryea and others (2006) compares labor mobility in nine middle-income countries and finds that it is highest in Mexico.

peting with China). As a result, there are times when job searches are easier (or more difficult), when moves between formality and informality are more (or less) frequent, and when moves are direct or involve a longer (or shorter) period of unemployment as an intermediate step.[36]

*But none of such short-run considerations should distract from a feature of Mexico's labor market that is central to social policy design: most workers experience periods of formality and informality during their working lives.* I argue that that feature is central because social interventions cannot be designed around transient and unpredictable characteristics of workers, in particular their labor status. By their very nature, many social interventions take a long-term perspective, whether the goal is helping a worker to save for a house or for retirement, improving people's health, protecting workers from disability, or protecting a worker's offspring in the event of the worker's sudden death.

*Mobility of workers from one labor status to another may be voluntary or involuntary.* At times a salaried worker may decide to try his luck as an entrepreneur; at other times he may be fired from his firm. Many different situations may be observed, as the earlier heuristic discussion based on ethnographic case studies illustrates. That is consistent with the large variance in wage movements observed in table 5-10: in some cases workers may voluntarily move from one sector to the other and thereby earn a higher wager; in other cases they may do so involuntarily and earn a lower wage.

*But from the standpoint of the government's social objectives, whether workers' formal-informal transits are voluntary or involuntary is not a central consideration.* What is central is whether workers are saving for their retirement pension and for their housing loan; whether they are covered by work-risk and disability insurance; and the conditions under which they have access to medical care. As long as the government's social objectives are fulfilled only when workers are engaged in salaried employment, formal-informal transits—voluntary or involuntary—are equally troublesome.

Mexico is a fairly small country in the international economy, subject to exogenous changes in world prices and shifts in comparative advantages. It experiences continuous shocks, many of which are beyond its control. There is unavoidable uncertainty in each firm's demand for labor resulting from idiosyncratic shocks; there are systemic shocks resulting from the weather and natural disasters; there are changes in workers' preferences throughout their life cycle that lead them to try different occupations, at times salaried and at times not; and there are mistakes in macroeconomic management. The large job and worker flows documented in this chapter as well as the changes in wage rates are, at the end of the day, a reflection of all those phenomena. But as things stand today, the majority of workers are not subject to long-term, stable social interventions to protect them systematically from

36. See Calderón (2000) and Bosch and Maloney (2006).

various risks, which is one of the core objectives of the government's social policy. That does not mean that workers are not getting transitory benefits from various social programs; as the figures presented in chapter 1 show, they are, increasingly so. But it does mean that those benefits are transitory and erratic, because social programs passively follow workers through their moves within the labor market.

I posit that formal-informal mobility raises fundamental questions for Mexico's current combination of social security and social protection programs. *It makes patently obvious the incongruence between the workings of the labor market and the everyday lives of workers, on one hand, and the design of social programs, on the other.* The fundamental problem is that social policy is based on legal categories of labor status that are

—unfair from the point of view of workers because they exclude some from certain benefits during all or part of their lives

—ineffective from the point of view of the government because they do not permit the imposition of its preferences on all workers all of the time

—costly from the point of view of the competitiveness of Mexican firms.

I posit also that the increasing reliance on social protection programs to extend benefits to workers when they are in the informal sector is the wrong response to the formal-informal dichotomy; as is shown in the next four chapters, that response increases informality and the social and economic costs associated with it. And I posit that that response, contrary to what is generally believed, is especially harmful to poor workers.

I end with five observations that arise from the results of this chapter, and turn in the next chapter to a framework that allows for assessment of some of these observations. First, the expressions "formal" and "informal" worker, although extremely common, are inexact and largely misleading. It is more accurate to speak of "a worker currently employed by a firm that registered her with IMSS" and "a worker currently employed in the informal sector because the firm that hired her did not register her with IMSS, because the firm offered her a job as a *comisionista,* or because she is self-employed." That is not a semantic difference; it is a substantive difference that calls attention to the fact that social interventions *on the same worker* change depending on the peculiarities of her working life or of the firm that hires her. What is the appropriate adjective for the average low-wage worker shown in figure 5-4 who was a formal employee 49 percent of the time during the ten-year period? Is it "formal" or "informal"?

Second, workers in Mexico save for retirement through various channels. When formally employed, they do so through their Afore account and perhaps through some other financial or physical asset. When informally employed, they do not save in an Afore (even if they have access to one, as shown in chapter 3), and they may or may not save through some other financial or physical asset. An implication of mobility is that millions of workers move between forced and voluntary saving. What is the impact of that pattern of saving for retirement on total national savings? What is the effect on income replacement rates?[37]

Third, workers' changes of labor status matter to firms. The costs of labor to firms depend on whether workers are legal and whether they are salaried. What are the effects on labor productivity when two workers with similar abilities earn different wages or cause firms to incur different costs depending on their labor status?

Fourth, as workers change from formal to informal status, they receive social security and social protection benefits that are financed differently, in one case through wage-based contributions and in the other through government subsidies. What is the redistributive impact of social security contributions and of government subsidies to social programs when workers move continuously from one labor status to another?

Fifth, as workers shift from one labor status to another, the fiscal costs of social programs vary because the per-worker subsidies for social protection programs are larger than for social security programs. What are the fiscal implications of the formal-informal dichotomy?

37. In the literature on pensions, the income replacement rate is the ratio of a worker's income during retirement to his income during his working life, where income during retirement is assumed to derive only from the worker's pension. The more that workers move between formal and informal status, the fewer the resources that accumulate in their retirement account and the lower their income replacement rate.

# 6

## Social Programs, Welfare, and Productivity

It is important to understand how workers and firms react to social programs, because their reactions affect the composition of employment, labor productivity, wage rates, workers' utility, and the achievement of the government's social objectives. To increase that understanding, I begin by sketching the objectives of the actors and the processes through which they interact to determine outcomes in those dimensions. The results are driven by the following logic:

—Workers maximize utility, choosing between salaried employment with social security benefits or *comisionista* or self-employment with social protection benefits. They make their choices on the basis of the wages that they earn in each case and the value that they attach to the social benefits associated with the different forms of participation in the labor market. Their ownership of productive assets influences their choices.

—Firms choose output and employment levels to maximize profits. In this chapter I assume that firms and workers comply with the law, so that all salaried employment is formal. (In chapter 7, I modify that assumption: depending on expected net benefits, including the possibility of fines, firms and workers might evade the official governance mechanisms that apply to salaried labor, giving rise to illegal salaried employment.) In this chapter I also assume that firms' capital stocks are given (in chapter 8, I modify that assumption, allowing for investment).

—I assume that all workers' valuations of social programs are the same. However, based on the arguments in chapter 4, later in the discussion I consider differences in poor and non-poor workers' valuations. When those differences occur, workers self-select into salaried or nonsalaried employment, affecting outcomes in the labor market.

—The independent choices of firms and workers jointly determine the distribution of the workforce across types of labor status: salaried, self-employed, and *comisionista* (and later illegal salaried). That distribution in turn determines the share of the labor force covered by social security and the share covered by social protection programs.

—In turn, given the differences in social benefits, the formal-informal distribution of the labor force determines the extent to which the government's social objectives are accomplished. If all workers are covered by social security, the government's social objectives are completely met; if some are covered by social protection, those objectives are partly met. I do not aggregate the coverage of social programs into a single indicator of social welfare; I just point out the changes in the coverage of health, disability, and life insurance; retirement savings; and so on, across the labor force.

—Similarly, the independent choices of firms and workers jointly determine the level and composition of aggregate output and the productivity of labor in each form of employment. That determination provides a link through which social programs affect aggregate labor productivity. The productivity effects in this chapter are only static. I leave the impact of social programs on the size distribution of firms and the composition of output for chapter 7 and discuss the impact on firms' investments and other dimensions of their behavior that generate dynamic productivity effects in chapter 8.

—The distribution of the labor force across the types of labor status has fiscal implications given the differences in the form of financing social protection and social security programs. The revenues that need to be raised to pay for social protection programs generate efficiency costs that add to the efficiency costs associated with differences in labor productivity across sectors. The total efficiency costs of social policies depend on the nature of the fiscal adjustments made to pay for them. If part of the adjustment occurs through reduced public investment, there is a third link between social policy and productivity and, potentially, growth. These are the subsidiary hypotheses mentioned in the introduction and explored in chapter 9.

The analysis in this book centers on low-wage, unskilled labor. I make explicit the key simplifying assumptions and point out where they matter for results. Two assumptions should be mentioned at the outset. First, workers are assumed to have similar abilities at work and full information about jobs and social programs. Second, workers are assumed to consume the package of benefits corresponding to their labor status, so that formal workers covered by social security do not access social protection programs and vice versa.

## Demand for Salaried and Nonsalaried Labor

Separating the demand for salaried and nonsalaried labor is necessary given the institutional set-up of Mexico's social programs; in turn, separating nonsalaried labor into *comisionistas* and self-employed workers is required because the role played by firms varies in each case. Analyzing the components of the total demand for labor separately allows for identifying the impact of social programs on workers and firms in each case.

### Demand for Self-Employment

I begin the analysis with workers who own productive assets: perhaps one or two hectares of low-quality, rain-fed land (which is a large holding by the standards of Progresa workers, as shown in chapter 4), a fishing boat, or a stand and a mixer for making fruit juices for sale in the streets; intangible assets like access to a busy street corner also fall in this category. Such workers seek to maximize their income, $Y_s$, given by the sum of quasi-rents on their productive assets and their labor income. For them the key decision is how much time to devote to working as a self-employed person given the possibility of participating in the labor market as a salaried worker or *comisionista*.

A key determinant of that decision is the market wage rate, here labeled $w$ and, until the next section, taken as exogenous. Workers' income is maximized by setting the marginal product of their labor produced with their own assets equal to the opportunity cost of working for somebody else, which is the market wage.[1]

Figure 6-1 explores alternative decisions depending on the market wage. Assume first that the wage is $w^1$. In that case the self-employed person works only for himself; he neither participates in the labor market by looking for helpers nor works for anyone else. That is because the amount of labor that he devotes to work with his own asset, $L_s$, equals his endowment of labor time, $\underline{L}_s$.

Assume now that the market wage falls to $w^2$. The worker's opportunity cost of working with his own assets falls, but because he already is fully self-employed,

---

1. These workers produce output according to $Q_s(K_s, L_s; K_p)$, where $K_s$ is their own productive asset, $L_s$ is labor devoted to work with their asset, and $K_p$ is the stock of public capital (rural roads, electricity lines to power their mixer, street lights). Output is sold at the exogenously given world price $p^w$, and the workers' problem is to choose $L_s$ to maximize $Y_s = p^w Q_s(K_s, L_s; K_p) + w(\underline{L}_s - L_s)$, where $\underline{L}_s$ is their endowment of labor time. The first term is the gross value of output and the second the net wage bill, which is positive or negative depending on whether the workers work only for themselves all of the time, work part of the time for themselves but also participate as net sellers of labor in the market, or also hire extra help at the market wage rate $w$ besides working for themselves all of the time.

Figure 6-1. *The Self-Employment Decision*

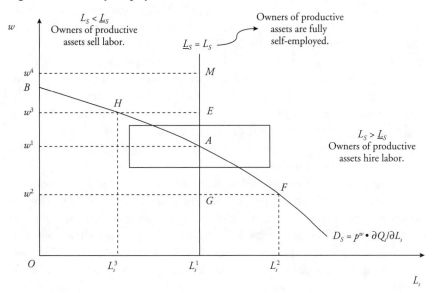

Source: Author's analysis.

he needs additional help, equal to $(L_s^2 - \underline{L}_s)$ workers in figure 6-1.[2] His total income consists of imputed wages on his own labor (which fall as the market wage falls), plus quasi-rents on his own asset (which increase as it is used more intensely), minus the cost of the additional helpers.[3]

The additional help could be provided by one of his relatives, so that a monetary wage need not be paid; instead, there could be some implicit payment in kind related to the opportunity cost of his relative's time. Alternatively, he might form a joint venture with someone else. The point is that a salaried labor relationship need not be involved. Nonetheless, if a one-person firm expands beyond a small limit, such contractual arrangements become increasingly difficult, and as the scale of operations grows, additional helpers—beyond, say, two or three—would tend to be salaried workers. In that case, the one-person firm evolves into a micro-enterprise, and the previously self-employed worker becomes a boss.

2. I ignore this worker's labor-leisure choice. I also assume that there are no indivisibilities in labor inputs; the distance $(L_s^2 - \underline{L}_s)$ might be the half-time equivalent of a worker. Recall that we are dealing here with very small scales of output and labor. If indivisibilities in getting help are introduced, the worker might not be able to expand operations and will have to remain at point $A$ despite the lower market wage.

3. In terms of figure 6-1, his income at the wage rate $w^1$ is $Y_i(w^1) = OL_sAw^1 + w^1AB$. When the wage falls to $w^2$, it changes to $Y_i(w^2) = OL_sGw^2 + w^2FB - w^2(L_s^2 - \underline{L}_s)$; he earns more quasi-rents and less imputed wages, and he has to pay for the helpers.

Assume now that the wage rate is $w^3$. Because the opportunity cost of his time is higher, the worker now devotes only part of his time to work with his own asset and participates in the labor market the rest of the time: at point H, he is a self-employed worker part of the time $(O - L_s^3)$ and a worker working for someone else part of the time $(\underline{L}_s - L_s^3)$. Finally, for wage rates like $w^4$ or higher, the opportunity cost of his time is so high relative to the quasi-rents that he obtains on his productive asset that he does not exploit it at all.[4] At that point he lets his land lie fallow, he sells or puts away his mixer and his fruit stand, or he gives up his valuable street corner. He now is a full-time salaried worker or a *comisionista*.

I want to make three points. First, the market wage determines the border between a purely self-employed worker and a self-employed small entrepreneur, between a part-time self-employed worker and a part-time salaried worker or *comisionista*, and between a full-time salaried worker and a *comisionista*. That is the key parameter that in the absence of social programs measures the opportunity cost of a worker's time. Second, when social programs are introduced, that parameter changes. The opportunity cost of the worker's time is the market wage and the value of the social programs that he can access if he is not self-employed (compared with his imputed wages and the social programs that he can access if he is self-employed). Social programs affect the opportunity cost of his time: valuable social security benefits increase the opportunity cost of being self-employed and, all things being equal, lead him to salaried employment; valuable social protection benefits decrease the cost and, all things being equal, lead him to self-employment. Third, as elaborated on below, market wages themselves are a function of social programs. As a result, *social programs influence the self-employment decision both directly, by affecting the value of the social benefits of one form of employment or another, and indirectly, because wages are endogenous to social programs.*

The analysis above assumes the continuous reallocation of a worker's time in response to any marginal change in wage rates or output prices. It is difficult to imagine that that is the case in practice. A worker might not give up his valuable street corner or sell his mixer and juice stand if he thinks that the shift from $w^1$ to $w^4$ is transitory. There may be, as noted, indivisibilities in hiring labor that are relevant at such a small scale of output. There also may be entry or exit costs. In figure 6-1, I try to depict such situations by drawing an arbitrary rectangle around point $A$, where for a range of wage or price shifts the self-employed worker remains fully self-employed. But that observation should not distract from a more fundamental one: self-employed workers are in the labor market, and even though they may not be hiring anyone or working at all for anyone else, the market wage rate is a crucial determinant of their income and of their decision to be self-employed.

---

4. At wages $w^3$, his total income is made up of imputed wages, market wages, and quasi-rents, so that $Y_i(w^3) = OL_i^3Hw^3 + L_i^3\underline{L}_iEH + w^3HB$. At wages $w^4$, he earns only wages, so that his total income is $Y_i(w^4) = \text{no quasi-rents} + O\underline{L}_iMw^4$.

Figure 6-1 also illustrates the case of workers who regularly move between self-employment and salaried employment. When the wage rate in Sinaloa increases to $w^4$, workers from Oaxaca migrate north, letting their land lie fallow or temporarily closing their handicrafts operations to take salaried jobs; when the wage rate in Sinaloa falls to $w^1$, they return to self-employment in Oaxaca (see figure 5-3). In this case, assets are not sold because workers are fully aware of the transitory nature of the wage increase.

Think now, more generally, of the effects of formal-informal mobility on the behavior of the self-employed. According to the patterns shown in the previous chapter, although many self-employed workers are sometimes able to obtain formal salaried jobs, they do not experience a stay in formality that is stable enough to persuade them to sell or give up their productive assets and become permanently formal. In addition to entering formal employment, which they certainly can do and do, they need to stay long enough to feel safe in leaving self-employment permanently behind and they need higher wages to compensate them for the quasi-rents that they lose if they do so. Under erratic stays in formality—as is the case for low-wage workers in Mexico—*the equilibrium level of self-employment is higher.*

Historically, sustained and relatively stable increases in market wages and social security benefits associated with salaried employment have led workers to gradually abandon self-employment in order to become full-time formal workers. But if that process is obstructed, self-employment will tend to persist. One of the effects of the formal-informal dichotomy in Mexico is to lower the wage relevant to the self-employed *and thereby to stimulate self-employment.*

The employment statistics in Mexico do not allow for separating *comisionistas* from self-employed workers. Table 5-1 shows that in 2006 those two categories accounted for 17.6 million workers, or 40 percent of the labor force; of those, 67 percent were low-wage and poor workers. One can speculate that some of the 11.8 million (17.6 million * 0.67 percent) workers were engaged in sharecropping arrangements in agriculture, fishing, and the like and that many were sales personnel hidden behind the label of *comisionista.* But despite the difficulty of separating the two categories, a relevant segment of the 11.8 million workers probably were truly self-employed, working in agriculture and, more likely, in myriad odd jobs in the streets of Mexico's cities because their opportunity cost of not being employed somewhere else was low. The discussion about the determinants of self-employment is very relevant for Mexico.

### Demand for Comisionistas

Firms may have nonsalaried relationships with workers when they are unable to observe their workers' labor input completely, because, for example, workers are out in the streets working at times of their own choosing. As a result, payments are structured in the form of commissions rather than wages in order to elicit effort (or to share some risk); however, one can think of commissions in wage-equivalent terms. More important, the amount of the commission offered is determined by market wage rates because those rates are the measure of the opportunity cost of workers' time *and firms needing* comisionistas *must compete with firms hiring salaried labor to attract workers.* As a result, for the purposes of what follows, it is sufficient to speak of firms' demand for *comisionistas,* which is similar to any firm's demand for labor. The key exception is that from the legal standpoint, firms are not hiring workers and paying them a wage; therefore they are not obligated to comply with the official governance mechanisms that apply to salaried labor.

## Demand for Nonsalaried Labor

Adding the demand for self-employment and the demand for *comisionistas* results in the demand for nonsalaried labor, labeled $D_i$ in the figures that follow. I refer to it as the demand for informal labor because so far I have assumed that all salaried workers are covered by social security and therefore are formal workers. (In chapter 7, illegal behavior by firms is considered; informal labor includes illegal salaried workers.)

## Demand for Salaried Labor

The demand for salaried labor derives from profit-maximizing firms whose production technology requires salaried labor (to monitor processes directly, ensure quality, manage inventories, and so on). Adding firms' individual demands for labor yields $D_f$, the market demand for salaried labor, which in the absence of illegal behavior by firms is also the demand for labor in the formal sector.

It is useful to note that individual firms' demand for labor shifts in response to systemic or idiosyncratic shocks, changing in turn the level and composition of formal employment. Figure 6-2 exemplifies that shift, assuming that there are two firms, *A* and *B,* facing a positive and a negative price shock between periods $t$ and $t + 1$, respectively.

In that example there are no net job flows in the formal segment of the labor market; *aggregate formal employment* is constant at $L_f^t = L_f^{t+1}$. But as firm A lays off and firm B hires personnel, there are worker flows. Those leaving firm A and those entering firm B need not be the same individuals; whether they are depends on the sector and location of each firm, among other factors. It might be that the workers leaving firm A find jobs in the informal sector, that the workers hired by firm B come from the informal sector, or that the persons laid off by firm A are hired by firm B. Obviously, there are many possibilities.[5] The point here is that

---

5. Kaplan, Martinez, and Robertson (2005), using the same social security registries used in chapter 5, finds that over the period 1985–2001 worker flows in Mexico were almost double job flows. Interestingly for the discussion of chapter 7, it also finds that smaller establishments exhibit higher rates of both worker and job flows and that job and worker flows are similar for men and women.

Figure 6-2. *Firm-Level Shocks and Demand for Salaried Labor*

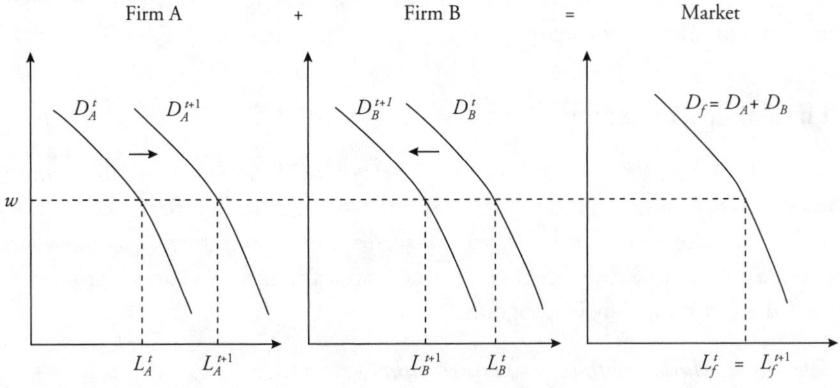

Source: Author's analysis.

there can be a great deal of formal-informal mobility along with stagnant formal employment.

In this chapter I ignore firm-specific shocks, placing the emphasis on the determinants of aggregate formal and informal employment and on the welfare and productivity implications of those aggregates. To do that, I assume that individual firms' demand functions for salaried and nonsalaried labor are constant and focus on the *net* changes in formal and informal employment. That approach contrasts with the analysis in the previous chapter, in which the individual mobility of a worker was highly relevant because it showed how the same worker would receive one or another social program given his or her labor status. The distinction made in chapter 5 between "a formal worker" and "a worker currently employed in the formal sector" notwithstanding, I shift focus here to the structural impact of social security and social protection programs on aggregate formal and informal employment and away from the implications for individual workers.

Critical economic phenomena are associated with the division of the total labor force between formal and informal employment. For a given distribution of land ownership, that division determines land/labor ratios in different forms of production (how many agricultural workers are self-employed, working their own plots; how many are sharecropping or working as salaried employees on someone else's plot). For a given distribution of capital stock, it determines capital/labor ratios (how many workers use their own old sewing machine to make jeans at home or use someone else's more modern sewing machine to make jeans in a maquiladora). In other words, the productivity of capital and land is much affected by the division of the labor force between $L_f$ and $L_i$. From the point of view of low-income workers, that division is critical also because it determines the productivity of their labor, which in most cases is their main productive asset (if not the only one, as seen in chapter 4, for the majority of poor workers). It is critical because, ignoring transfers and benefits from social programs, their productivity is the main determinant of their income.

## The Labor Market with Formal and Informal Sectors

In analyzing the welfare and productivity effects of the formal-informal dichotomy, I begin by assuming that there are no social programs, so that reference to a formal sector where salaried employment occurs and to an informal sector where nonsalaried employment occurs carries no implications for welfare or productivity. I then introduce social programs.

### The Labor Market without Social Programs

The simplest scenario is depicted in figure 6-3. The demand for salaried labor is drawn from the left-hand side (LHS) and the demand for nonsalaried labor from the right-hand side (RHS).[6] Note that the sum of formal and informal employment equals the total labor force. When social programs are introduced, the distribution of the labor force between the formal and informal sectors reflects the coverage of social security and social protection programs across the labor force.

Four observations are relevant to the discussion below. First, throughout I take output prices as exogenous because I assume that all goods are tradable, and rather than indexing them individually I take them to be a Hicks composite good whose relative prices are fixed. Attention centers on wage rates (in this chapter and the next) and on rates of return on capital (in chapter 8).

The second is that the solution depicted in figure 6-3 is *efficient in the sense that the marginal product of labor (MPL) in salaried employment is equal to the MPL in nonsalaried employment.* That implies that the allocation of labor maximizes the country's GDP at world prices.[7] It also implies that there is an efficient level of

---

6. In the labor market depicted in figure 6-3, the wage rate and the distribution of the labor force are endogenously determined as the solution to

$p^w \partial Q_f / \partial L_f - w = 0$ (firms hiring salaried workers maximize profits)
$p^w \partial Q_i / \partial L_i - w = 0$ (firms hiring non-salaried workers maximize profits)
$L_i + L_f = L$ (all workers are employed),

where $L$ is the total labor force, $p^w$ the world price of goods, and $Q_f$ and $Q_i$ the production functions in the formal and informal sectors respectively. The assumption of an exogenous supply of labor is not essential, and one could introduce some function $L(w)$ with a positive value assigned to leisure. If that is done, total employment would adjust in response to social policy, generating another channel through which social programs affect productivity. Doing so, however, makes it difficult to present diagrammatic solutions and provides few additional insights, as the impact of social programs on leisure-work choices has been extensively studied.

7. If a social planner solved the problem Max $p^w[Q_f( ) + Q_i( )]$ s.t. $L_i + L_f = L$, the solution would be the same as the one depicted in figure 6-3.

Figure 6-3. *The Labor Market without Social Programs*

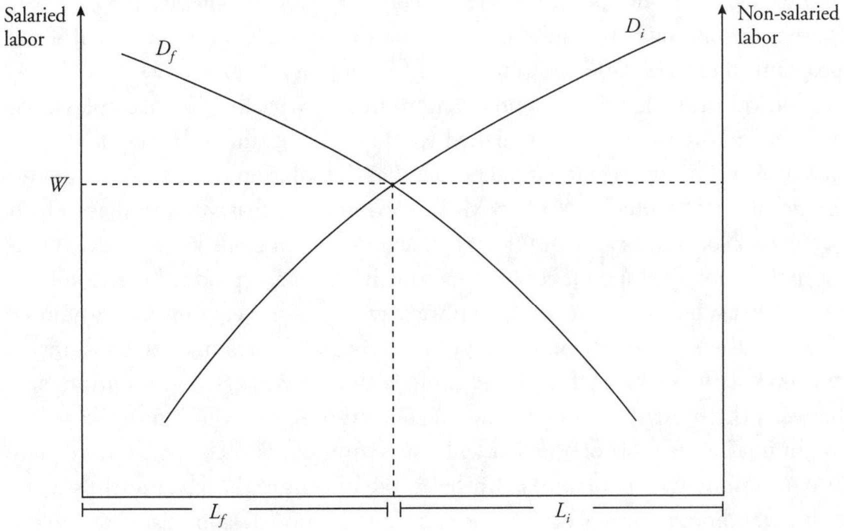

Source: Author's analysis.

nonsalaried employment in the economy or, in other words, that *there is an efficient level of informal employment.* Note that the efficient allocation of labor depends only on elements that are exogenous to social policy: world prices, technology, seasonal factors, pattern of ownership of productive assets, and contractual arrangements between owners of productive assets and workers that depend on the nature of the production function and the incentives required for eliciting effort or sharing risk.

The third observation is that this is a frictionless labor market in which workers move cost-free across sectors until wage rates are equalized. But there are many reasons why wage rates may not be equalized, even when there is full labor mobility. In particular, some workers might have a preference for the flexible schedules or absence of hierarchy associated with nonsalaried jobs.[8] Those considerations could be captured by adding some factor that produces a gap between the formal and the informal wage. If that factor was a function of social programs, it would

8. Maloney (2004) reviews sociological evidence related to preferences for being an employee or being "your own boss," arguing that those preferences may sustain wage differentials between formal and informal employment; see also Levenson and Maloney (1988). Later in the chapter, I explore the case in which workers self-select into formal and informal employment as a result of differences in valuations of social benefits, but the analysis can be extended to other dimensions of workers' valuation of work status aside from wages and benefits like flexibility and hierarchy. My point here, however, is that *given those preferences,* workers' choices are affected by the wages and social benefits associated with each occupation. At some combination of wage and social security benefits, the man preferring his taco stand will give it up to work as a salaried employee for a large chain of taco restaurants.

be important for the purposes of the hypothesis advanced in this volume. In what follows, however, nonpecuniary elements of a job are not modeled. I therefore ignore such considerations and center attention expressly on the effects of social programs on workers' decisions to search for a job in a given sector.

The fourth and last observation is that the market wage for salaried employment and the imputed wage for nonsalaried employment, $w$, might be very low compared with some other standard. The fact that the solution depicted in figure 6-3 is efficient in the sense that $\text{MPL}_f = \text{MPL}_i$ does not imply that worker welfare is high (or low) or socially acceptable (or not). The only meaning of efficiency here is that given the labor force and the country's productive assets and production technology, the market wage rate is the maximum wage rate that the economy can sustain.

From the standpoint of social policy, however, there may be substantive reasons why workers' welfare or the composition of workers' consumption (say, between the present and the future) associated with the solution in figure 6-3 might not be desirable or acceptable. It is the purpose of social policy to remedy any such undesirable outcomes. However, the pursuit of the government's social objectives should not generate a wage and a distribution of labor distinct from the one depicted in figure 6-3, because if it does, the cost of reaching those objectives will increase. Workers will not be as productive as they could be; their wages will be lower; and because GDP will be reduced, there will be less output to consume, redistribute, or invest.

## The Labor Market with Social Programs

Two critical changes occur in the labor market when social security and social protection programs are introduced. The first is on the side of formal firms, which then must include, in addition to wages, the costs of the official governance mechanisms that apply to salaried labor, $T_f$, as part of their labor costs. Consequently, profit-maximizing formal firms hire workers up to the point where the marginal product of labor is equal to $(w_f + T_f)$ and not, as before, to the point where it is equal to the wage only.

The second change is on the side of workers, who then choose between formal and informal employment on the basis of the wages and social benefits associated with each labor status. I capture that change by using equation 5-3, introduced in chapter 5 and reproduced here for convenience:

$$(w_f + \beta_f T_f) = (w_i + \beta_i T_i)$$

(6-1)        utility of formal    utility of informal

                employment     employment.

I next explore the impact of those changes on the labor market and compare them with the solution depicted in figure 6-3, proceeding in three stages. First, I assume that there are no social protection programs (so that $T_i = 0$) and that social

Figure 6-4. *The Labor Market with Complete Valuation of Social Security*

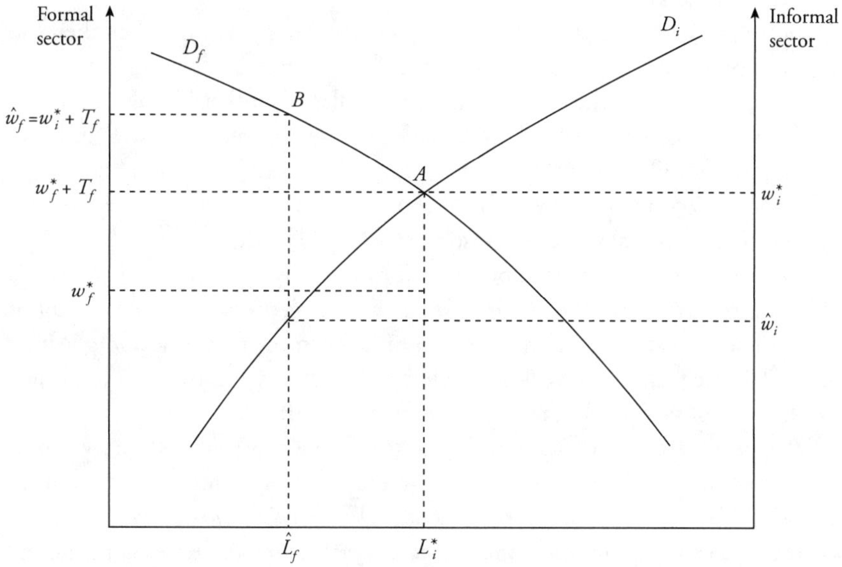

Source: Author's analysis.

security is fully valued by workers (so that $\beta_f = 1$). Second, I again assume that there are no social protection programs but that social security is not fully valued (so that $\beta_f < 1$ but $T_i = 0$). Finally, I consider the case in which social security is not fully valued and there are social protection programs (so that $\beta_f < 1$ and $T_i > 0$).[9]

#### FULLY VALUED SOCIAL SECURITY

Figure 6-4 shows wage rates and labor allocations when $\beta_f = 1$ and $T_i = 0$, using an asterisk to refer to the variables. At point $A$, formal and informal firms maximize profits. Formal employment is $L_f^*$; informal employment is $L_i^*$. However, to avoid clutter in this and the following figures, $L_i^*$ is not drawn, although it can be measured starting from the right side of the horizontal axis up to $L_f^*$; it is equal to $(L - L_f^*)$. Workers are indifferent to the choice between working in the formal or

9. Formally, I explore various solutions to the system of equations given by

$$p^w \partial Q_f / \partial L_f - (w_f + T_f) = 0$$
$$p^w \partial Q_i / \partial L_i - w_i = 0$$
$$w_i + \beta_i T_i = w_f + \beta_f T_f$$
$$L_i + L_f = L,$$

depending on the values of $\beta_f$ and $T_i$. Note that the analysis assumes that all workers value social security programs in the same way and that all workers value social protection programs equally. Appendix 6 shows that *this assumption is not essential* and that the results obtain even if valuations of social security or social protection programs differ between workers.

the informal sector because utility in one case, $U_i = w_i^*$, equals utility in the other case, $U_f = (w_f^* + T_f)$.

Clearly, this solution is the same as that depicted in figure 6-3, when there are no social programs. When social security is fully valued, it has no impact in the labor market except in the form of payment to salaried workers in the formal sector. What they get in social security benefits is compensated for exactly in lower wages, with the difference being exactly $T_f$. If social security was eliminated, wages in the formal sector would rise to the level of the informal sector, but the level and composition of formal workers' consumption would be the same.

There is a very important implication for productivity when social security is fully valued: *it does not affect the distribution of labor between sectors.* As a result, it is still the case that the marginal product of labor in the formal sector, given by $(w_f^* + T_f)$, is equal to the MPL in the informal sector, given by $w_i^*$. That is just another way of saying that the allocation of labor is efficient.

Who pays for social security contributions? They are fully paid by formal workers, not by formal firms. The level of output and formal firms' profits are the same as they would be in the absence of social security. *When social security is fully valued by workers, it does not redistribute profits (or quasi-rents) to wages.* In terms of the figures presented in table 3-9, the implication is that workers consider the 345,240 million pesos, or 3.9 percent of GDP, that was internalized as part of the transactions between them and formal firms to be worth 345,240 million pesos of benefits. The workers are indifferent to the choice between receiving them in the form of wages or in a claim to the bundle of present and future services provided by IMSS, Infonavit, the Afores, and the labor tribunals that determine severance payments. The point is that the 345,240 million pesos are not additional benefits on top of the wages that workers would receive without them. In other words, profits of formal firms did not fall by 345,240 million pesos; in fact, they did not fall by one peso.

That result is very important, and it is useful to look at it more closely. Go back to figure 6-4, and assume that there is no social security. The equilibrium wage for salaried workers equals the wage earned by informal workers, $w_i^*$. Now introduce social security, and assume formal firms pay for it. Starting from point A, where formal employment is $L_f^*$ at the wage $w_i^*$, formal firms face higher labor costs; in particular, their labor costs increase to $\hat{w}_f = (w_i^* + T_f)$. But at those higher labor costs, formal firms do not employ $L_f^*$ workers; they employ only $\hat{L}_f$ workers, at point B, not A. The $(L_f^* - \hat{L}_f)$ workers laid off by formal firms have to be absorbed by the informal sector, and that can happen only if wages there fall to $\hat{w}_i$. But with labor mobility, this situation is not sustainable. Because workers in the informal sector earn the lower wage $\hat{w}_i$ and workers in the formal sector earn the higher wage plus benefits $(\hat{w}_f + T_f)$, workers move from the informal to the formal sector. Wages fall in the formal sector until the point that $w_f^* + T_f = w_i^*$, which is point A, with formal employment at $L_f^*$ and formal sector workers receiving the wage $w_f^*$, which is lower than $w_i^*$ by exactly $T_f$.

*The legal obligation to deliver social security contributions to IMSS, Infonavit, and the Afores is fulfilled by firms. But the incidence of the contributions falls on workers, even though social security legislation stipulates that both firms and workers contribute to social security. The point is that there is a difference between what the Social Security Law formally stipulates and the nature of the adjustment that occurs in the labor market as a result of the law.*

That is a critical implication of the discussion of informal-formal mobility in chapter 5, and it is useful to state it in different terms: *under the best of circumstances (that is, $\beta_f = 1$), social security is not redistributive.* Under those circumstances there is neither redistribution from firms to formal workers or between formal and informal workers.

There is another critical implication: even though the solution depicted in figure 6-4 is efficient in the sense that it maximizes the productivity of labor, *it is suboptimal from the standpoint of the government's social objectives* unless the government has reason to believe that formality implies myopic behavior, moral hazard, and contracting problems in insurance markets and that informality does not. The discussion in chapter 3 is relevant at this point. If the government wants *all* workers to have a claim to the bundle of goods and services contained in $T_f$, that objective is not met even if social security is fully valued. There are $L_i^*$ non-salaried workers who may not be saving for their retirement, may lack access to health insurance, may not get a housing loan, and so on.

*That is a problem for the government, not for informal workers:* they have the same utility as formal workers. In fact, because the allocation of labor is efficient, they are getting the maximum possible utility given the technology of the economy and its productive assets. But the government faces this problem because it does not impose its preferences on informal workers and does not solve their problems in insurance markets. As a result, the government may feel the need to correct for this situation, and that is where social protection programs come in. But before considering them, I explore what happens when social security is not fully valued.

INCOMPLETELY VALUED SOCIAL SECURITY

I now assume that $\beta_f < 1$ (the results in chapters 3 and 5 give the basis for that assumption). The important point here is that from the point of view of formal firms, the fact that workers do not fully value social security does not change their legal obligation to cover the full cost of social security contributions.

Figure 6-5 describes the labor market in this case, where I use an apostrophe to denote the associated wage rates and labor allocations and compare them with those denoted by an asterisk, which correspond to the case in which social security is fully valued. Note first that workers are unwilling to work in the formal sector for the same wages observed when social security was fully valued.[10] As workers

10. That is because $(w_f^* + \beta_f T_f) < w_i^*$.

Figure 6-5. *The Labor Market with Incomplete Valuation of Social Security*

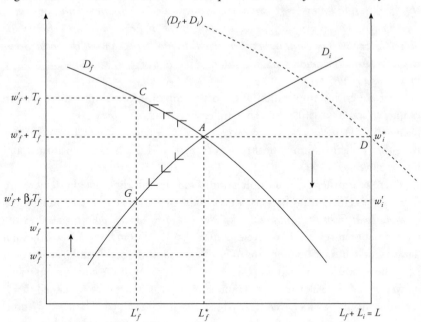

Source: Author's analysis.

move out of the formal sector, the formal wage increases, but if those workers are to be absorbed in the informal sector, wages in the informal sector must fall, so wages move in opposite directions. Formal firms maximize profits at $C$, pay $(w'_f + T_f)$ per worker, and employ $L'_f$ workers. Informal firms maximize profits at $G$, pay $w'_i$ per worker, and employ $L'_i$ workers. Workers' utility in the formal sector, $(w'_f + \beta_f T_f)$, equals workers' utility in the informal sector, $w'_i$.

One might ask at this point why wages do not fall in the formal sector so that more workers can get a formal job and access to social security. *The answer is that workers have the option of being informal.* The marginal productivity of labor in the informal sector sets a reference point for formal workers: workers are never going to work in the formal sector for less than $w'_f$ plus benefits of $\beta_f T_f$ because they can always work in the informal sector for $w'_i$.

Next I identify the impact of social security on labor productivity, wages, prices of productive assets, and the accomplishment of the government's social objectives, as well as the incidence of social security contributions. Consider first labor productivity. Incompletely valued social security increases employment and output in the informal sector and reduces employment and output in the formal sector. Because the allocation of labor when social security is fully valued maximizes the productivity of workers, any change in that allocation must lower it. In other words, *social security lowers aggregate labor productivity by inducing a reallocation of workers from more productive to less productive uses.*

It should be emphasized that low labor productivity in the informal sector is caused by excessive employment in that sector, not because the sector is intrinsically less productive. There is nothing inherently unproductive about employment in the informal sector; as just seen, there is an efficient level of informal employment. The problem is that social policy leads workers and firms into a situation in which the efficient level is exceeded. Indeed, if social policy provided incentives for excessive formal sector employment—that is, employment higher than $L_f^*$—the problem would be the opposite: there would be relatively low-productivity formal employment and high-productivity informal employment. The inefficiency that I highlight here exists from the social point of view, caused by the fact that social policy distorts the price of salaried relative to that of nonsalaried labor; *it does not exist because firms or workers in the informal sector are less efficient than those in the formal sector.*

Turn next to wages. Incompletely valued social security narrows the wage gap between sectors, given that wages in the informal sector fall while wages in the formal sector increase. If one ignored the valuation issue, that could be seen as evidence of rationing in the labor market, because informal sector workers are "worse off" than formal sector workers. The observation would be that the sum of wages and benefits in the formal sector exceeds wages in the informal sector, or that $(w_f' + T_f) > w_i'$. In fact, it could be argued that informal sector workers must be lining up for formal sector jobs. But there is no rationing, and informal workers are not lining up because utility is equal in both sectors. The point is that when social benefits are available, a comparison of wages across sectors says little about mobility in the labor market.[11]

On the other hand, note that wages in the formal sector do not increase as a result of technical innovations or new investment by firms. *Formal wages rise because the supply of labor to the formal sector falls.* As a result, output in the formal sector falls. In other words, one could say that undervalued social security lowers the profitability of production in the formal sector.

Consider the prices of productive assets. Wage changes affect quasi-rents on capital (or land). In the formal sector, the future flow of quasi-rents on capital goods falls as formal sector wages increase; the opposite happens in the informal sector, where productive assets become more valuable as informal wages fall. In fact, productive assets in the informal sector that at $w_i^*$ might not be used at all are

---

11. Discussing wage differentials in Mexico, Maloney makes the point that "unfortunately, the analysis cannot assume that workers fully value benefits [that is, that $\beta_f = 1$] or that the unobservables are negligible. For example, the value of not having a boss is difficult to measure. In sum, neither these nor any previously reported sectoral [wage] differentials are reliable measures of segmentation" (Maloney 1999, p. 284). I complement Maloney's observation below by noting that when $T_i > 0$, wage differentials tell even less about segmentation in the labor market.

exploited at $w_i'$ (see figure 6-1). *That helps to explain why some assets that, prima facie, would be worthless have economic value,* such as the half-hectare of rain-fed land with steep slopes and very low yields, the old mixer and weather-beaten juice stand, the small fishing boat. Land that would otherwise be put to rest is exploited (or used for agriculture instead of grazing) and old machines that should be put away are put to use.

What happens to the government's social objectives? Incomplete valuation puts the government further away from reaching its objective—forcing all workers to consume the bundled set of goods and services associated with social security— as the number of formal workers falls.

Finally, what is the incidence of social security contributions? They are paid by workers in *both* sectors and by formal firms, while informal firms receive the equivalent of a labor subsidy because for them, the cost of labor falls. In other words, incompletely valued social security redistributes income away from all workers to a subset of firms, those in the informal sector. *Crucially, it does not redistribute income in favor of workers; in fact, all workers are worse off.* Moreover, while formal firms' profits fall, they do so, so to speak, for the wrong reason: not because social security works well but because it does not.[12]

The negative effects of social security on welfare and productivity strengthen as $\beta_f$ gets closer to zero. Formal sector employment, output, profits, and aggregate labor productivity and wages fall along with workers' valuation of social security, while self-employment and *comisionista* employment become more profitable. That has substantive implications for Mexico. A social security system that does not work well creates a drag on the whole economy, reducing the productivity of all workers. Through the labor market, its costs extend to workers in the informal sector.

Even if social security covers only salaried workers, it behooves all to make it function well. In other words, the quality of services provided by IMSS, Infonavit, the Afores, and the labor tribunals that administer firing and severance pay regulations is not only an issue with respect to the welfare of the workers enrolled in social security; *it is a crucial issue for the composition of employment and the productivity of all workers in Mexico.*

---

12. IDB (2004) and Heckman and Pagés (2004) survey the evidence on the incidence of social security contributions and severance pay regulations in Latin America and conclude that "all in all, the available evidence for Latin America suggests that at least part of the costs of the non-wage benefits is passed on to workers in the form of lower wages. A few studies find evidence that workers pay for the entirety of benefits, but the majority find that employers bear a share of the cost. . . . Therefore, the evidence is fairly robust that although a large share of benefits is likely to be paid by employees, mandatory benefit regulations have a cost in terms of lower [formal] employment" (IDB 2004, p. 208). Those findings are fully consistent with the analysis above: in the unlikely case that $\beta_f = 1$, workers bear all the costs, and when $\beta_f < 1$, those costs are shared—but not only by firms and workers in the formal sector, as IDB and Heckman and Pagés suggest, *but also by workers in the informal sector* (unless there are barriers to mobility, which, as shown in chapter 5, do not pertain in Mexico).

SOCIAL PROTECTION PROGRAMS

Consider now what happens in the labor market when social protection programs are introduced, that is, when $T_i > 0$. Take the view that most people hold—that social security programs are more valued than social protection programs, or that

(6-2) $$\beta_i T_i < \beta_f T_f.$$

I show below that results are stronger if the inequality in expression 6-2 is reversed, but I use this example to illustrate that it is not true that incentives are "well aligned" in favor of formality just because the per-worker costs of social security are higher than the per-worker costs of social protection ($T_f > T_i$) or because social security programs are more valued by workers than social protection programs ($\beta_f T_f > \beta_i T_i$). That view considers only the costs and benefits of social programs; to get a fuller picture, one must look also at wages received by workers and labor costs paid by firms, because employment outcomes depend on the adjustment in the labor market that occurs as a result of the independent decisions of firms and workers.

The critical change that occurs when social protection programs are introduced is that the utility of informal employment increases relative to that of formal employment. However, informal firms continue only paying wages to their workers.

Figure 6-6 illustrates that case, using a double quote mark to denote the corresponding wage rates and labor allocations and, as before, an asterisk and an apostrophe to denote the solution values when only social security programs are in place, with $\beta_f = 1$ and $\beta_f < 1$, respectively. Because social protection programs increase the utility of working in the informal sector, workers move out of the formal sector. As they do so, wages in the formal sector increase, $w_f'' > w_f'$. Formal sector firms therefore move from $C$ to $K$, reducing employment from $L_f'$ to $L_f''$, given that at $K$ they face labor costs of $(w_f'' + T_f)$ compared with $(w_f' + T_f)$ at $C$. The workers flow to the informal sector, reducing wages there from $w_i'$ to $w_i''$; informal sector firms move from $G$ to $M$, increasing informal output and employment from $L_i'$ to $L_i''$ (not shown). At $K$ and $M$ workers are in equilibrium, obtaining utility $(w_f'' + \beta_f T_f)$ in the formal sector and $(w_i'' + \beta_i T_i)$ in the informal sector.

As before, I identify the impact of that change on labor productivity, wages, and the accomplishment of the government's social objectives. By design, there are no direct incidence effects of social protection programs because there are no "social protection contributions." (The fiscal impact of social protection programs is discussed in chapter 9.)

Consider first labor productivity. Social protection increases informal employment over and above the inefficient level caused by the undervaluation of social

Figure 6-6. *The Labor Market with Social Security and Social Protection*

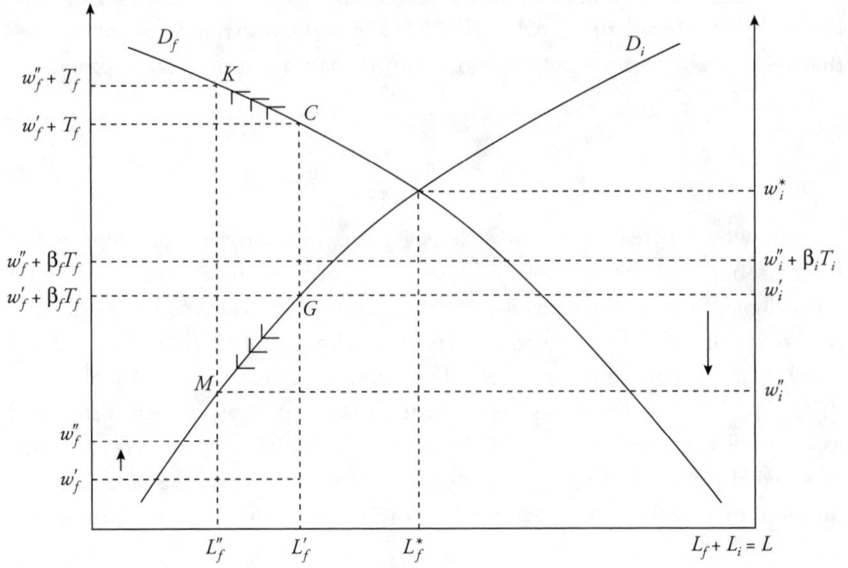

Source: Author's analysis.

security. *The loss of aggregate labor productivity caused by* $\beta_f < 1$ *is augmented by* $T_i > 0$. More low-income workers find it profitable to be self-employed, exploiting their little plots of low-quality land or peddling goods in urban areas. I emphasize that that happens even if social security programs are more costly than social protection programs ($T_f > T_i$) and even if they are valued more ($\beta_f T_f > \beta_i T_i$).

Social protection programs further narrow the wage gap as wages increase in the formal and fall in the informal sector. But if one compares the wage gap with and without social protection, one would find that it is wider with social protection.[13] As a result, it would appear that workers in the informal sector are worse off with social protection than without (so more would be lining up for formal jobs than before!). *But because that conclusion ignores the fact that workers in the informal sector receive benefits through social protection programs, it is wrong.*[14]

13. That is, $[(w_f'' + T_f) - w_i''] > [(w_f' + T_f) - w_i']$. Even when a correction for workers' valuation of social security is made, one still finds that $[(w_f'' + \beta_f T_f) - w_i''] > [(w_f' + \beta_f T_f) - w_i']$.

14. This is a point that I believe is missed by and large in the discussion and interpretation of econometric estimates of formal-informal wage differentials. Furthermore, the effects of social protection programs on wages are not small; the programs provide informal workers with benefits worth at least 1.7 percent of GDP. What would happen to the supply of labor to the formal sector if informal workers knew that they could access public health, housing, pension, and day care programs only if they had a formal job? What would be the values of $w_f$ and $w_i$ in that case?"

Note that if the inequality in expression 6-2 is reversed, so that social protection is valued more than social security, then $w_i'' < w_f''$. There would be a wage premium for formal sector workers, even ignoring social security benefits. That would strengthen the view of those who think that workers in the informal are worse off than workers in the formal sector, so that there should be a long queue of workers searching for formal employment. The argument would be that even ignoring social security benefits, wages in the formal sector are higher than in the informal. But, again, there is no queue; utilities are equalized.

This discussion brings out the extreme difficulty of gauging the extent of barriers to mobility in the labor market from formal-informal wage comparisons. The analysis shows that it is not necessarily the case that wage differences correlate with utility differences, that is, that

$$(6\text{-}3) \qquad \text{sign}\left(w_f - w_i\right) \to \text{sign}\left(U_f - U_i\right).$$

Clearly what matters from the point of view of workers is utility, not wage, differentials.

Observing that $\beta_i T_i > \beta_f T_f$ is not at all far-fetched in Mexico, particularly in small urban or rural areas, where, as discussed in chapter 3, hardly any IMSS health infrastructure exists but social protection health infrastructure does; where there is hardly any Infonavit housing but there may be social protection housing; where there are no IMSS day care centers; and where credit constraints increase the opportunity costs of saving for retirement for the large majority of poor workers. In those areas, social security is little more than a large tax on salaried labor (of up to 35 percent!); in addition, per-worker social protection benefits are larger than the average value of 5,670 pesos a year (approximately 10 percent of $w_i$), shown in table 3-9, given the large variance in the provision of social benefits. In such areas, the observation that $w_f > w_i$ may not be an indication of how much better formal jobs are than informal jobs; it may be an indication of how much lower the valuation of social security benefits is than the valuation of social protection benefits. Alternatively, in those areas there may be no formal employment at all, so that one does not observe the inequality $w_f > w_i$ for the reason that $L_f = 0$ and only $L_i > 0$ is observed (or only illegal salaried employment is observed, as elaborated on in chapter 7).

One last but critical observation should be made regarding wages. Despite the fact that social protection reduces wages in the informal sector ($w_i'' < w_i'$), workers are better off with social protection than without because ($w_i'' + \beta_i T_i) > w_i'$. At the same time, however, workers in the informal sector do not capture the full benefits of social protection, because their wages go down (as $w_i'' < w_i'$). In the context of labor mobility, part of the benefits of social protection is captured by workers in the formal sector, in the form of higher wages (in the same way that part of the costs of the incomplete valuation of social security benefits is shifted from formal to informal workers in the form of lower informal wages). *Social protection appears to make all workers better off.*[15]

This result is crucial: on one hand, more workers are occupied in informal activities with lower labor productivity and fewer workers are occupied in formal activities with higher labor productivity. Obviously, therefore, aggregate output is less. On the other hand, all workers enjoy higher utility. But workers' higher living standard does not result from their higher productivity; on the contrary, workers are less productive than before. Their higher living standard results from the fact that they are enjoying something that apparently no one is paying for, because from the point of view of workers and firms, social protection is free.

This discussion raises the issue of whether social protection is redistributive in the sense of increasing workers' utility at the expense of someone else's utility, in contrast with social security, where it is clear that it is not, because the utility of all workers is lowered. The issue can be framed as follows: can social protection programs make all workers better off? To answer that question, it is necessary to ask how the resources to pay for the programs are made available—or, using the data from table 3-9, to ask where the 1.7 percent of GDP used in 2006 for social protection programs came from. If that is not considered, one could simply set $T_i$ very high, shut down the formal sector, and permanently improve the welfare of all workers (given that there is a free good). To assess the distributive impact of social protection programs, it is necessary to consider the incidence of the taxes used to pay for them. As elaborated on in chapter 9, *it is not necessarily correct to state that because informal workers receive social benefits, income is being redistributed in their favor.*

Turn finally to the government's social objectives. Now all workers have social benefits in one form or another, which was not the case in the absence of social protection programs. So it could be argued that even if the economy is less efficient, the country is closer to achieving the objective of providing social benefits to all workers. *I argue here that this line of reasoning ignores a trade-off that needs to be considered.* Note two characteristics of the equilibrium when social protection programs exist: first, fewer workers are covered by social security because some move to the informal sector; second, informal workers might not necessarily consume all the benefits of social protection programs. The bundled and obligatory nature of social security and the unbundled and voluntary nature of social protection matters here.

To see the implications, assume that social security and social protection programs provide only health insurance and retirement pensions and that the government

---

15. In Levy (2006c) I show that social protection may make an otherwise binding minimum wage in the formal sector nonbinding. I do not argue that that is necessarily the case in Mexico, but certainly if millions of informal workers sought formal employment, $w_f$ would be pressed downward, potentially making a currently nonbinding minimum wage binding. The point is that informal workers are not pressing $w_f$ downward. Of course, if they did, the equilibrium value of $w_f$ still could settle above the minimum wage.

wants all workers to consume both. Assume, however, that workers value health services but are not willing to save voluntarily for retirement in the Afores (as chapter 3 shows). The government's social objectives, therefore, are only partly met because even though social protection permits informal workers to save for a pension, they will not save voluntarily. In that case, when social protection programs are introduced fewer workers save for retirement than without the programs, given that formal employment falls. In other words, *through social security, the government forces workers to save, but through social protection, it subsidizes workers' decision to avoid saving.*

On the other hand, all workers have access to health insurance, whereas before informal workers did not, and that is a clear gain. Thus there are contradictory effects on the government's social objectives, and further information on the government's welfare function is required to ponder them. Of course, given that social security offers more benefits than social protection, the situation is more complex. In particular, in Mexico social security includes disability and work-risk insurance as well as severance pay when layoffs occur; however, social protection does not. Consequently, having social protection programs implies that fewer workers than before are covered by the two insurance programs and fewer receive severance pay when fired.

## The Static Efficiency Costs of the Formal-Informal Dichotomy

An initial discussion of the impact of social programs on economic efficiency is presented here; chapters 7 and 8 complement the discussion, incorporating other effects that are relevant to Mexico.

### Fiscal Costs and Efficiency Costs

Recall two separate dimensions in the analysis of a tax. On one hand, revenues are collected and used to pay for some public policy; those paying the tax lose and those benefiting from the policy gain. Both the taxes collected and the expenditures made are recorded in the government's fiscal accounts and can be clearly identified and measured. Those are the fiscal dimensions of a public policy.

On the other hand, those being taxed generally modify their behavior to minimize the impact of the tax. An example is found in the previous discussion: when $\beta_f < 1$, social security acts partly as a tax on salaried labor, causing workers and firms to change their behavior, the former by moving to the informal sector and the latter by reducing employment. But the loss of output in the formal sector is not recorded in the government's fiscal accounts. At the same time, because there are more informal workers, output in the informal sector increases; that output gain is not recorded in the government's fiscal accounts either. If the output loss in the formal sector equals the output gain in the informal sector, the responses of firms and workers to social programs offset each other. But if it does not, and in particular if the former exceeds the latter, then the tax associated with social security generates a *net* loss.

Output losses unaccompanied by any countervailing gains are the efficiency costs of a tax. Those costs are not recorded in the government's fiscal accounts, but their absence in the federal budget should not distract from a simple but powerful truth: *the higher the costs, the poorer Mexico is as a whole. There is less to redistribute, invest, or consume; on average, everybody loses.*

### Labor Productivity Differences between Sectors

The productivity of workers is measured by the value of their marginal product in the relevant sector. As noted earlier, the marginal product of labor in the formal sector is $(w_f + T_f)$ and the MPL in the informal sector is $w_i$. Because the MPL in the formal sector is higher than the formal wage, there is a difference between comparisons of wage rates and comparisons of labor productivity. In other words, it need not be the case that

$$(6\text{-}4) \quad \text{sign}(w_f - w_i) \rightarrow \text{sign}(MPL_f - MPL_i) = \text{sign}[(w_f + T_f) - w_i].$$

That does not imply that comparing wage rates is irrelevant; it just means that the comparison is an intermediate step, not the final step, in measuring labor productivity differentials. In turn, the differentials are important because they imply that if workers could be reallocated from low- to high-productivity sectors, GDP would increase.

When social programs are introduced, the difference in labor productivity between sectors is as follows:[16]

$$MPL_f - MPL_i = [(1 - \beta_f)T_f \quad + \quad \beta_i T_i]$$

$$(6\text{-}5) \qquad\qquad\qquad\quad \text{tax on} \qquad\quad \text{subsidy to}$$
$$\qquad\qquad\qquad\quad \text{formal labor} \quad\; \text{informal labor}$$

Equation 6-5 identifies two sources of loss of GDP. The first is loss of output caused by incompletely valued social security, and it is greater the lower the value of $\beta_f$ and the higher the value of $T_f$. This source is associated with the tax on salaried labor. The second is the loss of output caused by social protection, and it is greater the higher the value of $\beta_i$ and the higher the value of $T_i$. That source is associated with the subsidy to nonsalaried labor. Note that $\beta_f$ and $\beta_i$ have opposite effects: improving the valuation of social security augments productivity as employment in the formal sector increases, but improving social protection lowers productivity by inducing overemployment in the informal sector. Note also that even

---

16. That follows from $[(w_f + T_f) - w_i]$ and rearranging equation 6-1 so that $w_i = w_f + \beta_f T_f - \beta_i T_i$.

if social security is fully valued, social protection programs induce productivity differentials and that even if there were no regulations on severance pay, there still could be productivity differentials.

The total GDP forgone is given by the size of the productivity differential between sectors multiplied by the number of workers that change from one sector to the other, which here is labeled $\Delta L$. In terms of figure 6-6, $\Delta L$ is equal to the difference between $L_f^*$ and $L_f''$ and has two components that mirror the tax on salaried labor and the subsidy to nonsalaried labor in equation 6-5: the shift from $L_f^*$ to $L_f'$ as a result of $\beta_f < 1$ and the shift from $L_f'$ to $L_f''$ as a result of $T_i > 0$.[17]

It follows that the annual loss of GDP from lower labor productivity is given by

$$(6\text{-}6) \qquad \text{Annual GDP loss from lower labor productivity} = \left[ MPL_f - MPL_i \right] \times \Delta L.$$

## Additional Efficiency Costs of Social Protection Programs

A standard interpretation of equation 6-6 is that it represents the counterpart to the government's social objectives. There is a trade-off between efficiency losses and the accomplishment of the government's social objectives (with a subset of the labor force); in other words, some loss of output is an inevitable consequence of social security, as is the case with almost any tax imposed for some public policy purpose.

*When social protection programs are introduced, that view becomes incomplete.* Social protection programs have fiscal costs. As a result, it is necessary to raise revenues somewhere to pay for the programs, and taxes imposed for that purpose also generate efficiency losses. In other words, from the standpoint of efficiency, social protection programs generate two losses: one, they act as a subsidy to informal employment, *adding* to the distortion in labor allocation caused by undervalued social security, as shown by equation 6-5; two, they generate efficiency costs because revenues need to be collected *somewhere* to pay for the subsidies.

To measure the second costs, one must identify what taxes are imposed on whom and how those taxed might change their behavior in ways that could induce an output loss similar to the one measured by equation 6-6. Alternatively, one has to identify whether debt is being contracted or other sources of revenue are being used (like oil rents). I leave that discussion to chapter 9, pointing out here only that there would be additional efficiency costs associated with social protection programs unless the government in Mexico were able to tax someone without prompting any changes in his or her behavior.

17. Note that $\Delta L$ is not equal to the elasticity of demand for labor in the formal sector multiplied by the change in formal sector wages ($\Delta w = w_f'' - w_f^*$). That is because the shape of the demand for labor in the informal sector determines how much wages in that sector must fall to absorb a given quantity of workers who leave the formal sector.

In sum, the efficiency costs of the formal-informal dichotomy are the costs of the distortions introduced in the labor market by the tax on salaried labor and the subsidy to nonsalaried labor measured by equation 6-6, *plus* the costs of the distortions introduced to raise revenues for social protection programs. Therefore, the relevant trade-off is between those costs and the social gains in the form of bundled social security benefits for workers in the formal sector and unbundled benefits for workers in the informal sector.

*That trade-off is not inevitable, and there may be others that are less costly.* In particular, the productivity losses observed in the labor market are caused by the fact that the government solves the contracting problems in insurance markets and imposes its preferences only on a subset of workers. If the government carried out its interventions on all workers, the losses could be avoided.

In particular, if the government extended to all workers the social benefits that it thinks that they should consume by means of an "alternative mechanism" and did not pay for them with wage-based contributions, there would be no distortions in the labor market and therefore no productivity differentials. To see how that would work, go back to figure 6-5. The dotted line adds $D_i$ to $D_f$ to obtain the aggregate demand for labor $(D_f + D_i)$. That intersects the vertical axis at point $D$, with all workers receiving the equilibrium wage $w_i^*$ and no one paying for any social security contributions. All workers are then provided $T_f$ in social benefits, which they all value at $\beta_f T_f$. At the same time, at $w_i^*$, employment in the formal sector is $L_f^*$ and in the informal sector $L_i^*$. There is no loss of labor productivity despite the fact that $\beta_f < 1$. The relative profitability of investing in salaried or nonsalaried labor activities is unchanged. Equally important from the social point of view is that the government's social objectives are completely fulfilled. Call this scenario "universal social entitlements without wage-based contributions."

Table 6-1 makes explicit the trade-offs between workers' utility, static efficiency costs, fiscal costs, and the fulfillment of the government's social objectives. The table compares four possible states, two including the formal-informal dichotomy (labeled A and B) and two without (labeled C and D).[18]

Mexico's current situation is best approximated by case B, which reveals the dilemma in which the government is caught as a result of the formal-informal dichotomy. Doing nothing, as in case C, maximizes efficiency and workers' wages, but it is unacceptable to the government because it leaves all workers without the social benefits that the government believes that they need. Providing only social security, as in case A, has low efficiency costs and no fiscal costs, but it also is unacceptable because it means that the government's social objectives are not achieved at all with respect to informal workers. But trying to protect workers in

---

18. Table 6-1 misses three important dimensions relevant for these trade-offs: large illegal salaried employment, illegal behavior by firms that has dynamic productivity effects, and government subsidies for social security. They are discussed in the following three chapters and summarized in table 10-1.

Table 6-1. *Trade-Offs between Workers' Utility, Static Efficiency Costs, Fiscal Costs, and the Government's Social Objectives*

| Measure | With formal-informal sectors | | Without formal-informal sectors | |
| --- | --- | --- | --- | --- |
| | *Case A (social security only)* | *Case B (social security and social protection)* | *Case C (no social programs)* | *Case D (universal social entitlements)* |
| Workers' utility | Lower utility than in case C | Higher utility than in case A | Highest possible wage, no social benefits | Highest possible wage plus value of social benefits |
| Static efficiency costs | GDP loss from tax on formal labor | Larger GDP loss than in case A from —tax on formal labor —subsidy to informal labor —distortions from raising revenues for social protection programs | None | GDP loss from distortions from raising revenues for social benefits for all |
| Fiscal costs | None | Costs of social protection programs | None | Costs of social programs for all, higher than in case B |
| Government's social objectives | —Complete for all formal workers —Absent for all informal workers | —Complete for a lower number of formal workers than in case A —Partial for a larger number of informal workers than in case A | Absent for all workers | Complete for all workers |

Source: Author's analysis.

the context of the formal-informal dichotomy, as in case B, is costlier in terms of productivity and does not really accomplish the government's social objectives because protection from risks is incomplete for large numbers of informal workers and erratic for workers who move between formal and informal employment. Furthermore, the more the government tries to improve benefits for informal workers, the greater the distance from its own social objectives grows because fewer workers are covered by social security and the larger the country's productivity losses as well as its fiscal costs become.

The relevance of case D is that it indicates that if an alternative mechanism to finance social programs existed, the nature of the trade-offs could be modified to be more favorable to the government's social objectives and to workers' productivity. If social security is just a mechanism to solve contracting problems in insurance markets and to change the composition of workers' consumption by imposing the government's preferences on workers, under some circumstances mechanisms other than wage-based contributions can be used to pay for those benefits without distorting labor relations throughout the economy. Of course, raising revenues through the alternative mechanism would also generate efficiency losses *somewhere*. I postpone discussion of that issue until chapter 10. However, I note at this point that it is feasible to find alternative mechanisms to pay for universal social benefits for all workers that are more efficient than those currently used.

## Empirical Estimates of Static Efficiency Costs

A proper estimate of the static efficiency costs of social programs requires specification of a computable general equilibrium model and the econometric estimation of various elasticities of demand for salaried and nonsalaried labor and other parameters, a fairly complicated task that exceeds the scope of this volume. Nevertheless, it is useful to provide estimates of the orders of magnitude of at least some of those effects.

Here I provide estimates only of the loss of GDP resulting from differences in labor productivity because I could not find any studies of the efficiency costs of taxation in Mexico. That is an important shortcoming given that the fiscal costs of social protection programs are on the order of 1.7 percent of GDP. For that reason and others discussed below, the figures provided clearly underestimate the static efficiency costs of the formal-informal dichotomy, perhaps quite substantially.

The approach followed here takes advantage of the results presented in tables 5-12 and 5-13, which show that mean wage rates for workers who moved between sectors were similar. The estimated wage rates allow direct computation of the differences in the marginal products of labor without having to estimate $\beta_f$ and $\beta_i$ individually. A weighted average of the wage rates of female and male high- and low-wage workers who changed labor status indicates that the formal wage rate equals 26.60 pesos an hour. Given that the costs of the official governance mechanisms that apply to salaried labor are 35 percent of the formal wage, it follows that $T_f = 9.31$ pesos an hour. From that it can be inferred that

(6-7)

$$MPL_f = \left(w_f + T_f\right) = 26.60 + 9.31 = 35.91 \text{ pesos an hour}$$

$$MPL_i = w_i = 26.60 \text{ pesos an hour.}$$

Equation 6-7 indicates that the loss of output associated with the *marginal* worker employed in the informal rather than the formal sector equals 9.31 pesos an hour. That is equivalent to an annual loss of GDP of 19,364 pesos per worker (compare that with the annual minimum wage, 17,590 pesos).

How many workers in Mexico would be salaried rather than nonsalaried in the absence of the formal-informal dichotomy? Or, in other words, what is the value of $\Delta L$ in equation 6-6? That is a difficult question to answer, but, jumping ahead to the results in chapter 7, a lower-bound estimate can be offered. As shown there, when $\beta_f < 1$ firms and workers engage in illegal salaried labor, it implies that there is a segment of informal employment made up of salaried workers that would not exist if $\beta_f = 1$.

Of course, in the absence of the formal-informal dichotomy nonsalaried employment also would be lower, as shown previously in this chapter. That implies that $\Delta L$ is made up of two components: one, those who already are salaried employees but illegally so and who therefore are informal employees, as identified in the next chapter; two, those who currently are nonsalaried employees but would be salaried in the absence of the tax on salaried employment and the subsidy to nonsalaried employment, as identified in the discussion in this chapter. An estimate of the former is provided by table 5-1, which shows that there were approximately 8.1 million illegal salaried workers in Mexico in 2006; an estimate for the latter is difficult to obtain without a proper estimate of the elasticities of demand for formal and informal labor. Ignoring nonsalaried employees who would be salaried, I take 8.1 million workers to be the lower-bound estimate of $\Delta L$. That implies that there would be no change in the share of salaried employment in total employment in the absence of the formal-informal dichotomy, just a change in its composition between legal and illegal workers.[19]

Multiplying 8.1 million workers by an annual loss of 19,364 pesos per worker yields a total GDP loss of 156.8 billion pesos, or 1.8 percent of GDP in 2006. However, because that calculation assumes that the marginal and the average product of labor are constant in both sectors, it is incorrect. As workers shifted from the informal to the formal sector, the marginal product of labor in the informal sector would rise, and as more workers joined the formal sector, their marginal product would fall. A standard procedure to account for those

19. That still leaves Mexico with a lower share of salaried employment than comparable countries; see table 5-2.

effects is to divide the GDP loss in half.[20] That implies that the average loss of GDP for each worker inefficiently employed in the informal sector is 9,682 pesos a year. That in turn *yields an estimate of the annual GDP loss associated with the formal-informal labor productivity differential of 78.4 billion pesos, or 0.9 percent of GDP in 2006.*

Three reasons suggest that that figure is an underestimate. First, the assumptions made to construct table 5-1 were systematically biased in the direction of underestimating evasion; see appendix 4. In fact, if the figure for salaried employment estimated for Mexico by the International Labor Office was used instead of the figure in table 5-1, the number of illegal salaried workers would be 11.4, not 8.1 million (see table 5-2). Under those assumptions, *the annual GDP loss would be equivalent to 1.24 percent of GDP in 2006.*

Second, the costs of the official governance mechanisms that apply to salaried labor are probably closer to 40 percent than to 35 percent of the wage, as discussed in chapter 1. If the higher estimate of $T_f$ is used in equation 6-7, the estimated range of the loss of output changes to 1.02 or 1.44 percent of GDP, depending on whether the estimate of 8.1 or 11.4 million illegal salaried workers is used.

Third, as already noted, the calculation assumes that the total number of non-salaried workers does not change when the tax on salaried employment and the subsidy to nonsalaried employment is removed—in other words, that no self-employed worker or *comisionista* would want to be a salaried employee despite the fact that he or she would be better off as such. Determining the number of *comisionistas* and self-employed workers who would be salaried is extremely difficult, but that number would add to the 8.1 or 11.4 million illegal salaried workers used above as an estimate of $\Delta L$, increasing the size of the GDP loss.

On the other hand, the estimates presented here capture only the efficiency costs associated with differences in labor productivity between sectors. In chapters 7 and 8, however, I argue that informality also affects efficiency through channels that are absent from these calculations: the size distribution of firms, Coase-type transaction costs, investments in job training, and distortions in the composition of output that produce a more "informality prone" production structure. Such dynamic effects add to the static effects approximated here.

Is an annual GDP loss of 0.9 to 1.44 percent of GDP large or small? In comparison with similar calculations of the efficiency costs of tariffs or other taxes, the numbers obtained here are large. Nevertheless, it could be argued that the loss is not large if in return the government provides social benefits to workers that it

20. That provides a measurement of the triangle formed between the curves representing the demand for formal and informal labor, or in terms of figure 6-5, area CAG. Alternatively, note that equation 6-6 approximates the value of GDP loss only for a marginal, or "small," $\Delta L$. Clearly 8.1 million is not small. Dividing by two the rectangle that results from the product of 8.1 million workers and the loss of 19,364 pesos of GDP from the marginal worker employed in the informal sector serves to approximate equation 6-6 or area CAG better.

otherwise could not. To gauge whether the costs identified above are large or small, they must be compared against relevant alternatives. Hardly any public policy objective can be reached without some cost; the relevant question is whether the same policy objective can be reached more effectively and at a lower cost. If an alternative policy can do that, then the costs estimated here, even ignoring the dynamic efficiency costs explored in the next two chapters, are very large. If not, then they are simply the costs of providing workers with social benefits, period, for the simple reason that not providing social benefits to millions of workers in Mexico evidently is not an option. I return to this issue in chapter 10.

## The Labor Market with Different Valuations for Poor Workers

Chapter 4 showed that poor workers have relatively better access to the benefits of social protection programs and that non-poor workers have relatively better access to the benefits of social security programs. On that basis, I argued that even if poor and non-poor workers had the same preferences, they valued social security and social protection programs differently. That was captured in expression 4-1, reproduced here for convenience:[21]

$$\beta_f^P < \beta_f^{NP};\ \text{poor workers value social security less than non-poor workers do.}$$

$$(6\text{-}8)\quad \beta_i^P > \beta_i^{NP};\ \text{poor workers value social protection more than non-poor}$$
$$\text{workers do.}$$

Consider a division of the labor force between poor and non-poor workers, $L^P$ and $L^{NP}$, respectively. Both types are employed in the formal and informal sectors, so that extending the notation used before, we have

$$(6\text{-}9)\qquad\qquad L_f^P + L_f^{NP} + L_i^P + L_i^{NP} = L.$$

In Mexico, poor workers are overrepresented among informal workers. They account for 23 percent of the labor force but 39 percent of informal employment; furthermore, 45 percent of non-poor workers but only 6 percent of poor workers are formal employees (see table 5-1). One would expect the opposite: that precisely because poor workers have fewer productive assets than non-poor workers, they would tend to be concentrated in salaried employment (in principle, formal employment).

---

21. The comparisons of mean wage rates presented in tables 5-12 and 5-13 are consistent with expression 6-8 to the extent that while there is evidence of a wage premium for high-wage workers employed in the informal sector (suggesting that they value social security programs more than social protection programs), the premium is not present in the case of low-wage workers.

The discussion in this chapter sheds some light on those patterns.[22] As can be inferred from expression 6-8, the tax on formal employment is higher for poor than for non-poor workers, as is the subsidy to informal employment. Appendix 6 shows that under those conditions, poor workers will self-select into the informal sector and non-poor workers into the formal sector. If the productivity of workers were the same regardless of what sector they were employed in, that outcome would not be so relevant. But if, as shown before, the productivity of informal jobs is lower than that of formal jobs, it is relevant. What is important to highlight here is that while the interphase between social security and social protection programs lowers the productivity of all workers, *that effect is concentrated in poor workers because the programs induce relatively more poor workers than non-poor workers to take informal employment.*

*These results are strengthened by making informal labor status a condition of poor workers' access to some social protection programs.*[23] Clearly, the programs increase poor workers' utility. But by inadvertently locking them in low-productivity informal jobs, they make it harder for poor workers than for others to obtain formal jobs and higher wages. The prevalence of informality among the poor is especially pernicious because it implies that they fail to benefit from training programs because they are employed by small firms and microenterprises that exist on the border between the formal and informal sectors and have higher failure rates; because they move more frequently and erratically from job to job; because they develop few firm-specific assets; and because they are always the first to be affected by output and employment shocks (see chapter 7). Under those conditions, poor workers might permanently need targeted income transfers, despite the positive effects of Progresa-Oportunidades.

It is critical to note that *this problem arises not because of the design of Progresa* but because of the formal-informal dichotomy, on one hand, and the differences between the benefits of social security and social protection programs for poor and non-poor workers, on the other. It also is critical to note that if attempts are made to remedy the problem by adding new components to Progresa that make it deviate from its original objective of human-capital formation, the problem will only worsen.[24]

In Levy (2006a) I argue that Progresa-Oportunidades needs to continue to focus sharply on its objective of transferring income to the poor—contingent on

22. However, in the case of the poor an important share of informal employment is associated with illegal salaried employment. That is discussed in the next chapter, where I argue that precisely because the tax on salaried employment is higher for the poor than for other employees, there is relatively more evasion in their case, so the factors discussed here are equally relevant.

23. Like Seguro Popular or the new day care program started in 2007; see chapter 1.

24. That was the case, for instance, with the retirement saving scheme introduced in 2006 as one more component of Progresa-Oportunidades that subsidized poor workers' savings for retirement as long as they had no formal job (see chapter 1). Fortunately, it was abandoned in 2007.

their investment in their own human capital—without further altering incentives in Mexico's already overregulated labor market. I also argue, on the basis of the discussion in this chapter, that programs that provide benefits conditioned on labor market status, like the social security and social protection programs, should not create special benefits for poor households in addition to the benefits that Progresa already provides. In my view, the best policy combination for poor workers is to maintain and improve the efficiency with which Progresa-Oportunidades delivers its benefits and to address directly the substantive obstacles that poor workers face in the labor market, not to skew them with new social protection programs or enhanced benefits for existing programs, which, although they may reflect the government's best intentions, inadvertently end up contributing to the persistence of poverty. I return to this discussion in chapter 8.

# 7

## *Productivity and Illegal Firms*

Chapter 6 associated formal employment with salaried workers and informal employment with nonsalaried workers and traced the impact of social programs on the distribution of the labor force between the two types of employment. But as table 5-1 shows, in Mexico there is a large category of employment made up of illegal, informal salaried workers that has not been captured in the analysis so far. This chapter explores the illegal dimensions of informality, first explaining why illegal employment occurs and then expanding the framework presented in chapter 6 to incorporate informal salaried workers. It gives reasons why some firms choose to be legal and others illegal and discusses how that choice affects the size distribution of firms and labor productivity. It then explains the coexistence of formal and informal workers in the same firm—a widespread phenomenon in Mexico—and discusses the impact of informality on the composition of output.

### The Labor Market When Social Security Is Evaded

Social programs have implications for firms' labor costs: firms hiring salaried workers pay $(w_f + T_f)$, while firms having relationships with nonsalaried workers, including the one-person firm of the self-employed individual, pay $w_i$. Salaried labor is indispensable for many economic activities, but depending on formal and informal wage rates, the difference in the costs of salaried and nonsalaried labor can be close to 50 percent.[1] In the absence of alternatives, such a large difference in the relative costs of labor would distort the composition of output: the economy would be characterized by a large share of GDP from self- and *comisionista* employment and a small share from activities in which salaried labor is indispensable. But firms and workers do have an alternative: *to bypass the official governance mechanisms that apply to salaried labor, generating illegal salaried employment* (here labeled $L_{if}$ to denote informal workers who should be formal).

This section explores the implications of evasion within the simple general equilibrium framework of chapter 6 in order to identify how evasion affects the distribution of the labor force between sectors and the structure of wages. I ignore differences in evasion among firms hiring salaried labor and so imply that all formal firms evade equally regardless of firm size. That in turn implies that all formal workers have the same productivity (as in chapter 6). In the sections following this one, I focus on the differences in the ways that firms evade the law depending on their size. The objective is to show that when differences among firms hiring salaried workers are considered, firms endogenously divide into formal and informal camps and that productivity differentials arise among salaried workers as well as between salaried and nonsalaried workers.

## The Equilibrium Level of Evasion

Workers and firms evade social security when the gains from doing so exceed the costs. Firms want to expand salaried employment but save on labor costs; workers want to be compensated for the loss of the value that they attach to the social security benefits that they are entitled to as salaried employees. A precondition for evasion is that $\beta_f < 1$. Because formal firms pay $T_f$ for each worker hired (in addition to his wage) but, in the worker's opinion, he receives only $\beta_f T_f$, an incentive exists for both to try to capture the "waste" of $(1 - \beta_f)T_f$ by evading IMSS. *Without a wedge between firms' non-wage labor costs and workers' valuation of benefits, there are no incentives for either party to break the law.*

In 2006, 8.1 million salaried workers evaded social security and only 14.1 million were enrolled (see table 5-1). One is tempted to use that fact and the information in table 3-9 to gauge the magnitude of evasion. If one did so, the interpretation would be that in 2006 the costs of the official governance mechanisms that apply to salaried labor were 345,240 million pesos, or 3.9 percent of GDP. A linear calculation would then suggest that without evasion, those costs would have been 543,569 million pesos ([(14.1 + 8.1)/14.1] * 345,240), or 6.1 percent of GDP. One

---

1. The ratio of salaried to nonsalaried labor costs is $(w_f + T_f)/(w_f + \beta_f T_f - \beta_i T_i)$. At one extreme, if $\beta_f = 1$ and $T_i = 0$, the ratio equals one; at the other, if $\beta_f = 0$ and $\beta_i = 1$, it equals $(w_f + T_f)/(w_f - T_i)$. Table 3-9 indicates that $T_i$ is 0.23 of $T_f$. Given that $T_f$ is 35 percent of $w_f$, if $w_f$ is normalized at unity, then $T_i$ is 8 percent of $w_f$ and the ratio equals 1.47.

could then argue that through evasion the costs of the governance mechanisms were reduced by the equivalent of 2.2 percent of GDP. But that calculation is misleading, because 14.1 million and 8.1 million are the post-evasion number of legal and illegal salaried workers. As I show later, *if there were no tax on salaried employment and no evasion, the number of salaried workers would be higher than 22.2 (14.1 + 8.1) million,* although that number cannot be observed. In fact, evasion in Mexico reduces the costs of the governance mechanisms that apply to salaried labor by more than 2.2 percent of GDP, which is a very large amount. On the other hand, a telling number that *can* be observed, imperfectly, is that at least 36.6 percent of salaried workers evade. The incentives to evade are great, and so is the extent of evasion.

Consider now how firms behave when evasion is possible. In Mexico the legal obligation to enroll workers in social security falls on firms, as does the punishment for failing to do so. Punishment takes the form of monetary fines, which I denote here by F, per worker evading. Obviously the fines for evading must be larger than the costs of the governance mechanisms being evaded, otherwise all firms would always evade.[2] The Social Security Law states that fines for evading are between 40 and 100 percent of the amount of the social security contributions evaded; when caught, firms also have to pay the amount of the contributions evaded. In addition, accrued interest since the time that contributions should have been paid also is added to the total. Since $T_f$ is 35 percent of the wage, the minimum fine is at least 15 percent of the wage bill, although actual fines in most cases are higher. The point is that fines matter to firms because they can increase labor costs by 35 percent above the labor costs that the firms should have paid (that is, costs including social security contributions). *Fines for evading social security are highly relevant to Mexican firms.*

However, IMSS cannot supervise the more than 3 million firms in Mexico individually (see table 7-2). As a result, there is a probability that IMSS will find and fine evading firms, here denoted by $\lambda$, and that probability plays a key role in firms' behavior.

When evasion is possible, firms face the problem of how to choose a mix of legal and illegal workers that will maximize profits. That choice is based on the non-wage costs of legal labor ($T_f$), the probability that they will be fined if they are caught by IMSS ($\lambda$), and the size of the fines that they would have to pay in that case ($F$). From the standpoint of the production function, legal and illegal workers are perfect substitutes—that is, they are equally productive. But the costs to firms of legal and illegal workers are not the same. On one hand, a legal worker costs ($w_f + T_f$). On the other, if firms hire illegal workers it must be because the cost of doing so is lower than the cost for legal workers, otherwise firms gain nothing by evading. Thus, two wages are paid to salaried workers: $w_f$ when they are legal, and $w_{if}$ when

2. In other words, it must be that $F > T_f$.

they are illegal. In addition, however, because firms hiring illegal workers run the risk of being fined by IMSS, the cost of hiring them is $(w_{if} + \lambda F)$—that is, the wage plus the expected fine for breaking the law (which is simply the probability of being caught multiplied by the fine).

It is natural to assume that the probability of being caught increases with the number of illegally hired workers. In the end, the more the law is violated, the likelier it is that a firm will be caught; as a result, given $w_f$, the marginal cost of a legal worker is constant at $(w_f + T_f)$. But given $w_{if}$, the expected marginal cost of an illegally hired worker increases because the more workers hired, the greater the probability of detection. That implies a fine based on all illegally hired workers, not on just the last worker hired illegally whose hiring caused the firm to be caught. Therefore, one cannot ex ante compare the cost of legal workers, $(w_f + T_f)$, with the cost of illegal workers, $(w_{if} + \lambda F)$, to determine whether the firm hires legal or illegal workers.[3] The point here is that the marginal cost to the firm of an illegally hired worker increases with the number of workers illegally hired. It is useful to summarize that as follows:

(7-1)

$$\begin{array}{ll} \text{Cost to firms of} & = (w_f + T_f); \text{ the marginal cost} \\ \text{legal workers} & \text{of workers is constant.} \\[1em] \text{Cost to firms of} & = (w_{if} + \lambda_f); \text{ the marginal cost} \\ \text{illegal workers} & \text{of workers increases.}^{4} \end{array}$$

Turn now to how workers behave when evasion is possible, that is, when they can earn a wage as salaried workers but without receiving social security benefits. Without evasion, their utility is $(w_f + \beta_f T_f)$ working in the formal sector and $(w_i + \beta_i T_i)$ working in the informal sector.

What is their utility if they are salaried but illegal? A very important consideration comes into play at that point: *in Mexico the benefits of social protection programs are offered to all workers not covered by social security regardless of whether or not lack of coverage is a result of an illegal act.* As a result, with evasion they now have a mixed option: being salaried without social security benefits, receiving instead social protection benefits. In that case their utility is $(w_{if} + \beta_i T_i)$—the wage paid by firms to workers evading the law plus the value of social protection benefits.

When labor mobility exists, workers move between sectors until utilities are equalized. It is clear that now workers will move between being salaried and formal,

3. If that was done, there would be a "corner" solution whereby firms would hire only legal or illegal workers. Technically the point is that $\lambda$ is endogenous to the level of evasion; see appendix 7.

4. That follows from $MCL_f = (w_f + T_f)$, so that $\partial MCL_f / \partial L_f = 0$, while $MCL_i = w_{if} + \lambda F + \partial \lambda (L_{if}) / \partial L_{if}.F.L_{if}$, so that $\partial MCL_i / \partial L_{if} > 0$.

Figure 7-1. *The Labor Market When Social Security Is Evaded*

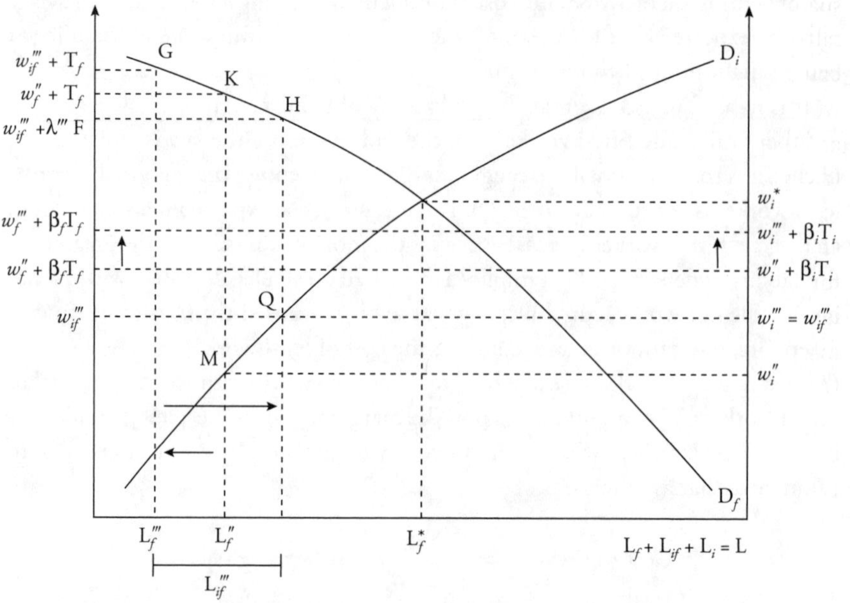

Source: Author's analysis.

salaried but informal (illegal), and nonsalaried and necessarily informal to maximize their utility. I summarize workers' behavior as follows:

(7-2)

$$(w_i + \beta_i T_i) = (w_{if} + \beta_i T_i); \text{ and } (w_{if} + \beta_i T_i) = (w_f + \beta_f T_f);$$

informal workers are indifferent to being salaried or not.

salaried workers are indifferent to being formal or not.

Figure 7-1 depicts the labor market when evasion of social security is possible (see appendix 7 for technical details). To identify the impact of evasion, I take as a reference point the situation wherein social security and social protection programs both are present but there is no evasion (as depicted in figure 6-6) and use " to denote the wage rates and labor allocations corresponding to that situation; I use ''' to refer to wage rates and labor allocations when there is illegal behavior. Before evasion, formal sector firms maximize profits at K, employing $L_f''$ workers, who obtain utility of $(w_f'' + \beta_f T_f)$, which is equal to what workers obtain in the informal sector, $(w_i'' + \beta_i T_i)$. At that wage, informal firms employ $L_i''$ workers (not shown) and maximize profits at M. That equilibrium is observed when all salaried workers are legal and all formal firms comply with the law.

I now allow for evasion. As formal firms evade, they offer $w'''_{if}$ above $w''_i$ to per-suade legal salaried workers, *comisionistas,* or self-employed workers to become salaried workers but without social security benefits. As wages rise, however, the cost of legally hired workers increases and formal firms convert some registered workers into unregistered workers, moving from K to G, with workers registered at IMSS falling to $L'''_f$. All the workers attracted from the informal sector and the $(L''_f - L'''_f)$ workers previously registered are illegally employed by formal firms.

The with-evasion equilibrium for formal firms is at point H, where they hire $(L'''_f + L'''_{if})$ workers but register only $L'''_f < L''_f$ workers. The equilibrium condition for legal and illegal salaried workers and self-employed workers and *comisionistas* is $(w'''_{if} + \beta_i T_i) = (w'''_i + \beta_i T_i) = (w'''_f + \beta_f T_f)$. Because informal wages increase, informal firms move from M to Q and *comisionista* and self-employment fall by $(L''_i - L'''_i)$, which is the net gain in salaried employment.

## The Impact of Evasion

Evasion affects the composition of employment, wages and profits, efficiency and productivity, and fulfillment of the government's social objectives.

Four implications arise with regard to employment. First, with evasion there are four types of workers. The first three are formal salaried workers registered at IMSS, self-employed workers, and *comisionistas,* as before. But there is now a fourth type: salaried workers who have a *relación obrero-patronal* with firms that never-theless do not register them with IMSS. Four factors combine to create that type of labor force composition:

—social security design features that exclude nonsalaried workers
—valuation problems with social security, which taxes salaried employment
—social protection programs that subsidize nonsalaried employment
—evasion of social security legislation.

The second implication is that one cannot interpret the sum of formal and informal salaried employment as the efficient level of salaried employment. As figure 7-1 shows, in the absence of the formal-informal dichotomy, salaried employ-ment would be $L^*_f$, higher than the observed level of legal and illegal salaried employment $(L'''_f + L'''_{if})$. Table 5-1 shows that in 2006 there were 14.1 million legal and 8.1 million illegal salaried workers, for a total of 22.2 million salaried workers (ignoring ISSSTE affiliates). Unfortunately, we cannot observe $L^*_f$, although we know that it exceeds 22.2 million. The point is that evasion cannot fully offset the effects of $\beta_f < 1$ because fines inhibit firms from ignoring com-pletely the official governance mechanisms that apply to salaried labor. *In other words, the efficient level of salaried employment in Mexico is higher than 22.2 million workers.*

The third implication is that providing social protection benefits to illegal workers increases the level of evasion. Clearly, if that was not the case, their oppor-tunity cost of accepting a salaried job without social security coverage would be higher and evasion lower.[5] Social protection facilitates evasion because even though workers lose $\beta_f T_f$ by evading, they receive $\beta_i T_i$ for evading. *There is a de facto subsidy for evasion: salaried workers receive free social benefits, but only if they are illegal.*

The fourth implication is that if there are differences in workers' valuations of social security programs, their incentives to evade differ too. As seen, a necessary condition for evasion is that $\beta_f < 1$. Clearly, the lower $\beta_f$, the higher the incentive to evade, so that for workers with a low $\beta_f$, evasion is higher. *To the extent that poor workers have a lower valuation of social security programs (that is, $\beta_f^P < \beta_f^{NP}$), the incentive for them to evade is higher than for non-poor workers.* Agricultural day laborers are an example. As discussed in chapter 4, they have a low $\beta_f$ because there are no IMSS health or day care facilities in the fields of Sinaloa, Sonora, and the Baja California peninsula where they migrate to work; because some may have plans to migrate to the United States permanently and do not value their future pension in Mexico; because there is no Infonavit housing for them; because they need cash now for a small investment project when they return home to Michoacán, Guerrero, or Oaxaca, for which they can get no credit; or because they know that because they are salaried workers during only half of each year, they will never accumulate enough weeks with IMSS to get a minimum pension.[6]

That is part of the explanation of why poor workers are overrepresented among informal salaried workers. But there is another side: because social protection programs are better for the poor than for the non-poor (that is, $\beta_i^P > \beta_i^{NP}$, as discussed in chapter 4), there are more incentives for poor salaried workers to be informal than for other workers. *Poor workers are overrepresented among illegal workers because they, and the firms that hire them, are rationally responding to the incentives offered by social security and social protection programs.*

Consider now the impact of evasion on wages and workers' utility. Self-employed workers and *comisionistas* get a higher wage as their numbers fall. Some urban workers leave the city streets to join a small clothing factory; some rural workers leave their plot of low-quality land to join a larger farm with better-quality land. Because wages in the informal sector increase, self-employed individuals and *comisionistas* get higher utility (note in figure 7-1 that $w_i''' > w_i''$). Next, legal salaried workers get a higher wage because their numbers fall (note in figure 7-1 that $w_f''' > w_f''$). Because they keep their social security benefits, they are better off. Finally, illegal salaried workers include two groups. The first includes those who were self-employed workers or *comisionistas* who already had social protection benefits but decided to become salaried because they got a higher wage and who

---

5. See appendix 7: that can be obtained from equation A7-1, rewriting equations A7-1d and A7-1e so that workers receive only $w_{if}$ and not $(w_{if} + \beta_i T_i)$. $L_{if}$ would be lower in that case.

6. In the case of *jornaleros*, evasion allows them to earn more in the close-to-the-U.S., high-productivity, irrigated lands of Sinaloa than in the far-from-the-U.S., low-productivity, rain-fed lands of Oaxaca, even if their bosses in Sinaloa do not register them with IMSS.

also are better off (note in figure 7-1 that $w_{if}''' > w_i''$). The second group includes workers who changed from legal to illegal salaried employment. Those workers, who had social security benefits but changed them for social protection benefits, get higher utility because their wages increase (note in figure 7-1 that $(w_{if}''' + \beta_i T_i) > (w_f'' + \beta_f T_f)$). The key point is this: *evasion makes all workers better off.*

Turn next to firms' profits. They increase in the formal sector (otherwise firms would not evade!). With the same capital stock, output expands because there is a net gain in salaried employment. On the other hand, profits or quasi-rents in the informal sector fall.

The impact of evasion on labor productivity is as follows. Salaried workers are less productive because employment increases with the same capital stock; for the opposite reason, labor productivity increases in nonsalaried employment. But because the situation without evasion is characterized by underemployment of salaried workers, there is a net gain: *aggregate labor productivity increases as workers are reallocated from low-productivity to high-productivity jobs.* That is why wages are higher for all.

There are two reasons why workers and formal firms are better off with evasion. One, before evasion there is a waste of $(1 - \beta_f) T_f$ per worker employed, to be distributed between workers and firms. With evasion, part of that waste is recovered through gains for formal firms and all workers (including informal workers).[7] Two, since there are more informal workers, the resources channeled to social protection programs increase, and as seen in chapter 6, neither firms nor workers pay for those resources. Formal firms save on part of their non-wage labor costs, passing them on to the government, and part of their savings are in turn passed on to workers.[8]

Turning to economic efficiency, one is tempted to argue that efficiency increases with evasion because the efficiency costs of labor misallocation are reduced. But that need not be true, because as informal employment expands, the costs of social protection programs increase *and the resources to pay for the additional benefits must come from somewhere.* To see the importance of that, return for a moment to table 3-9. In 2006 the total cost of social protection programs to provide benefits to 25.7 million informal workers was 146,351 million pesos; 17.6 million of the workers were nonsalaried, and 8.1 million were illegal salaried employees. Without evasion, the cost would be lower because informal employment would be lower. Again, one is tempted to say that the cost of social protection programs

7. But the waste cannot be fully recovered because some is still spent on a subset of workers who remain legal. However, formal firms maximize profits at that point given the fines and detection probabilities they face, and workers maximize utility given the alternatives in nonsalaried employment. One can think of the resources wasted by registering workers with IMSS as the cost of an insurance policy that formal firms pay to avoid fines.

8. Of course, the additional resources for social protection programs need to come from somewhere, so that, as before, the statement that firms and workers are better off with evasion is contingent on who pays (see chapter 9).

would have been 99,836 million pesos ((17.6/25.8) * 146,351) and that evasion generated an extra 46,515 million pesos worth of social protection programs for illegal salaried workers. But as before, that calculation is not accurate because if there were no incentives to evade, the number of nonsalaried workers would be lower (because, as shown, salaried employment would be higher). Whatever the hypothetical cost, the point is that as a result of evasion, more resources had to be channeled in 2006 to social protection programs than would have been needed without evasion. Depending on the revenue sources for the additional resources, the associated efficiency costs could offset the gains in labor productivity derived from the expansion of salaried employment. The static impact of evasion on economic efficiency therefore is ambiguous.

What happens if, in response to evasion, IMSS increases fines on firms? As fines get higher, the expected costs of illegal workers increase and firms respond by lowering their demand for illegal workers, until all evasion disappears and firms hire only legal workers. Note from figure 7-1 that that effect initially increases the number of workers registered with IMSS because some of the previously illegal jobs are turned into legal jobs, up to the point that all formal firms comply with the law and employment in the formal sector is $L_f''$. However, salaried employment will never be $L_f^*$, no matter how high the fines. There is an important message here: *the underlying problem caused by $\beta_f < 1$ cannot be corrected by increasing fines or having IMSS, Infonavit, and the Labor Ministry hire more inspectors.*

Conversely, when fines fall, evasion increases. As fines get closer to zero, all firms evade and all salaried employment lacks social security benefits; all workers get social protection benefits instead. At that point, the fact that $\beta_f < 1$ becomes irrelevant from the perspective of workers and firms because they all evade the implicit tax associated with what to them is a malfunctioning mechanism governing salaried labor. For fines that are positive but not too high, however, the labor market is characterized by some evasion. In turn, the labor force is composed of a mix of legal salaried workers making up formal employment, on one hand, and illegal salaried workers, self-employed workers, and *comisionistas* making up informal employment, on the other, as is the case in Mexico (see table 5-1).

What about the government's social objectives? Here there is a clear loss. With evasion, coverage of social security falls and fewer workers consume the bundle of goods in $T_f$ that is central to the government's social policy. More workers are informal, thereby receiving $T_i$ benefits, so they may or may not purchase life insurance, save for retirement, be protected from negative output shocks through severance pay regulations, and so on. This is not a minor issue. As seen in table 5-1, in 2006 there were at least 8.1 million workers evading IMSS and only 14.1 million registered workers, and as discussed below, approximately 2 million firms evaded IMSS as well. *Evasion is the concrete mechanism by which millions of firms and workers have avoided the official governance mechanisms that apply to salaried labor and trampled on the social objectives of the Mexican government. It is a major issue.*

## Concluding Remarks on Social Programs and the Labor Market

A few remarks are in order on the general equilibrium relationships observed in the labor market between social programs, labor allocation, and wage rates, because the remaining analysis in this chapter is carried out in a partial equilibrium context in which wages are exogenously given.

First, there is a direct relationship between Mexico's social programs and the composition of the labor force.[9] *The division of the labor force between salaried and nonsalaried and formal and informal workers shown in figure 5-1, as well as the size of the various subsets in table 5-1, is endogenous to social programs.*

Second, wages in Mexico reflect the impact of social programs. In particular, the wage rate for formal labor, $w_f$, reflects two facts:

—that many salaried workers are illegal, reducing the supply of labor to the formal sector

—that the supply of salaried workers as a whole is reduced by the stimulus given to nonsalaried labor.

In other words, wages in Mexico reflect, in addition to education, capital stock, short-run shocks, and so on (the standard determinants), *a system of taxes on and subsidies to different forms of labor and the partly legal and partly illegal reaction of workers and firms to that system through various levels of evasion.* As a result, it is not correct to interpret wage rates and employment levels as determined by a standard competitive market, even when there is full mobility of labor across sectors and even when neither firms nor workers exercise monopoly power. Wage rates reflect the influence of social programs, and that influence is large to the extent that the programs, measured as a share of GDP or of the wage bill, are large.

It is my view that in policy discussions in Mexico and, more generally, in the analytical literature on labor markets, a great deal of attention is placed on the mechanisms by which education, investment, and training programs, for example, affect labor allocations and wage rates. There also is a large literature on the effects of firing and severance pay regulations—that is, on the effects of a specific element of $T_f$. I believe that insufficient attention has been given to the fact that firing and severance pay regulations are bundled with other elements of social security and to the role played by the *interaction* between social security and social protection programs in a context characterized by significant illegal employment.

I also believe that an analysis of informal salaried labor cannot be carried out unless illegal behavior by firms and workers and the motivation for that behavior is modeled. Obviously I am not arguing that education, investment, and training programs are irrelevant. For some purposes they are fundamental. *But I am arguing*

---

9. One can think of a mapping $L = L[\beta_f, \beta_i, T_f, T_i; (\lambda, F); \Phi]$ and $w = w[\beta_f, \beta_i, T_f, T_i; (\lambda, F); \Phi]$, where $L$ is a vector of labor allocations $L_f, L_i, L_{if}$; $w$ is a vector of wage rates $w_f, w_i, w_{if}$; and $\Phi[K_f, K_i, K_p, p^w, \ldots\ldots]$ is a vector of other elements affecting the labor market: output prices, capital stocks, exogenous shocks, and so on.

Table 7-1. *Social Programs, Labor Allocation, and Wage Rates*[a]

| Allocation and rate | $T_f$ | $\beta_f$ | $T_i$ | $\beta_i$ |
|---|---|---|---|---|
| $L_f$ | − | + | − | − |
| $L_i$ | + | − | + | + |
| $L_{if}$ | + | − | + | + |
| $w_f$ | + | − | + | + |
| $w_i$ | − | + | − | − |
| $w_{if}$ | − | + | − | − |

Source: Author's analysis.

a. Cells refer to the general equilibrium effects of the parameters defining social programs on labor allocation and wage rates.

*that the analysis of the labor market and the design of social policy in Mexico needs to be complemented by a framework akin to the one sketched here.* In this context, $T_f$, $T_i$, $\beta_f$, and $\beta_i$ should not be seen as a concretion of social programs only; they need to be seen also as a set of taxes and subsidies on salaried and nonsalaried contractual arrangements between firms and workers that are quantitatively large relative to other taxes and subsidies that also have an incidence on the labor market. Similarly, the behavior of authorities in punishing firms when they evade the law also needs to be considered as a determinant of how those taxes and subsidies bind on firms and workers.

Table 7-1 summarizes the discussion of chapter 6 and this section and captures the *static* impact of social programs on the labor market.

Each column in the table captures the impact on the composition of employment and the structure of wages of changes in one of the four parameters defining social programs, *given the other three.* That caveat is important when interpreting the effects of changes to individual components of social policy. All else being equal, one would expect, for instance, that a pension reform that brings benefits closer to contributions would lead to an increase in formal employment (because the reform increases $\beta_f$). But if at the same time that the pension reform is introduced social protection changes as well—for example, because a new health program is introduced—the expected impact of the pension reform on formal employment will be diluted and potentially reversed (because the health program increases $T_i$).

I end this section with one last remark. At times the value of $T_f$ in Mexico is compared with that of other countries, particularly more developed ones, which are characterized by a larger share of formal employment in total employment than exists in Mexico (measured by $L_f/L$). The observation is made that the non-wage costs of labor are not significantly lower in those countries and that in many cases they are higher. That observation serves in turn to rule out social programs as an explanation for the higher share of informal employment in Mexico. The analyses in chapter 6 and in this chapter indicate why that line of reasoning is flawed. Comparisons of $T_f$'s across countries by themselves are not very illustrative, because the values of $\beta_f$, $T_i$, and $\beta_i$ may differ among countries. Workers in those countries may value the official governance mechanisms that apply to salaried labor more than workers in Mexico do (because in a broad sense those countries' mechanisms work better). In addition, social protection programs that are equivalent to Mexico's programs may not exist in those countries (because the critical association of social security with salaried labor is not made). Finally, in those countries illegal behavior is not subsidized by social programs. As a result, lower values for $T_f$ and $(L_f/L)$ in Mexico than in those countries are consistent with the casual links between social programs and informality that this volume emphasizes for Mexico.

## Illegal and Legal Firms

The remainder of this chapter focuses exclusively on firms hiring salaried labor and ignores self-employed workers and *comisionistas;* in the discussion that follows, therefore, informality equals illegality. In this section, my objective is to provide some preliminary insights on the decision of Mexican firms to operate legally or illegally and on the role played by social programs in that decision. Those insights are used in subsequent sections to discuss the impact of social programs on the size distribution of firms, the composition of employment within a firm between legal and illegal (or formal and informal) workers, and the composition of output. Because I focus on individual firms, I shift to a partial equilibrium setting in which wage rates are exogenous.

So far, illegal behavior has resulted only from firms' evasion of the non-wage costs of salaried labor. To capture firms' decisions in a more realistic setting, I incorporate two additional features of Mexico's tax and regulatory systems: taxes on firms' profits (*impuestos sobre la renta*) imposed by the Servicio de Administración Tributaria (SAT), the operational agency of the Finance Ministry in charge of collections,[10] and the registration costs of formality, including compliance with regulations like those that require titling the property on which the firm is established and registering it as a business premise.[11] I incorporate these two elements very simply: I assume firms have to pay profit taxes at the rate $t_\pi$ and registration costs of C; for simplicity I assume that C is independent of output.

---

10. The Servicio de Administración Tributaria, known to all firms in Mexico as SAT, is the Mexican equivalent of the U.S. Internal Revenue Service.

11. The last costs can take two forms. Some small firms occupy a house without declaring to the authorities that economic activity takes place on the premises; registration in such cases involves only a license to operate a small business, which is usually associated with higher operating costs (for example, electricity is charged at the industrial, not the household, rate). The other form occurs when the premises might have to be registered and titled for the first time in the Public Registry of Property (Registro Público de la Propiedad).

There are three benefits to a firm of being informal and illegal: savings of $T_f$ per worker hired, savings of C, and savings on profit taxes. On the other hand, firms face two risks of illegality: being caught by IMSS and being caught by SAT.[12] To simplify, I ignore fines for not registering a business with authorities other than IMSS or SAT, although there are implicit cost to firms for not doing so (for example, the value of their assets as collateral falls).

Assume that the capital stock in each firm is given. Assume also that the technology is such that salaried labor is required to produce output and cannot be replaced with nonsalaried *comisionista* labor. Each firm has to decide whether to exploit its capital stock legally, hiring $L_f$ workers, or illegally, hiring $L_{if}$ workers; as before, legal and illegal workers are perfect substitutes from the standpoint of the production function. To focus sharply on the key idea, I first treat that decision as a binary choice; I consider mixed cases later. In the binary case the decision hinges on the comparison of profits made when the firm is legal with those made when it is illegal.[13]

The decision is illustrated in figure 7-2. Panel A depicts the standard result, in which, in a context of legality, employment occurs at the point where the value of the marginal product of labor, $p^w \partial Q / \partial L_f$, equals its marginal costs, $(w_f + T_f)$. Firms' profits are indicated at the bottom of the panel: gross quasi-rents minus taxes on profits and registration costs.

Panel B, which illustrates two relevant changes associated with illegality, is more interesting. The first change is that if the firm evades IMSS, its labor costs are initially lower than if it does not because $w_{if} < (w_f + T_f)$.[14] However, that labor cost advantage is progressively eroded because the risks run by the firm increase with each worker hired, so the expected marginal cost of labor (MCL) slopes upward. The second change is that expanding output increases the exposure of the firm to being caught by SAT, *so the relevant demand for labor is the expected value of the marginal revenue product and not the value of the marginal product, as is the case under legality.* Given the two changes, if the firm is illegal, equilibrium is at E and the firm's (expected) profits are equal to area JEKD in panel B, which may or may not exceed the profits of being legal.

I want to make two points. First, *for a given capital stock, the behavior of a firm in terms of its levels of employment and output (and investment, as discussed in*

12. In what follows, fines for evading income taxes are proportional to output and not profits because the tax code in Mexico has established a regime under which small firms pay taxes proportional to sales (Régimen de Pequeños Contribuyentes), which is the relevant regime for the problem discussed here. As with IMSS, firms face a probability $\varphi$ of being caught, which is assumed to increase with a firm's output.

13. Formally $\Pi_f = [p^w Q(K_f, L_f) - (w_f + T_f) - C](1 - t_\pi)$ and $\Pi_i = [p^w - \varphi H]Q(K_f, L_{if}) - (w_{if} + \lambda F)L_{if}$ with $\varphi', \lambda' > 0$, where $\Pi_f$ and $\Pi_i$ are the profits made by being legal or illegal, where H is the fine per unit of output for violating the tax law, and where I assume that firms evade registration, profit taxes, social security, and severance pay regulations simultaneously.

14. As discussed, in addition to the wage, the cost of illegal labor includes the expected cost of being fined, but for the first worker hired illegally the probability of being fined is practically zero, so I ignore that cost.

Figure 7-2. *Firm Profits with Workers of Different Legal Status*

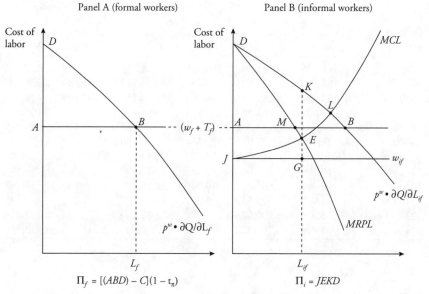

Panel A (formal workers)    Panel B (informal workers)

$\Pi_f = [(ABD) - C](1 - t_\pi)$    $\Pi_i = JEKD$

Source: Author's analysis.

*chapter 8) differs depending on whether it is legal or not.* Figure 7-2 makes the point that all else being equal, illegal firms would tend to be smaller than legal firms; in panels A and B, points B are the same, but in panel B, point E is left of B, so employment is less. In a sense, smallness is the price paid for illegality. It might not maximize efficiency, but it maximizes private profits.

Second, *in the case of firms hiring salaried workers in Mexico, informality and illegality derive from multiple regulations simultaneously, although they could derive from each set of regulations alone.* In panel B, the output and employment contraction derives jointly from the official governance mechanisms that apply to salaried labor, profit tax regulations, and registration costs. However, the firm could be illegal even if it did not evade social security but evaded only profit taxes, at point M; alternatively, it could be illegal even if it did not evade profit taxes but evaded social security, at point L.

## Informality and the Size Distribution of Firms

The following discussion concerns the implications of illegality for the size distribution of firms and labor productivity and the extent to which the choice of being legal or illegal is open to all firms or only to a subset of firms. It then elaborates on the interactions between social programs, illegal behavior, and productivity.

Table 7-2. *Numbers of Workers and Firms, Inegi and IMSS Registries, 2003*

| Firm size (number of workers) | Inegi (1) | | IMSS (2) | | Difference (1)–(2) | |
|---|---|---|---|---|---|---|
| | Firms | Workers | Firms | Workers | Firms | Workers |
| 0–2 | 2,118,138 | 3,011,902 | 350,459 | 488,727 | 1,767,679 | 2,523,175 |
| 3–5 | 581,262 | 2,078,023 | 183,432 | 686,515 | 397,830 | 1,391,508 |
| 6–10 | 153,891 | 1,135,021 | 95,886 | 725,253 | 58,005 | 409,768 |
| 11–15 | 47,601 | 604,387 | 38,855 | 494,430 | 8,746 | 109,957 |
| 16–20 | 24,361 | 433,741 | 21,342 | 379,795 | 3,019 | 53,946 |
| 21–30 | 25,171 | 627,011 | 22,399 | 556,830 | 2,772 | 70,181 |
| 31–50 | 20,927 | 812,729 | 19,125 | 743,225 | 1,802 | 69,504 |
| 51–100 | 16,100 | 1,135,608 | 15,337 | 1,077,909 | 763 | 57,699 |
| 101–250 | 10,898 | 1,683,740 | 10,526 | 1,629,298 | 372 | 54,442 |
| 251–500 | 4,029 | 1,379,532 | 3,804 | 1,314,357 | 225 | 65,175 |
| 501 and more | 2,636 | 3,199,628 | 2,626 | 3,082,169 | 10 | 117,459 |
| Total | 3,005,014 | 16,101,322 | 763,791 | 11,178,508 | 2,241,223 | 4,922,814 |

Source: IMSS (2005) and Inegi, Censos Economicos 2004 (www.inegi.gob.mx).

## Registered and Nonregistered Firms in Mexico

The 2003 census data are the most recent for firms in Mexico. It is important to note that the definition of "firm" used by Inegi *excludes* all activities in rural areas, organizations engaged in religious activities, public organizations providing health and social assistance services (like IMSS), public administrative organizations, public academic institutions, and urban transportation firms operating vehicles like taxis and buses. Equally important, it *excludes* all firms that do not have a fixed physical premise.[15] As a result, street markets (*tianguis*) and commercial activity by the self-employed or by firms operating in the streets are not included.[16]

Table 7-2 presents the result of an exercise in which IMSS registries of firms in 2003 were combed to match the definition of "firm" included in the 2003 census. Understandably, the matching is not exact because there is no official source of

15. Inegi states that "in the 2004 Economic Census the units of observation are fixed or semi-fixed economic enterprises; economic enterprises that carry out their activities in an ambulatory fashion or with installations that are not permanently fixed to the ground, or economic activities for own consumption carried out in the household . . . are not considered" (Inegi 2004, p. 4, my translation). Inegi refers to 2004 because that was the year that the census was published, but the data were gathered in the course of 2003.

16. De Soto vividly illustrates this activity: "In 1993, the Mexican Chamber of Commerce estimated the number of street-vendor stands in the Federal District of Mexico City at 150,000, with an additional 293,000 in forty-three other Mexican centers. These tiny booths average just 1.5 meters wide. If the Mexico City vendors lined up their stands on a single street with no gaps at intersections, they would form a continuous row more than 210 kilometers long" (De Soto 2000, pp. 28–29). That was in 1993, when there were approximately 19.9 million informal workers; in 2006, there were 25.8 million. *The point is that none of those firms are included in table 7-2.*

illegal salaried employment; nevertheless, the table allows a reasonable comparison of registered firms and workers (those in the IMSS registries) and nonregistered firms and workers (those in the census but not in the IMSS registries). In both cases firms are classified by size, measured by the number of workers. I reiterate that, given the nature of the census data, the table does not capture the universe of firms and salaried workers.

The contrast between Inegi and the IMSS registries is sharp indeed. According to the former, there were 3 million firms in 2003; according to the latter, there were only 763,791. If unregistered firms are illegal firms—which, according to the Federal Labor Law and the Social Security Law, they are—*in 2003, 75 percent of all firms in Mexico were illegal.* On the other hand, firms in the census account for 16.1 million workers, while firms registered with IMSS account for 11.2 million workers. In other words, evading firms captured by Inegi account for 4.9 million illegal workers.[17] The other side of large-scale evasion by workers of the official governance mechanisms that apply to salaried labor is large-scale evasion by firms.

Four more features in table 7-2 are worth highlighting. First, there is a very large number of small firms: of the 3 million firms, 2.7 million have five employees or fewer; of those, 2.1 million have two or fewer employees. Second, if large firms are defined as those with fifty-one employees or more, there are only 33,663 firms in that category, or 1.1 percent of the total (if the cut-off point is 100 or more employees, there are 17,563, or 0.6 percent). Third, medium-size firms—say, those with six to fifty workers—also are scarce: only 271,951, or 9 percent of the total (of which more than half have ten or fewer workers).

The fourth feature is that there is an inverse relationship between firm size and evasion. Figure 7-3 captures that relationship, showing the percent of illegal workers in the total number of workers hired for firms of various sizes. Figure 7-4 shows the percent of illegal firms in the total number of firms for firms of various sizes.

## Social Norms and Tolerance for Illegality

So far the discussion of illegality has been based on two important assumptions: one, that the probability of being fined for illegal behavior increases with size; two, that IMSS and SAT enforcement rules are known to all firms and that there is no institutional corruption, so detection means sanction. But that is not so. Even if one ignores corruption, there are enforcement costs, which imply that from the point of view of IMSS and SAT, the cost-benefit ratio of finding and fining firms varies with firm size.[18] Equally important, social norms influence the public's

17. The number of illegal workers here is lower than in table 5-1 because it refers to a different year (2006, not 2003) and, more important, because the number in table 5-1 includes all economic activities.

18. For IMSS and SAT, those are the costs of finding the evading firm and the costs of the legal procedures for collecting. Even if the five-to-ten employee firm is found, the costs to authorities of the legal procedures to collect might exceed the fines that eventually could be collected. Firms know that.

Figure 7-3. *Percent of Illegal Employees by Firm Size*

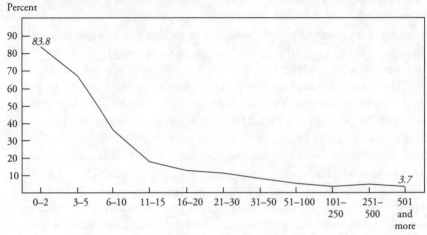

Source: Table 7-2.

Figure 7-4. *Percent of Illegal Firms by Firm Size*

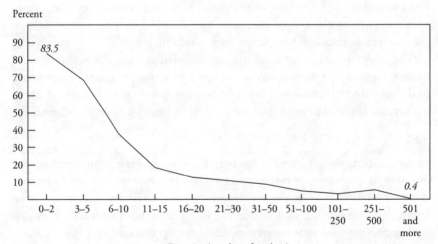

Source: Table 7-2.

expectations of authorities' behavior. As a result, the commitment of IMSS and SAT to fully enforcing the law is not equally credible to all firms.[19] Figure 7-2 seeks to convey the trade-offs between legal status and profits to indicate that formality is a decision variable of firms. However, the figure gives the impression that in Mexico firms are either legal or illegal, when what one observes are various combinations of illegal and legal salaried employment, depending on firm size.

I now pursue the notion that firms may adapt the size of their operations to avoid the costs of formality as part of their profit-maximizing strategy and elaborate somewhat on the complex environment in which firms and authorities interact in Mexico. In particular, I explore in more detail the probabilities of being fined by IMSS; mutatis mutandis, a similar description applies for SAT, so I do not discuss it here.

Firms in Mexico have expectations regarding how the Social Security Law and the Federal Labor Law apply to them. *Their expectations are based on a combination of written laws and unwritten social norms.* Firms know the level of fines, because they are included in the law, but the probability of being fined and sanctioned is not found in any law. Firms infer the probability with some uncertainty. That assessment is based on their estimate of society's tolerance for behavior that is contrary to law, as reflected in the conduct of IMSS; that estimate in turn is based on experience and information that is continuously updated through firms' observations of enforcement efforts.

Firms constantly update the information on which they base their expectations and continuously adjust the number of legal and illegal workers that they hire accordingly. That does not mean that they fire illegal workers and hire legal ones, interrupting the production process; it means that the same workers sometimes are registered with IMSS and sometimes not (recall the worker from Nuevo León in chapter 5). Production continues on the basis of market conditions.

In that regard, it is useful to note that in any given year, IMSS registers about 15 million instances of workers' enrollment, de-enrollment, and re-enrollment. Those changes are the result of adaptation to market conditions given exogenous shocks but also of firms' evasion of the law. At times workers may not even know that the firm has changed their status from formal to informal; keeping them in the dark is made easier by the fact that workers who have been enrolled in IMSS for eight weeks or more have the right to receive free medical care for eight weeks after losing formal status. Firms take advantage of that provision, which was intended

19. Basu, Chau, and Kanbur (2005) explores that problem in detail in the context of enforcing minimum wage laws. They make the point that if both firms and authorities know that there are enforcement costs, authorities may set the minimum wage higher than they would like it to be to serve as a sign of a credible commitment to enforce the law. The issue here falls within the class of problems that they analyze. I assume fines are exogenous but discuss the situation in which firms and IMSS both know that there are enforcement costs and, equally important, in which social norms tolerate some illegality.

to be a temporary aid to recently unemployed workers, to minimize labor costs by rotating workers and saving on social security contributions. Of course, during the time that workers are not registered with IMSS, they do not save for retirement or for a housing loan, although they still work for the same firm.

That does not mean that the Social Security Law is irrelevant. It is a very important reference point, just not the only reference point. When Mexico was a Spanish colony, many laws were issued in Spain for La Nueva España, which were to be "observed but not complied with," as, famously, a Spanish viceroy is said to have said.

With regard to the official governance mechanisms that apply to salaried labor, I posit that firms in Mexico behave as if the combination of social norms and the Social Security Law translate into

$$0 \text{ if } \left(L_{if} + L_f\right) < \underline{L}$$

$$(7\text{-}3) \quad \lambda\left(L_{if}, L_f\right) \approx \lambda_1\left(L_{if}, L_f\right) + \lambda_2\left(L_{if}, L_f\right) \text{ for } \left(L_{if} + L_f\right) \in \left[\underline{L}, \overline{L}\right]$$

$$0 \text{ if } \left(L_{if} + L_f\right) > \overline{L}.$$

In other words, firms behave as if there was some level of employment $\underline{L}$ below which the probability of being fined is extremely remote or, de facto, zero and equally as if there was a level of employment $\overline{L}$ above which the probability of being fined is almost certain or, de facto, one. $\underline{L}$ and $\overline{L}$ are not written in any law and change according to place, time, and type of activity. On the basis of table 7-2, $\underline{L}$ is around seven workers, but if the firm is in agriculture in a relatively faraway region, it may be thirty; on the other hand, if the firm is in Mexico City and is in manufacturing, it may be around five. At the other extreme, $\overline{L}$ is a number around 100, but if the firm is in agriculture it may be 250, and if the firm is in manufacturing it is probably 75.

Expression 7-3 also tries to capture the fact that the probability of being fined depends on the interaction between the total number of workers in the firm and the proportion of legal to illegal workers. A firm with seventy-five workers is more exposed to IMSS than a firm with sixty, but if seventy of the seventy-five workers in the first firm are legal and only five are illegal, while fifty of the sixty workers in the second firm are illegal and only ten are legal, the second firm is more likely to be fined than the first (see appendix 8).[20]

20. Firms look at other firms engaged in a similar type of activity for reference. What a firm's competitors are doing is very important because it tells the firm about its labor costs vis-à-vis theirs and about their willingness to bear risk. Firms cooperate and compete: if all firms in a line of activity cheat in similar ways, they are operating within the social norms and will protect each other (lobby jointly against IMSS and SAT, and so on). If a given firm is an outlier and cheats too much, other firms may denounce it to IMSS because its excessive illegality gives it an unfair advantage. Standards are a function of the business cycle: in hard times it is accepted and even expected that firms will cheat a little bit more, while in better times they are expected to cheat less. As a result, IMSS is expected to be laxer in tough times. IMSS knows that and adapts its behavior as well.

Figure 7-5. *Illegal Employment, Firm Size, and the Marginal Cost of Salaried Labor*

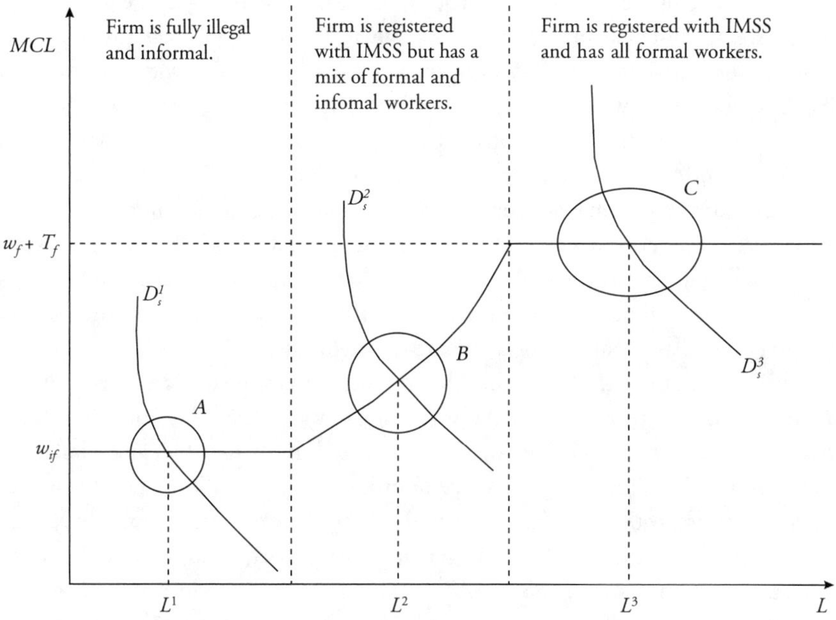

Source: Author's analysis.

## Firm Size and the Cost of Salaried Labor

Figure 7-5 provides a stylized description of the marginal costs of labor faced by firms hiring salaried workers in Mexico. As before, illegal workers get a wage of $w_{if}$; the average cost to firms of illegal workers is $[w_{if} + \lambda(.)F]$ and the marginal cost is $[w_{if} + \lambda(.)F + \lambda'(.)FL_{if}]$. Legal workers get a wage of $w_f$, and the average and marginal cost of a legal worker to the firm is $(w_f + T_f)$. Workers' utilities are equalized along the lines of the discussion at the beginning of this chapter. Three individual firm demand curves for salaried labor are included, which represent the value of the marginal product or the value of the marginal revenue product, depending on whether evasion of profit taxes is considered; I leave that vague to avoid focusing on SAT at this stage. I label the curves $D_s^1$ to $D_s^3$, drawn for given output prices and stocks of capital $K^1$ to $K^3$. I refer to the neighborhood of the points where those curves intersect the marginal cost of labor curve, drawing circles A, B, and C around them. That classification should be interpreted as a heuristic attempt to capture the context of microenterprises and small, medium-size, and large firms with capital and employment levels that cannot be pinned down with precision.

Two features of figure 7-5 are especially relevant. One is the distance between the vertical dotted lines at the points where the marginal cost of labor is positively sloped; appendix 8 shows that the points are close to $\underline{L}$ and $\overline{L}$. As shown immediately below, that distance determines the existence of an intermediate range of firms that are formal in the sense of being registered with IMSS but that hire some illegal workers. If the distance was very small, that range would disappear and the marginal-cost-of-labor curve in figure 7-5 would look like a two-step line with a jump given by the distance between $w_{if}$ and $(w_f + T_f)$.[21] But in Mexico that is not the case; as inferred from figure 7-3, the distance is about seventy to eighty workers.

The second feature is the distance between $w_{if}$ and $(w_f + T_f)$, which determines the maximum savings in labor costs realized through evasion. Given the wage comparisons in chapter 5, which show that for low-wage workers who move between the formal and the informal sector $w_{if} \approx w_f$, that distance is approximately equivalent to 35 percent of $w_{if}$, which is clearly significant and especially so for firms in which labor costs are an important share of total costs.

Firms with capital in the neighborhood of $K^1$ generating demand for labor like $D_s^1$ hire around $L^1$ workers, all of whom most likely are illegal; $L^1$ is anywhere from two to six and maybe up to nine workers (although in small urban and rural areas the number is higher). Those are the approximately 2 million small firms and microenterprises captured in table 7-2, which in practice operate completely outside the official governance mechanisms that apply to salaried labor because the probability of being fined by IMSS or SAT is extremely remote. Most of the firms are not registered with IMSS or any other authority. They also save on registration costs, and they may pay higher transaction costs in the sense argued by Coase, discussed in chapter 2, with suboptimal levels of vertical integration; however, that is practically impossible to measure. Call them fully illegal and informal firms.

Firms with capital in the neighborhood of $K^2$ hire around $L^2$ workers, composed of a mix of legal and illegal workers. Such firms—of which, according to table 7-2, there are around 270,000—are registered with IMSS (and probably with SAT and other authorities) and in that sense they are formal, but they comply only partly with social security regulations. As elaborated on below, at that level of employment firms optimally mix legal and illegal workers so that the expected marginal costs of a legal and an illegal worker are always equal to their marginal productivity (which is equal). *That implies that in the same firm there are formal and informal workers, some paid $w_f$ and getting social security coverage and some paid $w_{if}$ and getting social protection coverage, but both equally productive.* That also implies that the firms are larger, as measured by the number of workers, than the IMSS registries show. IMSS registries in table 7-2 show, for example, a firm having thirty workers when the firm has thirty-five or forty.

---

21. That jump would generate a discontinuity whereby for a range of shifts in demand firms do not change output and employment. The interesting observation is that the discontinuity derives not from an inherent nonconvexity in the technology but from the response of firms to a zero-one sanctioning behavior by IMSS: if they hire up to $\underline{L} = \bar{L}$ workers, they will not be audited, but if they hire one more, they certainly will.

Finally, firms with capital in the neighborhood of $K^3$ employ around $L^3$ workers, all legal; such firms are large (at least by Mexican standards), and they are registered with IMSS and SAT and other authorities. According to table 7-2, there were about 35,000 of those firms in 2006, setting their output and employment levels unbiased by concerns of illegality.

What determines such outcomes? There are many reasons, but I highlight one that I believe is central. In some activities, indivisibilities in capital requirements imply that the associated demand for labor cannot be substantially below $D_s^3$, as for firms with capital stock like $K^3$ and employment levels like $L^3$ in figure 7-5. Given the probability of being fined, as shown in expression 7-3, *the firm always chooses to be formal because being informal means that the firm most likely will be fined, thereby increasing its labor costs.* Think of automobile or steel production; in those activities there are no informal firms and no illegal salaried workers. Even if an automobile or a steel firm wanted to be small in order to evade the law, it could not be because the technology involved would not allow it to be small *relative to the probabilities of being fined given in expression 7-3.* Automobile firms cannot, so to speak, break $K^3$ into a number of smaller K's to produce cars in various plants with fewer workers, unseen by IMSS and SAT; even if the technology allowed them to do so, the transaction costs would be prohibitive. *For firms in such activities the marginal costs of labor relevant to them are constant and informality is not a consideration.* At the margin, their decisions are not affected by the official governance mechanisms that apply to salaried labor.

Circumstances require those firms to adopt a different logic: they do not invest any time in hiding from the IMSS and SAT inspectors, and their accounting is clear and organized. Some would call the firms "structured." They have access to formal sources of credit; they devote time and resources to technology adoption and innovation; and they train their workers and invest in firm-specific assets.[22]

But in some activities, indivisibilities in capital requirements imply output and employment levels that, relative to the probabilities of being fined given in expression 7-3, sometimes make some illegality a profitable option. Activities requiring capital like $K^2$ and generating demand for labor like $D_s^2$, as in figure 7-5, fit into that category. Firms engaged in those activities exhibit various degrees of compliance with the law. They are formal in the sense of being registered with IMSS and other authorities, and they may have access to formal sources of credit, but they hire various proportions of legal and illegal workers. The technology for such activities permits firms of various sizes to coexist, producing goods that are very close substitutes for each other or even the same—think of construction, agriculture, light manufacturing (toys, furniture, food preparation

22. Firms' investment in worker training is aided by the fact that most workers in such firms show little mobility.

and processing, textiles, apparel), some modes of transportation and distribution, and services in general.

There are large restaurant chains that have many employees, and there are many small restaurants that have only a few employees. There are large tortilla factories with hundreds of workers making tortillas, and there are small tortilla mills making tortillas with two to three employees. There are large construction companies building housing developments with hundreds if not thousands of workers and small construction companies building houses with a few workers. There are large agricultural firms with hundreds of hectares and thousands of workers picking tomatoes for sale in large supermarket chains, and there are smaller firms with ten-hectare plots with twenty to thirty workers who pick tomatoes for sale in the same supermarkets. Finally, there are large transportation companies with hundreds of employees moving cargo from one place in Mexico to another with a fleet of fifty to 100 trucks, and there are small transportation companies with two or three trucks that also move cargo from one place to another. The circumstances of $[K^2, L^2]$-type firms make it logical to invest some time in evading IMSS and SAT inspectors. They keep clear accounts for the inspectors to see, and they keep clearer accounts that they make sure the inspectors do not see. Such firms face increasing marginal costs of labor. Their average labor costs are somewhere between $w_{if}$ and $(w_f + T_f)$; as a result, they may obtain savings of, say, 20 to 30 percent of their labor costs by not running a completely legal operation. In the context of fierce international competition, that may make all the difference in a firm's survival.

Finally, for firms in the neighborhood of $K^1$ engaged in activities with no indivisibilities in capital requirements, informality and illegality is the most profitable option most of the time.[23] Such firms are fully illegal, and all of their six or seven workers are unregistered. These are the hundreds of thousands of firms represented in the Inegi column of table 7-2 and absent in the IMSS column. In small ranges, the firms face constant marginal costs of labor. A small entrepreneur operating a fruit juice stand on a corner in Mexico City with two assistants is not deterred from hiring a third by the effect of the additional assistant on the expected costs of those already hired as the business's exposure to IMSS and SAT increases. The same is true of the entrepreneur who hires three women illegally to make jeans with old sewing machines in the garage of his house; if demand expands, he can hire one or two more women at wages $w_{if}$ without worrying too much about the effects of that decision on his chances of being caught by IMSS or SAT (and in the worst-case scenario, he can always try to bribe the officials!). *But that is true only for small levels of output or employment.*

---

23. McKenzie and Woodruff (2003), using detailed data from the Encuesta Nacional de Micronegocios (ENAMIN), a special survey of microenterprises in Mexico, rules out the existence of nonconvexities in the production function that can serve as barriers to entry to the activities in which the firms engage (commerce, distribution, construction, services, and small manufacturing).

Firm owners have clear accounts of their business: they know who owes them money and whom they owe money, but that information is not kept in a computer spreadsheet managed with the latest accounting software because it is not necessary to do so. And if that structure makes the job of IMSS and SAT inspectors impossible, well, so much the better. The firms might appear simple, but that may be because the balance between vertical integration and arm's-length, market-mediated transactions tilts toward reduced vertical integration without making production unprofitable.

Reduced vertical integration implies that the scope of operations is limited. Firms in the $[K^1, L^1]$ range produce jeans and sports clothes, for instance, but they do not distribute them directly to large retailers or consumers. Rather, they sell their output to a separate firm, probably in the $[K^2, L^2]$ range, that concentrates the production of many small firms. The second firm may add a trademark to the clothes and sell them to a third firm, perhaps in the $[K^3, L^3]$ range, that also makes jeans and sports clothes, and the third firm sells the combined output to large retailers or exports it directly. In the end, the exporting firm is outsourcing some of its production to $[K^1, L^1]$ firms to minimize production costs indirectly by taking advantage of those firms' lower labor costs, even though the outsourcing is carried out through an intermediary, medium-size firm.

In the absence of all the distortions induced by the formal-informal dichotomy, perhaps the three types of firms—the micro $[K^1, L^1]$-type firms making jeans, the $[K^2, L^2]$-type firm buying jeans from many $[K^1, L^1]$-type firms and selling them to a $[K^3, L^3]$-type firm, and the $[K^3, L^3]$-type firm itself—would be a single firm. But all the transportation and transaction costs of suboptimal vertical integration might still be dominated by a 30 to 40 percent savings on labor costs and some other savings on registration costs. All the firms are maximizing private profits by evading formality through various mechanisms to spread and minimize the risk of detection and fines. All are very efficient at what they do, but clearly, from an economic point of view, they are incurring many costs that in the absence of the formal-informal dichotomy would not exist.[24]

The foregoing does not mean that all small firms in Mexico are illegal. As table 7-2 shows, 533,891 firms with up to five employees are registered with IMSS (of a total of 2,699,400).[25] The analysis here fails to capture other determinants of a firm's decision to be legal or not. A small firm might choose to be legal even if it has only five employees because it wants to supply goods or services to a government agency and can only do so if it has compliance certificates from IMSS and SAT, or because it wants to access a government-subsidized credit

---

24. The example above was related to the author by direct participants in the textile and garment industry in the state of Puebla; a similar model seems to apply in other industries, for example, toy manufacturing.

25. But note that many of the registered firms probably have more employees.

program. Many other possibilities exist. The labor costs that firms face are a critical determinant of their choices with regard to size and legal status, but they are not the only ones.

### Interaction between Social Programs and Firm Size and Legal Status

$[K^1, L^1]$-type firms and, overlapping them, $[K^2, L^2]$-type firms are very important in Mexico, for social and economic reasons. These firms are more fragile when exposed to exogenous shocks than $[K^3, L^3]$-type firms; they have the highest labor turnover and invest the least in job training and technology adoption (as discussed further in chapter 8). Their illegal status shuts them off from formal sources of credit. The workers that they hire are the ones who move the most between formal and informal employment, shown in the low-wage column of figure 5-4 in chapter 5. An individual $[K^1, L^1]$- or $[K^2, L^2]$-type firm is irrelevant, but in the aggregate, the firms are extremely relevant. As a result of their illegal behavior, more than 8 million workers are left without social security coverage, thwarting the government's social objectives.

Social norms and societal tolerance of illegality, in particular with respect to noncompliance with the official governance mechanisms that apply to salaried labor, matter for productivity. Those norms have complex origins, but they are not static; they evolve. Whether they evolve toward increasing tolerance or intolerance for illegality also matters for productivity. *I argue that social programs are factors that affect social norms.* I have shown that social protection programs facilitate evasion because, for given probabilities of being fined, they increase the gains from evasion; it pays to break the law a little bit more because the expected gains are higher.

But there is another side to that. *Social protection programs affect those probabilities.* The parameters of expression 7-3 are not exogenous. Social protection programs make evasion of social security more palatable from a social point of view and reduce political pressure to fight evasion. That is because workers who are not covered by social security are not as bad off as they might have been because now they have at least some social benefits. That may make it more difficult for IMSS, Infonavit, and the Labor Ministry to enforce the law and may explain why evading firms hiring salaried workers are in favor of social protection and want it extended: evasion becomes less risky; therefore more of it can occur.

An example of that view is found among the agricultural producers in the states of Sinaloa, Sonora, and the Baja California peninsula in northwest Mexico, who are large employers of *jornaleros agrícolas.* They hire salaried workers, and in principle they should be opposed to the implicit subsidy for firms hiring nonsalaried workers associated with social protection because the subsidy pushes the formal wage rate higher. Yet those producers, who also are large evaders, want social protection programs extended. From their point of view, when social protection programs exist, $[(w_{if} + \lambda F)]$ is the average cost of their illegal workers, who have a utility of $(w_{if} + \beta_i T_i)$, not the utility of $w_{if}$ that they would have without the programs. Moreover, with the programs, perhaps the parameters of $\lambda(.)$ in expression 7-3 can be modified, facilitating a little more evasion. Their workers are better off practically free of cost to them (and if the workers miss fewer days of work because they are healthier, so much the better). It is as if they had shifted part of their labor costs to the government.

It is common knowledge that although not all *jornaleros agrícolas* are poor, the vast majority are. Yet the government's commitment to enforcing the law among those workers is lower than with others. Despite lacking the legal authority to do so, the president has signed decrees reducing the social security contributions that workers and firms in agricultural activities must pay to IMSS.[26] Social norms with regard to the tolerance of illegality are more lax in agriculture than in other sectors not only because of the tacit association of agriculture with an activity that is strategic for national development and the incorrect association of agriculture with poverty but also because, *despite the fact that there is a large salaried agricultural labor force with full entitlement to social security, social norms associate social security with urban workers.* There are approximately 2 million *jornaleros agrícolas* in Mexico, all salaried, but as detailed in appendix 4, fewer than 250,000 are registered with IMSS.

More generally, social norms regarding tolerance of illegality with respect to poor workers are looser than those with respect to non-poor workers. As a result, firms hiring poor workers perceive lower probabilities of detection (that is, lower $\lambda$'s) when they hire poor workers, and so they evade more. That factor adds to the greater incentives that poor workers already have to evade IMSS: not only are their $\beta_f$'s lower and their $\beta_i$'s higher, but $\lambda$ also is lower. *In Mexico the interaction of social programs and social norms makes poor illegal workers relatively cheaper than non-poor illegal workers.*

Government officials in charge of promoting small and microenterprises also promote social protection programs without expressly recognizing that evasion of social security and low-productivity employment are being fostered along with them. The argument is that those firms need help in the face of increasing foreign competition and that social security is a luxury that they cannot afford. In their view, social protection programs provide a solution to the dilemma of workers' need for social benefits, on one hand, and the need for "job creation," on the other. Legal issues might be a minor technicality in that context, and the question of who pays for social protection programs lies beyond their realm of responsibility— that's for officials in the Finance Ministry to worry about. Yet, as the policy of promoting social protection programs for workers in microenterprises and small

---

26. Social security contributions are set by Congress in the Social Security Law and cannot be changed by presidential decree, yet that was done in 1998, 2006, and 2007.

firms is carried out, the Social Security Law and the Federal Labor Law are still on the books. But when government officials behave—de facto if not de jure—as if the official governance mechanisms that apply to salaried labor do not really apply to small firms, the outcome is the expansion of societal tolerance for illegality, more informality, and reduced productivity.

And, of course, government officials in charge of housing, health, and social development directly promote social protection programs. There are millions of informal workers without social security coverage, and whether or not that is the result of an illegal act is irrelevant to those officials. Their responsibility is to provide housing, health and day care services, and, if possible, pensions to workers and families not covered by IMSS, Infonavit, and the Afores. The fact that as social protection programs are enhanced or new ones are introduced productivity diminishes and evasion is further subsidized is not their concern. Their thinking is that the programs need to be in place until the day when all informal workers become formal—they do not recognize that their actions contribute directly to making it increasingly unlikely that that day will ever arrive.

Firms interpret all such measures as a soft government commitment to workers' rights and to the rule of law, government rhetoric notwithstanding. Sooner or later they internalize the fact that the dividing line between salaried workers and *comisionistas* shifts in favor of *comisionistas;* that the government is channeling an increasing amount of resources to social protection programs; and that instead of just winking at a little illegal activity by small and medium-size firms, the government is turning a half-blind eye to it. In other words, societal tolerance for illegality increases when the government promotes it, and over time $\lambda$ adjusts, the margin for informality increases, and labor productivity decreases.

It is useful to return for a moment to the discussion of the redistributive purposes of wage-based social security contributions presented in chapter 6. Although it is difficult to document, having "bosses" pay for the social security of "their workers" probably derives from the impression that most firms in Mexico are of the $[K^3, L^3]$-type in figure 7-5. Table 7-2 shows that that is not the case. Most firms in Mexico are of the $[K^1, L^1]$-type, and in many cases, the income of the "bosses" in such firms is not really much different from that of "their workers"; in some cases the "boss" and the "worker" are the same person or close relatives. What income could be redistributed from profits to wages in the hundreds of thousands of $[K^1, L^1]$-type firms?

*Most firms in Mexico cannot redistribute profits to wages in the sense that the Federal Labor Law, the Infonavit Law, and the Social Security Law want them to be redistributed.* And the legal attempts to do so are counterproductive, good intentions notwithstanding. Firms stay small and continue to evade; there is less innovation, adoption of technology, and labor training; workers end up without social security; aggregate output is less; and wages are lower. And, in that context, the attempt to provide salaried workers with substitute social protection benefits turns into a mechanism to subsidize and deepen that sad state of affairs. It is not, as with the Spanish viceroy in colonial Mexico, a case of "observe but do not comply"; it is a case of "observe and subsidize noncompliance."

## Informality and the Demand for Legal and Illegal Labor

What determines the combination of formal and informal workers within a firm? Figure 7-6 helps to answer that question, and appendix 8 provides further details. The upper panel depicts the marginal cost of labor faced by the firm. It also shows, for the same capital stock, two different demand curves for labor as a result of two different output prices, $p_1^w$ and $p_2^w$. The lower panel divides the level of employment given by the intersection of the MCL and the demand for labor into legal and illegal workers. The horizontal axis measures total employment $L$ and coincides with the horizontal axis of the upper panel; note that in both $\underline{L}$ is shown, which, from expression 7-3, is the number of workers below which firms consider the probability of being fined for hiring illegal workers to be zero. The vertical axis measures $L_f$ and $L_{if}$, and, by means of a 45 degree line, I ensure that $L = L_f + L_{if}$.

It is intuitive that if the firm employs fewer than $\underline{L}$ workers they are all illegal. As a result, in the lower panel up to $\underline{L}$, the demand for illegal workers coincides with the total demand for labor along the 45 degree line, and in the upper panel, the MCL of up to $\underline{L}$ workers is given by $w_{if}$. For employment levels higher than $\underline{L}$, the probabilities of being fined are positive and increase with the number of illegal workers hired; firms therefore increase employment by hiring some legal workers as well. In the upper panel, that translates into increasing MCL; in the lower panel, it translates into positive values for $L_f$ given by the difference between the 45 degree line and the inverted U-shaped curve, which depicts the demand for illegal labor. More generally, as employment expands, further illegal workers become relatively more expensive than legal workers (since the probability of being fined, $\lambda$, increases), and the proportion of legal to illegal workers shifts in favor of legal workers. In fact, when total employment is close to $\bar{L}$ (not shown), the probability of being fined is very close to unity and illegal workers are more expensive than legal workers, at which point the firm hires only legal workers. Accordingly, in the upper panel the MCL is given by $(w_f + T_f)$, with the firm facing constant marginal costs of labor after that point.

The most interesting aspect of figure 7-6 lies in the increasing range of the MCL, where I show two different equilibriums. The first is $E^1$ for given output prices $p_1^w$, with a total of $L^1$ workers employed by the firm, of which $L_{if}^1$ are illegal and $L_f^1$ legal. With a positive output shock, $p_2^w > p_1^w$, the firm expands total employment to $L^2$, made up of $L_f^2$ legal and $L_{if}^2$ illegal workers. What the figure makes clear is that the increase in legal workers exceeds the increase in employment, because as the firm expands, the optimal combination of legal and illegal workers shifts in favor of legal workers. That implies that when employment increases as a result of a positive

Figure 7-6. *Demand for Legal and Illegal Labor*

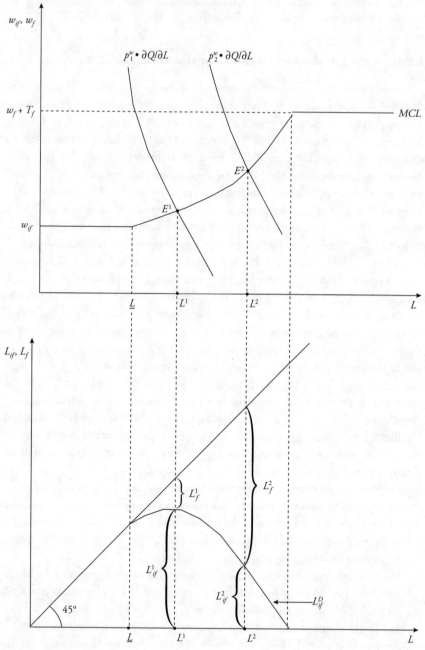

shock for firms in the range in which the marginal costs of labor are increasing, illegal workers within the firm are converted into legal workers. In other words, *the increase in formal employment registered by IMSS overstates the increase in salaried employment.*

Now consider the reverse, that is, a negative output shock. Assume $E^2$ is the initial equilibrium in the upper panel, with $L^2$ workers in the firm (although IMSS registries show only $L_f^2$ workers in the firm). Output prices fall from $p_2^w$ to $p_1^w$, the equilibrium shifts to $E^1$, and the firm adjusts employment to $L^1$. Firms absorb the shock partly by increasing the level of evasion as the demand for illegal workers increases, and the fall in legal workers is more than proportional to the fall in employment. In other words, *the fall in formal employment when there is a negative output shock overstates the fall in salaried employment.*

Figure 7-6 also suggests a different adjustment mechanism for responding to output shocks for microenterprises and small firms with up to $\underline{L}$ workers and for large firms with more than $\overline{L}$ workers. In both cases, output shocks translate one to one into changes in employment as firms face constant marginal costs of labor. But in the case of microenterprises and small firms, all the changes are absorbed by illegal workers and therefore would never be captured in the IMSS registries. In the case of large firms, all the changes are absorbed by legal workers and therefore are fully captured by the IMSS registries.

Two further remarks are useful. One, there is a difference between firms' expected labor costs and market wage rates, and for $[K^2, L^2]$-type firms the former can change even if the latter are constant as the mix of legal and illegal workers changes in response to shocks. Two, depending on the impact of a shock and its distribution across small, medium-size, and large firms, the change in IMSS employment registries may or may not provide a reasonable approximation of what is occurring to salaried employment in response to that shock. On the whole, the analysis suggests that changes in formal employment overstate changes in salaried employment. Figure 7-6 depicts a one-time price change in output prices, but as I show in the next chapter, the analysis extends to investments that augment the firm's capital stock and also shift the demand for labor. The kind of firm that is investing is an important determinant of the impact of firms' investments on formal and informal employment.[27]

27. This analysis is relevant for the interpretation of IMSS employment statistics. Every month IMSS publishes the change in the number of registered workers, which often is interpreted as the number of "jobs created" that month. The discussion indicates that some of the jobs were already there and were only "converted" from unregistered to registered. The expression "job creation," although very common, is largely misleading in a context like Mexico's, where the open unemployment rate is very low and most workers have a job. Public policies do not "create jobs"; they change the distribution of workers among various types of jobs. If jobs registered with IMSS is the desideratum of the government, then the policy issue is to convert unregistered salaried jobs and nonsalaried jobs to registered jobs. That is not a semantic issue; as elaborated on in chapters 9 and 10, it matters for policy design.

The formal, semi-formal, or informal status of firms matters for productivity. Four points are relevant here:

—In some cases a mix of legal and illegal workers engage in the same activities and sometimes work in the same firm.

—Firms with a mix of legal and illegal workers face increasing marginal costs of labor, so that for them hiring more workers and increasing output is, at the margin, more costly than for fully formal firms or fully informal firms.

—Within a firm, legal and illegal workers have the same productivity.

—Goods that are close substitutes or even the same goods are produced by firms of various sizes, with similar workers having different productivities.

As a result, first, the marginal productivity of salaried labor ranges from a low of $w_{if}$, where it coincides with the productivity of nonsalaried labor, to a high of $(w_f + T_f)$; second, the average of the marginal productivities of labor depends on the distribution of salaried workers across firms. *The greater the proportion of workers employed in informal or semi-illegal firms, the lower the average.*

This analysis provides a more nuanced picture of the determinants of labor productivity in the context of the formal-informal dichotomy than the one that emerges from chapter 6. At that point, all the differences in labor productivity were between salaried and nonsalaried workers, not among salaried workers. However, in the context of large evasion, as in Mexico, there is a continuum of labor productivities. Some salaried workers can be as unproductive as nonsalaried ones, while other salaried workers with similar abilities are more productive. Equally important, the average productivity of salaried labor in the economy is not independent of the size distribution of firms.

## Firm Size, Private Efficiency, and Productivity

*The analysis above does not mean that small firms are inefficient and large firms efficient.* All firms maximize profits. In particular, given their production function and capital stock, all hire workers up to the point that the value *to the firm* of the marginal product (or revenue product) of labor is equal to the expected marginal cost of labor *to the firm* (including the contingent costs of illegality). The productivity losses analyzed here do not arise because entrepreneurs in small firms are on average less able or competent than entrepreneurs in large firms. From the private point of view, large and small firms are equally efficient. The inefficiency analyzed here takes the form of lower aggregate labor productivity and therefore lower aggregate output. The same workers allocated differently between the same firms would produce more aggregate output and earn higher real wages. But precisely because all firms maximize profits, that cannot be observed, unless the cost of labor to firms was different from that associated with the formal-informal dichotomy.

In the analysis of the implications of the size distribution of firms for productivity, *it is essential to sharply separate private from social assessments.* Analyzing the dynamics of microenterprises in a recent report on informality, the World Bank stated that "young and small firms do tend to have higher costs and high failure rates and, at the same time, they are more likely to be informal. Although this description corresponds exactly to the standard picture of the stagnant, precarious, unprotected informal self-employment sector familiar in the literature, it is, in fact, the opposite. It emerges naturally from workers trying their luck as entrepreneurs (risk taking), often failing, and not engaging in the formal institutions until they grow. In sum, there may be nothing *pathological* [emphasis added] about the informal microfirm sector, and its existence may be largely unrelated to questions of labor market dualism or even credit market distortions."[28]

My point is that while there is nothing pathological from a private point of view when microenterprises and small firms maximize profits, the phenomenon is nonetheless "pathological" from a social point of view to the extent that firms' profitability rests on violating the laws that apply to salaried labor. It is pathological because, by their behavior, firms thwart the government's social objectives and reduce GDP (and, as shown in chapter 8, the rate of growth of GDP).

Informality does not mean that entrepreneurs are sloppy or inefficient; it just means that the labor allocation and output level derived from the aggregation of the individual actions of workers and private entrepreneurs in small, medium-size, and large firms are socially suboptimal. In other words, linking informality with low labor productivity does not require making any special assumptions about entrepreneurs on the basis of firm size or legal status. In the analysis in this chapter, no such assumptions were introduced. The only critical assumption is that differences in the indivisibilities of capital across activities associated with the nature of the production function in each activity imply that, relative to the probabilities of being fined and punished by the authorities, some firms find it profitable to hire more illegal salaried workers than others. The link is formed through differences in wage rates and the non-wage costs of labor, which by and large are exogenous to firms, which on that basis decide whether to be formal or not and determine the optimal mix of legal and illegal workers.

### Informality and Registration Costs

I end this section with some remarks on registration costs. *A distinction needs to be drawn between the marginal cost of labor and the marginal cost of output.* As seen in figure 7-5, unless $\underline{L}$ and $\overline{L}$ are the same, the curve representing the marginal cost of labor to firms is continuous and allows, so to speak, for a smooth transition between

---

28. World Bank (2007, pp. 139–40).

complete informality, semi-informality, and full formality as employment expands. But the firm's change from illegal to legal status might involve one-time registration costs and perhaps higher costs of intermediate inputs (for example, electricity, if it is no longer stolen from the grid or if it has to be paid for at the industrial and not the residential rate), which in turn might generate a discontinuity in the marginal cost of output curve. If so, $[K^1, L^1]$ firms might need to experience a large and sustained expansion in the demand for their output relative to their size to grow and become formal, which would require them to register at least some of their workers with IMSS in the early phases of their lives as $[K^2, L^2]$ firms.

As shown in Bruhn (2006) and Kaplan, Piedra, and Seira (2006), registration costs affect the behavior of firms in Mexico. The World Bank–International Finance Corporation finds that the cost of setting up a business varies significantly across Mexican states but that "even the best Mexican states are not internationally competitive in some indicators—18 days for property registration in Aguascalientes and 21 days in Sonora and Zacatecas compare poorly with Thailand, where it only takes 2 days. Another interesting comparison is that of Mexican states versus their regional competitors in Brazil. In general, Mexican states have faster procedures. However, doing business is generally more expensive in Mexico. A Brazilian firm must pay on average 10–13 percent of GDP per capita to open a business while the same type of firm in Mexico has to pay 20.4 percent. In addition, Mexican companies have to put up minimum capital, while their competitors in Brazil do not."[29] Since per capita GDP in Mexico was US$7,319 in 2006, that implies that registration costs are approximately US$1,493 or 16,423 pesos, which is a considerable sum, equivalent to almost eleven times the monthly minimum wage. That may help explain the very large number of illegal firms in Mexico in the range of up to two workers shown in table 7-2.

Those remarks highlight the complementarity between the de Soto "property rights–induced" informality and the "social programs–induced" informality analyzed in this volume. In the move from legality to illegality, registration costs are crucial. If they are large enough, they might serve to lock some firms into illegal status. However, after firms become legal in the sense of registering with the authorities, there are further obstacles to their growth because their marginal and average labor costs increase, in some contexts quite steeply. That also can serve to lock firms in informality. From the point of view of a subset of firms, it is important to solve the property rights problems and registration cost issues that de Soto has called attention to, but the point that I want to make is that for that subset of firms, as well as for the subset of firms that are registered but still engage in evasion, it is critical to remove the distortions in the labor market highlighted here, which are obstacles to increasing productivity.

---

29. World Bank–International Finance Corporation (2006, pp. 1–2).

Figure 7-7. *Informal Employment and the Composition of Output*

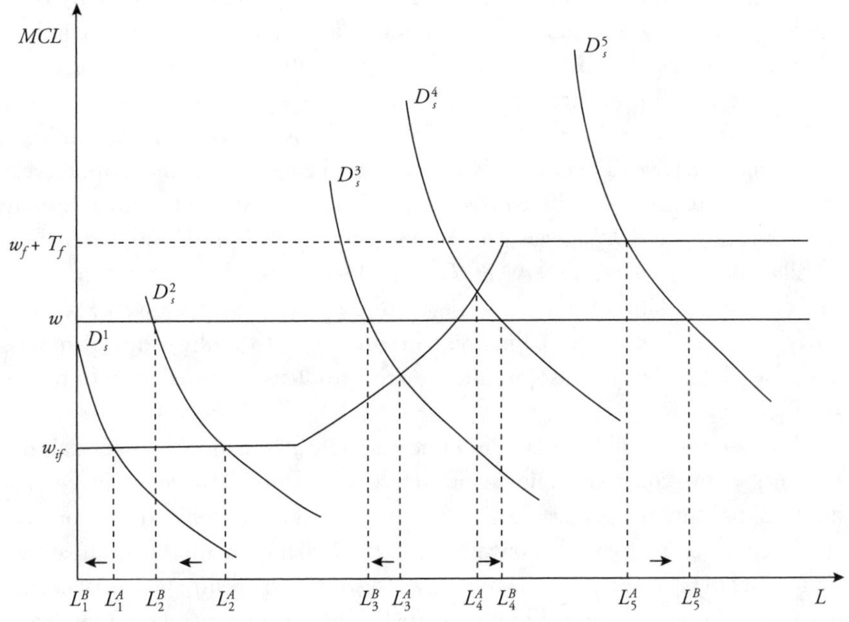

Source: Author's analysis.

## Informality and the Composition of Output

*Informality changes the relative profitability of activities.* Activities whose production technology places them in the neighborhood of point C in figure 7-5 face higher *average* labor costs than those at point B, which in turn face higher average labor costs than those at point A. The marginal costs of labor also are different. There are two effects. First, given output prices and all other parameters, the allocation of resources flows into activities with lower labor costs. In other words, the country's output mix tilts toward "informality prone" activities, meaning activities in which capital indivisibilities and the technology of production relative to the probabilities of punishment in expression 7-3 make some evasion profitable. Second, within activities the allocation of resources tilts toward firms that can best exploit the advantages of informality.

Figure 7-7 illustrates those two effects, comparing the situation denoted by superscript A, in which social programs make the costs to firms of salaried labor range from $w_{if}$ to $(w_f + T_f)$, with the hypothetical situation denoted by superscript B, in which there is a single wage rate for all salaried labor, either because social security programs are fully valued and there are no social protection programs or because there are universal social benefits funded without wage-based contributions (as in the proposal in chapter 10). It is important to note from the discussion in chapter 6 and earlier in this chapter that in such cases the wage rate paid by formal firms is lower and that paid by informal firms higher. That wage rate is denoted by w in figure 7-7; it is the one that clears the labor market in the simple general equilibrium setup presented before, when the allocation of labor is efficient. In figure 7-1, that wage rate is equivalent to $w_i^*$.

I drew the demand curves for labor for five firms of different size and legal status producing five different goods and compared employment and output levels in the two situations mentioned above. $D_s^1$ and $D_s^2$ correspond to fully informal firms hiring $L_1^A$ and $L_2^A$ illegal workers respectively and producing goods like tortillas and transportation services. $D_s^3$ and $D_s^4$ correspond to formal firms with a mix of legal and illegal workers hiring $L_3^A$ and $L_4^A$ workers respectively and producing, say, textiles and toys. Finally, $D_s^5$ corresponds to a fully formal firm hiring $L_5^A$ legal workers that also produces textile products. As usual, output prices are fixed.

Now assume that all firms face the same wage rate $w$ (situation B). Informal and fully illegal firms contract employment. In fact, at $w$, firm 1 closes down, given that it cannot produce tortillas at the higher labor costs; if the firm had three workers, an entrepreneurial boss and two workers, all three change to another occupation. That serves to make the point that for a given distribution of entrepreneurial talent, outcomes in terms of salaried or nonsalaried employment depend on wage rates. That point was discussed initially in chapter 6 with reference to self-employment, but it holds with respect to microenterprises too. According to table 7-2, there are at least 2 million entrepreneurs in Mexico owning firms with up to two workers. The question is how many of them would continue to be entrepreneurs if labor costs were, say, 20 percent higher than at present. Could they afford to hire workers? Would they still be entrepreneurs given that their opportunity cost of not being a salaried employee was higher?

Firm 2 does not close down, but it reduces output and employment (the latter to $L_2^B$). Perhaps the firm is in the business of moving cargo in a middle-size Mexican city, which it does with two old trucks. At labor cost $w_{if}$, it hired six employees, but at labor cost $w$, the firm keeps only four employees, and the other two find other occupations.

Firm 3, which produced shirts with, say, twenty workers, fourteen illegal and six registered with IMSS, also contracts because the lower labor costs for the workers that were legal in situation A are not offset by the higher labor costs for the workers that were illegal in situation A. The opposite occurs with firm 4, which produced toys with, say, fifty workers in total, forty registered in IMSS and ten unregistered. Savings on its legal workers more than offset the higher costs for its illegal workers, so the firm expands output and employment (perhaps hiring some of the workers laid off by the first three firms). Firm 5 saves fully on all its labor costs and expands production of textile products and employment.

In sum, changes in social programs change the composition of output. In the above examples, production of tortillas by a microenterprise disappears and transport with old trucks and production of textiles in small firms contract; on the other hand, production of toys and textiles in larger firms increases. The key point, however, is that *the output change is associated with increased average labor productivity* as workers relocate from small informal and illegal firms to medium-size and large formal firms.

Table 7-3 displays the distribution of firms in Mexico by size and activity, according to the 2003 census; table 7-4 displays the distribution of workers. In interpreting the tables it is useful to recall that firms carrying out their activities in the street or without fixed premises are excluded from the data and that agricultural and rural activities are excluded as well, as are all self-employed workers. That being said, it is noteworthy that in 2003, 1.2 million firms with up to two workers were in commerce and that an additional 0.6 million, also with up to two workers, were in services. Including firms with up to five workers brings *the number of firms in commerce and services to almost 2.4 million, or 79 percent of all firms in Mexico.*

It also is noteworthy that of all manufacturing firms, 58 percent had up to two employees and that an additional 25 percent had between three and five, so that *manufacturing firms with up to five employees made up 83 percent of all manufacturing firms.* It is difficult to believe that those firms, which are very small firms indeed, are fully exploiting the advantages of economies of scale or vertical integration.

Similar results occur in the transportation sector, in which 55 percent of all firms have up to two employees and an additional 17 percent have up to five. That fact is all the more relevant when one recalls that because Inegi excludes firms with mobile units, like taxis and buses for urban transport, they do not appear in tables 7-3 and 7-4. In other words, the firms included here are more in the business of transporting goods than people (although airline and interstate bus transportation companies are included).

Results in terms of employment are noteworthy as well. Table 7-4 shows, for instance, that manufacturing employment accounts for 25.6 percent of all employment by firms included in the census. But note that there are 581,613 manufacturing workers in 274,222 manufacturing firms of up to five employees, with an average number of 2.1 workers. Altogether there are 6.2 million workers in 2.8 million firms of up to ten employees, with an average firm size of 2.2 workers; at the other end, there are 7.4 million employees in 33,663 firms of fifty-one workers or more, with an average firm size of 220 workers. Average firm size for all firms listed in the census is 5.3 workers.

To be complete, the picture presented above needs to include information about self-employed workers and *comisionistas*. Unfortunately, there is no census of such workers, but as the previous quote from de Soto about ambulatory street vendors

Table 7-3. *Distribution of Firms by Size and Activity, 2003*[a]

| Size (number of workers) | Fishing | Mining | Manufacturing | Water and electricity | Construction | Commerce | Transportation | Services | Total |
|---|---|---|---|---|---|---|---|---|---|
| 0–2 | 14,050 | 1,014 | 190,692 | 417 | 1,435 | 1,204,644 | 23,009 | 682,877 | 2,118,138 |
| 3–5 | 2,077 | 643 | 83,530 | 674 | 1,625 | 271,223 | 7,229 | 214,261 | 581,262 |
| 6–10 | 1,348 | 446 | 24,456 | 536 | 2,027 | 57,998 | 4,083 | 62,997 | 153,891 |
| 11–15 | 818 | 247 | 7,405 | 189 | 1,660 | 16,798 | 1,839 | 18,645 | 47,601 |
| 16–20 | 588 | 139 | 3,995 | 99 | 1,169 | 8,231 | 1,057 | 9,083 | 24,361 |
| 21–30 | 784 | 166 | 4,205 | 129 | 1,575 | 8,002 | 1,313 | 8,997 | 25,171 |
| 31–50 | 748 | 146 | 4,124 | 114 | 1,399 | 5,969 | 1,317 | 7,110 | 20,927 |
| 51–100 | 524 | 112 | 3,814 | 103 | 1,262 | 4,007 | 1,099 | 5,179 | 16,100 |
| 101–250 | 272 | 77 | 3,357 | 67 | 854 | 2,682 | 611 | 2,978 | 10,898 |
| 251–500 | 40 | 26 | 1,620 | 29 | 276 | 862 | 192 | 984 | 4,029 |
| 501 and more | 3 | 26 | 1,424 | 80 | 162 | 171 | 150 | 620 | 2,636 |
| Total | 21,252 | 3,042 | 328,622 | 2,437 | 13,444 | 1,580,587 | 41,899 | 1,013,731 | 3,005,014 |

Source: Inegi, Censos Economicos 2004 (www.inegi.gob.mx).
a. Number of firms.

Table 7-4. Distribution of Workers by Firm Size and Activity, 2003[a]

| Size (number of workers) | Fishing | Mining | Manufacturing | Water and electricity | Construction | Commerce | Transportation | Services | Total |
|---|---|---|---|---|---|---|---|---|---|
| 0–2 | 18,086 | 1,375 | 278,448 | 623 | 2,090 | 1,721,570 | 30,442 | 959,268 | 3,011,902 |
| 3–5 | 7,416 | 2,443 | 303,165 | 2,646 | 6,378 | 956,144 | 26,830 | 773,001 | 2,078,023 |
| 6–10 | 10,544 | 3,454 | 180,478 | 4,029 | 15,869 | 423,227 | 31,002 | 466,418 | 1,135,021 |
| 11–15 | 10,555 | 3,177 | 93,926 | 2,438 | 21,338 | 212,728 | 23,486 | 236,739 | 604,387 |
| 16–20 | 10,457 | 2,505 | 70,985 | 1,768 | 20,925 | 146,405 | 18,823 | 161,873 | 433,741 |
| 21–30 | 19,709 | 4,184 | 104,888 | 3,185 | 39,317 | 198,421 | 32,770 | 224,537 | 627,011 |
| 31–50 | 29,261 | 5,695 | 161,018 | 4,393 | 54,223 | 230,205 | 51,949 | 275,985 | 812,729 |
| 51–100 | 35,497 | 7,829 | 273,922 | 7,189 | 88,586 | 282,078 | 76,088 | 364,419 | 1,135,608 |
| 101–250 | 38,754 | 11,433 | 529,562 | 10,161 | 129,895 | 417,623 | 93,646 | 452,666 | 1,683,740 |
| 251–500 | 14,037 | 8,751 | 567,973 | 10,623 | 94,122 | 282,209 | 65,296 | 336,521 | 1,379,532 |
| 501 and more | 2,166 | 25,142 | 1,571,485 | 174,280 | 179,644 | 126,756 | 178,969 | 941,186 | 3,199,628 |
| Total | 196,482 | 75,988 | 4,135,850 | 221,335 | 652,387 | 4,997,366 | 629,301 | 5,192,613 | 16,101,322 |

Source: Inegi, Censos Economicos 2004 (www.inegi.gob.mx).
a. Number of workers.

illustrates—and everyday experience on the streets of Mexico's cities confirms—most of them work in retail commerce, distribution, and services. So it is not the case, as could be inferred from table 7-4, that 4.4 million workers are engaged in commerce and services in informal establishments of up to five employees; to them one must add an indeterminate number of workers performing similar activities in the streets. Recall from table 5-1 that there are 11.8 million low-wage and poor self-employed workers and *comisionistas*. Many of them work in agriculture or in other rural activities, on plots of land and in firms of various sizes.[30] The majority, however, engage in all sorts of services and commercial activities in urban areas, many of them conducted on the street, with labor productivities that are not too different from those of the 6.2 million workers employed by firms of up to ten workers shown in table 7-4.

One cannot directly infer from table 7-4 that labor productivity is lower in smaller firms, nor, for the reasons given in chapter 6, can one infer productivity levels from a direct comparison of wage rates. The inference is indirect, based on the fact that firms' expected labor costs range from $w_{if}$ to $(w_f + T_f)$ and that the levels of evasion are significantly different across those firms, as shown in figures 7-3 and 7-4. What is certain is that

—there are many more workers who are self-employed or who work in small firms with a productivity of $w_{if}$ than there are workers in larger firms with a productivity of $(w_f + T_f)$

—on the basis of the comparisons of mean wage rates in chapter 5, the distance between $w_{if}$ and $(w_f + T_f)$ in the case of low-wage workers is about 35 percent of the formal wage, perhaps up to 40 percent

—there also exists a large number of workers with productivities within the range of $w_{if}$ to $(w_f + T_f)$, even though their wage rates are $w_{if}$

—workers with lower productivity concentrate in activities like commerce and services although they are spread out over all activities, including manufacturing

—at wages higher than $w_{if}$, most likely many of those workers would be employed in other activities or in other firms engaged in the same activities with higher labor productivity.[31]

In a context in which the marginal productivity of factors is equalized across activities, the composition of aggregate output is not very relevant. Labor and cap-

30. Unfortunately, lack of data precludes an across-activities analysis; therefore rural firms and workers are left out of tables 7-3 and 7-4. But the productivity problem is worse because, for the reasons given in the text, informality is higher in rural than in urban areas.

31. Duval (2006) observes a negative association between labor productivity and informal employment in Mexico. The author notes that sectors with the highest share of informal employment in total employment are also the sectors with the lowest productivity growth for the period 1988–2004. He finds that industries like financial services, mining, and electricity show constant and high rates of labor productivity growth, while industries like construction, personal services, agriculture, and commerce show practically stagnant labor productivity. Finally, he observes that after the 1994–95 crisis, the negative correlation between productivity growth and informality strengthened.

ital are equally productive in manufacturing, services, or construction. But when productivities are not equalized, the composition of output matters. It is illustrative in that context to quote from the McKinsey Global Institute study on productivity comparisons across countries, which is discussed in Lewis (2004): "Because productivity determines GDP per capita, the productivity of every worker matters. The average productivity of an entire economy is simply the average of the productivities of all workers. In today's rich countries, most workers work in service industries. Only about 20 to 25 percent work in manufacturing and about 5 percent in agriculture. That means the standard of living in the rich countries is determined primarily by the productivity of service industry workers. Thus, it's not high-tech workers in computers and biotechnology and it's not Wall Street. It's more the productivity of the massive number of workers in retailing, wholesaling, and construction that give the United States the highest GDP per capita in the world."[32] The point is that in Mexico the "massive number of workers in retailing, wholesaling, and construction" and, I would add, light manufacturing and transportation fail to contribute to giving Mexico "the highest GDP per capita in the world."[33]

I end this chapter with three remarks. First, I highlighted the incentives to informality created by social programs because labor costs are very important to most firms. That was not to argue that those incentives are the only cause of informality; as discussed at various points, registration costs and profit taxes also matter. But it was to argue that social programs strongly affect the shape of the marginal and the average cost curves of labor in ways that registration costs and profit taxes do not. *The informality caused by social programs is especially pernicious because it affects the cost of a fundamental non-traded input: labor.*

As figure 7-7 shows, in the absence of social programs–induced informality, all firms face the same marginal and average costs of labor regardless of capital indivisibilities or activities; the composition of aggregate output does not matter for productivity; the size distribution of firms is unaffected by social programs and fully reflects other factors that determine firm size: location, access to credit, the distribution of (unsubsidized) entrepreneurial talent, the optimal degree of vertical integration, economies of scale and scope, and so on. But in Mexico that is not the case. Illegality in the sense of evasion of the official governance mechanisms that apply to salaried labor and its effect on firm size are a direct result of the combination of social security and social protection programs. Even if there were no taxes on profits and no SAT and no registration costs, illegal

32. Lewis (2004, p. 10).
33. The arguments in favor of an active industrial policy in countries like Mexico need to be viewed in that light. In my view, the largest productivity (and welfare) gains would be achieved by focusing first on correcting the across-the-board distortions in behavior introduced by informality, which affect millions of workers and hundreds of thousands of firms. That is not to negate the existence of coordination failures or unexploited externalities that require targeted government intervention in specific activities but to weigh the relative importance of different policy reforms.

salaried employment would persist (in panel B of figure 7-2, the firm would be at point L, not E).[34]

Second, I focused only on firms hiring salaried labor. The size distribution of firms hiring *comisionistas* is unaffected by incentives to evade because they have no need to evade. One way to think about that in terms of the discussion in this chapter is to note that those firms also hire workers (although their remuneration is called a commission, not a wage) but that because of some special social norm, they act as if the probability of detection by IMSS is always equal to zero. In this case the social norm is, oddly, explicitly stated in the Federal Labor Law and the Social Security Law, which have established that *comisionistas* are not in a worker-boss relationship with their firm. In figure 7-5, such firms always hire workers at wages $w_i = w_{if}$, with constant marginal and average costs of labor at any level of employment. And for the same reasons discussed earlier, the output of goods and services produced by *comisionistas* also is subsidized. In Mexico, when users of cell phones stop at traffic lights, *comisionistas* associated with (hired by?) telephone companies approach their car window to sell them phone cards; *comisionistas* offer households health and beauty products and all sorts of services at their front door; and so on. There is a larger than socially optimal level of production of goods and services that require *comisionista* labor, and that also is a source of productivity loss.

The case of self-employment is similar, because overproduction of some goods and services is another source of productivity loss: too many workers in the streets washing windshields, too many people shining shoes, too many domestic servants, and so on.[35]

Finally, the framework explored here does not lend itself to a discussion of how informality affects the tradable/non-tradable composition of production because all output prices are assumed to be exogenously set by world prices. Yet one is tempted to make an association between informality and non-tradability to the extent that informality-prone activities tend to concentrate in services and commerce that by and large are non-traded. That association exists, but as shown, it is not strict. In Mexico there are many informal firms and workers producing tradable goods. But

34. More generally, the environment of illegality and the uncertain property rights associated with informality also affect the size distribution of firms. Using a sample of 70,000 firms from 107 countries, Aterido, Hallward-Driemer, and Pagés (2007) shows that microenterprises and small firms face greater interruptions in infrastructure services and pay more in bribes than larger firms and, more generally, that a weak business environment shifts the size distribution of firms downward.

35. Domestic servants are properly salaried workers: they are subordinated to a boss and receive a wage. Despite that, Mexico's Social Security Law makes an explicit exemption, treating them as if they were nonsalaried workers. There are approximately 2.2 million workers in this category, not registered with IMSS; see IMSS (2005, table 1.3, p. 22). In table 5-1, these workers were not included among evaders of social security. From a legal point of view, homeowners hiring domestic servants without registering them with IMSS are not evading the law, but the end result is that the vast majority of domestic servants are left without social security.

because labor costs differ across firms within the tradable sector, informality affects the composition of output in that sector, tilting it toward goods that require only simple technologies to produce, with few economies of scale, in firms with little vertical integration and reduced scope for innovation. One can hypothesize that the bias toward informality-prone activities within the tradeable sector acts as an obstacle to the international competitiveness of small and medium-size firms. However, the extent to which there is an association between informality and the pattern of exports and imports is left for further work.[36]

36. Chiquiar, Quella, and Ramos Francia (2006) analyzed the composition of Mexican exports over the period 1996–2004 and showed that Mexico was losing market share to Asian competitors as it continued to export unskilled labor–intensive goods while its competitors moved up the value chain. That, ex ante, appears consistent with the analysis here.

# 8

## Investment and Growth under Informality

This chapter focuses on the impact of social programs on the investment decisions of Mexican firms. I argue that the distortions introduced in the labor market by the formal-informal dichotomy spill over into the allocation of investment and reduce the productivity of capital even when there are no imperfections in the credit market; *as a result, the GDP growth rate is lower.* I also argue that social programs contribute to the persistence of informality and that economic growth per se will not eliminate it. Finally, I argue that when the growth path is characterized by persistent informality, it is unlikely that poor workers can access formal jobs with social security coverage even if, as a result of participation in Progresa-Oportunidades, they are healthier and better educated.

### Investment in the Formal and Informal Sectors

To focus sharply on the spillover from the labor market to the allocation of investment, I assume that the cost of credit to formal and informal firms in Mexico is the same. That assumes away all the relevant problems in the credit market: the uncertainty of property rights in the case of informal firms and its effect on the value of collateral, as noted by de Soto; differences in default rates between sectors; and monopolistic behavior by financial intermediaries, among others.[1] But I make that assumption to point out that even if the property rights–related reasons for

---

1. Haber (2007) points to difficulties in enforcing property rights and valuing collateral and monopolistic behavior by Mexican banks as the two main reasons for minimal lending to small and medium-size firms.

informality were absent and even if the credit markets had no imperfections, social programs–induced informality would distort the allocation of capital.

Consider the three firms depicted in figure 7-5, one fully illegal and informal, one formal but employing a mix of legal and illegal workers, and one formal and fully legal. The capital stock in each firm is $K_\tau^1$, $K_\tau^2$, $K_\tau^3$ respectively, where $\tau$ is an index of time periods. Associated with the capital stock is a level of employment in each firm, $L_\tau^1$, $L_\tau^2$, $L_\tau^3$ respectively. If each firm invested a total of $I^1$, $I^2$, $I^3$ resources, their capital stock and employment level would change in period $\tau + 1$ to

$$K_{\tau+1}^j = K_\tau^j + I^j$$

(8-1)                                for $j = 1,\ 2,\ 3$

$$L_{\tau+1}^j = L_\tau^j + \Delta L^j,$$

where $\Delta L^j$ represents the additional workers hired by each firm.[2] Of course, investment can be allocated to create new firms as well as to expand existing firms. As a result, GDP and employment grow through a combination of expansion and creation of firms.

I now focus on the formal-informal status of workers and firms when investment takes place. The main point is that new firms can be completely illegal and informal, formal but semi-illegal, or formal and fully legal. Existing firms also might decide to change their legal status when expansion is being considered; for example, a previously informal firm may decide to expand and as part of the process register with the relevant authorities, including registering some or all of its workers with IMSS. Table 8-1 considers six hypothetical options, labeled A through F; while they are not exhaustive, they suffice to illustrate the issue under discussion.

In option A, the fully illegal and informal firm invests but remains illegal and informal; in terms of the discussion of chapter 7, the firm continues to be a $[K^1, L^1]$-type firm (see figure 7-5). On the other hand, in option B, a new illegal and informal firm is created, adding to the number of $[K^1, L^1]$-type firms in the economy. The relevant point in option A is that expansion may raise the firm's expected marginal costs of labor due to higher exposure to IMSS and SAT.[3] That contrasts with option B, in which the new firm may face a lower probability of detection by IMSS and, as a result, lower labor costs. If options A and B were faced by the same firm, the question would be whether expanding employment left the firm below

---

2. The ratio $I^j/\Delta L^j$ measures the incremental capital-labor ratio in each firm; it then may be that $(K/L)_{\tau+1}^j \lessgtr (K/L)_\tau^j$, depending on whether firms grow by capital widening or capital deepening. That is not relevant here; the point is that firms expand with investment and their demand for labor increases.

3. That is because $\lambda(L_\tau^A + \Delta L^A) \geq \lambda(L_\tau^A)$,—that is, the probability of being fined grows as the firm hires more workers, increasing its expected costs.

Table 8-1. *Status of Firm and Workers under Various Investment Options*

| Option | Status in period τ | | Status in period τ + 1 | |
| --- | --- | --- | --- | --- |
| | Workers | Firm | Workers | Firm |
| A (existing informal firm grows but remains informal) | All informal | Informal and illegal | All informal | Informal and illegal |
| B (new informal firm is created) | Do not exist | Does not exist | All informal | Informal and illegal |
| C (informal firm turns formal but does not register all workers) | All informal | Informal and illegal | Mix of formal and informal | Formal but partly illegal |
| D (existing formal firm that previously cheated turns fully legal) | Mix of formal and informal | Formal but partly illegal | Informal converted to formal and new formal hired | Formal and fully legal |
| E (existing formal and fully legal firm expands) | All formal | Formal and fully legal | All formal | Formal and fully legal |
| F (new formal and fully legal firm is created) | Do not exist | Does not exist | All formal | Formal and fully legal |

Source: Author's analysis.

the threshold of workers at which the probability of detection was practically nil (below $\underline{L}$ in expression 7-3). If it did, expansion could provide more profits than a new venture; otherwise, a new venture would be started.[4] Note that in both options A and B, new investment expands the demand for informal workers.

In option C, the informal firm invests but turns formal and registers some of its workers, transitioning from a $[K^1, L^1]$- to a $[K^2, L^2]$-type firm. That option is interesting because by becoming formal, the informal firm minimizes the risk of detection created by its expansion.[5] Expansion involves paying the registration

---

4. That depends on the trade-off between economies of scale and scope, on one hand, and expected labor costs, on the other. In some cases, the increase in the latter may dominate the gains from the former, resulting in a productivity loss.

5. Note that following McKenzie and Woodruff (2003), I ignore indivisibilities in investment so that firms can invest as little as they desire. Nonetheless, as noted in chapter 7, registration costs do introduce a discontinuity to the extent that they are modeled as a fixed cost. A related issue not discussed here is whether firms perceive increases in demand as permanent or transitory. Intuitively, the move from informality to formality is easier in a context of steady economic growth than in a context of stop-go growth, because firms can expect to amortize their investment in registration costs. They also can enjoy the benefits of legality (access to formal credit, training programs, and so on) because the increased demand for their products is sustained. An interesting issue for further discussion is the extent to which macroeconomic instability fosters informality through increased uncertainty.

costs associated with formality, although the firm is not fully legal; depending on various parameters, demand might expand for both formal and informal labor or for formal labor only. In option D, the firm, which already is formal but mixes legal and illegal workers, becomes fully legal. In that case the expansion translates into an increase in formal employment beyond new hiring, because some of the workers now registered by the firm with IMSS were hired before the expansion, though illegally. In option E, the firm already is fully legal and formal; it just expands its demand for formal workers. In option F, finally, a new formal and legal firm is created. Note that in the last two cases, new registries in IMSS equal new jobs created by the firm.

## Social Programs and the Allocation of Aggregate Investment

Which of options A through F will be observed? I answer that question in two steps. First, I compute the additional or new profits, $\Delta\Pi$, associated with the investment made in each case (the details of the calculations are presented in appendix 8). Second, I compare the rates of return on the investments with the cost of credit faced by firms, which, as indicated, is assumed to be the same for all and denoted here by $r^*$. In particular, let

$$(8\text{-}2) \qquad r^k = \Delta\Pi^k / I^k \quad \text{for } k = a, b, \ldots, f$$

represent the rates of return of each investment option in table 8-1. A comparison of the rates of return given by equation 8-2 with $r^*$ determines the investment projects that are actually carried out; that in turn determines

—the distribution of aggregate investment between various firms and the change in the distribution of the country's capital stock

—the change in the size distribution of firms

—the change in the composition of formal and informal firms

—the change in the formal-informal distribution of workers.

How do social programs affect equation 8-2? I want to make two points. *One, unless $\beta_f = 1$ and $T_i = 0$, social programs increase the profitability of investments in informal firms relatively more than the profitability of investments in formal firms. Two, the economy's incremental capital-output ratio increases with the level of informality.*

To see the first point, recall from table 7-1 the impact of social programs on wage rates. As the parameters defining social programs change, wage rates for formal and informal labor also change, affecting in turn the profitability of investment options. Therefore it is possible to write $\Pi^k = \Pi^k(T_f, T_i, \beta_f, \beta_i)$—that is, to express the profits made in each option as a function of social programs. On that basis, I calculate the impact on rates of return of changes in the parameters defining social programs. The mechanism is straightforward: social programs directly impact firms' labor costs, and firms' labor costs in turn impact the profitability of investment options. The results are shown in table 8-2.

Table 8-2. *Social Programs and Rate of Return on Investment Options*

| Option | $T_f$ | $\beta_f$ | $T_i$ | $\beta_i$ |
|---|---|---|---|---|
| A (expand firm and stay informal) | + | − | + | + |
| B (create new informal firm) | + | − | + | + |
| C (register firm and mix workers) | − | + | − | − |
| D (become fully legal firm) | − | + | − | − |
| E (expand fully legal firm) | − | + | − | − |
| F (create new fully legal firm) | − | + | − | − |

Source: Author's analysis.

Consider the first column. As expected, increasing social security contributions, severance payments, or labor taxes reduces the profitability of investment options C through F associated with formality because all of the options require formal labor and increasing $T_f$ increases the tax on formal labor. Conversely, it increases the profitability of investments in illegal and informal firms because informal labor becomes cheaper than formal labor. The second column shows that if workers' valuations of social security increase, the incentive to evade and the tax on formal labor fall, lowering the rates of return on investment by informal firms and increasing those of formal firms. In fact, at the margin some firms may become formal as a result and register some of their workers with IMSS. Columns three and four work similarly: increasing social protection benefits or improving the valuation of existing benefits enhances the profitability of investments by informal firms and reduces that of formal firms.

Figure 8-1 reflects the impact of table 8-2 on the ranking of rates of return. The figure assumes that there is a portfolio of investment projects, each with a rate of return $r_n$ ($n = 1, 2, \ldots N$), where $N$ is a very large number (in the millions, because there are more than 3 million firms in Mexico and $N$ includes new projects as well). Those investment projects are evaluated twice. The first time, they are assessed in

Figure 8-1. *Social Programs and the Ranking of Rates of Return*

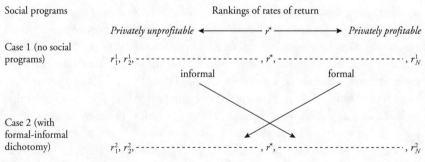

Source: Author's analysis.

the absence of social programs; I label that case 1 and order the rates of return from $r_1^1 \ldots < r_n^1 \ldots < r_N^1$. The second time, they are assessed under the formal-informal dichotomy; I label that case 2 and rank the rates of return in increasing order from $r_1^2$ to $r_N^2$. Rates of return on all N projects in both cases are compared with $r^*$.

Consider case 1. Because labor costs are the same for all firms in all activities, the ranking of privately profitable projects coincides with the ranking of socially profitable projects; as a result, investments go to the most efficient firms regardless of size or activity. In this case, in fact, the labels formal and informal are irrelevant.

Contrast that with case 2, in which the cost of labor in the informal sector is less than in the formal sector, increasing the profitability of investments of informal firms. The first point is that because social programs favor informality, the portfolio of privately profitable investment projects is modified, with some previously unprofitable options in the informal sector becoming profitable and vice versa for options in the formal sector. *At the margin, the allocation of capital tilts toward informality.*

To see the second point, assume that total investment is $I^*$. Investment is allocated in case 1 to all privately profitable investment projects with $r_n^1 > r^*$. Because no labor cost distortions exist, that allocation maximizes the productivity of labor and maximizes the additional GDP—that is, it minimizes the incremental capital-output ratio (ICOR). Contrast that with case 2 when $I^*$ is allocated to all privately profitable investment projects with $r_n^2 > r^*$. That allocation fails to maximize the productivity of labor and therefore the additional GDP because there is overinvestment (and overemployment) in the informal sector.[6] GDP in period $\tau + 1$ in case 1 and case 2 can be calculated as a result of investing $I^*$, which, subtracted from GDP in period $\tau$, is the GDP gained in each case by the *same* level of investment. The ratio of $I^*$ to the additional GDP provides the ICOR in case 1 and 2. It follows that

$$(8\text{-}3) \qquad ICOR^1 = I^* / \Delta GDP^1 < ICOR^2 = I^* / \Delta GDP^2.$$

That is the second point: *given the volume of aggregate investment, the more social programs tilt toward informality, the lower the GDP growth rate.* Because Mexico's current situation is that associated with case 2 under the formal-informal dichotomy, at present a large number of socially inefficient investment projects are being undertaken in the informal sector, which are lowering the country's rate of growth.

I emphasize again that the informal firms that result from expansion or creation are efficient in a private sense. Once the new or additional capital is in place, firms

---

6. In other words, investment resources can be distributed according to $I^* = \sum_{j=1}^{r_j^1 \geq r^*} I^j \left( r_j^1 \right)$ or $I^* = \sum_{j=1}^{r_j^2 \geq r^*} I^j \left( r_j^2 \right)$, so that the *same* aggregate investment results in a different distribution of capital stock across firms and activities.

will make the best use of it. As discussed, the problem is not with the productivity of firms once their capital stock is fixed (new or expanded). The problem is that capital investment in the firms occurs because their labor costs are lower than those of formal firms; at higher labor costs some of those capital allocations would not be observed.

That is the dynamic counterpart of the argument made in chapter 7. At that point I emphasized that given their capital stock, firms—large and small—were efficient and maximized profits by hiring workers up the point that their marginal product equaled the expected costs of labor. The argument repeats here. Given the capital stock that results from new investment, firms—large and small—are efficient and maximize profits in the same way. The addition here is to explain why, in a context in which there are no distortions in the credit market, investments are allocated to firms that lower the aggregate productivity of labor and capital. It is a significant addition because it brings up a very important point: *through continued investment in informal firms, illegal salaried employment will persist and may even expand.*

## Investments in Labor Training and Technology Adoption

The discussion above focuses on capital investment, ignoring other types of investment that also affect productivity. An analysis of firms' noncapital investments exceeds the scope of this volume, but it is useful to refer to some studies that suggest a negative link between informality and productivity that operates through firms' investment in labor training and technology adoption.

Fajnzylber, Maloney, and Montes Rojas (2006) studies the dynamics of microenterprises and small firms in Mexico, contrasting formal firms, which have access to credit from commercial and development banks, participate in business associations, pay taxes, and can benefit from government-sponsored training programs, with informal firms, which do not. The authors observe large informality in microenterprises and small firms, noting that less than 10 percent of such firms have received credit or training and that less than 17 percent participate in a business association. Their main finding is that *increases in formality broadly defined have the potential for increasing firms' profits and survival rates and bringing microenterprises closer to their optimal sizes.* Although they do not provide an explanation for the smallness of those firms, their findings are consistent with the hypothesis that informal firms are below their optimal size, noted in chapter 7.

López-Acevedo (2006) focuses on the relation between firm size and technology adoption in Mexico. Using firm-level data for 1992–99, the author finds that, aside from other attributes, the firms most likely to adopt new technology are large. López-Acevedo and Tan (2006) focuses on firms' investments in worker training and identifies positive impacts of such investments on labor productivity. Using the same data set used in López-Acevedo (2006), the authors find that *small firms and microenterprises are between one-fifth and one-sixth less likely than large firms to invest in worker training, either in house or through external providers.* Unfortunately, in neither case does the analysis distinguish between formal and informal firms, although, to the extent that a large share of small firms is informal, an indirect inference could be made from firm size (see table 7-2). That would suggest that the tax on firms' growth associated with social programs negatively affects technology adoption and worker training.

More generally, I quote at some length from the World Bank study on informality: "The empirical evidence on aggregate negative growth effects of informality is not conclusive, as informality tends to lose significance when other standard growth determinants are controlled for. This, however, could be due to the fact that many of the standard drivers of growth are also likely to affect informality—for example, low levels of human capital or institutional quality, leading to both lower growth and higher informality—and it is difficult to separate their direct growth effects from those that operate through larger informal sectors. The microeconomic empirical evidence, on the other hand, is still quite limited due to the econometric difficulties associated with distinguishing the effects of low productivity on informality from the reverse effects operating from informality to productivity. However, the available empirical evidence suggests that considerable efficiency gains could be derived from the transfer of production from low-productivity informal firms to their more productive formal peers. Similarly, the evidence indicates that the concerns associated with possible negative externalities generated by high levels of tax and social security evasion could well be justified, as firms operating in industries and regions characterized by high levels of sales and employment underreporting exhibit lower levels of labor and total factor productivity. Moreover, there is evidence indicating that exogenous increases in formality are associated with better firm performance, which should, in principle, translate into higher rates of economic growth."[7]

In ending this section, I have two comments. First, artificially increasing the rate of return on investment projects undertaken by self-employed workers or by microenterprises and small informal firms through the tax-cum-subsidy associated with social programs makes more workers become entrepreneurs than otherwise would and probably generates more firms as well. The hundreds of thousands, if not millions, of investment projects undertaken by those firms as a result of the combination of social protection and social security programs currently in place may give the impression that the informal sector is highly dynamic, with many

---

7. World Bank (2007, pp. 175–76). That is why I consider it important from a methodological perspective to construct a structural model in which informality is endogenous to the incentive structure faced by firms and workers and to use it to trace the channels through which informality affects static and dynamic efficiency, as chapters 6 through 8 have attempted to do with reference to social programs.

workers choosing self-employment and new firms continuously starting up, result-ing in abundant job creation. And that impression may be correct. But I argue that the adjective "dynamic" should not be confused with "socially efficient." Those microenterprises and small firms may be dynamic, but for the most part they also are illegal. And they continuously tap into Mexico's investment resources to create low-productivity informal jobs.

Second, none of the arguments presented here should be interpreted as argu-ing against workers "trying their luck" as self-employed entrepreneurs or as being against microenterprises and small firms. Nor are they against a particular distri-bution of the labor force among the agricultural, service, industrial, or commer-cial sectors or against nonsalaried contractual relationships between firms and workers. My point is simply that the size distribution of firms, the distribution of the labor force across activities, and contractual arrangements between workers and firms should not be biased by social programs, nor should the decisions of firms to pursue, for example, manufacturing or services or to invest more or less in capital goods, technology adoption, or labor training. As shown in chapter 6, there is an efficient level of nonsalaried employment. There is also an underlying distribution of talent, entrepreneurial ability, and other factors that should deter-mine the optimal size and number of firms, including one-person firms. Those factors need to operate apart from social programs if Mexico's economy is to become more productive and grow faster.

## Remarks on Saving under Informality

The previous analysis focused on the allocation of investment, taking its aggregate volume and, implicitly, the aggregate volume of savings as given. A discussion of the determinants of those aggregates is beyond the scope of this book, but it is use-ful to offer three observations related to social programs and the formal-informal dichotomy.

The first observation concerns forced saving. The impact of social security–induced forced saving on aggregate domestic savings and on growth has been ana-lyzed extensively, but in most cases assuming a given incremental capital-output ratio and a given efficiency of investment. The links are clear: higher domestic sav-ings resulting from forced saving have a positive impact on investment and for a given ICOR have a positive impact on the rate of growth.

Under informality that link becomes more complex for three reasons:

—because the impact of social protection programs on aggregate savings has to be determined (see chapter 9)

—because social protection programs reduce social security coverage and thereby the number of workers forced to save

—because the ICOR cannot be taken as given; it is endogenous to the distri-bution of investment between formal and informal firms.

The previous discussion focused on the third reason, because *regardless of how aggregate savings and investment are determined, the productivity of investment matters for growth.*[8]

But forced savings are important. Madero and Mora showed that in 2006 savings channeled through the housing and retirement sub-accounts of workers' Afore accounts represented 24 percent of all financial savings in that year.[9] That sum results from the forced savings of only 14.1 million workers enrolled in IMSS in the same year (see table 5-1). If forced saving increases the rate of economic growth, a relevant question is what the savings in Afores would have been if there had been no evasion in 2006 and 8.1 million additional salaried workers had been forced to save. What if all 41.4 million nonpublic workers, salaried and nonsalaried, were forced to save?

Those are difficult questions, and no attempt is made here to answer them.[10] I only observe that if it is believed that forced saving through the Afores increases aggregate domestic savings and that, despite Mexico's openness to international capital markets, aggregate domestic savings are a constraint on investment, *there are two negative effects on the rate of growth of GDP derived from the formal-informal dichotomy:*

—because as identified above, the efficiency of investment is lower or, in other words, the ICOR is higher

—because domestic savings are less, given that informality allows a majority of workers to escape from the obligation to save, in some cases legally (self-employed workers and *comisionistas*) and in others illegally (salaried informal employees).

The second observation is that the analysis helps to explain a puzzle observed in Mexico: why do workers invest in self-employment or in their own microenterprises

8. In the view of some observers, Mexico's openness to international capital flows allows the de-linking of domestic savings from domestic investment. In the view of others, access to international capital markets is restricted to a fairly small subset of large firms, so that increases in domestic savings facilitate access of small and medium-size firms to investment resources (for example, because Afores can invest in instruments with a long-term horizon, and so on). I do not take a position here, except to note that in either view the rate of return on investments is crucial and that those rates are distorted by the formal-informal dichotomy.

9. Madero and Mora (2006, pp. 8–9 and table 2). The authors also note that the share of Afore savings in GDP and in total financial savings increased rapidly from 1997 to 2006, from 3.9 to 12.9 percent and from 9.2 to 24 percent respectively. They also note that over time Afores have increased the share of resources invested in private projects. In 2006, 15 percent of all the resources that they administered went to finance firms, not to government bonds and other instruments.

10. Informality presents difficult challenges to identifying the links between social security and aggregate savings. On occasion those links are studied by assuming that a representative individual solving an intertemporal maximization problem is forced to save some share of his income; in that context the question is whether he reduces his voluntary savings by one peso for every peso he is forced to save. But when a worker enters and exits formality repeatedly throughout his life cycle, the context is different: first, because he may not know what his future path of work between formality and informality will be; second, because even if he does, it is not evident how that knowledge affects his pattern of saving. To the best of my knowledge, that issue has not been researched.

rather than save with a formal financial intermediary, such as an Afore, when saving would increase the pool of resources available to formal, legal firms to invest in projects that would allow the firms to hire the same workers as salaried employees, with both social security coverage and higher productivity? Why is the traditional circuit of financial intermediation modified so that workers invest their own savings in their own microfirms?

The answers to those questions, which involve the functioning of financial intermediaries and many other factors, are complex. But I believe that among them are four related to this analysis: one, the rates of return on investments in micro-enterprises are very high relative to the rates on projects by larger formal firms; two, those rates of return are high only if the projects are small; three, the rates of return on workers' savings in an Afore or comparable instrument are much lower; and four, the opportunity cost of being self-employed and starting a microfirm is low, given the constellation of wages and benefits in formal and informal employment. That is not to deny that entrepreneurial talent exists and that many workers prefer running their own business to being a salaried employee; accordingly, they prefer to channel their savings to their own business and not to an Afore. But it is to assert that the subsidies to informality associated with social programs induce more workers to become entrepreneurs than otherwise would and that the subsidies result in an inefficient allocation of investment.

The third observation is related to noncontributory pensions, which were briefly mentioned in chapter 1 as being relevant in Mexico. However, they were ignored afterward in the discussion of social protection programs because at this point they are still novel and it is uncertain whether they will have a measurable effect on a worker's choice between formal and informal status. But along with the development of health, housing, and day care programs for workers without social security, there has been a gradual increase in resources for elder people without a retirement pension.[11]

Noncontributory pensions can be an important redistributive instrument for low-income households with elder members. The pension programs have many dimensions, and I postpone their discussion until chapter 10. Nevertheless, I make

11. The pensions began first at the local level in the Federal District and in some states, but as of 2007 they had national coverage as a federal program. As noted, the 2007 federal budget contained 6,550 million pesos for the new Adults over Seventy program to provide a monthly pension of 500 pesos to adults seventy years of age or older who lived in communities with 2,500 inhabitants or less. One could argue that that amount compares unfavorably with the minimum pension for formal workers, which equals approximately 1,465 pesos a month. However, recall from chapter 5 that approximately half of all workers earning three times the minimum wage or less will not build up enough time in formal employment to qualify for the minimum pension. That is, they will not get a pension of 1,465 pesos a month even if they save 6.2 percent of their wages in their Afore accounts while they are in the formal sector (unless they work for fifty years or more). Contrast that with getting a pension of 500 pesos a month without saving in an Afore—and having the reasonable expectation that Congress or the president may at some point increase that amount.

two points here. First, to what extent are the pensions considered, de facto, a permanent entitlement, even though they have not been enacted into law by Congress? If they are, and if, as often occurs with other social programs in Mexico, political economy considerations lead to a gradual increase in their coverage and real value, *workers currently in the work force might expect that on retirement they too will benefit from the pensions.* In that context, it is an important issue to be researched, and it leads to the second point: to what extent do noncontributory pensions affect workers' saving patterns and their valuation of the forced-saving component of social security, given that they may have access to alternative sources of income after retirement without being forced to sacrifice current consumption?

## Growth and Job Creation under Persistent Informality

Social protection programs in Mexico at times are thought of as a necessary but *temporary* mechanism for providing informal workers with coverage against at least some of the risks that the government considers relevant as well as for redistributing income in the workers' favor. Although they are clearly inferior to social security in the sense that they do not necessarily accomplish all of the government's social objectives (given their unbundled and voluntary nature), it is nonetheless considered better from a social standpoint to provide some benefits to informal workers than no benefits at all. Furthermore, the network of social protection programs can be enhanced over time so that although social security and social protection might not be perfect substitutes, the degree of imperfect substitution between them can be reduced. Arguably, and ignoring political economy considerations, that line of reasoning is what justifies the programs and budgetary allocations described in chapter 1.

In that context, the expectation is that economic growth will create new jobs in the formal sector, gradually increasing the share of the labor force covered by social security. In other words, the dual social security–social protection system is considered a temporary feature of social policy that has persisted so far because successive macroeconomic crises and other obstacles have reduced Mexico's growth rate and therefore the creation of sufficient formal jobs. However, in a context of macroeconomic stability, accompanied perhaps by other reforms to boost the GDP growth rate, the expectation is that increasing formality will be observed until the desideratum of universal social security is achieved.

*I argue that that line of reasoning is flawed,* for two reasons. The first was given in chapter 6, where I showed that even under the best of circumstances—that is, when social security is fully valued by workers—informal workers will always exist given substantive reasons for nonsalaried contractual relationships between firms and workers and for self-employment. Universal social security cannot be observed in a system that by design excludes an important subset of workers from its intended coverage.

The analysis in this chapter brings up a second reason, which can be stated in two parts: first, informality lowers the rate of growth of GDP. Second, for any given rate of growth, informality increases the profitability of investments by informal firms and the profitability of self-employment, contributing to the persistence of informal employment as new informal jobs are continuously created or new workers choose to be self-employed. As a result, Mexico's social policy not only is inherently inconsistent in its approach to achieving the desideratum of universal social security, *it also is a central obstacle to achieving universal coverage because it continuously subsidizes the demand for informal labor.*

To make that argument more precise, I consider the factors determining the evolution of the composition of the labor force. Let the supply of labor change according to

$$(8\text{-}4) \qquad L_{\tau+1} = L_\tau + \Delta L.$$

Given the rate of growth of the labor supply, its distribution between formal and informal employment depends in an important way on whether or not the policy environment is conducive to the creation of formal jobs. Ignoring open unemployment, it must be that

$$(8\text{-}5) \qquad L_{\tau+1} = \left(L_{f\tau} + L_{if\tau} + L_{i\tau}\right) + \left(\Delta L_f + \Delta L_{if} + \Delta L_i\right),$$

so that the key issue is the change in the *composition* of the demand for labor. Informality will decline over time only if

$$(8\text{-}6) \qquad \Delta L_f \geq \Delta L \geq \left(\Delta L_i + \Delta L_{if}\right),$$

that is, only if formal jobs grow at least as fast as the labor force, implying that informal workers fall as a proportion of the labor force. That is a good outcome from the point of view of the government: the share of the labor force covered by social security expands. It also is a required condition if the argument that social protection programs are temporary is to hold.

What determines whether expression 8-6 is observed or not? In my view, the incentive structure faced by firms and workers is a central factor. The expected result of the process of growth is that formal jobs will increase, both because new salaried jobs are created and because illegal salaried jobs are converted to legal jobs. That process would be associated with a firm's shift from informal to formal status and with an increase in the share of legal workers within formal firms. The process also would result in higher labor productivity in salaried employment and, along with that, an increase in the opportunity costs of self-employment. The expectation is that, if the pace of investment is maintained, the process will translate into a secular decline in the share of informal employment in total employment. That is the natural, so to speak, process of economic growth, in which the economy becomes more formalized. And while it is difficult to document, that is the implicit expectation of Mexico's policymakers.

But that expectation is wrong. In Mexico, the process takes place with a permanent tax on formal labor ($\beta_f < 1$), which is not automatically eliminated just because the economy grows, implying that the incentives to evade social security—and therefore the motivation for informal salaried labor—are permanently present. Furthermore, the process occurs under a growing subsidy to informal labor ($T_i > 0$).

More pointedly, between 1998 and 2006, total resources for social protection programs increased from 77.1 to 150.8 billion pesos while informal employment increased from 23.5 to 25.8 million workers. That implies that spending on social protection programs per worker, $T_i$, increased from 3,280 to 5,840 pesos in the same period, or by 78 percent. On the other hand, it is difficult to make an assessment about the evolution of $\beta_f$ in the same period (there have been no legal changes affecting $T_f$). As discussed in chapter 3, the quality of services provided by IMSS has declined; however, the rates of return paid by the Afores and Infonavit as well as the number of Infonavit loans have increased since 2004. In the absence of better information, a reasonable assumption is that $\beta_f$ has been relatively constant.

The policy environment in Mexico has inadvertently lowered the rate of GDP growth and stimulated the creation of new informal jobs. Under such circumstances, formal firms must make a larger investment effort if growth in demand for formal labor is to outstrip growth in demand for informal labor. In other words, if the economy could grow faster, the rate at which formal jobs were created might exceed the rate at which informal jobs were created, despite the unfavorable policy environment; however, that requires a larger volume of investment or other measures to increase the profitability of formal firms. I am arguing that social policy in Mexico reduces the rate of growth, on one hand, and stimulates self-employment and investments in new informal firms, on the other; *as a result, it lowers the rate at which new formal jobs are created.*

Table 8-3 shows the change in the composition of employment and the growth rate of GDP over the last fifteen years. During that period the average growth rate was 2.9 percent, making real GDP 53 percent higher in 2006 than in 1991; similarly, the average growth rate of the labor force was 2.5 percent, making it 44 percent higher in 2006 than in 1991, for a net increase of 13.6 million workers. That increase was distributed as follows: 0.46 million workers in public sector employment; 3.97 million workers in formal salaried employment; 8.45 million workers in informal jobs (illegal salaried employees, self-employed workers, and *comisionistas*); and 0.89 million unemployed workers. Dividing the change in the different components of the labor force by the change in the total labor force results in the finding that *over the last fifteen years informal employment absorbed 62 percent of the total increase in the labor force, formal employment absorbed 32.5 percent, and open unemployment absorbed 6.5 percent.*

Table 8-3. *Percent of GDP Growth and Change in Employment Composition, 1991–2006* [a]

| Year | GDP growth | ISSSTE | IMSS | Formal | Informal | Unemployed | EAP |
|------|-----------|--------|------|--------|----------|------------|------|
| 1992–91 | 2.8 | 7 | −107 | −100 | 1,234 | 63 | 1,196 |
| 1993–92 | 2.2 | 52 | −182 | −130 | 1,263 | 63 | 1,196 |
| 1994–93 | 5.2 | 69 | 137 | 206 | 300 | 436 | 942 |
| 1995–94 | −7.0 | 47 | −814 | −767 | 1,273 | 436 | 942 |
| 1996–95 | 7.1 | 26 | 820 | 846 | 491 | −328 | 1,010 |
| 1997–96 | 6.7 | 43 | 611 | 654 | 1,464 | −376 | 1,742 |
| 1998–97 | 2.7 | 53 | 753 | 806 | 134 | −97 | 843 |
| 1999–98 | 5.4 | 29 | 701 | 730 | −442 | −211 | 77 |
| 2000–1999 | 4.7 | 37 | 525 | 562 | −199 | 224 | 587 |
| 2001–00 | −1.4 | 33 | −359 | −326 | 604 | 203 | 481 |
| 2002–01 | 2.0 | 13 | 51 | 64 | 425 | −36 | 453 |
| 2003–02 | 2.1 | −1 | −90 | −91 | 1,049 | 399 | 1,357 |
| 2004–03 | 4.8 | 11 | 260 | 271 | 426 | 105 | 803 |
| 2005–04 | 2.5 | 19 | 590 | 609 | 385 | −235 | 759 |
| 2006–05 | 4.3 | 23 | 896 | 919 | 50 | 247 | 1,215 |

Source: Table 5-3 and appendix 4.

a. Thousands of workers. ISSSTE includes other public sector workers with special social security regimes. Formal is the sum of ISSSTE and IMSS.

At this point one could argue that if wages in the formal sector were sufficiently flexible, then it should be able to absorb *any* increase in the labor force regardless of the rate of growth of GDP. One could then ascribe the persistence of informality to wage rigidity in Mexico. But that argument is incorrect, for the reasons given in chapter 6. The demand for labor in the informal sector sets a floor for wages in the formal sector—a floor that in Mexico is higher than the minimum wage. It is not that there is wage rigidity; it is that workers have alternatives and, given their valuation of social security, will not take jobs in the formal sector at lower wages if they can obtain higher wages and social protection benefits in the informal sector.

The key point is that given Mexico's investment efforts, the relative rates at which the demand for formal and for informal labor have increased have resulted in an insufficient number of new formal jobs to augment the share of the labor force covered by social security. There is little evidence of real wage inflexibility in the Mexican labor market, and except in 1995, open unemployment has not been the main variable accommodating increases in the labor supply. *Not enough formal jobs have been created because many workers have found and continue to find informal employment a comparable employment option and because firms have found and continue to find profitable investment projects in the informal sector.*

Certainly the 1994–95 crisis in Mexico played an important part in the low rate of growth of GDP and of the demand for formal labor, as did the slowdown in the U.S. economy observed in 2001 and problems with the supply of commercial bank credit, uncertain and costly energy supplies, and so on. It is extremely difficult to disentangle the various factors responsible. But my point is that in addition to macroeconomic crisis, difficulties with access to commercial credit, costly energy, and other factors, social policy has contributed to the outcome. If growth occurs under the weight of a permanent tax on legal salaried employment and an increasing subsidy to illegal salaried and nonsalaried employment, more jobs are created in the informal sector than would be otherwise. *Low growth produces informality, but the converse also is true: informality produces low growth.*

I believe that this analysis provides some insights with respect to suggestions that technological change and globalization are generating the phenomenon of "jobless growth." That is not really so if over the medium term there is reasonably full employment or if, ignoring short-run shocks, the open unemployment rate is around 3 to 4 percent on average, as has been the case in Mexico (see table 5-3). The expression "jobless growth" is used to describe what is really "economic growth with insufficient new formal jobs" (relative to the rate of growth of the labor supply). However, ignoring semantics, what really matters at the end of the day is whether economic growth results in jobs with higher labor productivity and whether the government's social objectives are met among an increasing share of workers— that is, whether social security coverage increases. The discussion shows that social policy in Mexico has worked against that objective.

## Static and Dynamic Efficiency Losses under Informality

Chapter 6 argues that the efficiency costs of the formal-informal dichotomy have two components: one, for a given distribution of capital stock, the loss of aggregate output resulting from over- and underemployment in the informal and formal sector respectively; two, the efficiency costs of raising revenue for social protection programs (see table 6-1). The substantive additions from chapters 7 and 8 are that the size distribution of firms and the allocation of aggregate investment are distorted by social programs. *As a result, the efficiency losses from informality are not repeated year after year but magnified year after year.*

Figure 8-2 illustrates that idea heuristically, depicting GDP and time on the vertical and horizontal axes respectively. Assume that up to period $\tau'$, social policy is characterized by the current combination of social security and social protection programs but that afterward the policy combination changes to one in which social security is fully valued and social protection programs disappear. Also assume that capital stock and employment levels adjust to that change immediately.

Conceptually, the discussion of chapter 6 captures a one-time gain in GDP as the economy becomes more efficient absent the labor tax-cum-subsidy implied by the formal-informal dichotomy. That gain was estimated to be on the order of 0.9 to 1.44 percent of GDP for 2006, although, as noted, that is most likely an

Figure 8-2. *Static and Dynamic Efficiency Losses under Informality*

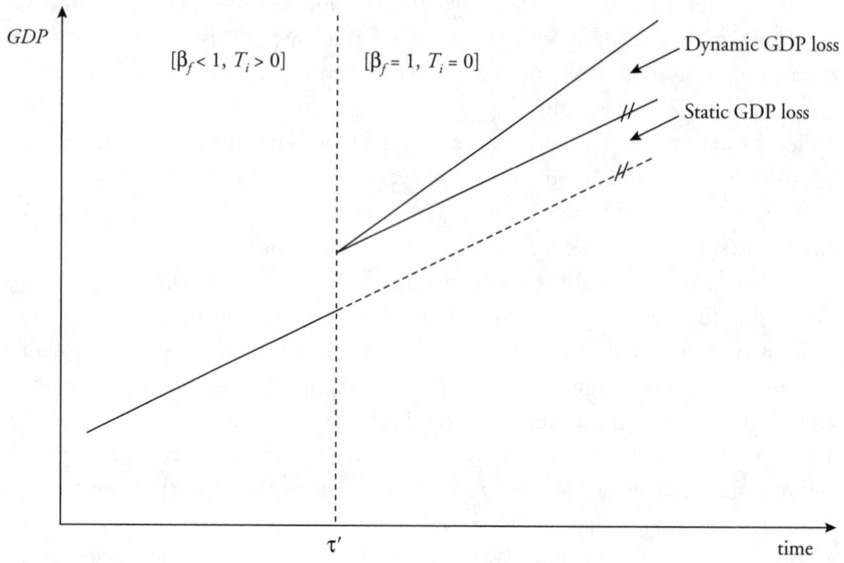

underestimate. At the same time, there was a one-time increase in real wages as the allocation of workers across sectors maximized labor productivity. But the (steady-state) rate of growth of GDP was not affected.

The discussion in chapter 7 and in this chapter, on the other hand, captures a change in the GDP growth rate, reflected in a steeper slope in figure 8-2, resulting from increased efficiency in the use of investment resources and other decisions by firms concerning training and technology adoption.[12] Meanwhile, real wages progressively increase, reflecting continuous increases in labor productivity as capital is allocated more efficiently, firms achieve economies of scale and scope unimpeded by evasion considerations or distortion of labor costs, and more firms invest in labor training and technology adoption.

Of course, from the point of view of the government, eliminating social protection programs is unacceptable because millions of workers would be left without benefits. But the figure illustrates sharply that *the formal-informal dichotomy has the Mexican government boxed in: on one hand, it must provide more social benefits to workers and protect them from various risks; on the other, it must increase the rate of growth of output, labor productivity, and workers' real wages.* As elaborated on in chapter 10, escaping from this dilemma is essential for Mexico.

---

12. If it is believed that forced saving increases aggregate national savings, the increased slope would also result from the greater volume of savings (and investment) as more workers are covered by social security, although that is not necessary for the result.

Table 8-4. *Age Distribution of Progresa-Oportunidades Beneficiaries, 2005*[a]

| Age range | Population | School scholarship | |
| | | With | Without |
|---|---|---|---|
| 0–5 | 1,727 | 0 | 1,727 |
| 6–10 | 3,349 | 1,588 | 1,761 |
| 11–15 | 3,861 | 3,049 | 812 |
| 16–21 | 3,573 | 657 | 2,916 |
| 22–59 | 9,658 | 0 | 9,658 |
| 60 or more | 1,894 | 0 | 1,894 |
| Total | 24,066 | 5,295 | 18,771 |

Source: Levy (2006a, table 5-1, p. 132).
a. Thousands of persons.

## Implications for Poverty Reduction and Progresa-Oportunidades

This chapter concludes with a discussion of the implications of my analysis for poverty reduction; the reader interested in the general argument can go directly to chapter 9. Chapters 6 and 7 argue that Mexico's current combination of social security and social protection programs provides stronger incentives to poor than to non-poor workers to look for informal jobs and to firms to hire proportionally more poor than non-poor illegal workers. This chapter shows that that combination reduces the rate of growth and creates conditions for persistent informality. Those results are central for designing poverty reduction measures in Mexico and for Progresa-Oportunidades, whose objective is not to "create jobs" but to provide temporary income transfers to poor households in order to increase their human capital.

Table 8-4 contains the age distribution of all Progresa-Oportunidades beneficiaries in 2005, dividing them into those who received a school scholarship from the program and those who did not. The presumption here is that in the range of eleven to twenty-one years, all those who were enrolled in school had a scholarship (it is rare for a poor youngster to attend school and not collect his or her scholarship because attendance is the only prerequisite).[13]

Progresa-Oportunidades began in 1997. It gradually extended its coverage until by 2003–04 it incorporated virtually all families living in extreme poverty. Because earlier coverage was incomplete and the scholarships for attending high school were not introduced until 2001, many poor youngsters currently do not

13. That presumption is not valid for children ranging from six to ten years of age because scholarships begin in the third year of primary school; in that age range there are more children in school than there are program scholarships.

attend middle or high school.[14] The program is increasing the number of years that children remain in school, but it is doing so gradually, and progress is more evident in the younger cohorts. The point here is that up to 2007, the number of poor workers *entering* the labor force having enjoyed the educational benefits of Progresa-Oportunidades is practically nil.

The intergenerational transmission of poverty will be broken only if future generations of poor workers earn higher incomes than current workers; improved nutrition, health, and education are necessary but not sufficient to achieve that goal. Chapter 4 shows that poor workers in Mexico own hardly any productive assets other than their labor; more precisely, it shows that the average number of hectares per working-age member of a poor rural household will fall from 0.45 hectare in 2005 to 0.18 hectare in 2012 (see figure 4-1). That implies that most poor workers will earn higher incomes only if they earn higher wages, which depends critically on their productivity once they enter the labor market.

From the standpoint of improvements in nutrition, school attendance, health, and current income, Progresa-Oportunidades already has had important effects. But the program has yet to have had any significant effect with respect to the *potential* benefits, in the form of higher real wages, that poor workers may enjoy once they enter the labor market.[15] From that perspective, the program is at a critical *initial* point, and the relevant question is this: when Progresa youth enter the labor force, will they be able to realize the potential for increased productivity and higher real wages associated with their improved human capital?

On the other hand, in 2005, 30 percent of all poor workers *already in the labor force* had received no schooling; 26 percent did not finish primary school; only 13 percent finished secondary school; and 7 percent moved beyond that level. Furthermore, not only is the number of poor workers with no or few years of schooling very large, but those workers will remain in the labor force for many years to come. In 2005, 80 percent of all poor workers were forty-five years of age or younger. Will those workers spend the rest of their lives working at the same low levels of productivity?

The foregoing poses two separate challenges for Mexico's poverty reduction efforts:

—to create conditions that permit new generations of poor workers to fully realize their potential for higher productivity

---

14. Evaluations show that those who dropped out of school three or more years before the program reached their community did not return to school. The program is effective in ensuring that children enter school and make the transition from one grade to another, leading to higher enrollment, promotion, and re-enrollment rates. But the impact on the education of the many sixteen- to twenty-year-olds who left school before the program started was negligible; see Levy (2006a, chap. 3) for a summary of the results.

15. The program already has had positive effects on the health status of poor workers and, of course, on the general welfare of the household; see Levy (2006a, chap. 3).

Figure 8-3. *Progresa-Oportunidades, Social Security, and Social Protection*

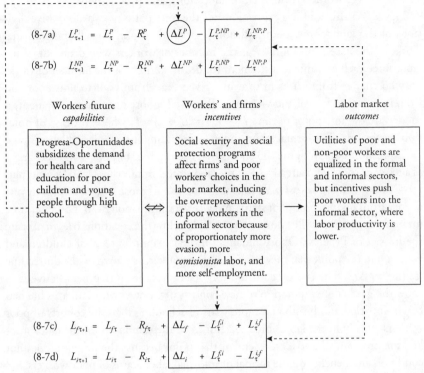

Source: Author's analysis.

—to create conditions that permit the productivity of poor workers already in the labor force to increase.

The two challenges are related, but separating them is necessary to identify with precision what falls within the realm of responsibility of Progresa-Oportunidades and what does not. In Levy (2006a) I argue that to make its maximum contribution to reducing poverty in Mexico, Progresa-Oportunidades should focus sharply on its own objective: *increasing the capabilities of the poor*. The program cannot resolve the problems created by Mexico's social security and social protection programs, which currently distort the behavior of workers and firms in the labor market, nor can it serve as a temporary substitute for social security for the poor. Moreover, attempts to convert it into such a substitute will further distort poor workers' incentives, to their detriment (see chapter 6).

Figure 8-3 contains three boxes that distinguish between building *capabilities* in poor children and youth through Progresa-Oportunidades; giving *incentives* to all firms and workers to be formal or informal through the interaction of social security and social protection programs; and generating *outcomes* in the labor market in terms of workers' utility, labor allocations, and productivity.

Figure 8-3 also contains expressions for the time-paths of two alternative divisions of the labor force: poor and non-poor workers and formal and informal workers. In those expressions, $R$ is the number of workers who drop out of the labor force each year due to retirement (or death) and $L^{m,n}$ is the number of workers who change from status m to n in a given year: from poor to non-poor and from informal to formal and vice versa. Because I ignore open unemployment, it follows that at any point in time $L^P + L^{NP} = L_i + L_f = L$, where, for ease of notation, I subsume all informal labor under $L_i$, including illegal salaried labor.

Expression 8-7a in figure 8-3 shows that the number of poor workers changes as a result of those who already are in the labor force, minus those who leave it, plus those *entering it for the first time,* plus the net effect of those who in any given year change from poor to non-poor status and vice versa. Equation 8-7b shows the same for non-poor workers. The box on the left side below the equations tries to capture the impact of Progresa-Oportunidades on the capabilities of poor children and youth up to the point that they enter the labor market, as shown by the dotted line leading to $\Delta L^P$. The critical contribution of Progresa from that perspective is to allow the gradual incorporation of new cohorts of workers who earlier in life had better nutrition and health and more years of schooling than the cohorts of poor workers already in the labor force, $L_\tau^P$. But from the standpoint of the labor market, the program's interventions end at that point because the program does not condition any benefits on the formal or informal labor status of poor workers.

What are the probabilities of observing a sequence in which $L_{\tau+1}^P < L_\tau^P$ so that the number of poor workers converges to zero? Consider now expressions 8-7c and 8-7d: independent of Progresa-Oportunidades, social security and social protection programs affect the incentives that workers and firms have to be formal or informal, and they also affect workers' productivity. The box in the middle summarizes the relevant aspects of the previous chapters, and the dotted line from that box to expressions 8-7c and 8-7d highlights that at present the incentive structure associated with social security and social protection programs leads poor workers into informal employment.

*Three processes are occurring simultaneously:* the health and educational levels of new cohorts of poor workers are gradually increasing as a result of Progresa-Oportunidades; poor and non-poor firms and workers are continuously choosing to be formal or informal, given the incentives offered by the social security and social protection programs; and poor and non-poor workers are being allocated into formal and informal jobs with different levels of labor productivity as a result of the interaction of the choices of firms and workers. Those three processes are interlinked, but it is essential to understand that they are driven by different factors.

If poverty is to decrease, the number of poor workers who pull out of poverty must exceed the number of poor workers entering the labor force plus the number of non-poor workers who may become poor as a result of some negative shock.[16] Given an exogenous poverty line, that occurs only if workers' real wages increase over time, which in turn requires increasing labor productivity. But whether poor workers can increase their productivity is not independent of the evolution of the formal and informal sectors—in particular, of whether new workers enter into informal or formal employment and whether, on average, more informal workers move to formal employment than formal workers move to informal employment. *Increased formal employment therefore is crucial to gradually reducing the number of poor workers.*

This volume is concerned with the "incentives" and "outcomes" boxes in figure 8-3. But from the standpoint of poverty reduction, a critical question is whether those boxes are compatible with the "capabilities" box; in particular, whether current social security and social protection programs facilitate increased formal employment of poor workers. Unfortunately for Mexico, the answer is no. They are, in fact, more conducive to increasing informal employment. I try to capture that effect in figure 8-3 by the dotted line that connects, through the "outcomes" box, the variables measuring workers' shifts from poor to non-poor and from formal to informal status. Because poor workers in Mexico have hardly any productive assets other than their labor, the expectation is that most of them are salaried and, in principle, formal, but the "incentives" box operates in the opposite direction. Furthermore, the programs and budgetary allocations described in chapter 1 point toward strengthening of the forces in the "incentives" box that generate that outcome. *Despite increased years of schooling for future cohorts of poor workers associated with Progresa-Oportunidades, firms are unlikely to offer them formal jobs and they are unlikely to seek formal jobs. The investments in workers' capabilities will not come to full fruition because the productivity of future workers will not increase.*

That is not to say that some poor workers will not find formal jobs, as they do today. Figure 8-3 obviously is very simplified and should not be understood as establishing a strict separation whereby all informal workers are poor and all formal workers are non-poor and labor productivity is completely stagnant. Even under informality, investment takes place in formal and informal firms, the self-employed learn new abilities, and labor productivity and real wages may increase; moreover, some poor workers are employed in the formal sector, although they are in the minority (as shown in table 5-1). Nevertheless, under informality, growth will benefit poor workers less than other workers because the incentive structure is biased against their formal employment. They will receive less job training than other workers, and they will work in smaller firms with lower capital-labor ratios. Unless the incentives change, proportionately more new cohorts of poor workers than new cohorts of non-poor workers will end up in low-productivity informal jobs. Although they will be healthier and more educated than their older

16. That is, $L_t^{P,NP} > (\Delta L^P + L_t^{NP,P})$.

peers, they will not earn progressively higher real wages. *The persistence of informality translates into the persistence of poverty in the context of a low-productivity, low-growth equilibrium.*

I close this chapter with four comments. First, in my view there has been a well-meaning but conceptually flawed attempt in Mexico to reduce poverty and increase workers' welfare as fast as possible through the creation and enhancement of a myriad of social programs without due concern for their incentive compatibility and impact on productivity and growth. *The analysis presented here shows that good intentions can translate into bad outcomes and persistent poverty.*

Second, instead of remaining a temporary program to increase the human capital of the poor and thereby contribute to breaking the intergenerational transmission of poverty, Progresa-Oportunidades runs the risk of becoming a permanent mechanism to transfer income to poor families whose children and grandchildren also will be poor. In addition, it runs the risk that as poor workers' earned income stagnates while non-poor workers' income increases, further attempts will be made to close the gap by adding more income transfers to those described in chapter 1, making the problem worse. Unfortunately, those efforts do not address the root problem: stagnant worker productivity.

But that is not all. There are many more programs to combat poverty in Mexico than Progresa-Oportunidades, among them programs to subsidize, through microcredits and other forms of support, new or existing microenterprises in rural and urban areas or small firms hiring low-wage or poor workers without social security coverage.[17] But at times the dividing line is tenuous between programs for productive support and programs that are labeled as such but are the de facto equivalent of income transfers. In the end, distortions through the credit market or through output subsidies are added to the distortions in the labor market created by the social security–social protection dichotomy. And while those programs do raise the incomes of those benefiting from them, that may be more a result of the transfer than of the profits from more productive firms. In other words, many such "productive" programs run the same risk of subsidizing informality and contributing to the persistence of low productivity run by many of the "social" programs discussed in this volume.[18]

17. On occasion such firms are called "social enterprises" (*empresas sociales*) to convey the idea that they serve a social purpose—for example, poverty reduction. But despite the label, the firms produce goods that are substitutes for goods produced by firms without that designation and they compete in the same markets. Furthermore, social enterprises are subject to the same official governance mechanisms that apply to salaried labor, although there may be greater societal tolerance for evasion in these cases. In the end, there is little difference between social enterprises and the $[K^1, L^1]$-type firms analyzed in chapter 7, except for the government subsidy and the label.

18. The 2007 federal budget contains forty programs that are potentially subject to these risks: twenty-one are in the Ministry of Agriculture, six in the Ministry of the Economy, five in the Ministry of Agrarian Reform, two in the Ministry of Social Development, and six in the Finance Ministry. The total budget allocation for the programs is 38.1 billion pesos, almost equal to the budget of Progresa-Oportunidades (39.5 billion pesos).

The third comment is related to education. Rates of return to education depend on the wage rates that workers earn once in the labor market.[19] But, as argued, if the current incentive structure persists, most new poor workers will become informal employees earning low wages. Rates of return to education will be lower and so will the incentives for poor youngsters to invest in education, despite Progresa-Oportunidades scholarships. What is the economic payoff from postponing entering the labor market to finish high school if having a high school degree makes hardly any difference in one's ability to obtain a better-paying job?

The fourth and last comment relates to the challenge of increasing the productivity of poor workers already in the labor force. Their reduced years of schooling are not an *absolute* impediment to increasing their productivity; that can be achieved through on-the-job training and employment in firms with higher capital-labor ratios. However, poor workers occupied in the two-to-five-employee firms discussed in chapter 7 or as self-employed workers or *comisionistas* peddling wares in the streets are unlikely to get much training, nor will workers exploiting one-third to one-fourth of a hectare of land.

Nonetheless, increasing the productivity of the almost 10 million poor Mexican workers currently in the labor force is possible. Moreover, it is imperative if poverty reduction in Mexico is to occur at a faster rate than that implied by replacement of the current generation of poor workers over the next decades. But for that to happen, poor workers currently in the labor force need to find jobs in larger firms willing to invest in their training or they have to exploit larger plots of land in order to benefit from the transfer of modern agricultural technologies.

While not all poor workers have to be salaried to benefit from on-the-job training, the majority probably needs to be salaried given their scarce ownership of non-labor assets. However, firms will invest in poor workers' training only if those investments are reflected in firm-specific assets, allowing firms to appropriate at least part of the benefits. That is facilitated if firms have a medium-term horizon and a relatively stable environment; if labor turnover is reduced because their workers are not formal today and informal tomorrow; if firms invest more time in thinking about innovation and technology adoption than in hiding from the IMSS or the SAT inspector and spend more money on new machines than on bribes for Labor Ministry officials; and, more generally, if firms grow and expand in a context of legality and certainty,

---

19. Unfortunately, I could not find any studies comparing rates of return to education for formal and informal workers in Mexico. Azevedo (2006) compares rates of return to education for poor informal workers in the slums of Rio de Janeiro with those of other workers in developing countries. The author finds that the former are on the order of 3 to 6 percent, while the latter are between 5 and 10 percent. He also finds that many of these poor Brazilian workers are young people who self-select into the informal sector (p. 127).

achieving economies of scale and scope on the basis of their unencumbered comparative advantages.

*Informality and low growth are the major deterrent to firms' investment in training poor workers, not workers' innate lack of ability or low levels of education.* I quote again from the McKinsey Global Institute study on productivity: "Lack of education of the Brazilian workforce is just an excuse today for poor economic performance. There are just too many examples, from banking to food processing and automotive, where firms have been able to match productivity levels at the economic frontier with the Brazilian workforce. These findings just reinforce what we found in every other country we studied. The primary means through which workers attain the skills to perform at the economic frontier is through on-the-job training. Brazilian workers are equally trainable in this regard to workforces all around the world. There are many important reasons to increase the educational level of the Brazilian people, including making Brazil's popular democracy work better. However, removing a constraint on current economic performance is not one of them."[20]

The McKinsey study did not focus on Mexico. Interestingly enough, however, in evaluating the productivity level of workers in the Brazilian construction industry, the study compared them with workers in the U.S. construction industry who were mostly poor Mexicans who had migrated to the United States. The educational level of the migrant workers was similar to that of workers shown in table 4-6. In this particular case, "we compared two similar subsidized housing projects in São Paolo and Houston. In both cases, many of the workers were illiterate and from agricultural backgrounds. However, in Houston the workers were from Mexico and most did not even speak English. Yet the Mexican workers in Houston were achieving close to best practice productivity. They had been trained sufficiently to work in the more productive operational and organizational systems used in Houston."[21]

Progresa-Oportunidades is an important component of Mexico's social policy generally and poverty reduction policy in particular. Despite shortcomings and clear room for improvement, the program has been effective in increasing years of schooling as well as in meeting the nutritional and primary health needs of the poor. The program needs to improve along those dimensions and consistently focus on its own objectives in order to continue to make a substantive contribu-

---

20. Lewis (2004, pp. 139–40).

21. Lewis (2004, p. 153). The study goes on to note that the Brazilian contractor had two productivity penalties: "The first was that his scale of operations was too small to keep his trained workers in different crafts fully utilized. . . . A second penalty was that he did not use heavy equipment, such as cranes and elevators, because they were not economic at Brazilian wage rates." (p.153). Note from table 7-3 that 50 percent of all construction firms in Mexico have less than fifteen workers; also recall that chapter 6 argues that under informality, prices of productive assets in the informal sector are artificially raised as wage rates for informal labor are lowered.

tion to reducing poverty. The program can best help the poor by doing that as effectively as possible and attempting nothing else.[22]

*However, Progresa-Oportunidades is patently insufficient to eradicate poverty in Mexico. Removing the tax on salaried employment and the subsidy to nonsalaried employment, both of which are larger for the poor than for the non-poor, is essential.* Along with Progresa-Oportunidades, what the majority of Mexico's poor workers need most is a formal firm that can offer them a relatively stable job and invest in their training while providing them with social security coverage. That need cannot be met by yet another social protection program that, while offering some temporary benefits, pushes them further into informal employment and permanent dependence on transfers of public funds. Mexico's poor workers need effective mechanisms that, in the context of increased international competition, translate good intentions into good jobs.

22. On the other hand, recent research results highlight the importance of interventions that promote early child development among poor children; see Young and Richardson (2007). This component of Progresa-Oportunidades could certainly be strengthened with potentially large gains over the medium term, without distorting workers' choices in the labor market.

# 9

## Social Programs and the Fiscal Accounts

S ocial programs have fiscal implications. Subsidies to social security have an impact on the labor market, increasing formality and the tax base. In contrast, because social protection programs subsidize evasion of social security, as informality increases the fiscal constraints under which social policy operates get tighter: more workers receive free social benefits, and the tax base erodes as fewer firms and workers pay taxes or contribute to social security. To analyze this issue, this chapter begins by introducing subsidies to social security within the framework presented in chapters 6 through 8 and then discusses the impact of social programs on the fiscal accounts.

At the same time, an important feature of the subsidies channeled to social programs is that they may redistribute resources from future to present consumption, not from high- to low-income households. On one hand, that reduces the effectiveness of social programs in reducing inequality in Mexico; on the other, it has a negative impact on growth as public investment is reduced to maintain fiscal balance. This issue is discussed in the last section of this chapter.

### Government Subsidies for Social Security

In Mexico, the federal government subsidizes social security health, retirement, and disability benefits. Furthermore, in 2007 the First Job program (Programa de Primer Empleo) was introduced to subsidize approximately 63 percent of the non-wage costs of labor when a firm registers a worker with IMSS who has never been registered before.[1]

Table 9-1 presents the amounts of those subsidies budgeted for 2007. (I do not use data for 2006, as in the rest of the monograph, because the First Job program started in 2007.) Three comments are relevant. First, the total non-wage costs of labor are 40.5 percent of the wage. Of that, the government pays 5.9 percent and firms and workers pay 34.6 percent. When the First Job program is included, the average amount paid by firms and workers falls to 34.5 percent and that paid by the government increases to 6 percent. Second, without the First Job program, government subsidies to social security are 14.5 percent (5.9/40.5) of the total non-wage costs of labor; with the program, they increase to 14.8 percent (6.0/40.5). Third, in 2007 those subsidies were budgeted to be 61,086 million pesos, or 0.66 percent of GDP. To put that in perspective, it is 55 percent *higher* than the budget of Progresa-Oportunidades for the same year.

*Impact on the Labor Market*

The easiest way to introduce subsidies to social security in the framework of this volume is as a wedge between the total non-wage costs of labor, which I continue to denote $T_f$, and the costs to firms. Let $\theta_f$ be the share of $T_f$ paid for by the government (that is, the 14.5 percent calculated above). The cost of legal salaried labor to firms is

$$(9\text{-}1) \qquad w_f + T_f - \theta_f T_f = \left[ w_f + \left( 1 - \theta_f \right) T_f \right].$$

Workers, on the other hand, receive bundled social security benefits for the full amount $T_f$, valued at $\beta_f T_f$. From the standpoint of firms' demand for labor, government subsidies for social security are equivalent to a subsidy to salaried employment. The analysis in chapters 6 to 8 can be repeated at this point, using equation 9-1 in all the relevant expressions and figures. Figure 9-1 provides a synthesis of the main impacts of that change in which, to simplify, I ignore evasion of social security and use a single quote mark and a double quote mark to denote the equilibrium values without and with subsidies, respectively.

---

1. The program's rules state that although the full amount of a firm's contributions to IMSS and the Afores is subsidized, the new worker must pay his or her share and that contributions to Infonavit are not subsidized. See IMSS, *Diario Oficial de la Federación* (Official Journal of the Federation), February 27, 2007. In terms of table 1-3, that lowers social security contributions from 29.5 to 7.4 percent of the wage. But given the bundled nature of all non-wage costs of salaried labor, the association of the subsidy with any of its individual components—or the distribution between the worker's share and the firm's share—is purely formal. Note also that the program is really the First Formal Job program or, more accurately still, the First Registry in IMSS program. As discussed below, that is not a semantic difference.

Table 9-1.   *Social Security Subsidies and Non-Wage Costs of Labor, 2007*
2007 pesos (millions)

| Contributions and subsidies | Percent of wages | Total costs |
|---|---|---|
| *Workers' and firms' contributions* | | |
| Health | 12.2 | 90,275 |
| Work-risk pensions | 2.5 | 19,171 |
| Life and disability pensions | 2.4 | 23,177 |
| Day care and sports facilities | 1.0 | 9,729 |
| Housing | 5.0 | 48,645 |
| Retirement pensions | 6.3 | 58,681 |
| Firing and hiring regulations[a] | 3.2 | 31,133 |
| Labor taxes[b] | 2.0 | 19,458 |
| Subtotal | 34.6 | 300,269 |
| *Government subsidies* | | |
| Health | 4.0 | 39,154 |
| Pensions[c] | 1.9 | 18,932 |
| First Job program[d] | (0.1) | 3,000 |
| Subtotal | 5.9 | 61,086 |
| Net workers and firms[e] | 34.5 | 297,269 |
| Total[f] | 40.5 | 361,355 |

Source: Appendix 1.

a. Following table 1-3, cost is estimated as 3.2 percent of the wage bill, although that figure does not appear explicitly in firms' accounts or as the revenue of any government agency.

b. Following table 1-3, cost is estimated as 2 percent of the wage, although these resources are collected by state governments.

c. Most of these resources are for retirement pensions, although there is a small component for disability pensions.

d. In principle, the First Job program subsidizes new workers, so a distinction needs to be made between the average and the marginal cost of labor to firms. The figure in table 9-1 is obtained by dividing resources budgeted over total firms' and workers' payments (3,000/300,269); see the discussion in text.

e. Subtotal of percent of workers' and firms' contributions minus percent of First Job program subsidy.

f. Subtotal of percent of workers' and firms' contributions plus subtotal of percent of government subsidies.

The without-subsidies equilibrium for formal firms is at K, with labor costs $(w_f' + T_f)$ and $L_f'$ workers. Informal firms are at point M, with labor costs $w_i'$. Workers' utility is $(w_f' + \beta_f T_f) = (w_i' + \beta_i T_i)$. The effects of subsidies to social security are as follows. As formal firms' labor costs fall, the firms expand output. But workers are attracted to the formal sector only if they are offered higher wages, which increases wages in both sectors. Equilibrium for formal firms is at Q, with labor costs $[w_f'' + (1 - \theta_f) T_f]$; for informal firms, it is at R, with labor costs $w_i''$. Formal workers' utility is $(w_f'' + \beta_f T_f)$, equal to utility of $(w_i'' + \beta_i T_i)$ for informal workers. Formal employment is $L_f'' > L_f'$, and informal employment is $L_i'' < L_i'$.

Figure 9-1. *Government Subsidies for Social Security*

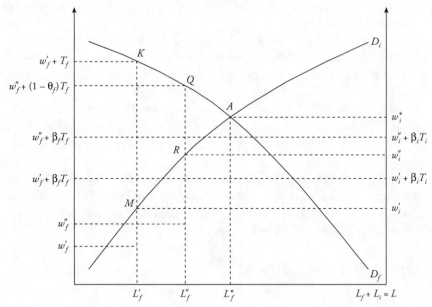

Source: Author's analysis.

For a quick summary of the effects of that change: workers are reallocated from lower-productivity informal jobs to higher-productivity formal jobs; profits (or quasi-rents) move in opposite directions, increasing in the formal and falling in the informal sector; wages increase in both sectors for the same reasons that they did under evasion—labor productivity increases. However, in contrast to the evasion scenario in chapter 7, higher wages are accompanied by an increase in social security coverage, bringing the government closer to accomplishing its social objectives. Ignoring the issue of who pays for the subsidies, workers' utility is higher, but unlike in the case of subsidies to social protection programs, increased workers' utility is accompanied by increased labor productivity.

Incorporating subsidies to social security sheds light on an insufficiently noticed implication of social programs in Mexico: because $\beta_f < 1$, social security taxes salaried employment, but because $\theta_f > 0$, social security subsidizes salaried employment. What is the net impact of $(\theta_f, \beta_f)$? To answer that question, note that with the exception of the First Job program, the subsidies listed in table 9-1 have been in place since the current Social Security Law went into effect in 1997; therefore they have been completely internalized by firms and workers and their effects are fully reflected in the labor allocations in table 5-1 and in the observed wage rates reported in tables 5-10 to 5-13. In that context, *it is noteworthy that despite subsidies of 14.5 percent of the total non-wage costs of labor, salaried employment is barely*

*53 percent of the non-public labor force; it is equally noteworthy that despite those subsidies, evasion of social security is large: although 14.1 million salaried workers are enrolled in IMSS, 8.1 million are not.*

The foregoing implies that notwithstanding subsidies to social security in the order of 0.66 percent of GDP, workers and firms in Mexico respond to the official governance mechanisms that apply to salaried labor through massive evasion of social security (and through *comisionista* and self-employment). Of course, the allocations in table 5-1 also reflect the subsidy to informal employment of 1.7 percent of GDP, which from that perspective plays the same role as undervalued social security: it partly nullifies the effects of subsidies to social security and augments informal employment.

Turning to the efficiency implications of $\theta_f$, I note that as in chapter 6, two effects are present: the impact on labor productivity and the efficiency costs of raising fiscal revenues to pay for the subsidies. Consider first labor productivity. A comparison of the MPL in each sector yields

$$(9\text{-}2) \qquad MPL_f - MPL_i = \underbrace{\left[\left(1-\beta_f\right)T_f\right]}_{\substack{\text{tax on formal} \\ \text{labor}}} + \underbrace{\beta_i T_i}_{\substack{\text{subsidy to} \\ \text{informal labor}}} - \underbrace{\theta_f T_f}_{\substack{\text{subsidy to} \\ \text{formal labor}}}$$

The relevant observation is that subsidies to social security reduce the output losses caused by social programs.[2] However, one has to consider the efficiency costs of raising 0.66 percent of GDP to pay for the subsidies. As a result, while the expectation is that the subsidies increase static efficiency, given that they reduce overemployment in the low-productivity informal sector, that cannot be ascertained.

One last point merits attention. On one hand, chapter 6 shows that social protection programs subsidize informal labor; on the other, the discussion here shows that subsidies to social security are a subsidy to formal labor. The point that I want to make is that because in Mexico social security and social protection programs are subsidized simultaneously, the government subsidizes formal and informal employment at the same time. In 2007, 0.66 percent of GDP is budgeted to promote formal employment through subsidies to social security, and 1.7 percent of GDP is budgeted to promote informal employment through subsidies for

---

2. Setting equation 9-2 equal to zero and solving for $\theta_f$ yields $\theta_f^* = (1 - \beta_f) + \beta_i(T_i/T_f)$, which shows, as expected, that the subsidy to social security that eliminates the loss of labor productivity increases with the size and valuation of social protection; it decreases when workers' valuation of social security increases. Because in 2006 $T_i = 0.23\,T_f$, that implies that $\theta_f^* = 23$ percent, assuming that social security and social protection benefits are fully valued. That compares with the observed subsidy of 14.5 percent. If, as argued, social security is not fully valued, the gap between the current 14.5 percent subsidy rate and $\theta_f^*$ is higher. Without arguing in favor of a specific number, I point out here that from the standpoint of productivity, subsidies to social security should be much higher.

social protection programs, for a total of 2.36 percent of GDP. *Those resources are substantial; they represent, for example, 38 percent of expected revenues from the value-added tax in 2007.*

## The First Job Program

The purpose of this volume is not to analyze any program in particular. Nevertheless, the framework developed here can be used to make some hopefully useful observations on the First Job program. Because the program subsidizes only *new* entrants, there is a difference between the *average* and the *marginal* $\theta_f$. As stated, with the program, the average rate increases from 14.5 to 14.8 percent; however, the marginal $\theta_f$ is 75.3 percent, which appears to be very significant.[3] The question is whether that can induce a permanent, relevant increase in $L_f$.

To assess the issue, note that an implicit assumption of the program is that there is a large stock of workers who have *never* been enrolled in IMSS. But as stated in chapter 5, the IMSS and Consar registries indicate that the number of workers who have been enrolled in IMSS at least once is very large. The First Job program departs from the assumption that entry into formality is the main constraint to increasing $L_f$. But the problem is *length of time* in formal employment, and that requires something other than a policy subsidizing *first* entry.

In that context, the effects are mixed. On one hand, given formal and informal wage rates, the reduction in $T_f$ associated with the program lowers the price of salaried labor relative to the price of nonsalaried labor and, within salaried labor, the price of legal labor relative to that of illegal labor. There will be an increase in legal employment, but a smaller increase in salaried employment; for the most part, what happens is that workers who already had been hired by firms are now registered with IMSS. On the other hand, in parallel with the First Job program, the 2007 budget increases the subsidies to informal employment from 150.8 billion pesos in 2006 to 162.4 in 2007, or 7.7 percent (see table 1-5). That implies that the effects of an increase in $\theta_f$ are offset by an increase in $T_i$. In other words, evasion is more profitable, and that fact lowers informal relative to formal wages, diluting— or even reversing the direction of change in—the price of salaried labor relative to that of nonsalaried labor and the price of legal labor relative to that of illegal salaried labor. The net effect of both policy interventions is ambiguous; it could result in an increase in informality.

A related observation is that the increase in $\theta_f$ from 0.145 to 0.753 when a new worker is hired applies only during the *first* year of employment. Beginning with the *second* year and thereafter, if the worker remains formally employed the subsidy associated with the First Job program is eliminated; in other words, $\theta_f$ returns

---

3. That is obtained as follows. Table 9-1 shows that $T_f$ is 40.5 percent of the wage. Without the First Job program, the government pays 5.9 percent of that 40.5 percent, so $\theta_f = 0.145$ (5.9/40.5); with the program, the government pays 30.5 percent of the same 40.5 percent, so $\theta_f = 0.753$ (30.5/40.5).

from its temporary value of 0.753 to its permanent value of 0.145. One has to consider whether, in the end, incentives inadvertently increase labor turnover (and reduce labor training). The reason is this: from the point of view of the firm, after a year has elapsed since it hired its first worker under the First Job program, the cost of hiring *another* new worker under the program is substantially lower than the cost of continuing to employ its first worker.[4]

## Feedback from Social Programs to the Fiscal Accounts

A critical question raised in chapter 3 is whether the current combination of social security and social protection programs is what the Mexican government wants or whether it is only the best that the government can do given the constraints that it faces in the second-best context in which policy is carried out in Mexico. Assuming the latter—because the argument that there are systematic differences in the behavior of salaried and nonsalaried workers or systematic asymmetries in insurance market failures with respect to those workers does not stand—it is clear that among the various considerations, fiscal constraints occupy center stage. I posit here that Mexico's social programs worsen those constraints.

Assume that the government argues that while from the standpoint of its social objectives, providing social security benefits to all workers is the desired outcome, at present it is unable to achieve that outcome given its budget constraints; as a result, it provides (temporary?) social protection benefits to informal workers. *The analysis here tries to show that that line of reasoning, when turned into policy, becomes self-reinforcing.* The point is this: on one hand, as informality increases, tax collections fall because GDP is lower and because the tax base erodes as evasion of income taxes and social security contributions increases; on the other hand, increased informality raises the fiscal costs of social policy because having more informal workers increases demand for free social protection programs. That creates a vicious circle. As social protection programs expand, the fiscal constraints on the government become more binding; more binding fiscal constraints make the goal of universal social security coverage ever more elusive; but because informal workers cannot be without social benefits, social protection programs must be enhanced and expanded; and so on.

A concise recapitulation of the sequence of conceptual exercises presented in chapters 6 and 7 is helpful in illustrating those points and highlighting their fiscal implications. Consider first social security with $\beta_f = 1$ and $\beta_f < 1$, but assume no

4. In that context, note also that subsidies for social security are included in the Social Security Law; firms and workers therefore perceive them as *permanent*. Subsidies for the First Job program are contained in the budget decree, which must be approved annually by Congress, so firms and workers may not consider them permanent, which may reduce their impact on long- term decisions. The program's rules state that the subsidy will last until 2012; nevertheless, that depends on annual approval.

social protection programs and no government subsidies for social security ($T_i = 0$, $\theta_f = 0$). It would appear that in those cases social security is fiscally neutral because there is no direct effect on either the revenue or the expenditure side of the federal budget. *But that is not so.* In the equilibrium with $\beta_f = 1$, total GDP and total fiscal revenues are higher than in the equilibrium with $\beta_f < 1$, because formal employment and formal firms' profits are higher and so are income taxes; wages also are higher and so are consumption taxes; and firms' evasion of social security contributions and income taxes is lower.

If one thinks of a process in which $\beta_f$ is initially equal to unity and then decreases for whatever reason, total fiscal revenues fall. Various options are available to deal with that change: decrease government investment; decrease ordinary government spending; increase income taxes or consumption taxes; extract more oil (or hope for a positive terms-of-trade shock); increase borrowing; or all or some combination of the above options.

Clearly, each option has different implications for public investment, the vulnerability of the economy to external shocks, the mix of present and future consumption, and the after-tax distribution of income between wages and profits (or quasi-rents). But one way or another, the inefficiency implicit in $\beta_f < 1$ is paid for. In other words, *although not expressly recorded in the fiscal accounts, an increasingly undervalued social security system costs the government money because total fiscal revenues are lower.*

Consider now social protection programs (while still ignoring subsidies for social security). They have a negative impact on the fiscal accounts for four reasons:

—because GDP, formal employment, and real wages fall further, inducing a contraction in income and consumption taxes

—because an explicit element appears on the expenditure side of the budget that was not there before: the costs of social protection programs

—because social protection programs increase evasion of social security contributions and, probably, income taxes[5]

—because the number of informal workers demanding free social benefits increases.

Finance Ministry officials in charge of spending see expenditures increase (which is something they did not expressly observe when $T_i = 0$), while Finance Ministry officials in charge of revenues see total taxes fall further because the increased informality of firms and workers reduces revenues collected by SAT and IMSS. To maintain equilibrium in the fiscal accounts, the government has the same six options given above.

---

5. Most of the hundreds of thousands of small firms that do not register their workers with IMSS do not register with the Ministry of Finance either. The same is true of many of the self-employed. The World Bank notes that "in Mexico, 63 percent of all urban micro-enterprises are not registered with the federal treasury, and 72 percent pay no taxes" (World Bank 2007, p. 150).

Finally, consider what happens with subsidies for social security. A new term appears in the expenditure side of the budget. There is an implicit saving in the costs of social protection programs because illegal salaried employment falls, along with self- and *comisionista* employment (see figure 9-1). At the same time, the revenue side of the budget strengthens as, at the margin, the incentives to evade social security and income taxes are reduced. But as before, if the additional revenues do not fully compensate for the additional expenditures, the six options listed before are available.

At this point the results of chapter 8 are relevant. To the extent that social policy places the economy on a path characterized by lower GDP growth and persistent informality, the fiscal implications are magnified year after year. Indeed, as new social protection programs are introduced or existing ones enhanced, the fiscal constraints become more binding each year because the number of informal workers receiving benefits increases; benefits per worker increase; evasion of social security contributions and income taxes increases; and the low GDP growth rate limits the rate of growth of total income and consumption taxes.

*From the fiscal standpoint, social policy in the context of the formal-informal dichotomy becomes increasingly more complex.* The tax base erodes while the number of beneficiaries receiving (claiming?) nonfunded benefits increases. Social security in Mexico generates fiscal pressures to the extent that a share of its costs is subsidized, but social protection creates greater fiscal pressures because it is fully subsidized and because the per worker fiscal subsidy is higher under social protection than under social security.[6] Neither social security nor social protection programs have an automatic source of financing in Mexico because no mechanism exists whereby fiscal revenues increase in step with spending. But there is a key difference between them: *social security augments the degree of formality in the economy, which facilitates increases in fiscal revenues; social protection does the opposite.*

Chapters 6 through 8 argue that the formal-informal dichotomy presents Mexico's government with a difficult dilemma: to provide social benefits to workers without social security coverage and thereby reduce labor productivity and the country's growth rate or to leave millions of workers exposed to various risks. Incorporating the fiscal dimension makes that dilemma even more pronounced, because while providing social benefits to workers without social security coverage reduces labor productivity and the growth rate, it also erodes the tax base and increases expenditures. In that context, the policy challenge posed by informaltity is,

—from the social standpoint, to ensure that instead of giving some workers social security coverage all the time, some workers social protection coverage all the

---

6. In 2006 the per worker subsidy was 3,648 pesos if the worker was formal and 5,670 pesos if he or she was informal (see tables 3-9 and 5-1).

time, and some workers social security and social protection coverage at various points in time, all workers get the same social benefits all the time

—from the economic standpoint, to provide benefits through programs that bypass the current distortions in the allocation of labor and capital and thereby place the economy on a higher growth path, with faster increases in productivity, and to ensure that the programs are fiscally sustainable.

That policy challenge is discussed in chapter 10.

## Is Social Policy Redistributive?

Here I present some thoughts on the redistributive impact of social security and social protection programs in Mexico, for two purposes. The first is to argue that all sources of funds used to finance those programs need to be analyzed simultaneously to assess their distributive impact and that it is not necessarily the case that even if the programs do a good job of targeting low-wage workers, they are redistributing income in those workers' favor. The second is to argue that it is necessary to separate three different government social objectives that at times are lumped together:

—to redistribute income from other groups in society to workers

—to protect workers from various risks by solving their contracting problems in insurance markets

—to force workers to consume a set of goods that they otherwise would not consume.

It is useful to recall some results from chapter 6. When the labor market is characterized by mobility of workers and there are no subsidies (that is, $\theta_f = 0$), social security contributions are paid with a combination of reduced formal firm profits and lower wages for *all* workers, formal and informal. Although social security is not an effective tool for increasing workers' consumption, it is effective in solving contracting problems in insurance markets and in imposing the government's preferences on workers; however, in both cases its effectiveness is limited to the periods when workers are formally employed. Social protection programs, for their part, can solve *some* of the contracting problems that workers have in insurance markets, but they are not fully effective in forcing workers to consume a bundled set of goods that otherwise they would not consume. At the same time, because social protection programs are fully subsidized by the government, they can increase the level of consumption of formal and informal workers, although to assess that it is necessary to determine who pays for the subsidy.

The earlier discussion in this chapter modifies those results in the sense that subsidies to social security may increase workers' consumption, but as with subsidies to social protection, that depends on who pays for them. In other words, the same problem created by the fiscal costs of social protection programs exists with regard to the fiscal costs of subsidies to social security. In both cases, one needs to determine who pays to assess whether the subsidies are redistributive. *Unsubsidized social security does not redistribute income from formal firms to workers. The question is whether the net effect of partly subsidized social security programs and fully subsidized social protection programs is redistributive.*

## The Relevant Incidence Question

I now argue that the incidence question needs to take into account the joint effects of social security and social protection programs. In policy discussions it is common to assume that the two programs are independent and operate separately, but the evidence presented in chapter 5 contradicts that assumption. As argued, mobility of workers across sectors implies that the relevant beneficiaries of social programs are not "formal workers" and "informal workers" but "workers currently employed by firms who register them with IMSS" and "workers who currently do not have that labor status." Workers move constantly from the formal to the informal sector. While in the formal sector, they pay wage-based contributions directly and *potentially* benefit from the subsidies to social security, but they also *potentially* benefit from the subsidies to social protection programs because those programs raise the utility of all workers. While in the informal sector, they pay social security contributions indirectly, and they *potentially* benefit from the subsidies to social security and social protection programs.

Policymakers can assume that contributions to social security are paid for the most part by formal firms; they also can assume that the number of workers employed in the informal sector and the wage rates that they receive are invariant to social security contributions. Policymakers can focus separately on subsidies to social security and to social protection programs and argue that the utility of "formal workers" is increased by 0.66 percent of GDP through the first and that the utility of "informal workers" is increased by 1.7 percent of GDP through the second. They can justify the corresponding budget allocations by the claim that the former get benefits paid by the firms that hire them that the latter do not get. *But all that is an accounting convention or, if the reader wishes, an expenditure classification exercise; it is not a behavioral description of Mexico's labor market, and it is very misleading to base the government's redistributive policy on it.*

In a context of labor mobility and wage flexibility, from the point of view of workers, social security and social protection are just two labels under which the government spends a total 2.36 percent of GDP in subsidies to increase their utility. And because formal and informal workers have to pay 3.24 percent of GDP in social security contributions as an inevitable consequence of participating in the labor market, from their point of view those contributions cannot be treated separately from the 2.36 percent of GDP in subsidies that they also get for participating in that market. At the end of the day and labels notwithstanding, from the workers' point of view what matters is whether they are better off as a result of the government's social interventions. In other words, I argue that in the case of Mexico, the relevant incidence question is the following: *what is the incidence* *of the mix of wage-based contributions and general revenues used to finance the social benefits that some workers always receive in the form of $T_f$, some receive at times in the form of $T_i$ and at other times in the form of $T_f$, and some always receive in the form of $T_i$?*

My point of view is that it is more useful to think in terms of the Mexican government operating a single system of social benefits for all workers. That system is labeled social security when workers are hired by a firm that registers them with IMSS and social protection when workers have any other labor status. The system costs 5.6 percent of GDP.[7] Two sources of revenues are used to pay for it: wage-based contributions and undetermined funds. Wage-based contributions pay for 84.5 percent of the costs of "social security" and 0 percent of the costs of "social protection"; undetermined funds pay for 15.5 percent of the costs of "social security" and 100 percent of the costs of "social protection."

### Three Government Social Objectives

Table 9-2 evaluates Mexico's system of social benefits on the basis of its ability to meet three government social objectives:
    —solving workers' contracting problems in insurance markets
    —forcing workers to consume a bundle of goods that they otherwise would not consume
    —redistributing income toward workers from other households.

Because the ability of social security and social protection programs to accomplish the first two objectives already has been discussed, I focus here on the third, depicted in the last column of the table. Are the programs redistributing income in favor of workers in the sense that their level of consumption is higher than it would be without them? That is a difficult question, and no definite answer is given. What follows are some observations that I hope provide part of the answer, in the understanding that a full assessment requires a much more elaborate framework than the one presented here (in particular, one that distinguishes between workers and households of different income levels and quantifies the intertemporal effects of different adjustment options).

Note that of the cost of the entire system of social benefits, equivalent to 5.6 percent of GDP, wage-based contributions pay for 58 percent (3.24/5.6). The fact that more than 50 percent of the cost of the system is not financed through an instrument that can redistribute income suggests that if any redistribution is taking place, it must derive from subsidies. It also suggests that, *at best,* social security and social protection programs redistribute 2.36 percent of GDP from other households in Mexico to workers. It also suggests that 28 percent of the potential redistribution takes place through social security (0.66/2.36) and 72 percent through social protection (1.7/2.36). Those results are important: at most, 42 percent of

---

7. That is the total cost of the system of social benefits given by $[T_f L_f + T_i(L_i + L_{if})]$.

Table 9-2. *Evaluation of the Government's Social Objectives in Mexico's System of Social Benefits*

| Program | Solving problems in insurance markets | Imposing government's preferences on workers | Redistributing income toward workers |
|---|---|---|---|
| Social security | Yes | Yes | Share paid with wage-based contributions [0.855] (3.24 percent of GDP): No |
| | | | Share paid with undetermined funds [0.145] (0.66 percent of GDP): Maybe |
| | | | Share paid with wage-based contributions [0.00] (0.0 percent of GDP): No |
| Social protection | Partly[a] | Maybe[b] | Share paid with undetermined funds [1.00] (1.7 percent of GDP): Maybe |

Source: Author's analysis.

a. Workers employed in the informal sector can buy health insurance like Seguro Popular or the Incorporación Voluntaria al Regimen Obligatorio (IVRO) insurance offered by IMSS; workers can buy life insurance when purchasing Seguro Popular or IVRO insurance; informal workers can save for the future in an Afore. However, informal workers cannot buy work-risk and disability insurance or insurance against being fired or otherwise losing their job, such as severance pay.

b. Informal workers may choose any combination of the options offered by the government, but the government cannot force them to purchase any.

the funding for Mexico's system of social benefits has the potential to redistribute income from other households to workers, and almost three-fourths of the potential amount to be redistributed is channeled to programs that are less effective at meeting the other two components of the government's social objectives: solving contracting problems in insurance markets and changing the composition of workers' consumption.

Turn now to the nature of the potential redistribution associated with the 2.3 percent of GDP in subsidies to social programs. Table 9-3 divides the six options

Table 9-3. *Sources of Funds to Pay for Subsidies to the System of Social Benefits*

| Effects absorbed in one period | Effects absorbed over time |
|---|---|
| Reducing government current spending in other programs | Reducing public investment |
| Increasing consumption taxes | Extracting more oil (or hoping for a positive and sustained price shock) |
| Increasing income taxes | Borrowing money |

Source: Author's analysis.

identified previously to pay for the subsidies into those whose effects are absorbed in the same period in which the subsidies are provided and those whose effects are distributed over time. That reveals that there are two forms of redistribution, one with and one without intertemporal effects.

Consider the first column. There are two noteworthy considerations. First, subsidizing social programs involves no indebtedness or potential sacrifice of future growth because public investment is compressed, nor are oil rents used to increase workers' *present* consumption. Second, nevertheless, the fact that subsidies to social programs are financed with increased taxes or reduced spending does not necessarily imply that they are redistributive. For that to be the case, another condition must be met: reduced government spending must focus on programs that do not provide benefits to workers or additional income or consumption taxes must be paid by other households—or both. Clearly, if the government increases taxes on workers and uses the proceeds to subsidize social security and social protection programs, it is changing the composition of workers' consumption but it is not increasing its level; similarly, if the government cuts training or educational programs for workers and uses the proceeds to finance subsidies to social programs, it is not increasing the utility of workers. *In other words, in the absence of intertemporal effects, subsidies to social programs redistribute income from other households to workers only if they are paid for by reductions in government spending benefiting other households or by additional income or consumption taxes on those households.*

To make that point explicit—and to pave the way for the policy discussion in chapter 10—it is useful to rewrite the expressions for workers' utility, allowing for the taxes that they pay. Therefore, let $t_w$ denote worker's per capita consumption taxes, so that

(9-3)
$$U_f = w_f + \beta_f T_f - t_w$$
$$U_i = w_i + \beta_i T_i - t_w,$$

with labor mobility ensuring that $U_f = U_i$. In that context the point is whether

(9-4)
$$t_w \left[ L_f + L_{if} + L_i \right] \lessgtr \left[ \theta_f T_f L_f + T_i \left( L_i + L_{if} \right) \right],$$

that is, whether the government subsidies for social security and social protection programs for workers exceed government taxes on workers. In the absence of intertemporal effects, social security and social protection programs would redistribute income from other households toward workers when the left side of expression 9-4 is less than the right side.

Consider now the second column in table 9-3. It is qualitatively different from the first in the sense that redistribution does not entail lower *present* consumption by any household. In this case, the redistribution that occurs is from future to present consumption. The net impact of that intertemporal redistribution on workers depends on the instrument used and on the households that will have to reduce their future consumption to pay for current benefits. If subsidies to social programs are paid for with oil rents that could have been invested in productive infrastructure or, more directly, through reduced public investment, then all households' future consumption is reduced, including that of workers.[8] The redistribution in that case is from workers' future consumption to workers' present consumption, *not from other households' consumption toward that of workers*. Similar arguments apply when subsidies are paid for by borrowing: eventually the debt has to be paid, and it is important to know whose future taxes will be raised.

For analytical purposes, I make a sharp contrast between the two columns in table 9-3. As shown below, however, in Mexico subsidies are paid for through a mix of options from the two columns. *What the discussion indicates is that the fact that 2.3 percent of GDP is channeled to subsidizing social security and social protection programs does not necessarily imply that Mexico's workers are receiving a redistribution of that magnitude through those programs.* To the extent that a mix of options is used, the actual redistribution is lower.

At the same time, the discussion indicates that more precision is needed when using the word "redistribution," clarifying whether it is from other households toward workers or from future workers' consumption to present workers' consumption. It also indicates that the simple observation that public subsidies to social programs are increasing—as shown in figure 1-3—is not equivalent to the observation that redistribution in favor of Mexico's workers is increasing.

This discussion is not academic; it is crucial to gauging the redistributive impact of Mexico's social programs. At times an implicit association is made between the targeting of the benefits of a program and the redistributive effect of the program. Analyses are presented showing that a given social program focuses its benefits on a subset of workers—say, poor workers—on the basis of the distribution of the program's resources by income decile or by the geographic location of beneficiaries. But there is a difference between targeting benefits to low-wage or poor workers and funding those benefits through an instrument that lowers somebody else's present or future consumption. The first does not necessarily imply the second. The difference is fundamental. When benefits are paid by lowering public investment or using (temporary?) oil rents that could have been invested, *the contribution of the programs to reducing Mexico's income inequality is diminished and, from a dynamic perspective, potentially nullified.*

*Budget Figures*

Table 9-4 shows the evolution of key fiscal indicators for the period 1998–2007; for reference, the last line shows the value of GDP. Item 6 includes revenue-sharing

---

8. Similarly, if subsidies are paid for with increased oil rents that prove to be temporary, the sustainability of the system of social benefits or the increased vulnerability of the economy to external shocks may become an issue.

Table 9-4. *Selected Fiscal Indicators, 1998–2007*
2007 pesos (billions)

| Item | 1998 | 1999 | 2000 | 2001 | 2002 | 2003 | 2004 | 2005 | 2006 | 2007 |
|---|---|---|---|---|---|---|---|---|---|---|
| 1 (budget surplus) | −77.80 | −77.00 | −80.80 | −51.60 | −88.10 | −55.90 | −23.20 | −10.90 | 8.30 | −22.00 |
| 2 (tax revenues)[a] | 497.80 | 563.00 | 619.90 | 662.40 | 679.30 | 724.20 | 733.20 | 790.30 | 890.70 | 929.10 |
| 3 (oil rents)[b] | 134.20 | 147.30 | 145.10 | 132.50 | 181.70 | 204.80 | 211.30 | 198.80 | 326.60 | 338.30 |
| 4 (social programs)[c] | 120.10 | 136.80 | 150.20 | 161.80 | 176.70 | 184.40 | 199.10 | 217.80 | 233.20 | 257.20 |
| 5 (investment)[d] | 183.40 | 169.20 | 172.40 | 160.90 | 146.00 | 169.50 | 177.70 | 154.30 | 208.60 | 147.80 |
| 6 (other spending)[e] | 869.74 | 920.64 | 1,073.19 | 1,113.02 | 1,227.10 | 1,342.46 | 1,374.32 | 1,495.10 | 1,616.98 | 1,602.28 |
| GDP | 6,982.00 | 7,357.00 | 7,704.00 | 7,599.00 | 7,750.00 | 7,914.00 | 8,298.00 | 8,504.00 | 8,867.00 | 9,186.00 |

Source: Ministry of Finance and Public Credit.

a. Income taxes (ISR) plus value-added taxes (VAT) plus other consumption taxes (IEPS).

b. Net of income taxes paid by Pemex and excluding all other contributions as well as revenues of public enterprises.

c. Subsidies to social security and social protection programs as defined in the text, plus resources for Progresa-Oportunidades only. Resources for all other social programs are excluded.

d. Public investment in infrastructure, excluding investments in the energy sector financed with private credit and registered separately (in Mexico's accounting terminology these are the *Pidiregas* projects).

e. All other spending net of interest payments, public investment, spending by public enterprises, and spending on social programs (in Mexico's terminology this equals programmable spending plus transfers to state and municipalities less items 4 and 5 and public enterprises).

Figure 9-2. *Index of Selected Fiscal Indicators, 1998–2007*[a]

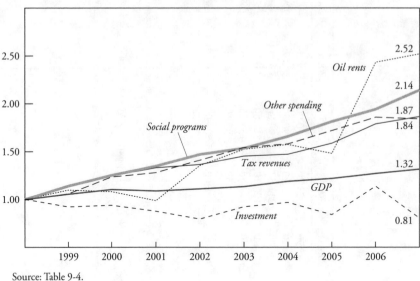

Source: Table 9-4.
a. 1998 = 1.00.

transfers to state governments but excludes spending by federal public enterprises like Pemex, Mexico's petroleum and gas company, and the electricity companies. Item 2 excludes revenues from those companies. In turn, the spending registered for social security within item 4 refers only to government subsidies because contributions from workers and firms are netted from both sides of the accounts.[9] Excluding the performance of public enterprises, those numbers give a broad view of Mexico's public finances over the last decade.

The table shows, foremost, that over the decade there was a consistent effort to exercise fiscal discipline. The budget deficit shows a downward trend, both in absolute terms and as a share of GDP. That allows one to draw a very important conclusion: *social programs were not paid for by increasing indebtedness,* ruling out one source of intertemporal redistribution identified in table 9-3.

To assess the role of the other items, figure 9-2 depicts an index for each, with 1998 equal to unity. I exclude the budget surplus from the figure on the basis of the observation made above regarding the decline in the budget deficit. Five facts should be noted. First, GDP in 2007 is expected to be 32 percent higher than in 1998 while tax revenues are expected to be 87 percent higher, indicating

9. Note that the sum of items 4, 5, and 6 minus items 2 and 3 does not equal item 1. That is primarily due to the fact that the federal government on its own runs a deficit, which is compensated for by including the surplus from public enterprises in the federal budget. The budget surplus reported in item 1 results from consolidating the federal government with public enterprises.

that over the decade there is a significant effort to increase tax revenues as a share of GDP. Second, other (nonsocial) government spending mirrors the behavior of tax revenues almost exactly, and in 2007 it is expected to be 84 percent higher than in 1998. Note that as a share of GDP, it is slightly higher than tax revenues in most years.

Third, oil rents increase by 152 percent, raising their share in GDP by the equivalent of 1.8 points (from 1.9 to 3.7 percent). Fourth, public investment is stagnant: with the exception of 2006, in all years its share of GDP is lower than in 1998 and in some years it is lower in absolute terms. Fifth, spending in social programs is the most dynamic of the three expenditure items considered. In 2007 it is expected to be 114 percent higher than in 1998, and in each year it has grown faster than tax revenues or GDP.

The data strongly suggest that, at the margin, none of the additional oil rents translated into increased public investment; one can argue that instead those revenues were used in part to reduce the budget deficit and in part to finance other government spending and social programs (the net increase in oil revenues exceeds the reduction in the budget deficit).

What does that imply for the redistributive impact of social programs? There are two possible answers. One is that all the additional tax effort was absorbed by additional government spending on other items and that all expansion of social programs was financed by a mix of oil rents and reduced public investment. In that case, social programs implied no redistribution of income from higher-income households toward workers but rather redistribution from future to present consumption. And to the extent that public investment contributes to the overall performance of the economy, the programs resulted in reduced growth.

But a second answer could be offered by presenting a different decomposition of the expenditure side of the budget, shown in table 9-4. In this case, social programs are included within other government expenditures and some other items (education, public security, and so on) are excluded. The argument would be that the additional tax effort served to pay for increased spending in social programs and that spending on other items was financed through a mix of oil rents and lower public investment.

At this level of generality, one cannot discriminate between the alternatives. Yet both have in common that the additional tax effort was insufficient to pay for the sum of the increases in other government spending and social programs *and that given the commitment to fiscal discipline, it was not possible to allocate any of the additional oil revenues to growth-promoting public investment.*[10]

10. The argument does not imply that all oil rents should be invested in physical assets (public infrastructure) or financial assets (reduced budget deficits or repurchased public debt). Given a social discount rate, some share of oil rents should be used to increase present consumption, but one needs an extremely high discount rate to justify reducing public investment when oil rents increase (and an optimistic assumption regarding the permanence of those rents).

I close this chapter by restating a fundamental result for the policy discussion in chapter 10: wage-based social security contributions are not redistributive. Article 123 of the Constitution, the Federal Labor Law, and the Social Security Law notwithstanding, *patrones* in Mexico are not redistributing profits toward *obreros* through the institutions of social security.[11] In the end, leaving aside rhetorical considerations, the argument for those contributions rests on *budgetary convenience,* given the difficulty of raising revenues through other means and the greater administrative ease of taxing the wage bill of a small but relevant subset of firms than of taxing income or consumption. Those are substantive arguments that cannot be minimized. What also cannot be minimized is that there is a vast difference between budgetary convenience and effective redistribution.

From that perspective, there is a different justification for wage-based social security contributions: *they are easy to collect.* Yes, the tax on legal salaried labor is a large, costly, and very pernicious distortion indeed, and yes, taxing legal salaried labor is far from redistributing resources to workers. But that tax no longer needs to be approved by Congress, firms, or workers: *it already exists.*

In my view, the claim that (rich) firms should pay for the social security of their workers as part of the redistributive aim of social policy is harmful rhetoric. That does not mean that the rich should not pay proportionately more or that redistribution toward low-income workers is not necessary; it means even less that the government should give up on its social objectives. It just means that in Mexico's current circumstances, the instruments used to accomplish those objectives must be different if policies are to be effective.

Chapter 3 asked whether the Mexican government really wants the combination of social security and social protection programs that it now has or whether that is just the best that the government can do given the constraints that it faces. As indicated, it cannot be argued that what the government has is what it wants. The conclusion is inescapable: the current combination of programs exists because the government considers that combination the best that it can do—poverty reduction, productivity enhancement, and growth promotion notwithstanding. At this point, it can be pointed out that the most prominent of the constraints on the government is the fiscal one. Ultimately, at the core of the formal-informal dichotomy lies a deep fiscal problem: *the difficulty of financing social programs by raising taxes on higher-income households, bypassing wage-based contributions on salaried workers. Nevertheless, as the social and economic losses that arise from informality persist year after year, the failure to solve that problem makes most workers in Mexico worse off.*

---

11. Recall from table 7-2 that there are more than 3 million firms in Mexico but only about 760,000 are registered with IMSS. Even if the incidence of social security contributions fell on firms, only about 25 percent of all firms would be redistributing income toward workers. Furthermore, 350,000 of the 760,000 registered firms have around two workers. Some of those firms probably are owned by the same workers, in which case redistribution is from the workers to themselves.

# 10

## Can Social Policy Increase Welfare and Growth?

Mexico's government needs to escape the dilemma posed by the formal-informal dichotomy. An alternative model is required, one that will both provide social benefits to all workers and accomplish the government's social objectives more effectively, bypassing the distortions in the allocation of labor and capital. There must be deep change in the scope and financing of social security, and that change must be carried out in the context of a strategy that integrates social and economic policy. This chapter presents such an alternative, elaborates on the fiscal changes required to sustain it, and sketches its redistributive impacts. Appendix 9 elaborates on the implications of the proposal, with an emphasis on retirement pensions.

### The Case for Reform

Table 10-1 summarizes the impact of Mexico's social security and social protection programs in five separate dimensions: the government's social objectives; workers' utility; static efficiency costs of the programs; dynamic efficiency costs; and two economic objectives of the government: fiscal sustainability and economic growth.

It is not unusual for discussions of social programs to ignore their impact on growth and productivity because those issues belong to the realm of "economic policy." A view that emphasizes only the efficiency effects of the programs without considering the government's social objectives obviously is unsatisfactory. Mexico's social programs exist because the Mexican government has social

Table 10-1. *Main Trade-Offs in the Formal-Informal Dichotomy*

| Dimension | Outcome |
| --- | --- |
| **Government social objectives** | |
| Provide insurance Impose government preferences | Yes. The government provides insurance for and imposes its preferences on 14.1 million formally employed workers and does so partially and erratically with 25.7 million informally employed workers. |
| Redistribute income | Yes. Up to 2.36 percent of GDP is redistributed, although some redistribution is from future to present consumption, not from high- to low-income households. |
| Reduce poverty | No. Government policy induces poor workers to take illegal and informal jobs, and poor workers face greater impediments than other workers to increasing their productivity. |
| **Workers' utility** | Workers' wages are lowered by overemployment in the low-productivity informal sector, although workers' utility is increased by subsidies to social security and social protection programs. |
| **Static efficiency costs** | Between 0.9 and 1.4 percent of GDP is lost each year from labor misallocation in addition to the efficiency costs of raising 2.36 percent of GDP in revenues to subsidize social security and social protection programs. |
| **Dynamic efficiency costs** | |
| Firms' size | Firms with low capital indivisibilities and little vertical integration predominate; up to 75 percent of firms are illegal, and the vast majority are small. |
| Composition of output | The reduced supply of labor to the formal sector lowers formal sector output; informal sector output is biased toward commerce, services, and light manufacturing; there is overproduction of goods and services by self-employed workers. |
| Allocation of investment | The profitability of small informal firms is artificially raised; the efficiency of investment falls; and the incremental capital output ratio increases. |
| Savings | Only 14.1 million workers are forced to save for retirement, while 25.7 million are not, potentially lowering aggregate domestic savings. |
| Innovation and job training | There is very little innovation or job training in the majority of firms given their illegality, small size, and high rate of failure. |
| **Government economic objectives** | |
| Economic growth | There is lower GDP growth with persistent informality; stagnating public investment also fails to contribute to growth. |
| Fiscal sustainability | The tax base erodes as firms and workers evade taxes and social security contributions, while the number of informal workers demanding free social benefits grows. |

Source: Author's analysis.

objectives; to evaluate those programs while ignoring their raison d'etre clearly will not do. But the opposite also is true: it does not do to consider only the programs' achievement of social goals while ignoring their impact on productivity and growth. Social programs have economic effects on firms and workers; they also have to be paid for. Ignoring their economic dimensions sooner or later hurts the households that they are meant to help, particularly the poor. As this volume has tried to show, the question is not just one of good intentions. A purely "social" view of social programs is as incomplete as a purely "economic" view. Table 10-1 highlights that *the social and economic effects implied by the formal-informal dichotomy are inseparable.*

In a nutshell, Mexico's current conundrum is this:

—Social policy provides 14.1 million workers with health insurance, retirement pensions, housing loans, severance payments, and coverage against other risks that the government considers relevant while providing 25.7 million workers with partial coverage against some of those risks. The numbers refer to average coverage levels, not to specific individuals, who may alternate between social security and social protection programs at various points during their working life, and coverage is more erratic and incomplete with low-wage and poor workers.

—Government subsidies to social security and social protection programs increase workers' current utility, although that is not completely a result of redistribution of income from higher-income households. It is unlikely that 2.3 percent of GDP is being redistributed from high- to low-income households, implying that the contribution of social security and social protection programs to reducing income inequality in Mexico is weak. Some redistribution is from future to present consumption, in the form of lower public investment and use of oil rents, and to that extent it reduces workers' future utility.

—In exchange for partial coverage against risks and a minor redistributive effect, the combination of social security and social protection programs induces static and dynamic efficiency costs, reflected in reduced labor productivity and a lower GDP growth rate respectively. The annual loss of output is in the order of 0.9 to 1.44 percent of GDP; the reduction in the GDP growth rate is difficult to estimate because it operates through the inefficient allocation of capital, distortion in the size distribution of firms, and reduced adoption of technology and investments in job training.

—The combination of social security and social protection programs also induces systematic evasion of the laws meant to protect salaried workers and erosion of the tax base. Only about 25 percent of all firms hiring salaried workers are legal and comply with the official governance mechanisms that apply to salaried labor, and at least 8.1 million workers are illegally employed as salaried workers.

—With respect to poverty reduction, poor workers already in the labor force are led into low-productivity informal jobs with little prospect for increased real wages. In addition, the absence of incentive compatibility between social security and social protection programs, on one hand, and between those programs and Progresa-Oportunidades, on the other, implies that the expected medium-term benefits of Progresa may be partly lost.

—The trade-offs mentioned are inherent in the current design of social policy in Mexico, and as long as that design persists they will be inescapable because it lies at the root of informality. As the numbers of informal workers and social protection programs increase, those trade-offs will become increasingly costly. Economic growth itself will not eliminate informality, but it will be slower because of it.

The conundrum just described also defines, in a nutshell as well, the case for reform—*a case that, in my view, is very strong when based on any one of the elements above and that is compelling when those elements are considered together.*

## A Reference Equilibrium: Universal Social Entitlements

Any case for reform must be built on the existence of an alternative proposal that on balance can be considered better than the status quo; my proposal, I believe, fits that description. This section provides a general overview of the proposal, which is discussed in more detail in the sections that follow. I begin with four premises: first, that there are substantive reasons for the government to impose its preferences on workers, forcing them to consume a bundle of goods that they may otherwise not consume; second, that the justification for the imposition applies to all workers, not just salaried ones; third, that the government's objective in imposing its preferences is different from its objective in redistributing income in favor of low-wage workers, although, given Mexico's deep inequities, that is equally important.

The fourth premise is perhaps the most important at this point: *what matters are the results, not the intentions, of policies; consequently, the instruments used to pursue them need to be chosen pragmatically to achieve the desired results.* That implies that the challenge is to find an administratively feasible and effective combination of instruments that will in fact produce the desired outcome in the international context faced by Mexico today: to provide all workers with protection against basic risks, to redistribute income toward those with low incomes to avoid increasing the country's fiscal vulnerability, and to align the incentives of workers and firms to increase productivity and efficiency.

### The Core Proposal

The core proposal can be simply described: *to provide all workers with the same social entitlements paid for from the same source of revenue.* To contrast it with the status quo, let $T^{CP}$ be the monetary cost per worker of the social benefits provided

Table 10-2. *Social Policy: Status Quo versus Core Proposal*

| *Status quo (social security and social protection)* | *Core proposal (universal social entitlements)* |
|---|---|
| **Benefits** | |
| Benefits are bundled and obligatory for formal workers and unbundled and voluntary for informal workers. | Benefits are bundled and obligatory for all workers (although benefits are fewer than current benefits for formal workers). |
| **Firms** | |
| Those hiring salaried labor mix legal and illegal workers and cover the costs of social security contributions and the expected costs of fines; those hiring nonsalaried workers and the self-employed pay only the informal wage. | All firms pay the same wage; there are no non-wage costs of labor. |
| **Workers' utility** | |
| $w_f + \beta_f T_f = w_i + \beta_i T_i = w_{if} + \beta_i T_i$ <br> formal   informal   informal <br> salaried  nonsalaried  salaried | $w_f + \beta^{CP} T^{CP} = w_i + \beta^{CP} T^{CP}$ <br> salaried    nonsalaried |
| **Government budget constraint** | |
| The budget includes the cost of subsidies to social security and social protection programs. | The budget includes the cost of universal social entitlements. |

Source: Author's analysis.

to all workers under the core proposal and let $\beta^{CP}$ be workers' valuation of those benefits. I do not yet describe the specific benefits contained in $T^{CP}$, except to note that it includes those that the Mexican government wants all workers to consume. At this point it is helpful to keep the discussion at a general level. There are two important points about $T^{CP}$:

—Benefits are the same for all workers.[1]

—Benefits take the form of entitlements or legal rights.

Table 10-2 provides a broad comparison between the status quo and the core proposal. First and foremost, in the core proposal the government's social objectives are achieved with all workers, *regardless of their salaried or nonsalaried status or their shifts between the two.*

Second, in the status quo there are formal and informal workers, including among the latter illegal salaried workers; in the core proposal there are salaried and nonsalaried workers and all are legal (although to avoid introducing new notation, I keep the subscripts f and i).

Third, salaried employment is higher in the core proposal than in the status quo and nonsalaried employment lower. More particularly, the distribution of the

---

1. That is why there are no subindices on $T^{CP}$ and $\beta^{CP}$.

labor force between salaried and nonsalaried employment in the core proposal is similar to that observed in the case discussed in chapter 6, where either $\beta_f = 1$ and there was no social protection or there was no social policy at all (see the discussion of figures 6-4 and 6-5). The key difference in this case is that there are social entitlements for all, even if $\beta^{CP} < 1$. *In other words, workers' valuations of social benefits are irrelevant from the standpoint of efficiency in the allocation of labor.*

Universal social entitlements allow separating the workings of the labor market from the government's social objectives. The allocation of labor is driven only by the economic rationale for different forms of contractual relationships between firms and workers, based on considerations regarding the distribution of ownership of productive assets and entrepreneurial ability across workers and the risk-sharing and effort-eliciting agreements between firms and workers briefly discussed in chapter 1. Those relationships are not distorted by attempts to avoid a tax on salaried employment or to enjoy the benefits of a subsidy to nonsalaried labor. Equally, workers who choose self-employment do so because of their inherent comparative advantages as entrepreneurs and the quasi-rents on the efficiently priced value of any productive assets that they might own—not because of the implicit subsidy to entrepreneurship and the artificially high prices for their assets associated with depressed informal wages. As a result, *in the core proposal, aggregate labor productivity and aggregate output are higher.*

Fourth, in the core proposal there are no incentives to evade and no implicit taxes on a firm's growth from evading social security because there are no wage-based social security contributions. As a result, average firm size is larger than under the *status quo*, with more fully exploited economies of scale or scope and lower Coase-type transaction costs providing another source of efficiency gains. Further, because the cost of labor is the same to all firms regardless of size or type of activity, there are no distortions provoked by social programs in the composition of output or in the allocation of investment. The latter condition implies that there are no implicit subsidies to investment in privately profitable but socially inefficient projects that increase the economy's incremental capital-output ratio (ICOR); *as a result, the rate of growth of GDP is higher.*

Fifth, wages in salaried and nonsalaried employment are higher in the core proposal than under the *status quo* because labor productivity is higher. Nevertheless, the cost of labor to firms demanding salaried workers in the core proposal is lower because firms save on the cost of the official governance mechanisms that apply to salaried labor; that is why salaried employment increases. Profits and quasi-rents in firms hiring salaried workers also are higher in the core proposal because output and employment expand as a result of lower non-wage labor costs. On the other hand, profits and quasi-rents are lower in nonsalaried employment because wages (or commissions) are higher.

An implication of higher labor costs in nonsalaried employment is that the price of productive assets used in some nonsalaried activities is lower in the core proposal, perhaps leading to some assets being laid to rest (for example, the half-hectare of low-quality, rain-fed land that was profitably exploited only when the opportunity cost of a worker's own labor was very low).[2] The same could occur when small firms that hire salaried workers evade social security laws. As chapter 7 argues, higher wages could cause small backyard workshops that hire salaried workers illegally to close down, with those workers being absorbed in salaried employment by firms that previously did not evade (see the discussion of figure 7-7). Self-employment most likely would decrease too, because the opportunity cost of working on one's own would increase; as a result, the price of old mixers used to make fruit juice for sale on city streets would fall and street corners where all sorts of wares could be sold would become less valuable.

Sixth, finally, in the core proposal poor workers face the same incentives as other workers; there are no social policy–induced reasons for poor workers to be over-represented among illegal salaried workers. More poor workers have salaried jobs with firms that are, on average, larger. The incentives of Progresa-Oportunidades are compatible with the incentives of other social programs, in contrast with the the status quo. *Poor workers have improved access to higher-productivity jobs and can earn higher wages, eventually escaping poverty through their own efforts without the need for government transfers.*

In short, the universal social entitlements model eliminates the tax on formal labor and the subsidy to informal labor that currently characterize Mexico's labor market, removing a crucial obstacle to higher productivity and growth. That does not imply that informality would disappear. Firms could still be informal in the sense of not registering with relevant state and municipal authorities, and they could still evade income taxes; informality could still exist from the standpoint of there being substantial property that was not registered or titled and therefore not available to use as collateral for financial transactions. But it does imply that *from the standpoint of social policy, formality and informality would no longer be relevant categories.* Subject to various qualifications made below, my argument is that, in a general sense, Mexico would be better off under a system of universal social entitlements than under the present dualistic system of social provisioning.

## Is Efficiency Necessarily Higher under Universal Social Entitlements?

To determine whether efficiency is necessarily higher under universal social entitlements, it is useful to contrast the efficiency costs of the core proposal with those

2. Of course, in a misguided attempt to use agricultural pricing policies to stimulate employment, subsidies to output prices still could induce workers to exploit their low-quality land. The results of those policies are similar to the ones discussed in this book: they trap workers in low-productivity jobs.

observed under the status quo. The left side of expression 10-1 captures the latter; the right side captures the former:

$$(10\text{-}1)\quad \begin{bmatrix}\text{lost productivity from labor}\\ \text{misallocation + lost productivity}\\ \text{from capital misallocation and other}\\ \text{obstacles to firms' growth + efficiency}\\ \text{costs of raising 2.3 percent of GDP}\\ \text{in subsidies to social protection}\\ \text{and social security programs}\end{bmatrix} \leqslant \geqslant \begin{bmatrix}\text{efficiency costs of raising}\\ \text{? percent of GDP in}\\ \text{subsidies for universal}\\ \text{social entitlements}\end{bmatrix}.$$

Note that while under the core proposal the productivity costs of labor and capital misallocation disappear, the efficiency costs of raising revenues to pay for universal social benefits must be considered. Obviously, unless more information is provided about $T^{CP}$ and the sources of revenue used to pay for it, one cannot tell whether the right side of expression 10-1 is lower than the left side. As a result, even though from the standpoint of the government's social objectives universal social entitlements are clearly preferable to the status quo, from the standpoint of efficiency the costs to the economy are not necessarily lower. For that to be the case, an alternative source of revenue must be found to pay for the costs of universal social entitlements that creates fewer distortions than the present combination of wage-based contributions and other sources of revenue discussed in chapter 9. If universal social entitlements are paid for with external debt, with temporary oil rents, or with further reductions in public investment, the cure could end up being worse than the disease as the economy plunges into macroeconomic uncertainty and budget deficits appear that sooner or later end up making everybody worse off.

I argue below that universal social entitlements should be paid for with consumption taxes and that wage-based social security contributions should be eliminated. That argument rests on two lines of reasoning. First, in an economy open to international competition, consumption taxes create fewer distortions than a tax on salaried labor accompanied by a subsidy to nonsalaried labor. In other words, a distortion in the price of a key non-traded input is exchanged for taxes that do not affect the distribution of employment, the composition of output, or the allocation of investment. Two, with an appropriate combination of consumption taxes and subsidies, the government also can achieve the objective of redistribution.

*Universal Social Entitlements without Redistribution*

To elaborate on the core proposal, I proceed in two steps, separating the government's redistributive objective from its objectives of changing the composition of workers' consumption and solving their contracting problems in insurance markets. Table 10-3 contrasts workers' utility and the fiscal costs of social programs

Table 10-3. *Financing Social Policy without Redistribution*[a]

| Status quo (formal-informal dichotomy) | Core proposal (universal social entitlements) |
|---|---|
| **Workers' utility** | |
| $U^{SQ}_f = w^{SQ}_f + \beta_f T_f - t_w$ | $U^{CP}_f = w^{CP}_f + \beta^{CP} T^{CP} - (t_w + \Delta t_w)$ |
| $U^{SQ}_i = w^{SQ}_i + \beta_i T_i - t_w$ | $U^{CP}_i = w^{CP}_i + \beta^{CP} T^{CP} - (t_w + \Delta t_w)$ |
| $U^{SQ}_f = U^{SQ}_i$ | $U^{CP}_f = U^{CP}_i$ |

**Impact on government budget**

| $(t_w)L$ | $\leq \geq [\theta_f T_f L^{SQ}_f + T_i (L^{SQ}_i + L^{SQ}_{if})]$ | $(t_w + \Delta t_w)L = T^{CP}L$ | |
|---|---|---|---|
| taxes paid by workers | cost of subsidies to social protection and social security programs | taxes paid by workers | cost of universal social entitlements |

Source: Author's analysis.
a. The superscripts SQ and CP refer to the status quo and the core proposal, respectively.

under the status quo and the core proposal. As in chapter 9, I leave open the question of whether there is some redistribution under the present combination of social security and social protection programs. The point that I want to emphasize here is that in the core proposal there is an increase in consumption taxes paid by workers, $\Delta t_w$, so that the total amount of the taxes that workers pay equals the cost of the universal social entitlements that they receive.

The relevant aspect of table 10-3 is the column on the right side, which depicts the case in which the government's social interventions change the composition of workers' consumption but are neutral from the redistributive perspective; there is no redistribution of income from future to present or from other households to workers. The government accomplishes its objective of protecting all workers against the risks that it considers relevant without affecting its fiscal position.[3] In particular, the taxes that the government takes away from workers with one hand are returned to workers with the other hand in the form of $T^{CP}$, the bundled set of goods and services that the government wants workers to consume. If all workers were salaried, that situation would be qualitatively identical to the one described in chapter 6 (see the discussion of figure 6-5). The only difference in comparison with that scenario is that instead of social security contributions being deducted from gross wages at the workplace when the workers are paid, the equivalent amount is deducted at the store in the form of consumption taxes when workers make their purchases. In both cases net wages after social security contributions, or net disposable income after consumption taxes, are the same.

3. That is not completely accurate because under the formal-informal dichotomy, the taxes that workers pay may be more or less than the subsidies that they receive through social security and social protection programs. In fact, if, as discussed in chapter 9, those subsidies currently are being paid in part with oil rents, the proposal *improves* the government's fiscal position because now all social entitlements are paid with taxes.

However, because not all workers are salaried, social security contributions and consumption taxes are not equivalent. Under the formal-informal dichotomy, workers can avoid social security contributions through informal labor, whereas under universal social entitlements they cannot avoid consumption taxes by changing labor status. From that perspective, the proposal just changes the point of collection from the workplace to the store. The advantage is both simple and powerful: *all workers have to pay regardless of labor status.* Although workers value at $\beta^{CP} T^{CP}$ something that they pay $T^{CP}$ for, there is nothing they can do to avoid the "pure" tax of $(1 - \beta^{CP}) T^{CP}$. In particular, workers gain nothing by changing from salaried to any form of nonsalaried employment[4] and firms gain nothing by altering the labor contracts that they offer workers or by changing their employment and output decisions to avoid detection and punishment by IMSS.

Are workers better off? To answer that question, compare workers' utility in each case. Focusing on salaried workers (the same holds for nonsalaried),

$$(10\text{-}2) \qquad U_f^{CP} - U_f^{SQ} = \left( w_f^{CP} - w_f^{SQ} \right) + \left( \beta^{CP} T^{CP} - \beta_f T_f \right) - \Delta t_w .$$

The first term on the right side is clearly positive because the higher labor productivity associated with a more efficient allocation of labor translates into higher wages (see figure 6-5 and the discussion thereof). The third term is clearly negative because workers pay higher consumption taxes. The term in the middle is ambiguous; its direction depends on the value that workers attach to universal social entitlements relative to the value that they attach to social security benefits—that is, to the bundle of goods included in $T^{CP}$ relative to the bundle included in $T_f$. One cannot make a definite assessment; at this point, I just make a preliminary conclusion: *in the absence of any redistribution toward workers, a fiscally neutral change from the current combination of social security and social protection programs toward universal social entitlements has an ambiguous effect on workers' utility and a positive effect on productivity.*

It is important to highlight here that the comparison in equation 10-2 is with the status quo. If universal social entitlements are compared with a no-social-benefits equilibrium, from the point of view of workers there would be a clear loss or, at best, no gain. The reason is discussed in chapter 6: workers prefer to keep their full income and spend it as they like, and, unless $\beta^{CP} = 1$, they always are worse off when the government imposes its preferences on them. This discussion reiterates, from a different perspective, an argument made in the previous chapters: unless there are subsidies from other households to workers, a policy of universal social entitlements cannot increase workers' utility more than the no-social-policy case does.

*However, from the point of view of the government, that comparison is irrelevant.* As argued in previous chapters, what matters to the government are its own social

---

4. I assume that the change in consumption taxes is permanent, so workers cannot avoid them by consuming less today and more tomorrow. They face the same taxes every year.

objectives. And from that perspective it is highly relevant to note that even without government subsidies, a change from the current dualistic structure of social provisioning to universal social entitlements has the potential to increase workers' utility while realizing the government's social objectives with all workers.

## Universal Social Entitlements with Redistribution

Having the potential to increase workers' utility and actually doing so are two different things. Regardless of whether utility is higher under the core proposal, the government still might want to redistribute income to workers—or at least to a subset of low-wage workers—in addition to imposing its preferences on all workers.

In order to achieve the redistributive objective in the context of universal social entitlements an additional instrument must be introduced, namely, a pure income transfer to workers. The combination of consumption taxes on all households with a pure income transfer to a subset of households serves to redistribute income and attain balance in the fiscal accounts. To see how, let $s^{CP}$ be a pure monetary subsidy per worker to be freely spent, so that the change in workers' utility is

$$(10\text{-}3) \quad U_f^{CP} - U_f^{SQ} = \left(w_f^{CP} - w_f^{SQ}\right) + \left(\beta^{CP}T^{CP} - \beta_f T_f\right) - \Delta t_w + s^{CP},$$

where $s^{CP}$ is chosen so that workers are at least as well off in the core proposal as under the status quo and potentially better off.

What is the effect of the transfer on the government's fiscal accounts? To isolate its fiscal impact, assume that universal social entitlements and pure income transfers cannot be paid by using oil rents, taking on further debt, or reducing public investment or spending on other goods and services. That is a strong assumption, but it is useful here to rule out any intertemporal redistribution or indirect costs to economic growth of the change in social policy. The following expression identifies the impact of the pure income transfer:[5]

$$(10\text{-}4) \quad \left(R_{ct}^{CP} + R_{\pi}^{CP}\right) - \left(R_{ct}^{SQ} + R_{\pi}^{SQ}\right) \geq T^{CP}L - \left[\theta_f T_f L_f^{SQ} + T_i\left(L_i^{SQ} + L_{if}^{SQ}\right)\right]$$

(additional revenues from consumption taxes on nonworker households plus additional income taxes on firms)   (net fiscal costs of universal social entitlements).

---

5. Let $R_{cw}$ and $R_{\pi}$ be total consumption taxes paid by workers and other households respectively and $R_{\pi}$ be income taxes paid by firms. The difference between taxes and the fiscal costs of subsidies to social security and social protection programs is given by $[R_{cw}^{SQ} + R_{ct}^{SQ} + R_{\pi}^{SQ}] - [\theta_f T_f L_f^{SQ} + T_i(L_i^{SQ} + L_{if}^{SQ})]$. The difference between taxes and the fiscal costs of universal social entitlements together with the fiscal costs of the income transfer is given by $[R_{cw}^{CP} + R_{ct}^{CP} + R_{\pi}^{CP}] - [T^{CP}L + s^{CP}L]$. The constraint that workers pay no more *net* additional consumption taxes than under the status quo is equivalent to $R_{cw}^{SQ} = R_{cw}^{CP} - s^{SP}L$. Combining that with the two previous expressions yields expression 10-4 in the text.

Expression 10-4 is very useful. It can be interpreted in two steps: first, consumption taxes are increased on all households, but the additional amount paid by workers is returned to them via a direct income transfer, so that the net gain in tax revenues comes only from nonworker households and higher income taxes paid by firms. Second, to pay for universal social entitlements, the additional revenues collected, net of the amount returned to workers, are used to complement the resources already budgeted for subsidies to social security and social protection programs. Of course, whether the inequality in expression 10-4 is observed depends not only on the net additional taxes collected, but also on $T^{CP}$—that is, on the bundle of social entitlements that is to be provided to all workers. Because the content of $T^{CP}$ is central to the proposal, I discuss it in more detail in the following sections.

The main point to be made at this stage is that there are two alternatives to pay for universal social entitlements: one in which workers pay fully for the additional costs of the entitlements and one in which they do not pay at all. In both cases, the government accomplishes its objective of imposing its preferences on all workers and solving their contracting problems in insurance markets; in both cases the allocation of labor is efficient and there are no impacts on firms or on the allocation of investment; and in both cases there is no redistribution from future to present consumption in the form of reduced public investment or increased used of oil rents to pay for social programs. The key difference is in the extent of redistribution that occurs from other households toward workers: at one extreme, none; at the other, the change in social policy is fully redistributive.

Of course, many intermediate cases can be constructed, with the value of $s^{CP}$ chosen so that workers bear some of the costs of the change toward universal social entitlements.[6] Rather than pinpointing a specific case, the discussion stresses three points:

—The redistributive objective must be separated from the objective of changing the composition of consumption.

—A different instrument must be used to pursue each objective.

—The instruments used to pursue the objectives must be the same for all workers.

Is an increase in consumption taxes indispensable if the government is to offer universal social entitlements in Mexico? In my view, yes. The reader could argue

6. A limitation of the analysis here is that it treats all workers equally and returns to each worker the additional consumption taxes paid. Of course, there is significant variance in workers' wages and some redistribution within workers is desirable, indeed unavoidable, because higher-income households also have workers. One way of achieving that is to set the value of $s^{CP}$ at, say, the level at which workers in the third decile of the income distribution pay no additional taxes and return the same $s^{CP}$ per worker. That would imply that workers in the first three deciles would be overcompensated and those from the fourth decile onward would pay net taxes. Dávila and Levy (2003) discusses this in detail.

that income tax rates could be raised as well (and loopholes in the income tax laws closed). A proper assessment of why that is unlikely to succeed is beyond the scope of this volume, but two points are noteworthy. One, increases in income taxes could strengthen firms' incentives to be illegal, because while firms no longer would have to pay for social security contributions, they would have to pay higher income taxes. Any such incentive would partly offset the efficiency gains sought by removing wage-based social security contributions. Second, in the context of international capital mobility, income tax rates have limits. Large firms can easily engage in tax arbitrage across countries, with little revenue gained. That does not mean that loopholes should not be closed and compliance strengthened (and procedures simplified!) or that the higher revenues thus obtained could not contribute to financing universal social entitlements. But it does mean that there are narrow limits to the extent to which additional income tax rates on firms can be raised in Mexico (as opposed to increasing tax collections through better enforcement).

Must consumption taxes be raised for all? In my view, yes. Attempts to redistribute income through consumption taxes are very ineffective for a reason that is sad but, for the purposes of the core proposal, convenient: Mexico's extremely concentrated distribution of income and consumption.[7] In that context, exemptions from consumption taxes on various goods transfer more income to higher-income than to lower-income households, even if lower-income households allocate a larger share of their income to purchasing the goods subject to exemptions.

The value-added tax (VAT) is Mexico's main consumption tax. The general VAT rate is 15 percent, but there are two special regimes, justified on redistributive grounds: an exemption regime at every stage of the production process for food items and a zero-rate regime at the last stage of the production process for medicines and education. Dávila and Levy (2003) shows that of every peso of revenue forgone under the zero-rate regime, only around 30 centavos reaches the poorest half of the population and that of every peso of revenue forgone under the exempt regime, only 18.3 centavos reaches that group.[8] It also shows that in the context of VAT reform to eliminate the special regimes, it is feasible to carry out a Slutsky-type compensation to fully compensate all households in the first two to five deciles of the distribution and still leave substantial net resources.

At the same time, given the administrative complexities (and opportunities for corruption) associated with a system of multiple VAT rates, there are large leakages of revenue that do not benefit low-income households. The net result is this: because only 55 percent of the total consumption basket pays the VAT rate

---

7. Mexico has one of the highest concentrations of income in Latin America and probably in the world. The poorest 20 percent of the population receives only 4.4 percent of total income, while the richest 20 percent receives 54.5 percent.

8. Dávila and Levy (2003, p. 364).

of 15 percent, the average rate is approximately 8 percent,[9] and total VAT revenues as a share of GDP were only 4.2 percent in 2006.[10]

In fact, because in Mexico the distribution of income is so skewed, the higher the VAT rate the more the redistribution that can occur while leaving a larger remnant of resources. A basic finding of Dávila and Levy (2003) is that if the VAT rate was changed and set at a uniform rate of 15 percent with no exemptions—under the very conservative assumption that the increase in the VAT would be fully translated into consumer prices, with no reduction in firms' profit margins—of every peso of additional revenue raised, 9.3 centavos would be sufficient to fully compensate all households in the first two deciles of the income distribution and 27 centavos would be enough to fully compensate all households in the first five deciles.[11] In other words, for every peso of additional gross revenue there would be between 90.7 and 73 centavos of net after-compensation revenue, depending on whether compensation reached the poorest 20 or 50 percent of the population.

*The basic point is that consumption taxes exist to raise revenue, not to redistribute income,* and that, good intentions notwithstanding, attempts to use them to redistribute income in a context like Mexico's, where the distribution of consumption is highly skewed, are counterproductive. Yes, workers pay less for certain goods, but they also get less of other goods—the set of goods that are at the center of the government's social objectives. And as other sources of revenue are used to finance those other goods, namely social security contributions, the distortions created along the way end up hurting everyone, particularly low-wage and poor workers. That is one of the central messages of this book. Because income is so unequally distributed in Mexico, redistribution will not function through an instrument that fails to distinguish between household income levels—one, in fact, that in absolute terms ends up reducing the tax burden on higher-income households more than on lower-income households. And because the government ends up with less revenue, it is forced to choose between diverting oil rents and sacrificing growth-promoting public investments to finance social programs or leaving millions of workers unprotected. The choices made by the Mexican government in the last decade were documented in chapter 9 (see table 9-4 and figure 9-2). Although those choices are understandable, they will not lead to higher growth, increased productivity, and faster poverty reduction.

That does not mean that the VAT rate should be increased indefinitely, because that would generate problems with evasion. But it does mean that in the case of Mexico, substantial room currently exists to increase the average rate, compensate

9. Dávila and Levy (2003, section 10.3)
10. Mexico has one of the lowest tax burdens in the world. In 2006 total taxes were only 9.9 percent of GDP; see table 9-4. That was composed of 4.2 percent VAT, 4.9 percent income taxes, and 0.8 percent other taxes (on gasoline, liquor, imports, and so on). By international standards, the VAT is the most abnormally low of all taxes in Mexico.
11. Dávila and Levy (2003, table 10.2, p. 374).

low-income households, and have something left over for other uses. The proposal in this chapter is that *the special VAT regimes should be removed, using the proceeds to eliminate what is probably the most distorting tax in Mexico today, the tax on legal salaried labor, and to fund universal social entitlements through tax-cum-expenditure reform that increases equity and is more conducive to higher productivity and growth.*

## Is the Proposal Administratively Feasible?

With some qualifications discussed below, the proposal is administratively feasible. To elaborate it is necessary to provide more detail regarding what is contained in $T^{CP}$, as I do in the following discussion. However, to avoid distracting the reader's attention at this point, I assume momentarily that $T^{CP} = T_f$. From the administrative standpoint, the proposal works as follows:

—First, all workers are assigned a social security number and a social security card for which they must pay an annual fee of, say, twenty pesos;[12] all workers are required to register with the Finance Ministry and declare their occupation and income; and all workers are required to open an individual account with the Afore of their choice if they do not have one.[13] No worker can have an Afore account without registering with the Finance Ministry, and no worker can receive any benefits without his or her social security card.

—Second, out of general tax revenues, the government sets aside $T_f$ per worker registered with the Finance Ministry and with an Afore.

—Third, the government transfers $T_f$ per worker to IMSS, which then proceeds as if $T_f$ had been obtained from wage-based social security contributions: it distributes the corresponding share of $T_f$ to the housing sub-account and the retirement sub-account of each worker's Afore account and to the medical, disability, work-risk, and day care funds of IMSS.

12. An important element of the proposal is that all workers would have a social security number (the *Clave Unica de Registro de Población* assigned to all Mexicans at birth) and that no worker could access any government program without it (that would extend to programs operated by all federal ministries and agencies). The fee is symbolic; it could be set even lower, say, at ten pesos a year. The point is that *all workers have to comply with an obligation before receiving any benefits and that there is a formal point of intersection between the worker as citizen and the state.* Mexico's previous experience in that regard has been successful: since the mid-1990s, all citizens have had to have a card to exercise their voting rights, and even citizens in the most remote rural areas of Mexico have a card and use it. The exercise of the right to vote is contingent on an obligation: to obtain a voting card first. I note here that all households that are beneficiaries of Progresa-Oportunidades already are registered with the Ministry of Social Development and periodically provide the government with information about their household characteristics, so even the poorest workers can comply with the obligation suggested here. The basic obstacle to a universal social security card is an internal government problem: unifying the many databases dispersed throughout various ministries and agencies.

13. Recall from table 5-8 that at the end of December 2006 there were 37.4 million Afore accounts and from table 5-1 that there were 41.4 million workers (excluding ISSSTE affiliates). If there were no duplications, that would indicate that in fact only about 4 million workers do not have an Afore account already. But even considering duplications, the numbers show that the majority of workers have an account.

—Finally, IMSS, Infonavit, and the Afores proceed with their normal operations, *except that they cover 41.4 million rather than 14.1 million workers.*

In other words, the basic administrative capabilities and operational procedures for providing universal social entitlements in Mexico already exist or can be developed in a reasonable amount of time with existing information technologies. That does not mean that the ministries and agencies administering those procedures and providing services work perfectly. As the discussion in chapter 3 illustrates, that is not the case. But the point here is that no radically new mechanisms, procedures, or institutions are needed. On the contrary, Mexico's previous efforts and recent experience can be put to good use. Of course, the proposal requires improvements in the modus operandi of ministries and agencies, but those improvements are urgently needed with or without universal social entitlements.

What about the compensation mechanism to return $s^{CP}$ to workers, given the redistribution considered appropriate? The mechanism to do so already is in place. Because each worker has his or her own Afore and the law regulating Afores already takes into consideration that workers can periodically draw resources from the sub-account in which they put their voluntary savings, the government would transfer to IMSS not only $T_f$ per worker, but $T_f$ plus $s^{CP}$. IMSS would then use the mechanisms already in place to deposit $s^{CP}$ into each worker's Afore account at the same time that it deposits the retirement and housing components.[14] Workers could draw $s^{CP}$ from their accounts on a periodic basis (say, every month) for current consumption or, if they wish, voluntarily save some or all of it for the future, adding to the obligatory saving occurring with the retirement component of $T^{CP}$.

I end this section by noting that while in the discussion I referred to consumption taxes, perhaps it would be more proper to call them "universal social entitlements contributions." That distinction is irrelevant here, although not from a legal standpoint because in Mexico contributions must have a specific purpose and taxes can be used for any purpose. By making a "universal social entitlements contribution," workers would have full certainty that their consumption taxes would be returned to them in the form of $T^{CP}$ and not diverted to any other use. Members of Congress, particularly those from opposition parties, would have the same certainty. Dávila and Levy (2003) briefly discusses the issue of trust in the context of VAT reform and argues that any proposal to increase the VAT must be accompanied by a proposal of equal legal weight to obligate the government to provide ben-

---

14. Recall from chapter 3 that the government already contributes to each worker's retirement pension with a subsidy—the *cuota social para el retiro,* which is channeled to each worker's Afore account. That subsidy goes to the worker's retirement sub-account and cannot be used until retirement. Using exactly the same mechanism, the government would also deposit $s^{CP}$, except that workers could use it for current consumption.

efits to workers. Clearly a "Tax me; I trust you to provide me with social benefits" attitude will not do. The same holds with regard to pure income transfers: payments of $s^{CP}$ to workers would be included in the Social Security Law, making the compensation a credible, legal obligation of the government.

## What Should Universal Social Entitlements Be?

The previous discussion purposely glossed over the contents of $T^{CP}$ to focus attention on the issues of universality and fiscal and administrative feasibility. This section addresses two issues: the nature of the benefits contained in $T^{CP}$ and whether all benefits should be delinked from workers' labor status.

### Partially Unbundling Social Benefits

Recall the present contents of the official governance mechanisms that apply to salaried labor in Mexico, captured by $T_f$ in equation 3-1, which is reproduced here for convenience:

$$(10\text{-}5) \quad T_f = \left[\text{social security} \,|\, \text{firing and severance pay} \,|\, \text{labor taxes}\right]$$

$$= \left[\text{health insurance} \oplus \text{retirement pensions} \oplus \text{disability pensions} \oplus \text{housing loans} \oplus \text{work-risk pensions} \oplus \text{day care centers} \oplus \text{sports and cultural facilities} \oplus \text{life insurance} \oplus \text{firing and severance pay regulations} \oplus \text{labor taxes}\right].$$

Is it desirable that $T^{CP} = T_f$? Or, from a different angle, what are the social benefits to which all Mexican workers should be entitled? I try to separate the answer to that question from that of who should pay for the entitlements to focus attention on the analytical reasons, as opposed to historical inertia or administrative convenience, that should underlie $T^{CP}$. The discussion in chapter 3 provides four elements that I believe need to be considered:

—whether benefits cover the individual or the family

—whether benefits respond to failures in insurance markets that prevent workers from buying insurance against some risks even when they want to

—whether benefits are such that workers would not be willing to purchase them even if they were available

—whether benefits are intrinsically associated with salaried labor.

I argue that

—health, life, and disability insurance, along with retirement pensions, belong to $T^{CP}$

—work-risk pensions and firing and severance pay regulations require separate treatment as benefits relevant only for salaried workers

—housing loans, day care centers, and access to sports and cultural facilities require yet a different treatment

—taxes on salaried labor belong to a different category.

The first two statements respond to the classical reasons for government social intervention, with the important difference that the first applies to all workers. It is important to note that retirement pensions and life and disability insurance are included in the first group because there is no argument other than administrative convenience for exempting nonsalaried workers from the obligation to save for their retirement and to protect themselves from disability or sudden death. The inclusion of retirement pensions is especially critical in the case of Mexico, given the extent of labor mobility (see chapter 5).

Providing insurance to protect workers from work-related risks as well as from negative output and employment shocks in the form of firing and severance pay regulations is, on the other hand, intrinsically associated with salaried labor and with the existence of a boss who fires a worker or who fails to enforce safety standards in the workplace. One could argue that there is no need for the government to obligate parties to provide insurance in such cases, because wages would reflect the risk premiums of various jobs in terms of variability in the level of employment and exposure to work accidents without the government's intervention (and workers also would self-select into jobs on the basis of risk aversion). One also might argue that the government should try to solve only informational failures that prevent parties from internalizing such risks efficiently. There is long debate on that topic, which at this point I skew in my favor because I think that in Mexico's case intervention is necessary.

On the other hand, it is difficult to argue that Infonavit's interventions in housing are required because Mexican workers would not willingly purchase housing otherwise. Nor is it easy to argue that there are large risks that cannot be insured by private firms or informational failures, myopia, or moral hazard with regard to housing. On the contrary, other than the administrative convenience for Infonavit of funding itself out of easy-to-collect taxes on the wage bill, it is difficult to find support for the proposition that contributions to a housing fund need to be obligatory and to apply to salaried workers only. It is even more difficult to find support for the proposition that loans for higher-wage workers should be subsidized with the forced savings of lower-wage workers, as occurs with Infonavit's current modus operandi.

In a context of increased macroeconomic stability, there is substantial room for a private market for long-term mortgages to develop in Mexico. It may have been the case that workers had no access to housing loans in the past, but that was primarily a result of substantive distortions in financial markets that have been corrected in part over the last decade (see Haber 2007). Of course, workers' income level may impede them from obtaining a housing loan, but that is not equivalent to workers' suffering from myopia or there being large informational problems in the housing market.

The point that I am trying to make is that while there may have been reasons in the past for the Mexican government to lump housing and social security together, *those reasons do not exist today.* That does not mean that the government should completely disregard housing; it means only that there are substantive differences between the markets for health insurance or retirement pensions and the market for housing that call for a different type of intervention. Equally, that does not mean that the government should not subsidize housing; it means only that it is difficult to argue that housing should be a universal social entitlement in the same category as health or retirement benefits. From that perspective, should access to food not be a universal social entitlement?

Similar arguments apply to day care centers. There are no substantive failures in the market for day care services, nor do parents need to be forced to consume them. There are no large economies of scale, and there is ease of entry; the technology to provide services is well known and easily accessible. Again, that does not mean that the government should refrain from subsidizing day care centers or intervening to ensure appropriate quality, but it does mean that it is difficult to think of day care as a universal social entitlement.[15] Without further discussion, it is clear that the same arguments apply with greater force to sports and cultural facilities.

Finally, it is clear that the taxes currently collected on salaried labor by state governments are unrelated to social benefits. Those taxes are levied because Mexico's fiscal laws give state governments few alternative sources of taxation.[16] But in this case the issue is conceptually simple: replacing the revenues that state governments receive from labor taxes with an alternative source of revenue. Given Mexico's revenue-sharing formulas, that occurs automatically whenever income or value-added taxes increase. Without providing numerical details, the proposal to increase the VAT automatically generates a mechanism to replace state taxes on salaried labor with shared revenues from this tax.

## The Nature of Universal Social Entitlements

A few observations are in order regarding the four social entitlements included in $T^{CP}$. The first concerns retirement pensions. One central feature is that workers save for their retirement during their entire working life, regardless of their labor status or moves between types of status. Another central feature is that the amounts channeled to workers' individual accounts are the same for all workers regardless of wage level (or income level, in the case of self-employed workers or *comisionistas*), set so

15. IMSS experience with subrogated day care services illustrates that subject to established norms, private providers deliver services appropriately. At the end of 2005, IMSS directly operated 142 day care centers providing services to 30,000 children and outsourced services to 1,217 private firms that provided services to 160,000 children. IMSS sets norms with respect to the feeding and care of children while they are at the centers and norms for educational programs, including early child stimulation; see IMSS (IMSS 2005, p. 83).

16. Income from revenue-sharing formulas on taxes collected by the federal government and transfers from the federal budget account for more than 90 percent of states' revenues.

that at the end of their working life, they have sufficient resources accumulated in a retirement account to enjoy a basic pension or the minimum pension considered socially appropriate. Of course, workers can make additional voluntary contributions to their Afore account. In the case of salaried workers, that could be the result of contractual negotiations with firms, but it could also result from individual decisions, as in the case of self-employed workers and *comisionistas*. The social entitlement takes the form of a basic, not a maximum, pension, and all workers would be free, at the margin, to save according to their preferences.[17]

The same holds for life and disability insurance. Workers would be forced to buy life and disability insurance regardless of labor status or changes of status, and the premiums paid would be the same for everyone. Again, workers could enhance their coverage by purchasing additional insurance with private insurance providers, either with their own funds or through contractual negotiations with firms.[18]

On the other hand, the Social Security Law and the Health Law in Mexico already have established equality of health benefits regardless of wage or income level. Given the changes in Mexico's epidemiological and demographic profile, major challenges have appeared in the health care arena. The proposal allows for a more effective response to those challenges, for example, by facilitating more efficient use of the public medical infrastructure owned by IMSS and federal and state health ministries and agencies. It also opens up the possibility of extending to all workers a health protocol that emphasizes prevention of disease first and treatment second. In addition, by pooling risks over the entire universe of workers, the proposal solves the current adverse selection problem faced by IMSS in which workers with more complex diseases self-select into the formal sector for that reason alone.

Finally, it is obvious that *a proposal to provide the same entitlements to all workers regardless of income level and to pay for them with consumption taxes that by their*

---

17. An important question is whether the government wants to force workers to save the same amount or an amount proportional to their income. The proposal here assumes the former and provides a basic pension, which is the same for everyone. But the government might want to force workers to save in proportion to their income. The system then would offer a basic pension in the form of an equal, universal entitlement and a complementary pension proportional to income. However, the government could force workers to save for the complementary pension only while they were salaried. A related issue is whether the basic pension would be a right of workers or a right of citizens, because some people might go in and out of the labor force during their lifetime. Appendix 9 discusses those issues in more detail.

18. Incentives for rehabilitation also need to be reinforced. Contrary to the general perception, in Mexico most pensions are not granted because workers retire but because they have an accident at work or become disabled. In 2004 *six of ten beneficiaries of a permanent pension received it for work-risk or disability reasons at an average age of forty-eight years;* see IMSS (2005, p. 517 and p. 539, table X.11). The point is that the number of work-risk and disability pensions is abnormally high and results from giving workers and IMSS the wrong incentives. A study should be done of the possibility of changing the system so that those pensions become temporary, providing renewable benefits for workers while they are in rehabilitation, with permanent pensions granted only at retirement age or in case of indisputable medical evidence of irreversible disability. See IMSS (2005, chap. 10).

*nature are proportional to income level is inherently redistributive.* Even if low-wage workers are not compensated for their reduced current consumption as a result of higher VAT rates, the proposal increases their future consumption proportionately more than that of high-wage workers and implies a cross-subsidy for health services and life and disability insurance, which can be consumed at any point in a worker's lifetime. The proposal implies extending social entitlements to 16.9 million low-wage workers, which would *more than double the number (8.1 million) of those workers who currently have social security coverage* (see table 5.1).

Poor workers would gain the most, but not only because of the redistribution in their favor and their increased access to social benefits. For the poor, the improved possibilities of obtaining a salaried job and being trained by a firm in the context of legal and more stable work relationships is equally valuable. *A radical change in the incentives given to firms and workers in the labor market is required if poor workers are to find better jobs.* The proposal offers such a change. Under the proposal, those workers eventually will require no redistribution because they will have pulled out of poverty through their own efforts.

### The Nature of Salary-Specific Social Entitlements

Let $T_f^{CP}$ denote the monetary costs per worker of social entitlements that apply only to salaried labor: firing and severance pay regulations and work-risk insurance. It is natural to introduce the parameter $\beta_f^{CP}$ to represent workers' valuation of $T_f^{CP}$. Take special note that $T_f^{CP}$ includes only benefits that pertain to an individual worker.[19]

*Work-risk insurance and firing and severance pay regulations imply that social entitlements should not be fully delinked from labor status.* Clearly, risks that are exclusive to salaried labor should be covered only for salaried workers. Parties in salaried relationships need to have the right incentives to minimize those risks. As a result, the costs of work-risk insurance should be covered by wage-based contributions, as they are today, with premiums reflecting the individual firm's accident record and offering appropriate incentives to workers and firms to make the workplace safer.

Following the discussion in chapter 6, to the extent that $\beta_f^{CP} < 1$, a wedge is introduced between the benefits perceived by workers and the costs to firms, generating a "pure" tax on salaried labor of $(1 - \beta_f^{CP})\, T_f^{CP}$. But the productivity loss generated by the tax would be substantially lower than that of the current tax because the costs of $T_f^{CP}$ are about one-seventh the costs of $T_f$ (see below) and because the fact that all benefits in $T_f^{CP}$ are appropriated by the individual worker and take the form of a monetary payment suggests not only that $\beta_f^{CP} > \beta_f$ but also that $\beta_f^{CP}$ could be close to unity.

---

19. As a result, there would be no disincentive to one married partner seeking salaried employment when the other partner already is salaried; more generally, family composition would not affect labor status choices.

On the other hand, at present firing and severance pay regulations are characterized by uncertainty and significant transaction costs that create a large wedge between the benefits received by workers and the contingent costs paid by firms.[20] In the context of universal social entitlements, workers would be protected by health insurance and would accumulate resources for their retirement even if temporarily unemployed. That opens the possibility of exploring more effective mechanisms to protect salaried workers from output and employment shocks. In particular, replacing severance pay with well-designed unemployment insurance that exploits the fact that all workers have an individual account is a possibility that merits further attention. The idea would be to allow for longer search periods and better matches between workers' individual abilities and firms' needs while avoiding moral hazard problems and aligning incentives in the direction of work.[21]

One possible mechanism is to make unemployment insurance similar to work-risk insurance, with firms paying ex ante a premium to be deposited in a separate sub-account of each worker's individual account. Those resources could be used by workers during periods of unemployment; unused resources would increase their retirement pensions.[22] This issue is complex and exceeds the scope of this book, but it is nonetheless worth a brief mention to include it in the general discussion of how to design more effective instruments to protect workers while minimizing productivity costs to the economy.

### Universal and Salary-Specific Social Entitlements and Social Benefits

*In summary, I argue for deep change in the scope and nature of Mexico's social policy:* eliminating social protection programs; turning social security for salaried workers into a system of universal social entitlements; keeping only a small subset of social entitlements specific to salaried workers; potentially replacing the current system of severance pay with unemployment insurance; introducing direct income transfers to workers to protect low-income households from the regressive effect of changes to the VAT; ceasing to treat housing and day care as an entitlement of workers, while keeping open the government's options to subsidize those benefits to the extent fiscally possible; and, at the same time, maintaining the operation of Progresa-Oportunidades. Figure 10-1 summarizes my proposal.

Two implications of this proposal should be highlighted. First, as represented by the ⊕ sign, *universal social entitlements take the form of a bundle of benefits.*

---

20. See Dávila (1994) and Calderón (2000).

21. See IDB (2004) and Blanchard (2004).

22. A feature of this mechanism is that it would protect workers from a firm's bankruptcy because benefits would be prepaid on a flow basis while the firm is in operation. At present many workers, particularly those working for small and medium-size firms, fail to collect their severance pay because the firm declares bankruptcy. While their legal rights to collect are preserved, it is costly to seize and auction the assets of the bankrupt firm to pay workers. Often assets somehow disappear one day before bankruptcy is declared.

Figure 10-1. *Proposed Social Entitlements and Social Benefits*

| Social program | | Beneficiary |
|---|---|---|
| $T_i$ ⟶ 0 | | Nobody |
| $T_f$ | $T^{CP}$ = [health insurance ⊕ retirement pensions ⊕ life insurance ⊕ disability insurance] | All workers |
| | $T_f^{CP}$ = [work-risk insurance ⊕ severance pay (unemployment insurance?)] | Salaried workers |
| | Other social benefits = [housing loans + day care centers (not entitlements)     + sports and cultural facilities] | All workers |
| $s^{CP}$ ⟶ | Direct income transfers to compensate for VAT; no income transfers or subsidies through income taxes | All workers same amount |
| Progresa-Oportunidades ⟶ | Income transfers to households contingent on investments in human capital | Poor households |

Source: Author's analysis.

Certainly $T^{CP}$ bundles fewer benefits than $T_f$, but a complete unbundling of benefits is not appropriate. That does not mean that the benefits listed in $T^{CP}$ should be provided by the same agency, but it does mean that mechanisms are needed to ensure that all workers consume the benefits jointly.[23] Note that social entitlements for salaried workers, $T_f^{CP}$, also are bundled. Again, that does not mean that those benefits have to be provided by the same agency; it means that salaried workers need to be protected against the risks simultaneously. Consequently, some benefits continue to be linked to salaried labor status.

Second, the proposal modifies substantially the nature of the federal budget. On the revenue side, labor taxes would be replaced by consumption taxes; revenues from VAT would increase significantly; the tax base also would expand as income tax evasion by firms was reduced (as well as the evasion of VAT associated with multiple rates); and income transfers carried out through the revenue side of the budget would disappear.[24] *Taxes would concentrate on what taxes are supposed to do: raising revenues as efficiently as possible.*

23. In other words, the challenge in Mexico is not to provide universal health insurance by itself, disregarding the implications of the mechanisms to do so for workers' access to pensions, for instance. More generally, if the government wants all workers to have access to the goods contained in $T^{CP}$, then it cannot focus its attention on individual components of $T^{CP}$ separately; it needs to consider all of them at the same time.

24. Mexico's income tax law (Ley del Impuesto Sobre la Renta) includes a negative income tax in the form of a wage-subsidy justified on redistributive grounds. By design, benefits can accrue only to formal workers. The proposal eliminates that feature of the income tax law and consolidates income transfers in $s^{CP}$, allowing for a redistribution of income to all low-wage workers regardless of labor status. An important by-product would be a significant simplification of the income tax law.

On the expenditure side, social protection programs would disappear. In addition to Progresa-Oportunidades, *core social spending would take the form of four programs only, which would provide universal benefits to 41.4 million workers:* health insurance, retirement pensions, life insurance, and disability insurance. In addition, social spending would include direct income transfers to workers, salaried or non-salaried, to mitigate the impact of higher VAT rates. Subject to the relevant constraints, the budget also would include resources for housing, day care, and other programs; however, eligibility would not depend on labor status, and the resources made available would not take the form of entitlements.[25] The government would achieve its objectives of redistributing income and protecting households against risk through separate instruments. A critical point is that all legislated social entitlements, permanent by their very nature, would have a legislated and therefore permanent source of funding. *Mexico's system of social benefits would be put on a stronger fiscal footing. In addition, a larger share of oil rents could be channeled to public investments, providing another source of growth and productivity gains that eventually would translate into higher real wages.*

## How Much Would Universal Social Entitlements Cost?

A careful estimate of the costs of universal social entitlements requires a detailed analysis that is beyond the scope of this book. Nonetheless, table 10-4 presents a mechanical but, I hope, illustrative calculation. The table is based on the current costs of providing medical services for workers enrolled in IMSS (as shown in table 9-1) and simply extrapolates it to all workers currently not covered.[26] In addition, it assumes a contribution for retirement pensions and for life and disability insurance equal to that associated with workers earning three times the minimum wage.

*The fiscal cost of the proposal is approximately 4.3 percent of 2007 GDP.* To pay for it—ignoring additional income tax revenues from firms resulting from increased

25. Of course, there also would be other social programs targeting groups with specific needs (for example, programs to promote gender equality, combat alcoholism, protect abandoned children, and so on). Such programs have not been discussed in this volume, but they clearly are a necessary part of a more encompassing social policy.

26. Actuarial calculations show that if IMSS did not have to pay for the pension liabilities of its own workers (the RJP regime discussed in chapter 3), the existing premiums for medical insurance would need to be raised by 20 percent of the current level to cover estimated medical expenses over the next fifty years (see IMSS 2005, figure XI.2 and pp. 592–96). That suggests an underestimation of similar magnitude of the medical costs presented in table 10-4, at least over the medium term. On the other hand, those costs incorporate high labor costs arising from the allocation of a large number of IMSS workers to nonmedical tasks and do not include the effects of preventive health programs on the medium-term epidemiological profile of the population. More detailed calculations are needed, but in principle existing premiums might be sufficient if those issues were tackled. The more important point is that the accumulated RJP pension liabilities would have to be absorbed by the federal government and would no longer be serviced by IMSS. See Levy (2006d) for further discussion.

Table 10-4. *Estimated Net Fiscal Costs of Universal Social Entitlements*
2007 pesos (millions)

| Entitlement | Workers' and firms' contributions | Government contributions | Total (14.1 million workers) | Total (41.4 million workers) |
|---|---|---|---|---|
| Health insurance | 90,275 | 39,154 | 129,429 | 375,344 |
| Retirement pensions | 58,681 | 18,932 | 77,613 | 184,561[a] |
| Life and disability insurance | 23,177 | 0 | 23,177 | 54,896[b] |
| Gross total | 172,133 | 58,086 | 230,219 | 614,801 |
| Minus resources already in budget[c] | | | | 218,586 |
| Net total | | | | 396,215 |
| Percent of 2007 GDP | | | | 4.3 |

Source: Author's analysis.

a. This is calculated as 276 pesos of wage-based contributions plus 95.5 pesos of government subsidies for retirement pensions (*cuota social para el retiro*) per month, multiplied by 12 times 41.4 million workers.

b. This is calculated as 105 pesos of wage-based contributions plus 5.5 pesos of government subsidies for insurance per month, multiplied by 12 times 41.4 million workers.

c. This is the sum of 61,086 million pesos for subsidies to social security and 157,500 million pesos for subsidies to social protection programs budgeted for 2007; see tables A1-1 and A1-6 in appendix 1.

output and reduced evasion—tax collections from the VAT would have to double from 4.2 to 8.5 percent of GDP.[27]

From the point of view of workers, the additional 4.3 percent of GDP allows for

—depositing the equivalent of 8.5 percent of an annual wage of three times the minimum wage in the individual retirement savings account of 41.4 million workers, ensuring that all workers retire with a pension higher than the currently guaranteed minimum

—providing life and disability insurance for 41.4 million workers, with benefits equivalent to those provided to the worker earning three times the minimum wage

—providing health insurance for 41.4 million workers and their families, with benefits equal to those currently offered by IMSS

—providing work-risk insurance and severance payments to salaried workers in case of loss of employment, proportional in each case to their own wages (or unemployment insurance instead of severance payments).

27. A linear calculation implies that the average rate would have to be raised from the current 8 percent to 16 percent, but that probably is an overestimate because the introduction of a uniform rate would reduce evasion, although its impact would be hard to estimate. A uniform rate of 15 percent probably would generate sufficient revenues. *That is not a high rate by international standards, nor are VAT revenues of 8.5 percent of GDP high.* On the contrary, the current average rate of 8 percent and overall VAT revenues of 4.2 percent of GDP are abnormally low.

From the point of view of firms, the additional 4.3 percent of GDP allows for

—reducing wage-based contributions to social security from 35 to 5 percent of the wage: approximately 2 percent for work-risk insurance and 3.2 percent for the contingent costs of firing and severance pay[28]

—fewer constraints on firms' growth and lower costs in dealing with the government.[29]

Various observations on those results are important. First, the aggregate tax burden would not increase by 4.3 percent of GDP. To see that, note from table 9-1 that wage-based social security contributions would fall by 2.7 percent of GDP. *The net increase in the tax burden equals 1.6 percent of GDP.* That makes clear that the proposal implies a major shift away from wage-based taxes to consumption taxes.

Second, the Afore contribution of all workers, both high and low wage, would be based on a wage of three times the minimum wage. But note that the loss of contributions from high-wage workers would be more than offset by the increase in the number of workers contributing. The net impact of the proposal is this: the flow of resources to the Afores would more than double, *increasing by the equivalent of 1.15 percent of GDP.*[30] If the forced savings were not offset by diminished voluntary savings, total domestic savings would be higher. Those savings would belong to workers and be managed by the Afores, as they are at present; in principle, they could contribute to stimulating domestic private investment.

Third, the previously calculated gross and net increases in the tax burden of 4.3 and 1.6 percent of GDP respectively are measured with respect to 2007 GDP. But because the proposal raises both the level and the rate of growth of GDP, the additional tax burden as a share of GDP could be lower, particularly if GDP grows faster than the labor force. In any event, the numbers are extremely rough and could change significantly if benefits are set at a different level. The estimates take as a reference point the current medical costs of IMSS, which certainly can be reduced. Furthermore, there is no allowance for economies of scale or savings from

---

28. If severance pay regulations were replaced by some form of unemployment insurance, with deposits made in individual accounts, the unemployment insurance fee could be 3.2 percent of the wage. However, depending on the design of the system, it could be higher or lower.

29. An important point here is that IMSS and Infonavit would no longer have the authority to collect social security contributions, eliminating a significant source of administrative costs (and corruption).

30. In 2006 the average wage-based contribution to a worker's Afore was 392 pesos a month. Adding 95.5 pesos from the government subsidy yields a total of 487.5 pesos per worker, which, multiplied by twelve months and by 14.1 million workers, yields an annual flow of 82,483 million pesos. Under the proposal, 372 pesos a month would be deposited into an Afore for 41.4 million workers, yielding an annual flow of resources into the Afores of 184,363 million pesos. The increase in forced savings would be 101,880 million pesos, or 1.15 percent of GDP.

eliminating duplication of functions.[31] In addition, resources can be saved by modifying the eligibility criteria for disability pensions; introducing more competition among providers of medicine and medical supplies; further strengthening competition between the Afores; and lowering labor costs in the provision of public health services.[32]

With what reference point should the fiscal cost of the proposal be compared? The temptation is to compare it with the fiscal cost of the status quo, as in table 10-4. But an important implicit assumption needs to be made explicit if that comparison is made: that the fiscal cost of the status quo will remain constant (say, as a share of GDP). That in turn implies that there will be no further increases in the cost of social protection programs—particularly for health care, day care, and retirement benefits—and that the government will remain passive when a large share of the current generation of low-wage workers retires without any pension.

*Recent experience contradicts that assumption.* As documented, resources for social protection health programs have increased steadily as a share of GDP over the last decade (see table 1-7). Furthermore, in the case of Seguro Popular the government has a legal commitment to extend coverage to all informal workers by the end of 2013. In addition, as of 2007 there was a new noncontributory federal pension program, the Adults over Seventy program.[33]

*In other words, the relevant reference point for comparing the fiscal cost of the proposal is not the cost of the status quo in 2007 but the trend in the cost of the status quo* as Mexico's population begins to develop increasingly complex health problems and the share of retirees in the total population grows. Moreover, an important share of that population, particularly those with low incomes or living in poverty,

31. For example, approximately 23,000 of IMSS's 360,000 workers currently collect social security contributions, and an additional 24,000 workers provide day care services and administer sports and cultural facilities, none of which would be needed for health care purposes (IMSS 2003b, figure I.1, p. I.5). The Ministry of Health has its own administrative unit to operate the budget for Seguro Popular, and thirty-one state governments also have personnel in charge of administration and revenue collection (as opposed to provision of medical services). The Ministry of Labor operates its own system of labor tribunals to solve worker-firm disputes associated with firing and severance pay regulations, among other tasks. The Ministry of Social Development has personnel administering its housing and day care programs. Infonavit has personnel dedicated to supervising and auditing firms (even though IMSS is in charge of collections), and so on.

32. Each of those issues has its own complexities and needs to be tackled even if the status quo persists. IMSS (2003a) provides a discussion of incentive problems in disability pensions and evidence of insufficient competition in the market for annuities. IMSS (2005) discusses problems with the pricing of medicine; Levy (2006d) discusses competition problems in the Afores. But because the market for all such goods and services would expand under the proposal, tackling those issues should, in principle, be easier. In essence, providers would face lower margins but greater volume.

33. While the pension currently is restricted to adults living in localities of up to 2,500 inhabitants and pays only 500 pesos per month, it is not far fetched to suggest that political pressure will gradually lead to expanding coverage to, say, localities of up to 5,000 inhabitants or more and increasing the 500 pesos to 600, then to 700, and so on.

will reach retirement age with no retirement income because they have been informal most of their working life. If informal workers today are going to receive a pension wholly financed from the federal budget tomorrow, why not start saving for it today? Would it be inconvenient to legalize a mechanism to ensure an orderly and fiscally sound transition to a system of universal health insurance and retirement benefits? If not, why not at the same time align incentives in the direction of higher productivity and growth rather than channel additional resources into subsidizing informality, evasion, and low-productivity jobs?

## Implications for Noncontributory Pensions

What about the relationship between the proposal and noncontributory pensions? The issue is how to deal with the irreversible legacy of past informality. Many low-wage workers do not have much saved for retirement in an Afore account because their stays in formal employment have been erratic and short. As discussed in chapter 5, some may stay long enough to reach the guaranteed minimum pension, but most will not. As a result of population aging, if the status quo continues in the years ahead, the Mexican government will face another dimension of the dilemma created by the formal-informal dichotomy: *letting poor retired workers experience poverty during old age or increasing the scope of noncontributory pension programs like the Support for Older Adults and the Adults over Seventy programs* (see the discussion in chapter 1).[34]

The first option contradicts the social objectives of the government, and as the emergence over the last few years of various noncontributory pension programs suggests, it probably is politically unsustainable. The second option has two drawbacks: one, pressures on the federal budget will increase as the number of low-wage workers reaching old age increases; two, as noncontributory pensions programs expand and take the form of a de facto entitlement, the incentives for informality and free riding will increase. Expectations will grow among low-wage workers currently in the labor force that they will receive a noncontributory pension on retirement.

The proposal in figure 10-1 solves that dilemma over the medium term because all workers, regardless of labor status and income level, would save for retirement. *Eventually, noncontributory pensions could be phased out because all workers would have saved for a pension during their working life.* But that will happen only over the medium term. Given that some low-wage workers already are close to retire-

---

34. Language here can be confusing. I use the adjective "noncontributory" in the traditional sense, referring to a pension that is not financed from wage-based contributions. In a sense all pensions are contributory, because somebody has to contribute to pay for them. In fact, using the traditional terminology, under the proposal in figure 10-1 all retirement pensions would be noncontributory because none would be paid for with wage-based contributions. In the discussion, I stick to the traditional use of the word.

ment age, even if the proposal was put in place tomorrow, they would not have enough time to accumulate sufficient resources in an Afore to retire with a minimum pension.

Table 10-5 illustrates that point, showing the results of a hypothetical exercise that assumes that the proposal in figure 10-1 is adopted immediately and, given the age distribution of workers, calculates the pensions that could be obtained at retirement using Consar's life-expectancy tables (retirement age is set at sixty-five, as under the status quo). The table assumes, as before, that each month the government deposits 8.5 percent of three times the minimum wage, or 372 pesos, in each worker's account and computes the resulting pension under two real rates of return: 3.5 percent and 5.3 percent, the average rate currently paid by the Afores.[35]

As expected, results vary depending on the rate of return. If one assumes a 3.5 percent rate, all workers born before 1972, who account for 40 percent of the labor force, would not accumulate enough funds to obtain a pension worth more than the monthly minimum wage (the guaranteed minimum pension). Under the more optimistic 5.3 percent rate of return, that changes to all workers born before 1967, or 29 percent of all workers in the labor force today.

Table 10-5 overestimates the magnitude of the problem because not all workers born before 1967 or 1972 earn low wages and because it ignores the resources that some workers have accumulated in their Afore accounts up to the present. Nonetheless, it points out that unless workers increase their savings for retirement immediately, the pressures for increased noncontributory pensions to reduce old-age poverty will intensify.

Assuming that old-age poverty is to be avoided, the question is how to design noncontributory pensions so that they benefit only the current generation of older workers. In other words, *how can one ensure the intertemporal consistency of noncontributory pension programs with the incentives to save for young workers?* Noncontributory pensions are needed today because workers engaged in informal employment over the last decades, but those pensions should not contribute to more informality tomorrow, requiring the maintenance or even expansion of noncontributory pensions in the future. The issue is exactly the same as that discussed in chapter 6 with regard to social protection programs: because informal workers currently in the labor force cannot be left without social benefits, programs are introduced today, but those programs lead to more informal workers tomorrow, who in turn need more of the programs, and so on.

*Policy needs to change today if noncontributory pension programs are not going to become permanent.* Young low-wage workers should save for their retirement today just as any other workers do, and mechanisms need to be found to eventually

35. I use the average net rate of return based on Afore commissions in July 2007 for workers who were voluntarily affiliated as opposed to the net rates of return observed in the last decade, reported in table 3-4 (see www.consar.gob.mx). I also use a 3.5 percent real rate to provide a more conservative scenario; that is the rate used by IMSS for its actuarial valuations.

Table 10-5. *Monthly Pensions per Age Range, Retirement at Age 65*
(2007 pesos)

| | Workers[a] | | Real annual return of 5.3 percent | | | Real annual return of 3.5 percent | | |
| | | | | Monthly pension[c] | | | Monthly pension[c] | |
| Year of birth | (number) | (percent) | Savings at retirement[b] | (pesos) | (multiple of minimum wage) | Savings at retirement[b] | (pesos) | (multiple of the minimum wage) |
|---|---|---|---|---|---|---|---|---|
| 1947 and before | 1,811,091 | 4.37 | 0.00 | 0.00 | 0.00 | 0.00 | 0.00 | 0.00 |
| 1947 to 1951 | 1,353,417 | 3.26 | 25,829.77 | 167.70 | 0.11 | 24,424.42 | 158.58 | 0.11 |
| 1952 to 1956 | 2,135,487 | 5.15 | 60,034.68 | 390.95 | 0.27 | 53,512.52 | 348.48 | 0.24 |
| 1957 to 1961 | 2,977,251 | 7.18 | 105,330.33 | 684.37 | 0.47 | 88,154.77 | 572.78 | 0.39 |
| 1962 to 1966 | 3,872,300 | 9.34 | 165,312.82 | 1,073.80 | 0.73 | 129,411.72 | 840.60 | 0.57 |
| 1967 to 1971 | 4,671,173 | 11.27 | 244,744.28 | 1,590.23 | 1.08 | 178,546.39 | 1,160.11 | 0.79 |
| 1972 to 1976 | 5,067,761 | 12.22 | 349,930.90 | 2,273.57 | 1.55 | 237,062.96 | 1,540.25 | 1.05 |
| 1977 to 1981 | 5,212,933 | 12.57 | 489,223.65 | 3,178.07 | 2.17 | 306,752.86 | 1,992.71 | 1.36 |
| 1982 and after | 14,356,967 | 34.63 | 673,681.24 | 4,377.38 | 2.99 | 389,749.54 | 2,532.48 | 1.73 |

Source: Author's analysis based on data from the last quarter of the 2006 ENOE, Consar's registries, and Consar's on-line calculator (www.consar.gob.mx).

a. Excludes "ISSSTE and other" workers assuming that they have the same age distribution as the total EAP.

b. Computes total savings for workers who were born at the lower bound of the year of birth range.

c. Calculated on the basis of Consar's tables for annuities given workers' life expectancies.

phase out the probably unavoidable noncontributory pensions associated with the legacy of past informality. The proposal in figure 10-1 has the virtue of contributing to an intertemporally consistent solution to the problem of noncontributory pensions. To the extent that all workers save for their own pension and the amounts accumulated over a lifetime are sufficient to acquire a minimum pension, noncontributory pensions will not be needed because retired workers will not face poverty in old age.

That implies, in turn, that *the design of noncontributory pensions should not be separated from the design of the rest of the system of social entitlements and social benefits.* In other words, programs like Adults over Seventy and Support for Older Adults need to be incorporated in the discussion of retirement pensions as a universal social entitlement. If the proposal in figure 10-1 is adopted, a transitional system of noncontributory pensions to combat old-age poverty based on calculations like those presented in table 10-5 needs to be legislated as part of the proposal. The transitional pensions could be based on the year in which workers were born and perhaps some means testing at old age. In addition, *a binding prohibition needs to be established against funding noncontributory retirement pensions with public monies, except the transitional pensions for workers born before a particular year.* Once a consistent system of retirement pensions is designed, it needs to be enacted in law and not tinkered with because of short-run political decisions that undermine workers' incentives to save; if not, workers could develop the expectation that, in addition to the basic pension, they would get yet another pension. That would undermine the health of public finances as well as workers' incentives to save.

I have one last comment. No claim is made that the proposal presented here is the best possible one or that all the details have been fully worked out—far from it. Many aspects of the proposal certainly can be improved, and further empirical work is required to determine the appropriate level of various tax rates, costs, and benefits. The concern here is with the broad architecture of an alternative to the current social security–social protection dichotomy. But the claim that is made here is that *a feasible alternative exists that simultaneously ensures better social and better economic policy.*

## From Here to There: Isolated Reforms versus Step-by-Step Reform

To increase welfare and growth, Mexico's social policy should be modified to shift from the status quo toward the proposal described. Four points should be noted. One, it is essential to have a clear vision of the ultimate goal of what would be a long and complex reform process. Two, social policy reform should not be viewed in isolation (and reforms to its various components should be viewed that way even less); on the contrary, a harmonious design that integrates social and economic policy is required. Three, a consistent strategy is an essential element of the reform process. Four, the most important aspect of the transition from the status quo to the desired goal is its credibility and internal consistency, not its speed. It is not just a matter of crafting the various pieces of a puzzle; to ensure that the puzzle produces the desired outcome, it is necessary to visualize how the pieces will eventually fit together and in what sequence.

## A Clear Vision

It is not unusual for policy discussions in Mexico to focus on "pension reform," "labor market reform," "health care reform," "poverty policy reform," and "fiscal reform" and to treat each area separately.[36] Nor is it unusual to focus on the social implications of, say, "health reform" or "poverty policy reform" without considering the economic impact of any such reform beyond its obvious budgetary implications—or, at best, to focus on the economic impact of reform in each area in isolation. This book argues that such a narrow focus is wrong, because workers and firms react to the incentive structure set by social policy, not to the incentives of individual programs.

Moreover, it is not unusual to argue that some workers lack health benefits, or others lack housing, or still others lack day care services or retirement pensions and then introduce a new program to take care of the problem. This book argues that it is necessary first to understand why existing programs are not reaching those workers and to evaluate whether introducing new programs might actually reinforce the conditions that prevent workers from benefiting from existing programs. Why are more than 8 million salaried workers not benefiting from social security? Under what conditions could one expect informal workers to be covered by social security, considering that almost 2 percent of GDP is spent on those workers contingent on their being informal?

*This book is a plea for internal consistency in social policy*—an internal consistency that must treat informality not as a minor nuisance or temporary phenomenon but as a central feature of Mexico's economy that determines the efficacy of the country's social programs even as it is determined by those programs.

---

36. In Mexico that phenomenon has various causes: the organizational structure of the federal government, in which each ministry and agency has a vertical view of public policy and is generally, if not exclusively, concerned with the programs and policies under its domain; the organization of Congress, in which the various committees (social security, housing, health, labor, social development) discuss and evaluate individual pieces of legislation; bureaucratic battles for turf among ministries and agencies, at times heightened by the desire of high public officials for recognition; and overlap in the areas of responsibility of the federal and state governments. Designing effective social policies requires a horizontal view of programs and policies that cuts across ministries, agencies, and levels of government. The point is that substantive changes in the organization of ministries and agencies and in their responsibilities and incentives must be *an integral part* of the proposal made here to reform social policy. In the absence of such changes, even if the proposal had the backing of Congress, the natural tendency of ministries and agencies would be to block it or subtly sabotage it. Levy (2006a) discusses this phenomenon in the context of poverty programs in Mexico, arguing that a program's institutional design is as important as its technical design. This point is highly relevant to the proposal made here, which is much broader than previous reforms of poverty programs.

*This book also is a plea for integrating social and economic policy.* It is understandable that given Mexico's long history of costly macroeconomic crises, attention has centered on stabilizing the economy, balancing the fiscal accounts, strengthening the financial sector, and maintaining a low rate of inflation. That was as it should have been. But after a decade of persistent efforts to exercise fiscal and monetary discipline—without putting the country's macroeconomic achievements at risk—it is high time to widen the focus of economic policy to address the substantive distortions that are limiting Mexico's growth. The double role of social programs needs to be explicitly recognized: they are instruments for redistributing income and protecting workers against various risks, but they also are instruments that affect the microeconomic behavior of firms and workers, which in turn has spillover effects on productivity and growth. It is not enough to maximize social spending in the context of a given budget constraint in the hope that the more social programs the better; *it is necessary to recognize that the composition of spending is as important as the level and that social programs modify the behavior of firms and workers—in other words, that social policy is economic policy.* That recognition needs to be fully internalized by those responsible for economic policy as well as by those responsible for social policy.

In that context, this book argues that two inputs are necessary before any reform of social programs is undertaken: one, a clear sense of the desired goal of the system of social benefits considered as a whole; two, an understanding of the mechanisms by which different social programs affect firms and workers and produce outcomes. If the government is to carry out similar interventions on similar workers as part of its effort to expand social inclusion and enhance equity—and if universal social entitlements are going to be a true goal of social policy, not just a rhetorical device—then the design of new social programs and reforms to existing ones need to be carried out with an understanding of how they affect the ultimate goal. Isolated reforms will not do. The government needs to envision and undertake changes to individual programs as steps in an integral process of broader reform.

## A Gradual and Consistent Strategy

It may be argued that Mexico's current political equilibrium rules out any substantive changes to the laws regulating social programs and the labor market, let alone changes in the VAT rates. That may be so. Nevertheless, that does not necessarily imply that the programs and budgetary allocations described in chapter 1 reflect the best that the government can do. The point is that while the political equilibrium determines public policy, it also is endogenous to public policy; *it is not immutable.* The initial steps of an integral reform could occur gradually and initially almost imperceptibly. The important point is to advance in the desired direction, making changes that contribute to creating conditions in which today's immutable political constraints sooner or later can be converted into yesterday's not-so-immutable constraints.

Policymaking in a second-best context generally rules out large systemic reform; political or fiscal constraints limit policymakers to making changes at the margin. But second-best arguments should not serve as carte blanche to indulge the notion that any social program is a good program, even if its beneficiaries are well targeted. Certainly there are political constraints, but there also are trade-offs that need to be considered, and to the extent that changes in social policy—major or minor, fast or slow—are feasible, it is essential to be clear about the direction in which those changes lead.[37] *The relevant trade-off for Mexico is not "integral" versus "piecemeal" reform but "consistent step-by-step reform toward an internally consistent and coherent social policy" versus "ad hoc isolated reforms to existing programs or implementation of new social programs."*

Much can be done to advance in the direction of reduced informality and increased productivity without initially having to carry out major legal reform of the Federal Labor Law or changes to the VAT. A few brief suggestions follow, with no particular order or hierarchy:

—Consider a moratorium on new social protection programs and expansion of current ones. To the extent that fiscally sound resources are available for social spending, gradually increase subsidies to social security, ensuring that the change is permanent, not temporary, and that it applies to new and existing workers (unlike the First Job program).

—Phase out Infonavit's financing through wage-based contributions, replacing it with fiscal subsidies if doing so is indispensable (and perhaps consolidate various dispersed housing programs). A gradual reduction of the contribution rate from the current 5 percent to 0 percent over five years is a possibility, although other paths are feasible.

—Improve the functioning of Progresa-Oportunidades, but do not increase the size of transfers to households or add another pension or energy component. Do not create any other cash or in-kind income transfer programs for the poor, in the understanding that poverty cannot be eliminated with income transfers only and that excessive transfers can contribute to the permanence of poverty.

—Envision how, over the medium term, existing noncontributory pension programs to combat old-age poverty can be integrated with the pension programs for workers currently in the labor force.

—Focus efforts to provide all workers with a social security number (the *Clave Única de Registro de Población*). Develop the administrative ability to issue a single social security card with a view to eventually operating a unified system of social benefits.

---

37. If changes in the opposite direction are made, it is equally essential to know that policy is advancing in the wrong direction so that a change for the better can be effected. That is especially relevant in an area like social policy, which lends itself to rhetorical excess, hyperbole, and demagoguery.

—Continue current efforts to enhance competition in the Afores and extend those efforts to the market for annuities. Strengthen the application of competition laws in the market for medicine and medical supplies and eliminate artificial trade barriers disguised as sanitary regulations in order to lower monopoly rents and bring prices closer to marginal cost.

—Homogenize the tax base of the Income Tax Law and the Social Security Law for the purpose of collecting income taxes and social security contributions in order to lower firms' compliance costs and fight evasion.

—Consolidate the registries of firms maintained by IMSS, SAT, and the Labor Ministry.

—Ensure that subsidized credit and related programs for microenterprises and small firms are not enhancing informality or promoting firms that are not contributing to productive jobs.

—Consolidate under a single authority the registries of beneficiaries of all social security, social protection, and targeted poverty programs currently operated by the Health Ministry, the Social Development Ministry, IMSS, Infonavit, and other ministries and agencies.

—Merge the registries of beneficiaries of all social programs with the Finance Ministry's registry of persons paying income taxes.

—Tackle the problem of the pension regime for IMSS's workers (the RJP regime), complying with rather than eluding the 2004 reforms to the Social Security Law. In that context, transfer IMSS's accumulated pension liabilities to the federal government, releasing resources to improve the quality of IMSS medical services. Under no circumstances increase wage-based contributions to cover those liabilities.

—Modify IMSS administrative procedures and internal regulations with respect to work-risk and disability pensions to strengthen incentives for rehabilitation and reincorporation of workers into the workforce.

—Design an unemployment insurance scheme that aligns incentives in the direction of efficiency and facilitates better matching of firms and workers to eventually replace current firing and severance pay regulations. At the same time, narrow the gap between firms' contingent payments for severance benefits and the benefits that workers actually receive, improving the functioning of labor tribunals (Juntas Federales de Conciliación y Arbitraje).

The list can be extended, but that is not the point here, nor is it to debate the individual merits of any of the suggestions made. The point is that much would be gained if the government undertook an internally consistent program of change to advance simultaneously toward greater formality, legality, and productivity. None of the changes suggested is large enough in its own right to make a significant difference, but the accumulated effect of these and similar changes not listed here would make such a difference, from at least three perspectives. One, the changes would signify a departure from observed trends in social policy over the last years; two, they would reduce the cost of formality to firms and workers; and three, they would help to prepare the terrain for more substantive changes to the legal and institutional architecture of Mexico's social policy.

Ensuring that the actions taken are consistent will improve the incentives to firms and workers to formalize and slowly create synergies among different social actors. Sooner or later that may open up space for more substantive legal reforms, including a reform of the VAT tied to the financing of social entitlements along the lines sketched previously. The point is to advance *consistently* in the right direction. If there is going to be a sustained process of reform leading toward more effective, inclusive, growth-promoting social policy, *the government needs to send a clear, crisp message to everyone declaring its commitment to promoting higher-productivity formal jobs with social security coverage; moreover, it needs to demonstrate that commitment by channeling its administrative, political, and budgetary resources toward that end.*

Of course, successful reform requires much more than just the orderly implementation of a coherent sequence of changes. It also is necessary to have an understanding of the political economy behind the various groups that support the status quo, and it is equally necessary to probe deeper into the nature of the links between social programs and the political legitimacy of the government. Furthermore, it is necessary to modify the old habits of political parties with regard to manipulating social programs for electoral purposes. Those extremely complex issues, which deserve a book of their own, are as important for policy reform as the technical considerations discussed in this book. It is evident that if a reform process along the lines suggested in this chapter is undertaken, new coalitions need to be built, others strengthened, and yet others belonging to the *ancién regime* abandoned. A consensus for change needs to be forged. A task as complex and ambitious as the substantive transformation of Mexico's social policy cannot be achieved by the government alone, even less in the context of Mexico's evolving democracy. *But the government must lead.*

## A Final Word

This book does not claim that informality is the only explanation for Mexico's lackluster growth and productivity performance over the last decade. As discussed at various points in the volume, many factors have contributed to that outcome and it is extremely difficult to separate the role played by each. Nor does the book claim that informality results only from social policy. As also discussed at various points, other policies contribute to informality. Nor, finally, does the book claim that informality is a new phenomenon resulting from recently introduced social protection programs. Informality has characterized Mexico's economy for a period longer than the one examined in this volume, and many of the social security and social protection programs that partly account for it have been in place for many decades.

This book does claim that Mexico's social policy—in particular the recent notable increase in resources for social protection programs—contributes to informality and that informality, aside from thwarting the government's social goals, diminishes the country's economic potential, to the detriment of all. The book supports that claim by showing, within a simple framework and without recourse to any ad hoc assumptions, how the actions of profit-maximizing firms and utility-maximizing workers interacting in a labor market characterized by intersectoral mobility and wage flexibility are biased against efficiency and productivity because of the incentives generated by social programs; by showing how those actions have harmful social effects; and by providing empirical evidence suggesting that their social and economic effects are quantitatively relevant.

Many public policies need to be modified if Mexico is to grow faster. But this book's emphasis on social policies stems from a qualitative difference between social policies and other policies affecting Mexico's growth. That is the fact that social protection programs use a large and increasing quantity of fiscal resources to lower the productivity of labor, a non-traded input essential for competitiveness and whose returns are central to workers' welfare, and that at the same time that the productivity of labor is reduced, the productivity of capital also is reduced. One could argue that there is something troublesome about social protection programs—call it perhaps self-inflicted harm—that is all the more troublesome if they are at least partly financed with rents from a (temporary?) positive oil shock and by sacrificing growth-promoting public investments.

To the reader it may seem counterintuitive to argue that social programs can reduce productivity and growth, as a large literature argues that a healthier and more educated labor force is a positive factor for growth; furthermore, an equally large literature argues that a country with a more equitable income distribution is likely to experience a higher and more sustained rate of growth.[38] And clearly, in a country like Mexico, characterized by a highly unequal income distribution and a significant share of the population living in poverty, social programs are indispensable in redistributing income and promoting equality of opportunity.

I do not dispute those assertions; in fact, I strongly concur with them. In my view, not only are eradicating poverty and increasing equity valuable goals in their own right, they also are prerequisites for sustainable growth in Mexico. My point in this book is that the programs chosen for those purposes generate, de facto, a perverse incentive structure that works against the long-run interests of workers, particularly low-income workers, and that the contribution of those programs to reducing income inequalities is weak. The challenge, therefore, is to reform the programs so that they go hand in hand with increasing productivity and faster growth and become more effective in reducing inequality. The book's point is that unless Mexico escapes from the dilemma created by the formal-informal dichotomy,

---

38. An excellent summary of those arguments is found in World Bank (2005b).

workers' welfare and productivity will suffer for a very basic reason: a sustained increase in workers' standard of living cannot be divorced from a sustained increase in workers' underlying productivity unless there is a permanent and stable source of external rents. History shows, however, that such a source of rents is unlikely to be available and that it is very risky to have the welfare of millions of workers depend on it. Because in the end there is no trade-off between increasing workers' welfare and increasing workers' productivity, Mexico needs to reform its social programs in order to increase productivity and welfare; *social policy is economic policy.*

On the other hand, considerations besides those discussed in this volume highlight the importance of reforming social policy. Over the last decade, reforms essential for growth and productivity in Mexico—in energy, telecommunications, and education, to name a few—have stalled. Some might argue that it is because the benefits of previous reforms in the system of retirement pensions, privatization of some firms, deregulation of some industries, and trade liberalization were captured (or are perceived to have been captured) by a minority of households or concentrated in a few regions. Others might argue that precisely because the reforms have stalled, there is little growth and few "good" jobs.[39] Whatever the individual view, the result is that the social consensus for more reform, which is essential to regaining Mexico's competitiveness and attaining higher rates of growth, has weakened. Creating good jobs rapidly in a context of greater social inclusion and broader opportunities can reinforce the social consensus needed for growth-inducing reforms. But enough good jobs will be created only if incentives exist for firms and workers to create those jobs; today, however, those incentives are undermined by social programs. Increasing social inclusion and opportunities for workers requires eliminating the segmentation and perverse incentives created by social programs. Those are additional reasons why social policy reform needs to be high on the economic agenda. And if social reform implies more equity, as any serious reform would, so much the better—*social policy reform for equity and growth.*

The proposal in this book contributes to greater social inclusion as it institutionalizes the provision of the same social benefits to all workers, rich and poor, salaried and nonsalaried, urban and rural. Social programs would be a legal obligation of the government, sanctioned by Congress. Gradually, there would be a change in the relationships between firms and workers, on one hand, and between firms and workers and the state, on the other, based on a stronger emphasis on obligations as well as rights. All workers would have a right to social benefits, but they would pay higher consumption taxes and would have to register with the Finance Ministry, even if they did not pay any income taxes. Some would benefit from direct income transfers through transparent channels in the federal budget, resulting in more effective income redistribution than at present.

---

39. See Levy and Walton (2007).

The proposal also contributes to broadening opportunities. In a context of greater legality, a much larger number of workers and firms than at present would have increased access to credit from commercial banks, to job training programs, and to programs to facilitate the adoption of new technologies. More generally, they would be able to participate in and benefit from societal institutions, such as business associations and trade unions, designed to represent the interests of all, not just the small segment of firms and workers that are formal today and that are able to express their group interests to the president, Congress, the media, and the other powers that be.

The proposal, finally, contributes to improving Mexico's welfare along a dimension that may not be measurable in pesos and centavos but that nonetheless is essential to prosperity in a modern society: *strengthening the rule of law*. Gradually, society's current and arguably increasing tolerance for illegal activity by firms and workers with respect to core legal labor obligations would diminish. Compliance with the law would increase, first and foremost, because the government no longer would be channeling fiscal resources to social protection programs that subsidize the evasion of social security, and second, because laws regulating labor relationships would reflect more closely than they do today the realities faced by firms and workers in Mexico's labor market—and, more broadly, the realities imposed on Mexico by international competition.

For political reasons, it might not be possible to make the changes needed to implement a policy of universal social entitlements, at least not in the short run. But I believe that the analysis in this book is nonetheless important because it changes, I hope, the nature of the debate on social policy and in doing so opens new avenues of research on the persistence of informality and low productivity in Mexico. To illustrate, contrast the following two statements:

—The current architecture of Mexico's social policy, in the context of the formal-informal dichotomy, is correct, and it is desirable to continue the programmatic and budgetary trends observed over the last decade.

—The current architecture of Mexico's social policy cannot be characterized as even second best, and there is a feasible alternative that is better for fiscal sustainability, for growth and productivity, and for all workers, particularly those who are poor. However, Mexico's political system cannot process such a change.

At the end of the day, what it is important to understand is that informality is not a permanent state of nature, nor is it an inherent characteristic of Mexico's economy. Informality results from public policy, and it can be changed by public policy. This volume seeks to contribute to an understanding of some of the channels through which informality thwarts Mexico's development, focusing on the role played by social policy, and it offers a proposal for an alternative to the status quo. The alternative is far from perfect and requires more detailed analysis and discussion, but it is better than the status quo. It is confusing, frustrating, and demoralizing when in an area as critical to a nation's well-being as social policy, good intentions yield bad outcomes. *It is possible to turn good intentions into good outcomes.*

# 1

## Resources for Social Programs

This appendix describes the data sources and calculations used in tables 1-4 and 1-5. Figures in table 1-4 are derived mainly from IMSS financial statements for the years reported. Detailed data were gathered for Mexico's social security programs, shown in table A1-1.

With the exception of entry II.6, which corresponds to Infonavit, figures for the 1998–2006 series in sections I and II of table A1-1 come from the appendixes of the IMSS income-expenditure statements for those years (Estado de Ingresos y Gastos por Ramo de Seguro, Anexos Contables). They were obtained from IMSS in pesos for the corresponding year, as shown in table A1-2, and then converted into 2007 pesos. Resources for Infonavit were simply calculated as 5 percent of the wage bill, in accordance with the law (or five times the resources for day care centers, which, in accordance with the law, are equivalent to 1 percent of the wage bill).

Note that the program Seguro de Salud para la Familia, even though administered and thus reported by IMSS, is excluded because the program provides benefits to informal workers who voluntarily sign up for coverage. Therefore it is added to the resources pertaining to social protection programs. With that exception, the rest of the entries correlate directly with those reported in table A1-1. For 2007, all entries were extracted directly from the official IMSS budget for that year. Table A1-3 shows the consumer price index used to calculate all data in 2007 prices.

As discussed in chapter 1, the resources that IMSS pays each year to the special pension regime for its own workers (Régimen de Jubilaciones y Pensiones) must be subtracted from the IMSS budget for the social security programs that it administers. In particular, RJP payments reduce resources available for the health,

Table A1-1. *Resources for Social Security Programs, 1998–2007*[a]

2007 pesos (billions)

| Resources | 1998 | 1999 | 2000 | 2001 | 2002 | 2003 | 2004 | 2005 | 2006 | 2007 |
|---|---|---|---|---|---|---|---|---|---|---|
| I.   Public | 38.7 | 43.4 | 47.4 | 49.4 | 49.6 | 48.0 | 52.7 | 56.1 | 51.7 | 61.1 |
| I.1   Health insurance | 28.0 | 30.6 | 33.7 | 34.1 | 34.7 | 35.3 | 37.3 | 40.1 | 34.7 | 39.2 |
| I.2   Disability and life insurance | 0.8 | 0.8 | 1.0 | 1.0 | 1.1 | 0.8 | 1.1 | 1.2 | 1.3 | 1.4 |
| I.3   Retirement | 10.0 | 11.9 | 12.7 | 14.3 | 13.8 | 11.8 | 14.2 | 14.8 | 15.7 | 17.6 |
| I.4   First Job program | ... | ... | ... | ... | ... | ... | ... | ... | ... | 3.0 |
| II.  Private | 162.8 | 179.7 | 202.5 | 214.3 | 217.5 | 220.6 | 232.0 | 241.7 | 242.7 | 249.7 |
| II.1   Health insurance | 62.1 | 69.2 | 77.3 | 79.9 | 80.7 | 79.7 | 84.8 | 86.9 | 83.5 | 90.3 |
| II.2   Disability and life insurance | 15.8 | 15.9 | 17.8 | 19.2 | 19.8 | 20.5 | 21.8 | 22.9 | 23.2 | 23.2 |
| II.3   Retirement | 36.0 | 39.7 | 45.1 | 48.5 | 49.2 | 50.6 | 52.3 | 55.5 | 59.3 | 58.7 |
| II.4   Work-risk insurance | 12.3 | 13.4 | 15.5 | 16.3 | 16.4 | 17.2 | 18.1 | 18.5 | 18.0 | 19.2 |
| II.5   Day care and recreational facilities | 6.1 | 6.9 | 7.8 | 8.4 | 8.6 | 8.8 | 9.2 | 9.7 | 9.8 | 9.7 |
| II.6   Housing fund | 30.6 | 34.6 | 39.1 | 41.9 | 42.9 | 43.8 | 45.9 | 48.3 | 48.9 | 48.6 |
| III. Subtotal (I + II) | 201.5 | 223.0 | 249.9 | 263.7 | 267.1 | 268.6 | 284.7 | 297.9 | 294.4 | 310.8 |
| IV. RJP expenditure | 6.2 | 7.5 | 8.7 | 10.7 | 12.8 | 12.5 | 14.0 | 16.1 | 19.9 | 20.7 |
| IV.1 Health insurance | 5.2 | 6.3 | 7.2 | 9.0 | 10.7 | 10.5 | 11.7 | 13.4 | 16.6 | 17.3 |
| IV.2 Disability and life insurance | 0.4 | 0.4 | 0.5 | 0.6 | 0.7 | 0.7 | 0.8 | 0.9 | 1.2 | 1.2 |
| IV.3 Work-risk insurance | 0.4 | 0.4 | 0.5 | 0.6 | 0.8 | 0.7 | 0.8 | 1.0 | 1.2 | 1.2 |
| IV.4 Day care and recreational facilities | 0.3 | 0.4 | 0.4 | 0.5 | 0.6 | 0.6 | 0.7 | 0.8 | 0.9 | 1.0 |
| V.  Total (III – IV) | 195.3 | 215.5 | 241.3 | 252.9 | 254.3 | 256.1 | 270.7 | 281.8 | 274.5 | 290.1 |
| V.1  Health (I.1 + II.1 – IV.1) | 84.9 | 93.5 | 103.8 | 105.1 | 104.7 | 104.6 | 110.4 | 113.6 | 101.6 | 112.1 |
| V.2  Disability and life (I.2 + II.2 – IV.2) | 16.2 | 16.3 | 18.3 | 19.6 | 20.1 | 20.6 | 22.1 | 23.2 | 23.3 | 23.3 |
| V.3  Retirement (I.3 + II.3) | 46.0 | 51.7 | 57.8 | 62.7 | 63.0 | 62.4 | 66.5 | 70.4 | 75.0 | 76.2 |
| V.4  Work-risk insurance (II.4 – IV.3) | 11.9 | 12.9 | 14.9 | 15.7 | 15.7 | 16.4 | 17.2 | 17.6 | 16.8 | 17.9 |
| V.5  Day care and recreational facilities (II.5 – IV.4) | 5.8 | 6.6 | 7.4 | 7.9 | 8.0 | 8.2 | 8.5 | 8.9 | 8.9 | 8.8 |
| V.6  First Job program (I.4) | ... | ... | ... | ... | ... | ... | ... | ... | ... | 3.0 |
| V.7  Housing fund (II.6) | 30.6 | 34.6 | 39.1 | 41.9 | 42.9 | 43.8 | 45.9 | 48.3 | 48.9 | 48.6 |

Source: See discussion in text.

a. Three periods (. . .) indicates that the program did not exist for the year reported.

Table A1-2. *Selected Items from IMSS Income-Expenditure Statements, 1998–2006*
Pesos for each year (billions)

| Resources | 1998 | 1999 | 2000 | 2001 | 2002 | 2003 | 2004 | 2005 | 2006 |
|---|---|---|---|---|---|---|---|---|---|
| Public | 24.0 | 30.1 | 35.9 | 39.0 | 41.3 | 42.0 | 48.4 | 53.3 | 51.1 |
| Health insurance | 17.1 | 21.0 | 25.2 | 26.6 | 28.6 | 30.3 | 33.7 | 37.4 | 33.7 |
| Disability and life insurance | 0.5 | 0.6 | 0.7 | 0.8 | 0.9 | 0.7 | 1.0 | 1.1 | 1.2 |
| Seguro de Salud Para la Familia | 0.3 | 0.4 | 0.4 | 0.4 | 0.4 | 0.8 | 0.8 | 0.9 | 1.0 |
| Retirement | 6.1 | 8.2 | 9.5 | 11.1 | 11.4 | 10.2 | 12.9 | 13.8 | 15.2 |
| Private | 81.2 | 100.1 | 122.9 | 135.2 | 144.8 | 152.3 | 168.6 | 181.1 | 188.7 |
| Health insurance | 37.9 | 47.5 | 57.8 | 62.4 | 66.6 | 68.4 | 76.6 | 81.1 | 81.0 |
| Disability and life insurance | 9.6 | 10.9 | 13.3 | 15.0 | 16.3 | 17.6 | 19.6 | 21.4 | 22.6 |
| Work-risk insurance | 7.5 | 9.2 | 11.6 | 12.8 | 13.6 | 14.8 | 16.3 | 17.3 | 17.4 |
| Day care and recreational facilities | 3.7 | 4.7 | 5.8 | 6.6 | 7.1 | 7.5 | 8.3 | 9.0 | 9.5 |
| Seguro de Salud Para la Familia | 0.4 | 0.5 | 0.6 | 0.6 | 0.6 | 0.5 | 0.6 | 0.6 | 0.6 |
| Retirement | 22.0 | 27.3 | 33.7 | 37.9 | 40.6 | 43.4 | 47.2 | 51.8 | 57.6 |

Source: See discussion in text.

Table A1-3. *National Consumer Price Index, 1998–2007*[a]

| Index | 1998 | 1999 | 2000 | 2001 | 2002 | 2003 | 2004 | 2005 | 2006 | 2007[b] |
|---|---|---|---|---|---|---|---|---|---|---|
| Original index (base June 2002) | 76.19 | 85.58 | 93.25 | 97.35 | 102.90 | 107.00 | 112.55 | 116.30 | 121.02 | 124.65 |
| Transformed (2007 prices) | 61.1 | 68.7 | 74.81 | 78.11 | 82.56 | 85.84 | 90.30 | 93.31 | 97.09 | 100.00 |

Sources: Figures for 1998–2006 are from Inegi (www.inegi.gob.mx); figures for 2007 were derived from the official inflation estimate of 3 percent reported in the president's budget proposal for 2007 (Criterios Generales de Política Económica para 2007).

a. Figures are for December of each year.
b. Estimated figures.

Table A1-4. *RJP Total Expenditures, 1998–2007*
Pesos for each year (billions)

| RJP expenditure | 1998 | 1999 | 2000 | 2001 | 2002 | 2003 | 2004 | 2005 | 2006 | 2007[a] |
|---|---|---|---|---|---|---|---|---|---|---|
| Total | 3.9 | 5.3 | 6.7 | 8.7 | 10.9 | 11.1 | 13.1 | 15.5 | 20.0 | 20.0 |

Source: See discussion in text.

a. The expenditure for 2007 is reported in 2005 pesos because the estimate was made in that year.

disability, life, and work-risk insurance programs; for day care and recreational facilities; and for the family health insurance program (Seguro de Salud para la Familia). Data for RJP payments for 1998–2006 were obtained from the IMSS income-expenditures statements for those years. The estimate for 2007 was obtained from the estimate for that year made by IMSS in 2005. The RJP data are reported in table A1-4.

I used the consumer price indexes shown in table A1-3 to express the figures in table A1-4 in 2007 prices. I used the IMSS income-expenditure statements to distribute the total for each year among the five programs mentioned in the previous paragraph and applied the average for the 1998–2006 period to the data in table A1-2. The results are shown in table A1-5. The data were then used to construct the resources for social security, net of RJP, shown in section V of table A1-1.

Table A1-6 shows expenditures for all social protection programs reported in the federal budget (Cuenta de la Hacienda Pública Federal).

Other than for entries I.3 and I.4, data in section I of table A1-6 come from the Cuenta Pública for each year up to 2006. Data for 2007 were taken from that year's federal budget. Data for entry I.4 come from the source used above for other IMSS programs, the Estado de Ingresos y Gastos por Ramo de Seguro, Anexos Contables. Data for entry I.3 for 1998–2005 come from the statistical yearbooks (*Anuario Estadístico*) of the Ministry of Health and for 2006 and 2007 from a ministry estimate. The same sources were used for entries II.2 and II.3. Data for entry II.4 on fees paid by beneficiaries for the Seguro Popular program were obtained directly from the National Commission of Social Protection in Health, which is the Ministry of Health agency in charge of administering the program. Finally, because all data were given in then current pesos, I used the price index in table A1.3 to express all figures in 2007 pesos.

Table A1-5. *Distribution of IMSS Expenditures on RJP by Program, 1998–2006*
Average percentage

| IMSS expenditure on RJP | Work-risk insurance | Health insurance | Life and disability insurance | Day care and recreational facilities | Seguro de Salud para la Familia | Total |
|---|---|---|---|---|---|---|
| Average | 5.8 | 80.8 | 5.6 | 4.5 | 3.2 | 100.0 |

Source: See discussion in text.

Table A1-6. *Resources for Social Protection Programs, 1998–2007*[a]

2007 pesos (billions)

| Resources | | 1998 | 1999 | 2000 | 2001 | 2002 | 2003 | 2004 | 2005 | 2006 | 2007 |
|---|---|---|---|---|---|---|---|---|---|---|---|
| I. | Public | 75.7 | 82.3 | 89.2 | 96.4 | 100.6 | 108.9 | 117.8 | 128.4 | 146.4 | 157.5 |
| | I.1 IMSS-Oportunidades | 5.3 | 5.2 | 5.1 | 5.5 | 5.0 | 5.8 | 4.8 | 5.4 | 4.8 | 5.5 |
| | I.2 Federal transfers to states' health services | 26.6 | 30.3 | 33.9 | 35.6 | 36.2 | 39.8 | 38.9 | 40.6 | 41.8 | 41.6 |
| | I.3 State governments' expenditures in health | 38.0 | 41.2 | 43.9 | 49.1 | 51.9 | 53.2 | 59.5 | 61.9 | 64.4 | 65.0 |
| | I.4 Seguro de Salud para la Familia | 0.5 | 0.5 | 0.5 | 0.5 | 0.5 | 0.9 | 0.9 | 1.0 | 1.0 | 0.8 |
| | I.5 Seguro Popular | . . . | . . . | . . . | . . . | 0.3 | 0.7 | 5.0 | 9.3 | 17.7 | 26.0 |
| | I.6 Transfers to national health institutes | 3.6 | 4.1 | 4.4 | 4.6 | 4.6 | 5.0 | 5.0 | 5.6 | 6.1 | 6.4 |
| | I.7 First Generation program | . . . | . . . | . . . | . . . | . . . | . . . | . . . | . . . | . . . | 3.0 |
| | I.8 Subsidies to popular housing fund trust (Fonhapo) | 1.2 | 0.6 | 0.9 | 0.6 | 1.2 | 1.5 | 1.8 | 2.3 | 4.9 | 2.1 |
| | I.9 Subsidies to housing fund (Fovi) | 0.7 | 0.5 | 0.4 | 0.5 | 0.9 | 1.0 | . . . | . . . | . . . | . . . |
| | I.10 Subsidies to Habitat | . . . | . . . | . . . | . . . | . . . | 0.9 | 2.0 | 2.2 | 2.0 | 2.2 |
| | I.11 National Housing Commission (Conavi) | . . . | . . . | . . . | . . . | . . . | . . . | . . . | . . . | 3.7 | 3.9 |
| | I.12 Universal day care program | . . . | . . . | . . . | . . . | . . . | . . . | . . . | . . . | . . . | 1.0 |
| II. | Private | 1.7 | 1.7 | 1.6 | 4.1 | 4.5 | 4.8 | 4.5 | 5.0 | 5.1 | 5.5 |
| | II.1 Seguro de Salud para la Familia (SSF) | 0.7 | 0.7 | 0.8 | 0.7 | 0.7 | 0.6 | 0.6 | 0.6 | 0.6 | 0.7 |
| | II.2 State governments' health recovery fees[b] | . . . | . . . | . . . | 2.5 | 2.8 | 3.2 | 2.9 | 3.0 | 3.2 | 3.4 |
| | II.3 National health institutes' revenues | 1.0 | 1.0 | 0.8 | 0.9 | 0.9 | 1.0 | 1.0 | 1.1 | 1.2 | 1.3 |
| | II.4 Seguro Popular recovery fees[b] | . . . | . . . | . . . | . . . | . . . | . . . | 0.1 | 0.2 | 0.1 | 0.2 |
| III. | Subtotal (I + II) | 77.4 | 84.1 | 90.8 | 100.5 | 105.1 | 113.7 | 122.3 | 133.4 | 151.5 | 163.1 |
| IV. | RJP expenditure (from SSF) | 0.2 | 0.3 | 0.3 | 0.4 | 0.4 | 0.4 | 0.5 | 0.5 | 0.7 | 0.7 |
| V. | Total (III − IV) | 77.2 | 83.8 | 90.5 | 100.2 | 104.7 | 113.2 | 121.8 | 132.8 | 150.8 | 162.4 |
| | V.1 Health (I.1 to I.7 + II − IV) | 75.4 | 82.8 | 89.2 | 99.0 | 102.6 | 109.8 | 118.1 | 128.3 | 140.3 | 153.2 |
| | V.3 Housing | 1.8 | 1.1 | 1.3 | 1.1 | 2.1 | 3.4 | 3.8 | 4.5 | 10.5 | 8.2 |
| | V.4 Day care | . . . | . . . | . . . | . . . | . . . | . . . | . . . | . . . | . . . | 1.0 |

Source: See discussion in text.

a. Three periods (. . .) indicates that the program did not exist for the year reported.

b. "Recovery fee" (*cuota de recuperacion*) refers to the fees paid by private users of these services.

# 2

# *Regional Coverage of Social Programs*

There are no systematic data on the geographic coverage of social programs. What follows is a combination of various sources whose coverage and scope are inevitably different but that nonetheless provide a general overview of the phenomenon.

## Coverage of IMSS Health Services

The National Population Count for 2005—produced by Inegi (Instituto Nacional de Estadística, Geografía, e Informática/National Institute of Statistics, Geography, and Information Sciences)—is the broadest and most recent source of information on the distribution of Mexico's population. Using that information, I distributed Mexico's total population of 103.3 million for 2005 by state and size of locality. I divided localities into those with a population of up to 20,000 persons (which I designated the rural area of influence of IMSS health services) and those with population of more than 20,000 (the urban area of influence). Note that this rural-urban split is different from that used in the Progresa-Oportunidades surveys because I assumed that the area of influence might include a large number of smaller localities to which beneficiaries had reasonable access.

The Inegi population count includes a variable for the population covered by IMSS, which allows for distributing the beneficiaries by state and by rural or urban area of influence. Note that there is a difference between the beneficiary population registered in the population count and the population included in IMSS's estimate of its beneficiaries, which results from the fact that Inegi reports actual users while IMSS reports eligible users whether they use IMSS services or not. The population count yields 32.1 million beneficiaries (for 2005); the IMSS estimate yields 47.9 million persons (for 2006). I used the latter because it is a better approximation of the potential demand for IMSS services and the former already reflects any rationing resulting from insufficient facilities or inadequate quality. The total national population was updated to 2006 by using the population projections of the National Population Council (Consejo Nacional de Población), keeping constant the relative structure of beneficiary population by state and rural-urban area of influence. The net result is a state-level classification by rural-urban area of the IMSS potential beneficiary population for 2006. This exercise allows one to bypass the fact that IMSS's registries of its beneficiary population are based on where the firm employing the worker is registered and need not coincide with where the worker and his or her family lives.

The information on the regional distribution of the beneficiary population is combined with information from the 2006 directory of IMSS medical units, which is a very accurate and up-to-date catalog of all IMSS medical infrastructure by state and locality. The medical infrastructure is similarly classified by rural or urban area of influence. It also is classified into first-level facilities, which are measured by the number of doctors' offices in which medical examinations can be performed and primary care offered (basically preventive medicine and treatment of ailments that do not require hospitalization), and second- and third-level facilities, which are measured by the number of hospital beds available.

Table A2-1 presents the state and rural-urban estimates of the IMSS beneficiary population. Table A2-2 presents the state and rural-urban estimates of IMSS health facilities by level. The two tables allow for calculating the means and standard deviations of the urban and rural distribution of medical infrastructure per beneficiary by state discussed in chapter 3, and they also are the basis for the general remarks made throughout the text on the urban and rural distribution of IMSS health infrastructure. The results should be interpreted as indicative of the variance in access to medical benefits; they should not be interpreted in a rigorous sense. First, the quality of services varies within facilities because the age of facilities and equipment varies. Second, one needs a much more detailed analysis by geographic location because some beneficiaries might live in a locality that is classified within the rural sphere of influence but that nevertheless lies close to urban facilities. Third, IMSS pays the transportation costs for patients who are referred from states that do not have sophisticated facilities for complex medical interventions to cities where they can be treated, although the number of patients who benefit is very small.

## Coverage of Social Protection Health Services

Using the same criteria as used for IMSS, the exercise was repeated using data from the Health Ministry's *Yearbook 2006*. According to the yearbook, by the end of 2006 there were 64.7 million total beneficiaries of IMSS-Oportunidades and state health services combined. Results are reported in the same fashion as above in tables A2-3 and A2-4.

Table A2-1. *State and Rural-Urban Estimates of the IMSS Beneficiary Population, 2006*

| State | Total population | IMSS beneficiaries | Total population Up to 20,000 | Total population 20,000+ | IMSS beneficiaries Up to 20,000 | IMSS beneficiaries 20,000+ |
|---|---|---|---|---|---|---|
| Aguascalientes | 1,059,369 | 713,100 | 308,739 | 750,630 | 137,820 | 575,280 |
| Baja California | 3,027,728 | 1,841,356 | 489,828 | 2,537,900 | 230,540 | 1,610,816 |
| Baja California Sur | 515,527 | 334,037 | 267,928 | 247,599 | 161,782 | 172,255 |
| Campeche | 788,314 | 396,059 | 406,165 | 382,149 | 86,403 | 309,656 |
| Coahuila | 2,574,397 | 1,835,179 | 806,967 | 1,767,430 | 515,906 | 1,319,273 |
| Colima | 598,537 | 324,386 | 351,613 | 246,924 | 163,955 | 160,431 |
| Chiapas | 4,475,338 | 746,405 | 3,164,112 | 1,311,276 | 250,990 | 495,415 |
| Chihuahua | 3,490,734 | 2,153,103 | 795,328 | 2,695,406 | 264,182 | 1,888,921 |
| Federal District | 8,815,298 | 7,128,984 | 140,846 | 8,674,452 | 42,550 | 7,086,434 |
| Durango | 1,560,005 | 709,925 | 711,943 | 848,062 | 208,990 | 500,935 |
| Guanajuato | 5,101,377 | 2,295,567 | 2,034,309 | 3,067,068 | 403,807 | 1,891,760 |
| Guerrero | 3,269,745 | 753,996 | 1,983,890 | 1,285,855 | 137,796 | 616,200 |
| Hidalgo | 2,408,400 | 695,393 | 1,716,016 | 692,384 | 364,180 | 331,213 |
| Jalisco | 6,868,606 | 3,782,827 | 1,991,018 | 4,877,588 | 650,282 | 3,132,545 |
| State of México | 14,893,754 | 4,200,889 | 4,307,728 | 10,586,026 | 630,734 | 3,570,155 |
| Michoacán | 4,238,900 | 1,254,472 | 2,296,050 | 1,942,850 | 364,984 | 889,488 |
| Morelos | 1,735,816 | 588,730 | 828,935 | 906,881 | 189,811 | 398,919 |
| Nayarit | 1,003,921 | 398,417 | 615,721 | 388,200 | 189,953 | 208,564 |
| Nuevo Leon | 4,306,021 | 3,261,918 | 450,762 | 3,855,259 | 220,604 | 3,041,314 |
| Oaxaca | 3,738,823 | 681,041 | 2,906,817 | 832,006 | 367,259 | 313,782 |
| Puebla | 5,591,458 | 1,542,473 | 3,045,233 | 2,546,225 | 310,081 | 1,232,392 |
| Queretaro | 1,629,106 | 1,065,928 | 825,228 | 803,878 | 345,354 | 720,574 |
| Quintana Roo | 1,129,921 | 708,396 | 298,575 | 831,346 | 81,690 | 626,706 |
| San Luis Potosí | 2,418,946 | 1,114,345 | 1,326,781 | 1,092,165 | 304,436 | 809,909 |
| Sinaloa | 2,794,000 | 1,357,124 | 1,221,447 | 1,572,553 | 406,139 | 950,985 |
| Sonora | 2,524,706 | 1,394,853 | 872,863 | 1,651,843 | 364,259 | 1,030,594 |
| Tabasco | 2,093,095 | 621,965 | 1,444,440 | 648,655 | 290,573 | 331,392 |
| Tamaulipas | 3,220,502 | 1,864,526 | 632,602 | 2,587,900 | 186,354 | 1,678,172 |
| Tlaxcala | 1,088,812 | 309,267 | 749,566 | 339,246 | 185,123 | 124,144 |
| Veracruz | 7,315,156 | 2,407,873 | 4,384,295 | 2,930,861 | 929,424 | 1,478,449 |
| Yucatan | 1,830,893 | 851,383 | 764,432 | 1,066,461 | 222,860 | 628,523 |
| Zacatecas | 1,417,952 | 584,232 | 948,309 | 469,643 | 240,621 | 343,611 |
| Total | 107,525,207 | 47,918,149 | 43,088,486 | 64,436,721 | 9,449,342 | 38,468,807 |

Source: Inegi, II Conteo Nacional de Población y Vivienda (National Population Count for 2005) (www.inegi.gob.mx) and IMSS registries.

Table A2-2. *State and Rural-Urban Estimates of IMSS Health Infrastructure, 2006*[a]

| | Rural | | Urban | |
|---|---|---|---|---|
| State | Beneficiaries per doctor's office | Beneficiaries per hospital bed | Beneficiaries per doctor's office | Beneficiaries per hospital bed |
| Aguascalientes | 68,910 | . . . | 6,253 | 1,868 |
| Baja California | 9,606 | . . . | 8,261 | 1,728 |
| Baja California Sur | 10,785 | 7,034 | 4,306 | 1,267 |
| Campeche | 21,601 | . . . | 7,373 | 1,935 |
| Coahuila | 14,740 | 11,998 | 5,341 | 994 |
| Colima | 23,422 | . . . | 4,336 | 1,099 |
| Chiapas | 12,550 | . . . | 8,542 | 1,828 |
| Chihuahua | 6,952 | 13,209 | 7,293 | 1,762 |
| Federal District | | . . . | 8,600 | 1,157 |
| Durango | 6,531 | . . . | 5,692 | 1,128 |
| Guanajuato | 36,710 | . . . | 7,597 | 1,652 |
| Guerrero | 15,311 | . . . | 6,486 | 1,736 |
| Hidalgo | 28,014 | . . . | 4,800 | 1,200 |
| Jalisco | 7,068 | 10,004 | 7,235 | 1,091 |
| State of México | 25,229 | . . . | 5,144 | 1,704 |
| Michoacán | 9,605 | 22,812 | 6,638 | 1,458 |
| Morelos | 10,545 | . . . | 5,114 | 796 |
| Nayarit | 7,302 | 3,452 | 5,959 | 1,304 |
| Nuevo Leon | 7,879 | . . . | 7,207 | 1,349 |
| Oaxaca | 13,602 | 30,605 | 4,903 | 1,382 |
| Puebla | 10,692 | 20,672 | 6,885 | 1,188 |
| Queretaro | 10,465 | . . . | 8,282 | 2,410 |
| Quintana Roo | 20,423 | . . . | 9,216 | 3,581 |
| San Luis Potosi | 10,498 | 60,887 | 7,499 | 1,749 |
| Sinaloa | 6,551 | . . . | 5,799 | 1,010 |
| Sonora | 4,670 | 10,714 | 6,871 | 1,187 |
| Tabasco | 12,107 | . . . | 7,204 | 1,632 |
| Tamaulipas | 4,051 | . . . | 9,022 | 2,049 |
| Tlaxcala | 7,405 | 1,596 | 4,281 | 2,387 |
| Veracruz | 14,522 | 3,017 | 6,211 | 1,085 |
| Yucatan | 12,381 | . . . | 5,465 | 910 |
| Zacatecas | 6,332 | . . . | 8,811 | 1,727 |
| National average | 14,724 | 16,333 | 6,645 | 1,542 |
| Standard deviation | 12,329 | 15,802 | 1,440 | 545 |

Source: IMSS registries.

a. Three periods (. . .) indicates that there were no doctor's offices or hospital beds in those areas.

Table A2-3. *State and Rural-Urban Estimates of Social Protection Health Services Beneficiary Population, 2006*

| State | Total population | Beneficiaries | Total population | | Beneficiaries | |
| | | | Up to 20,000 | 20,000+ | Up to 20,000 | 20,000+ |
|---|---|---|---|---|---|---|
| Aguascalientes | 1,059,369 | 492,912 | 412,868 | 646,501 | 192,102 | 300,809 |
| Baja California | 3,027,728 | 1,457,167 | 882,393 | 2,145,335 | 424,673 | 1,032,494 |
| Baja California Sur | 515,527 | 218,005 | 83,402 | 432,125 | 35,269 | 182,736 |
| Campeche | 788,314 | 475,795 | 236,088 | 552,226 | 142,493 | 333,302 |
| Coahuila | 2,574,397 | 837,142 | 2,213,926 | 360,471 | 719,925 | 117,218 |
| Colima | 598,537 | 314,040 | 105,768 | 492,769 | 55,494 | 258,546 |
| Chiapas | 4,475,338 | 3,779,092 | 1,259,123 | 3,216,215 | 1,063,236 | 2,715,855 |
| Chihuahua | 3,490,734 | 1,545,920 | 2,467,958 | 1,022,776 | 1,092,970 | 452,951 |
| Federal District | 8,815,298 | 4,274,573 | 2,008,476 | 6,806,822 | 973,918 | 3,300,655 |
| Durango | 1,560,005 | 837,060 | 24,925 | 1,535,080 | 13,374 | 823,686 |
| Guanajuato | 5,101,377 | 3,290,822 | 2,328,126 | 2,773,251 | 1,501,839 | 1,788,982 |
| Guerrero | 3,269,745 | 2,594,781 | 1,303,897 | 1,965,848 | 1,034,738 | 1,560,044 |
| Hidalgo | 2,408,400 | 1,757,135 | 1,461,277 | 947,123 | 1,066,127 | 691,008 |
| Jalisco | 6,868,606 | 3,764,319 | 4,893,970 | 1,974,636 | 2,682,126 | 1,082,193 |
| State of México | 14,893,754 | 9,071,369 | 4,317,286 | 10,576,468 | 2,629,538 | 6,441,831 |
| Michoacán | 4,238,900 | 3,176,572 | 1,226,020 | 3,012,880 | 918,762 | 2,257,810 |
| Morelos | 1,735,816 | 1,152,946 | 940,225 | 795,591 | 624,507 | 528,439 |
| Nayarit | 1,003,921 | 602,437 | 479,420 | 524,501 | 287,692 | 314,745 |
| Nuevo Leon | 4,306,021 | 1,433,526 | 2,640,954 | 1,665,067 | 879,205 | 554,321 |
| Oaxaca | 3,738,823 | 3,023,773 | 391,386 | 3,347,437 | 316,534 | 2,707,239 |
| Puebla | 5,591,458 | 4,235,977 | 4,347,183 | 1,244,275 | 3,293,339 | 942,638 |
| Queretaro | 1,629,106 | 896,279 | 887,247 | 741,859 | 488,133 | 408,145 |
| Quintana Roo | 1,129,921 | 647,061 | 572,365 | 557,556 | 327,770 | 319,290 |
| San Luis Potosi | 2,418,946 | 1,468,300 | 593,320 | 1,825,626 | 360,145 | 1,108,155 |
| Sinaloa | 2,794,000 | 1,403,035 | 1,390,522 | 1,403,478 | 698,264 | 704,771 |
| Sonora | 2,524,706 | 1,092,107 | 1,103,720 | 1,420,986 | 477,434 | 614,673 |
| Tabasco | 2,093,095 | 1,494,457 | 521,753 | 1,571,342 | 372,528 | 1,121,929 |
| Tamaulipas | 3,220,502 | 1,561,905 | 2,222,461 | 998,041 | 1,077,867 | 484,038 |
| Tlaxcala | 1,088,812 | 803,815 | 213,875 | 874,937 | 157,893 | 645,922 |
| Veracruz | 7,315,156 | 5,070,135 | 5,035,940 | 2,279,216 | 3,490,410 | 1,579,724 |
| Yucatan | 1,830,893 | 1,014,022 | 1,097,335 | 733,558 | 607,748 | 406,274 |
| Zacatecas | 1,417,952 | 965,580 | 592,022 | 825,930 | 403,148 | 562,432 |
| Total | 107,525,157 | 64,752,059 | 48,255,232 | 59,269,925 | 28,409,203 | 36,342,855 |

Source: Secretaria de Salud (2006) and Inegi, II Conteo Nacional de Población y Vivienda (National Population Count for 2005) (www.inegi.gob.mx).

Table A2-4. *State and Rural-Urban Estimates of Social Protection Health Infrastructure, 2006*[a]

| | Rural | | Urban | |
|---|---|---|---|---|
| State | Beneficiaries per doctor's office | Beneficiaries per hospital bed | Beneficiaries per doctor's office | Beneficiaries per hospital bed |
| Aguascalientes | 677 | 623 | 1,544 | 1,420 |
| Baja California | 1,946 | 2,073 | 3,869 | 4,122 |
| Baja California Sur | 2,098 | 1,287 | 1,434 | 879 |
| Campeche | 2,022 | 1,681 | 1,224 | 1,018 |
| Coahuila | 267 | 215 | 2,561 | 2,063 |
| Colima | 986 | 897 | 1,264 | 1,149 |
| Chiapas | 5,594 | 6,298 | 1,116 | 1,256 |
| Chihuahua | 3,456 | 2,318 | 2,081 | 1,395 |
| Federal District | . . . | . . . | 2,358 | 1,852 |
| Durango | 1,460 | 1,128 | 1,199 | 927 |
| Guanajuato | 2,130 | 2,079 | 3,735 | 3,644 |
| Guerrero | 1,742 | 2,800 | 1,836 | 2,952 |
| Hidalgo | 1,319 | 1,852 | 1,893 | 2,658 |
| Jalisco | 2,236 | 1,488 | 2,072 | 1,379 |
| State of México | 1,184 | 857 | 4,821 | 3,491 |
| Michoacán | 5,009 | 5,686 | 1,570 | 1,782 |
| Morelos | 1,771 | 3,043 | 2,115 | 3,633 |
| Nayarit | 985 | 1,434 | 1,598 | 2,326 |
| Nuevo Leon | 215 | 442 | 1,745 | 3,592 |
| Oaxaca | 8,660 | 11,435 | 619 | 818 |
| Puebla | 2,355 | 1,883 | 2,848 | 2,278 |
| Queretaro | 929 | 974 | 7,228 | 7,580 |
| Quintana Roo | 1,296 | 1,616 | 2,573 | 3,208 |
| San Luis Potosi | 2,116 | 2,001 | 1,956 | 1,848 |
| Sinaloa | 1,210 | 1,198 | 2,518 | 2,494 |
| Sonora | 1,704 | 953 | 1,981 | 1,108 |
| Tabasco | 1,512 | 1,765 | 1,504 | 1,755 |
| Tamaulipas | 7,428 | 5,037 | 7,386 | 5,009 |
| Tlaxcala | 2,643 | 2,898 | 2,157 | 2,365 |
| Veracruz | 2,304 | 2,175 | 2,104 | 1,987 |
| Yucatan | 3,175 | 2,689 | 1,606 | 1,360 |
| Zacatecas | 2,578 | 2,886 | 1,252 | 1,402 |
| National average | 2,355 | 2,378 | 2,368 | 2,336 |
| Standard deviation | 1,889 | 2,161 | 1,528 | 1,408 |

Source: Secretaria de Salud (2006).

a. Three periods (. . .) indicates that there were no doctor's offices or hospital beds in those areas.

# 3

# Land Holdings of Progresa-Oportunidades Households

To analyze the land holdings of Progresa-Oportunidades households, I used two different types of household survey: Encaseh (Encuestas de Características Socioeconómicas de los Hogares/Surveys on Socioeconomic Characteristics of Households) and Encreseh (Encuestas de Recertificación de los Hogares/Surveys for Recertification of Households). The Encasehs are used to determine whether households enter the Progresa-Oportunidades program; the Encresehs are used three and six years later to determine whether households that entered are eligible to continue in the program. Households covered by Progresa are divided into rural (living in localities with up to 2,500 inhabitants) and urban (living in localities with more than 2,500 inhabitants). The program covers a total of 5 million households, of which 68.8 percent are rural and 31.2 percent are urban.

To construct the rural database, I used a random sample of households for each of Mexico's thirty-one states. The sample contained 10 percent of all rural localities in each state. Once localities were chosen, I obtained all of the Encasehs available and complemented them with all the Encresehs for households for which an Encaseh was not available, using the most recent information. Encasehs and Encresehs contain pretty much the same data, and from each household survey I obtained information on household ownership or use of land, demographic composition, years of schooling per household member, and all the other variables presented in chapter 4. The average number of inhabitants in each rural locality was 685 people. Table A3-1 describes the rural sample.

In both the Encasehs and the Encresehs, some families reported owning land but did not specify the amount; the total number of families that failed to report

Table A3-1. *Characteristics of the Rural Sample*

| Survey | Families | Percent | Localities | Percent |
|--------|----------|---------|------------|---------|
| Encreseh 2000 | 19,385 | 7.16 | 509 | 5.47 |
| Encreseh 2001 | 118,318 | 43.69 | 3,683 | 39.58 |
| Encreseh 2002 | 62,825 | 23.20 | 1,894 | 20.35 |
| Encreseh 2003 | 1,327 | 0.49 | 54 | 0.58 |
| Encreseh 2004 | 26,119 | 9.64 | 1,503 | 16.15 |
| Encreseh 2005 | 4,866 | 1.80 | 179 | 1.92 |
| Encaseh 2001 | 3,478 | 1.28 | 42 | 0.45 |
| Encaseh 2002 | 7,442 | 2.75 | 166 | 1.78 |
| Encaseh 2004 | 27,057 | 9.99 | 1,276 | 13.71 |
| Total | 270,817 | 100.0 | 9,306 | 100.0 |

Source: Encresehs and Encasehs, various years, conducted by the Coordinacion Nacional del Programa de Desarollo Humano Oportundidades [National Coordinating Agency of the Human Development Program Oportunidades].

the amount was 19,556, or 7.2 percent of the total. In those cases I filled in the missing data by using the median number of hectares of land owned by families in the locality where those households lived. I also updated the age of all household members to 2005 and 2012 in order to calculate the number of hectares per working age member of each household. The key assumption, however, was that land ownership of each household stayed constant. The data on schooling, labor participation, access to social security, and family composition correspond to the year in which the survey was conducted.

The urban data set consisted of 154,514 families. I used the same procedure as the one described above for rural households in calculating land ownership and other variables.

Table A3-2 describes ownership patterns for rural and urban households for the samples just described, which consisted of a total of 425,331 families of a universe of 5 million, 270,817 rural (7.9 percent of all rural households) and 154,514 urban (9.9 percent of all urban households). I estimated rural and urban expansion factors of 12.65 for the rural areas and 10.1 for urban ones and used those factors to calculate the total land holdings of Progresa-Oportunidades households reported in chapter 4.

Table A3-2. *Use or Ownership of Land by Progresa-Oportunidades Households*

| Use or ownership | Rural households | Percent | Urban households | Percent |
|------------------|------------------|---------|------------------|---------|
| With land | 166,680 | 61.55 | 136,739 | 88.5 |
| Without land | 104,137 | 38.45 | 17,775 | 11.5 |
| Total | 270,817 | 100.0 | 154,514 | 100.0 |

Source: Encresehs and Encasehs, various years, conducted by the Coordinacion Nacional del Programa de Desarollo Humano Oportundidades [National Coordinating Agency of the Human Development Program Oportunidades].

# 4

# Estimation of Mexico's Economically Active Population

This appendix describes the data used to construct tables 5-1 and 5-3. Note that because several sources of information were used, various assumptions are required to make the data consistent. As a result, a degree of imprecision was inevitable; both tables therefore should be interpreted as indicative of the orders of magnitude rather than as precise estimates.

## Estimates for 2006

Because of the very nature of evasion of the Social Security Law, there are no official figures on its frequency. *Therefore I systematically made conservative assumptions in my analysis so that one could argue that evasion was underestimated.* As discussed in chapter 1, the dividing line between salaried workers and *comisionistas* is not precise and clearly some salaried employment is disguised as nonsalaried. The measurement of evasion reflects a strict definition of salaried employment, and I made no attempt to identify *comisionistas* who really were salaried workers. Consequently, because both the total labor force and the formal labor force were measured with much more precision than illegal salaried workers, the result was an overestimation of the informal labor force legally occupied in nonsalaried activities. Finally, the sources of information were too weak to separate nonsalaried employment between self-employed workers and *comisionistas*. That explains why they are aggregated in table 5-1 despite the fact that in the text the two forms of employment are analyzed separately.

## Division by Labor Status

The estimate of the economically active population (EAP) comes directly from ENOE (Encuesta Nacional de Ocupación y Empleo/National Survey of Occupations and Employment) for the last quarter of 2006, which is published by Inegi (Instituto Nacional de Estadística, Geografía, e Informática/National Institute of Statistics, Geography, and Information Sciences). According to the ENOE, at the end of 2006 the total EAP consisted of 44,447,032 workers, of whom 1.6 million were unemployed.

I calculated the formal segment of the EAP by adding up all workers affiliated with different social security systems in Mexico. Note that 2.9 million workers were registered with social security systems other than IMSS at the end of 2006; they are listed under "ISSSTE and others" in the first line of table 5-1.[1]

On the other hand, IMSS reported 14,080,367 affiliates at the end of 2006, equivalent to 31.7 percent of the EAP. Of those, IMSS reported 5.9 million workers making more than three times the minimum wage and 8.1 million making less than that. The first figure provides set F1 in table 5-1; the second provides (F2 + F3). To divide (F2 + F3) into its components, I used additional information detailed below.

The informal segment of the EAP was estimated to be the simple difference between the total EAP and formal and unemployed workers, resulting in the estimate of 25.8 million informal workers in table 5-1. That total was then subdivided in illegal salaried workers and nonsalaried workers.

## Illegal Salaried Workers

The ENOE reported 28,048,498 "subordinated and remunerated workers" in December 2006 (of which 2,136,975 were in agriculture). That is the closest estimate of total salaried workers in Mexico, and I used it here because, as chapter 1 argues, the combination of subordination and remuneration invariably reflects the existence of a worker-boss relationship (*relación obrero-patronal*). At least that many workers should be enrolled in social security. I made three deductions from the total estimate of subordinated and remunerated workers: 2,958,245 workers belonged to ISSSTE and other special social security institutes; 14,080,367 workers were enrolled in IMSS; and 2,887,369 workers were reported in the ENOE as

---

1. That includes 428,056 total workers (including temporary hires) in the Ministry of Defense and the Ministry of the Navy, who have their own social security institute, ISSSFAM (Instituto de Seguridad y Servicios Sociales de las Fuerzas Armadas de México/Institute of Social Security and Social Services of the Armed Forces of Mexico); 140,505 workers in the public oil monopoly, Pemex, who also have a special social security regime; and 2,389,684 public workers in national and subnational ministries and agencies, who are affiliated with ISSSTE (Instituto de Seguridad y Servicios Sociales para los Trabajadores del Estado/Institute of Social Security and Social Services for State Workers), the public workers' equivalent of IMSS. Data on affiliation were taken directly from ISSSFAM, Pemex, and ISSSTE.

not working in a business premise. The third group are workers who, despite being subordinated and remunerated, are not considered subject to obligatory enroll-ment in social security.[2] The remaining 8,122,884 workers is a lower-bound esti-mate of the number of workers who in December 2006 should have been enrolled in IMSS but were not. That provides (I1 + I2 + I3) in table 5-1.

Note that using the ENOE definition of "subordinated and remunerated workers" as a measure of total salaried employment results in an underestimation. Aside from the case of domestic workers, which is an explicit legal exemption, it excludes *comisionistas*, some of whom under some circumstances could be salaried workers, given that they have a worker-boss relationship with a firm. Indeed, under a more rigid interpretation of the current Federal Labor Law, the estimated level of social security evasion would increase. Contrast, for example, two cases. In one, a pharmaceutical salesperson works on and off for several different companies over different periods of time selling different products at different points of delivery; in the other, a cosmetics salesperson works twenty-five consecutive years for a sin-gle company that demands exclusivity from her, imposes sales goals on her, and requires her to attend training meetings where she receives instructions on how to market the company's products. The first salesperson clearly is a *comisionista;* the second one is, for all practical purposes, a salaried worker. Yet in the ENOE, both cases are treated equally and excluded from the estimate of "subordinated and remunerated workers." In table 5-1, all such ambiguous cases are treated as non-salaried workers, even though the example shows the shortcomings of doing so. That explains why the International Labor Office estimate of salaried employment in Mexico referred to in table 5-2 is larger than the estimate here.

*Informal Workers*

Given a total estimate of 25,777,123 informal workers and an estimate of 8,092,111 illegal salaried workers, I estimated the total number of self-employed workers and *comisionistas* as the difference between the two. That equals 17,685,012 workers and provides the estimate of (I4 + I5 + I6).

I separated sets (F2 + F3), (I1 + I2 + I3), and (I4 + I5 + I6). Because there is no direct measure of poor workers in the ENOE surveys, I used the Progresa-Oportunidades surveys mentioned in appendix 3 and synthesized in chapter 4 to construct one. I also used the Progresa-Oportunidades registry of beneficiaries, which reports the age composition of the 25 million program beneficiaries at the end of 2006. Given that information, I assumed that the labor participation rate for poor workers (EAP/working age population) is the same as the aggregate par-ticipation rate observed in the ENOE. That provides an estimate of 10,054,605

---

2. That is the case with domestic workers, who clearly are subordinated and remunerated and, in terms of the Federal Labor Law, are salaried workers. Nevertheless, the Social Security Law expressly exempts them (or, more precisely, their bosses) from the obligation to enroll in IMSS.

poor workers. From table 4-5, I estimated that poor workers covered by social security equaled 6.3 percent of all poor workers, or 636,788 workers. That provides F3 and, by subtraction, an estimate of 7,457,138 workers for F2, completing the division of formal employment.

To identify illegal poor workers (I3), I combined data from the ENOE, the IMSS registries, and the Progresa-Oportunidades surveys, proceeding in two stages, measuring evasion in agriculture and evasion in other activities. First, as mentioned, ENOE estimated 2,136,975 subordinated and remunerated workers in agriculture. The key assumption that I made was that all of them were poor. On the other hand, the IMSS registries showed a total of 186,342 agricultural workers, which I also assumed were poor. Subtracting the latter from the former provides an estimate of poor illegal workers in agriculture of 1,950,633 workers. Second, table 4-4 indicates that 32.1 percent of all poor workers were salaried employees in construction or manufacturing; on the other hand, table 4-5 reports that 86 percent of them were not enrolled in IMSS. Because the total number of poor workers is 10,054,605, that implies that of 3,227,528 poor salaried workers in construction and manufacturing, 451,446 were enrolled in IMSS and 2,767,207 were not. As a result, I estimate that 1,950,633 poor salaried workers in agriculture and 2,767,207 workers in nonagricultural activities were not registered in IMSS, providing an estimate of 4,726,307 workers for I3.[3]

Given 10,054,605 poor workers, of which 636,788 were registered with IMSS (F3) and 4,726,307 were salaried but not registered (I3), the remainder must be poor self-employed workers or *comisionistas*. That provides an estimate of 4,691,510 workers for I6.

The ENOE reports the earnings composition of self-employed and *comisionistas*. In particular, 32.9 percent of all *comisionistas* and self-employed workers earned three times the minimum wage or more in December 2006. Applying that percentage to the total provides an estimate of 5,818,360 workers for I4; given that figure and the estimate for I6 previously mentioned, I5 was estimated as the difference between the total estimate of self-employed workers and *comisionistas* and I4 plus I6, equal to 7,175,133.

The ENOE also reports the wage structure of all remunerated and subordinated workers. In December 2006, 63.8 percent earned three times the minimum wage or less and 36.1 percent earned more than that. There are no data to estimate the wage structure of illegal salaried workers, however. As a result, I assumed that their

---

3. I did not use the estimates in table 4-5 of agricultural workers with and without social security coverage because the Progresa-Oportunidades surveys do not separate *jornaleros agrícolas* and *peones agrícolas*. The first are salaried workers; the second are mostly nonsalaried workers in sharecropping and related activities. As a result, I used the ENOE estimate of subordinated and remunerated workers in agriculture and the IMSS registries. The estimated number of *jornaleros agrícolas* is of the same order of magnitude as that for other estimations of these workers.

wage structure was the same as that for all salaried workers (of which they are part in the ENOE statistics). That probably underestimates the number of low-wage illegal workers, because for the reasons discussed in chapters 6 and 7, evasion tends to concentrate in those workers. Nevertheless, lacking any other data, I estimate that 2,922,849 workers (8,092,111*36.1) were in the high-wage illegal category, or set I1. Given the total of illegal workers and the estimates of I1 and I3, set I2 is estimated as the difference, equal to 442,955 workers. That implies that low-wage but not poor workers are a small share of evading workers, a reflection of the fact that evasion in high-wage workers is overestimated (and probably also a reflection of the fact that some low-wage workers classified as *comisionistas* in set I5 are really salaried but not registered with IMSS).

The data are too weak to support division of nonsalaried workers between self-employed workers and *comisionistas*. The ENOE does report a figure for *comisionistas* of 1,638,928 workers, but it refers only to door-to-door salespersons. The figure excludes sharecropping and many other forms of nonsalaried labor relations between workers and firms. So it is clear that there are more *comisionistas*, but it is not possible to estimate how many more. As a result, while for analytical reasons I analyze the two categories separately in various chapters, in table 5-1 they are grouped together.

## Estimates for 1991–2006

The series in table 5-3 was constructed using data from three different sources: the ENOE for every quarter of 2005 and 2006; the National Employment Survey (ENE), published biannually by Inegi from 1991 to 1993, annually from 1995 to 1999 (in both cases with data from the second quarter of each year), and quarterly from 2000 to 2004; and the statistical appendixes to the Sixth Presidential Report to Congress (*Sexto Informe de Gobierno*) for 2000 and 2006, presented to Congress at the end of the administration of presidents Zedillo and Fox respectively.

EAP and unemployment series for 2005 and 2006 were extracted directly from the ENOE and correspond to the figures reported for the fourth quarter of each of those years. ENOE defines EAP as persons fourteen years of age or older who during the survey's reference period engaged in some sort of economic activity or actively looked for one at some point in the month before the day that they were interviewed.

On the other hand, the ENOE did not exist before 2005, so data for the years 1998-2004 were obtained from its official predecessor, the ENE. The definition of EAP in the ENE is almost identical to that in the ENOE, except for the fact that the former also includes persons between twelve and fourteen years of age at the time of the interview. However, ENE records give the age of those surveyed, so persons under fourteen years of age were excluded. The EAP obtained from the ENE, with that correction, is reported in table A4-1.

Table A4-1. *EAP for Persons Fourteen or Older and Unemployed Workers,*
*1998–2004*[a]
Thousands of workers

| Category | 1998 | 1999 | 2000 | 2001 | 2002 | 2003 | 2004 |
|---|---|---|---|---|---|---|---|
| EAP | 38,320 | 38,396 | 39,379 | 39,860 | 40,313 | 41,670 | 42,473 |
| Unemployed workers | 878 | 683 | 918 | 1,120 | 1,084 | 1,483 | 1,589 |

a. All figures correspond to the last quarter of each year, except those for 1998 and 1999, which correspond to the second quarter.

While figures for 2000–04 in table A4-1 are directly comparable with the ones from ENOE, before 2000 the ENE was collected only in the second quarter of each year, so data for 1998 and 1999 had to be standardized. That was done by applying to the figures reported a factor of 1.01 in the case of the EAP and of 1.03 in the case of unemployment, which resulted from averaging the fourth- and second-quarter ratios for each variable for every year in the 2000–06 period. That resulted in an EAP of 38.7 and 37.8 million workers for 1998 and 1999 respectively, with unemployment of 0.9 and 0.7 million workers for the same years.

Although ENE does have records for the years before 1998, they were not publicly available, so an indirect source was required for the 1991–97 period. I used the *Sexto Informe de Gobierno* for 2000, which uses the ENE data and therefore can be considered an almost perfect substitute. The data are reported in table A4-2.

Figures in table A4-2 are not directly comparable with the 1998–2006 series because the former are for the second quarter of each year and include persons between twelve and fourteen years of age. Hence, the previously described factors of 1.01 for EAP and 1.03 for unemployment were applied to those figures in order to standardize them to the fourth quarter of each year. To standardize the series so that only workers fourteen years of age and older were considered, I applied the factors 0.978 to the estimate of the EAP and 0.987 to the estimate of open unemployment. Those factors result from averaging each year's total EAP with the fourteen-or-older EAP (and similarly for unemployment) for every year in the 1998–2004 period. The results are shown in the nonshaded cells of table A4-3.

Table A4-2. *EAP for Persons Twelve or Older and Unemployed Workers,*
*1991–97*[a]
Thousands of workers

| Category | 1991 | 1993 | 1995 | 1996 | 1997 |
|---|---|---|---|---|---|
| EAP | 31229 | 33652 | 35558 | 36581 | 38345 |
| Unemployed workers | 695 | 819 | 1677 | 1355 | 985 |

a. All figures correspond to the second quarter of each year.

Table A4-3. *Standardized EAP and Unemployed Workers, 1991–97*
Thousands of workers

| Category | 1991 | 1992 | 1993 | 1994 | 1995 | 1996 | 1997 |
|---|---|---|---|---|---|---|---|
| EAP | 30,844 | 32,040 | 33,236 | 34,178 | 35,120 | 36,129 | 37,871 |
| Unemployed workers | 706 | 769 | 832 | 1,268 | 1,704 | 1,376 | 1,001 |

The shaded cells are equal to the average of the previous and the next year because there are no official data for those years.

Data regarding other social security systems, labeled "ISSSTE and other" in table 5-3, include the same set of public workers mentioned previously and used to construct table 5-1. Their number was obtained directly from the *Sexto Informe de Gobierno* 2006. Finally, informal employment was obtained by subtracting records from IMSS, ISSSTE and other, and unemployment from total EAP, as was done for table 5-1. Therefore both tables are comparable.

# 5

## Mean Wage-Rate Comparisons
## by Matching Methods

This appendix describes how tables 5-12 and 5-13 were constructed. As mentioned in chapter 5, mean wage comparisons between salaried workers who change labor status disregard the particular characteristics that the workers may have that might be the main reason for the changes. The only way of making sure that every characteristic is taken into account is to observe the *same* individual's decisions under different scenarios at the same time, but that is impossible. As a result, the best approach to comparing wage rates is a *counterfactual* analysis in which one compares the effects of a move on an individual's outcomes with the effects the worker would experience from staying where he or she originally was. That can be done on an average basis by comparing the expected outcomes of moving between sectors given a set of characteristics common to both *movers* and *stayers* as formally defined in equation A5-1 below.[1]

Let AEM be the average effect on the outcome of moving from one sector to another:

(A5-1)
$$AEM = E\left(Y_T - Y_C \mid D = 1, \boldsymbol{X}\right)$$
$$= E\left(Y_T \mid D = 1, \boldsymbol{X}\right) - E\left(Y_C \mid D = 1, \boldsymbol{X}\right),$$

where $Y_T$ is the outcome of the movers' group, $Y_C$ is the outcome of the stayers' group, $\boldsymbol{X}$ is a vector of observed characteristics, and $D$ indicates whether each individual was or was not a mover, taking the value of 1 if the individual was and 0 if he or she was not. *Assuming* conditional independence on any unobserved

---

1. This equation draws from the average treatment effect on the treated (ATT) technique, which is widely used in program evaluation.

variable, this technique allows for *the most similar* individuals to be compared with each other, the only difference between their outcomes being the effect of whether they moved or not.

Parametrically, that *similarity* can be captured by a *propensity score* defined by Rosenbaum and Rubin (1983) as the conditional probability of being treated given a set of defined characteristics. To estimate the propensity score, a probit model such as the one formally described in equation A5-2 was used.

(A5-2) $$p(X) \equiv Pr\{D = 1|X\} = E[D|X]$$

From the observable characteristics available from ENOE, the characteristics ultimately used to construct vector $X$ in equations A5-1 and A5-2 are shown in tables A5-1 and A5-2, along with the results of the associated probit models.

Table A5-1. *Probit Results for Male Salaried Workers*

| Treated | Description | Formal to informal | | | Informal to formal | | |
|---|---|---|---|---|---|---|---|
| | | Coefficient | Standard error | | Coefficient | Standard error | |
| Age | Age | −0.0849 | 0.0189 | *** | 0.0301 | 0.0207 | |
| Age2 | Squared age | 0.0010 | 0.0002 | *** | −0.0003 | 0.0003 | |
| Edu2 | Junior high | −0.1125 | 0.0959 | | 0.3087 | 0.1052 | *** |
| Edu3 | High school | −0.3548 | 0.1171 | *** | 0.5526 | 0.1428 | *** |
| Edu4 | High school + | −0.3764 | 0.1030 | *** | 0.4152 | 0.1487 | *** |
| Numwor1 | 1–10 workers | −0.2215 | 0.0976 | ** | 0.6977 | 0.1189 | *** |
| Numwor2 | 11–50 workers | −0.3898 | 0.0935 | *** | 0.5545 | 0.1219 | *** |
| Type1 | Written contract | −0.2894 | 0.0966 | *** | - | - | |
| Type3 | No written contract | −0.1842 | 0.1328 | | - | - | |
| Ten2 | 1 to 3 years' tenure | −0.0554 | 0.0878 | | −0.0941 | 0.0991 | |
| Ten3 | 4 to 6 years' tenure | −0.2021 | 0.0909 | *** | −0.0323 | 0.1012 | |
| Ten4 | 7 to 9 years' tenure | −0.3215 | 0.1368 | ** | −0.5945 | 0.1845 | |
| Ten5 | Ten years or more | −0.4827 | 0.1131 | *** | −0.1809 | 0.1269 | *** |
| Act1 | Agriculture | 0.5598 | 0.1922 | *** | −0.7596 | 0.1530 | *** |
| Act2 | Mining | −0.0690 | 0.2083 | | −0.7197 | 0.4190 | |
| Act3 | Electricity | 0.3479 | 0.1548 | ** | −0.1961 | 0.1495 | |
| Act5 | Manufacturing | 0.0706 | 0.1138 | | −0.1456 | 0.1458 | |
| Act6 | Commerce | −0.2867 | 0.2130 | | −0.0675 | 0.2813 | |
| Act7 | Transportation | 0.1922 | 0.1067 | * | −0.2302 | 0.1530 | |
| Act8 | Services | 0.3019 | 0.1077 | *** | −0.3340 | 0.1377 | ** |
| Urban | Urban location | −0.1919 | 0.0846 | ** | 0.2823 | 0.0967 | *** |
| C | Constant | 1.1007 | 0.3688 | *** | −1.2680 | 0.3739 | *** |
| Observations | | 3,710 | | | 1,124 | | |
| Log likelihood | | −819.09 | | | −628.28 | | |

Source: Author's analysis.

*Significant at the 90 percent confidence level; ** significant at the 95 percent confidence level; ***significant at the 99 percent confidence level.

Table A5-2. *Probit Results for Female Salaried Workers*

| Treated | Description | Formal to informal | | | | Informal to formal | | |
|---|---|---|---|---|---|---|---|---|
| | | Coefficient | Standard error | | | Coefficient | Standard error | |
| Age | Age | −0.0132 | 0.0329 | | | 0.0331 | 0.0324 | |
| Age2 | Squared age | 0.0001 | 0.0004 | | | −0.0003 | 0.0004 | |
| Edu2 | Junior high | −0.5016 | 0.1422 | *** | | −0.3317 | 0.1766 | |
| Edu3 | High school | −0.5709 | 0.1610 | *** | | −0.3078 | 0.1741 | |
| Edu4 | High school + | −0.7491 | 0.1347 | *** | | 0.0819 | 0.2066 | |
| Numwor1 | 1–10 workers | −0.1860 | 0.1202 | | | 0.7568 | 0.1678 | |
| Numwor2 | 11–50 workers | −0.4293 | 0.1256 | *** | | 1.0557 | 0.1789 | |
| Type1 | Written contract | −0.3275 | 0.1360 | ** | | | | |
| Type3 | No written contract | −0.0965 | 0.1830 | | | | | |
| Ten2 | 1 to 3 years' tenure | −0.0974 | 0.1169 | | | 0.1412 | 0.1311 | |
| Ten3 | 4 to 6 years' tenure | −0.1497 | 0.1217 | | | −0.0406 | 0.1404 | |
| Ten4 | 7 to 9 years' tenure | −0.4163 | 0.1996 | ** | | −0.2329 | 0.2542 | |
| Ten5 | Ten years or more | −0.3629 | 0.1587 | ** | | −0.4395 | 0.2068 | |
| Phom2 | Household head's spouse | −0.2693 | 0.1239 | ** | | −0.4678 | 0.2129 | ** |
| Phom3 | Daughter | −0.0871 | 0.1547 | | | −0.3322 | 0.1994 | * |
| Phom4 | Other position at home | −0.4030 | 0.2321 | * | | −0.1896 | 0.2252 | |
| Child1 | 0–3-year-old children | −0.3470 | 0.1810 | ** | | 0.1293 | 0.2366 | |
| Child2 | 4–11-year-old children | 0.1399 | 0.1090 | | | 0.0854 | 0.1428 | |
| Child3 | 12–18-year-old children | 0.1065 | 0.0933 | | | 0.0730 | 0.1272 | |
| Act1 | Agriculture | 0.3623 | 0.6857 | | | | | |
| Act3 | Mining | 0.5773 | 0.5136 | | | | | |
| Act5 | Manufacturing | 0.1630 | 0.3847 | | | 0.2409 | 0.2305 | |
| Act6 | Commerce | 0.5157 | 0.3804 | | | −0.3349 | 0.7142 | |
| Act7 | Transportation | 0.3465 | 0.3725 | | | 0.1932 | 0.2118 | |
| Act8 | Services | 0.7918 | 0.3830 | ** | | −0.8712 | 0.2207 | *** |
| Urban | Urban location | −0.2538 | 0.1237 | ** | | 0.3828 | 0.1536 | ** |
| C | Constant | −0.0177 | 0.7427 | | | −1.4494 | 0.6165 | ** |
| Observations | | 2,472 | | | | 764 | | |
| Log likelihood | | −472.98 | | | | −309.28 | | |

Source: Author's analysis.
*Significant at the 90 percent confidence level; ** significant at the 95 percent confidence level; *** significant at the 99 percent confidence level.

However, the propensity score by itself is not enough for calculating the ATT. Indeed, since $p(X)$ is a continuous variable, the chances of observing two individuals with the same propensity score is very low because it would require both of them to have exactly the same set of observed characteristics. Thus, matching individuals by their propensity scores requires further manipulation of the data, which in this case was done by using a *kernel* matching function.

From equation A5-1, the generalization of the AEM is as follows:

(A5-3)
$$AEM = \frac{1}{N^M} \sum_{i \in M} \left[ Y_{M_i} - \sum_{j \in S} w_{ij} Y_{S_j} \right],$$

where $Y_{Mi}$ is the outcome of treatment unit $i$ if exposed to the treatment, $Y_{Sj}$ the outcome of control unit $j$, and $w_{ij}$ is the weight on control $j$ in forming a comparison with treated $i$. When using kernel-based matching, AEM can be redefined as follows:

(A5-4)
$$AEM = \frac{1}{N^M} \sum_{i \in M} \left[ Y_{M_i} - \frac{\sum_{j \in S} Y_{S_j} G\left(\dfrac{P_j - P_i}{h_n}\right)}{\sum_{K \in S} G\left(\dfrac{P_k - P_i}{h_n}\right)} \right],$$

where $G$ is a kernel function, in this case a normal one, and $h_n$ is a bandwidth parameter, which for the referred experiment was set at 0.01.

Finally, once the match was performed, observations in the sample were divided in two sets, treatment and control; the control group included a number of individuals whose particular characteristics were most similar to those of the treatment group. For the purposes of the analysis in chapter 5, the sample was divided into three different subsets, defined in table A5-3:

Table A5-3. *Subsets of the Counterfactual Analysis Reported in Chapter 5*

| B | A | A* |
|---|---|---|
| Individuals in the sample who moved from one sector to another | All individuals in the sample except those in subset B | Members of subset A whose particular characteristics are more similar to those in the B subset |

# 6

# Equilibrium in the Labor Market with Differences in Workers' Valuations

This appendix discusses how the labor force is distributed between the formal and the informal sectors when workers have different valuations of social programs.

## The Labor Market with Social Security

The simplest case is the one in which there are social security but no social protection programs. Assume that there are two exogenously given types of worker, $L^A$ and $L^B$, so that $L^A + L^B = L$. Workers of each type have the same valuations, $\beta_f^A$ and $\beta_f^B$. Assume also that type A workers fully value social security but type B workers do not:

(A6-1) $$1 = \beta_f^A > \beta_f^B \geq 0.$$

Equations A6-2a through A6-2f describe the equilibrium conditions for firms and the labor market. Formal firms are not affected by differences in workers' valuations, because regardless of whom they hire, they have to (formally) pay the full amount of social security contributions. Informal firms also are unaffected. However, now two employment conditions must be simultaneously fulfilled: one, employment in the formal and informal sectors must be equal the total labor force; two, all type A and type B workers must be employed. Hence,

(A6-2a) $$(p^w \partial Q_f / \partial L_f) - (w_f + T_f) = 0.$$

(A6-2b) $$p^w \, \partial Q_i / L_i - w_i = 0$$

(A6-2c) $$L^A + L^B = L$$

(A6-2d) $$L_i + L_f = L.$$

Based on the reasoning in chapter 6, the equilibrium conditions for workers would be

(A6-2e) $$w_f + \beta_f^A T_f = w_i$$

(A6-2f) $$w_f + \beta_f^B T_f = w_i,$$

but given equation A6-1, it is clear that equations A6-2e and A6-2f cannot hold simultaneously.

To construct a solution to equation A6-2, it is useful to note that for a given wage rate, type A workers prefer jobs in the formal sector more than type B workers do. However, the number of exogenously given type A workers may exceed or fall short of the endogenously determined number of workers in the formal sector. There are three qualitatively different cases, depending on whether $L^A \lessgtr L_f^*$, which determine the outcomes in equations A6-2e and A6-2f.

To capture those cases, figure A6-1 includes the values of $L^A$ and $L^B$ on the upper horizontal axis, with $L^A$ measured from the left side (and $L^B$ from the right side, not shown). Consider case 1, in which $L^A = L_f^*$. Inspection of the figure shows that the equilibrium replicates the full-valuation equilibrium discussed in chapter 6, at point D. Workers in the formal sector get wages and benefits $(w_f^* + \beta_f^A T_f) = (w_f^* + T_f)$. Workers in the informal sector—of which there are exactly $L^B$—get a wage of $w_i^*$. Firms in the formal sector face labor costs of $(w_f^* + T_f)$ as a result of which they hire $L_f^* = L^A$ workers, and firms in the informal sector face labor costs of $w_i^*$, at which point informal employment is $L_i^* = L^B$. Note that in this case,

(A6-3) $$w_f^* + \beta_f^A T_f = w_i^* > w_f^* + \beta_f^B T_f \qquad \left( \text{with } L_A = L_f^* \text{ and } L_B = L_i^* \right).$$

This inequality says that at wage rates $w_f^*$ and $w_i^*$, type B workers prefer jobs in the informal sector and type A workers are indifferent to the choice between a job in the formal or the informal sector. In other words, workers who value social security less self-select into the informal sector. Note also that in this case, $MPL_f = MPL_i$.

From the above, I conclude that when type A workers fully value social security and the distribution of workers between type A and type B is such that $L^A = L_f^*$, self-selection of workers into informal sector jobs produces an efficient equilibrium. Furthermore, all workers obtain the maximum utility given their valuations. Note finally that equation A6-3 provides an answer to the impossibility of equations A6-2e and A6-2f holding simultaneously.

Figure A6-1. *Differences in Workers' Valuation of Social Security*

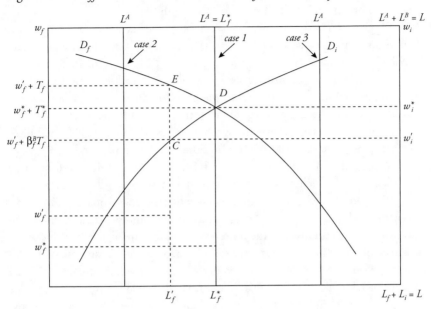

Source: Author's analysis.

Assume now that the distribution of type A and B workers is such that $L^A < L_f^*$. In that case (case 2 in figure A6-1) there are not enough workers willing to work in the formal sector at the wage rate $w_f^*$, so wages have to increase to attract some type B workers who at $(w_f^* + \beta_f^B T_f) < w_i^*$ prefer the informal sector. As formal sector wages increase, however, formal sector firms reduce employment. The equilibrium moves from point D to points E and C, with formal sector employment at $L_f'$, formal sector wages at $w_f'$, and informal sector wages at $w_i'$. Note the critical point that $L^A < L_f'$, so formal sector employment exceeds the number of type A workers. In other words, there are now some type B workers in the formal sector, because at this point

(A6-4) $\qquad w_f' + \beta_f^A T_f > w_i' = w_f' + \beta_f^B T_f \quad \left(\text{with } L^A < L_f' \text{ and } L^B > L_i'\right),$

The inequality in equation A6-4 captures two facts: first, type B workers are willing to work in the formal sector only at higher wages; second, since type B workers are now employed in both sectors, from their point of view the value of wages and benefits in the formal sector must equal wages in the informal sector.[1]

---

1. The reasoning can be thought of in terms of the complementary slackness theorem of linear programming. The comparison between $L^A$ and $L_f^*$ tells us whether the exogenously given constraint of $L^A$-type workers is binding or not; that determines whether an inequality is observed in equation A6-2e or A6-2.

To gain further insight, compare this equilibrium with the one in chapter 6, in which all workers undervalued social security with the same $\beta_f < 1$. To do that, assume for a moment that $L^A = 0$. The labor force consists of type B workers only, all of whom value social security at less than its cost. That is exactly the equilibrium described in chapter 6, by simply writing $\beta_f^B = \beta_f < 1$. The comparison is useful because it tell us what the formal sector wage will be in each case. In particular, a moment's reflection suggests that when there are no type A workers (that is, when all workers undervalue social security), the formal wage is higher than when there are some type A workers. If everybody undervalues social security, formal firms have to pay more for salaried labor; on the other hand, if some workers fully value social security (but not all that are needed, because $L^A < L_f^*$), formal firms need not raise wages as much to get the workers that they need as they need to when everybody undervalues social security (that is, when there were no type A workers). And because given $T_f$, wages in the formal sector determine salaried employment, it follows quite naturally that the more workers there are who fully value social security, the lower $w_f$, the greater the size of the formal sector, and the more efficient the economy. In sum, when $L^A = 0$, the wage in the formal sector is higher than when $L^A > 0$. I return to this line of reasoning below but first make some remarks on this equilibrium from the standpoint of workers, firms, and the government's social objectives.

Type A workers are better off when $L^A < L_f^*$ than when $L^A = L_f^*$ because $w_f' > w_f^*$. That result is intuitive: the fewer the workers in the labor force who fully value social security, the higher the wages for salaried labor. Note one additional implication: type A workers are willing to work in the formal sector for $(w_f^* + \beta_f^A T_f)$ but their utility is $(w_f' + \beta_f^A T_f)$, so they get a rent per worker of $(w_f' - w_f^*)$. Those rents, however, are not brought down to zero by entry of more workers into salaried employment because they are perceived as such only by type A workers, the only ones who value fully social security benefits.[2]

Type B workers, on the other hand, are worse off when $L^A < L_f^*$ as $w_i' < w_i^*$. That result also is intuitive: more workers do not fully value social security and prefer nonsalaried informal employment, lowering wages in that sector. Note one additional implication: those workers would not be any better off if more of them worked in the formal sector; the rents received by type A workers are not seen as such by type B workers. The effects on firms are the opposite of those on workers: profits of formal sector firms are reduced because fewer workers fully value social security benefits; for the same reason, profits (or quasi-rents) in the informal sector are higher. Finally, from the standpoint of the government's social objectives, results are straightforward and intuitive: the fewer the workers who fully value social

2. One could think of those rents as the standard producer surplus. This "workers' surplus" exists because despite the fact that all salaried workers get the same wages and social security benefits, a few of them value the benefits more than the rest.

security, the smaller the size of the formal sector and therefore the coverage of social security. The gap in the fulfillment of the government's social objectives increases with the distance between the government's preferences and workers' valuation of social security benefits.

What if $L^A > L_f^*$? That describes case 3 in figure A6-1, in which more workers would try to self-select into the formal sector. However, because I have assumed that $\beta_f^A = 1$, the equilibrium would be the same as in case 1. That is because formal firms would hire more workers than $L_f^*$ only if wages were lower than $w_f^*$. But if more workers were to be employed in the formal sector, wages in the informal sector would increase beyond $w_i^*$ and type A workers, despite the fact that they fully value social security, would be unwilling to work in the formal sector at a formal sector wage less than $w_f^*$. They would be especially unwilling if the informal sector wage was higher than $w_i^*$, as at that wage the utility of being informally employed would exceed $(w_f^* + \beta_f^A T_f)$, which is the utility of being formally employed. The limit to the expansion of the formal sector is given by the opportunity cost of employment in the informal sector, a cost that is invariant to workers' valuation of social security. As a result, in this case employment in the formal and the informal sector is $L_f^*$ and $L_i^*$ and wages are as in equation A6-3. There are no type B workers in the formal sector, and there are some type A workers in the informal sector, getting a wage $w_i^*$ that compensates them for the fact that they get no social security benefits, which they value at $\beta_f^A T_f = T_f$.

It is illustrative to return to the discussion above in which $L^A = 0$, as it suggests that the model with social security and homogeneous workers' valuations presented in chapter 6 is a special case of the more general model presented here. Let $\phi \in [0,1] = L^A/L$ measure the proportion of the labor force that fully values social security. When $\phi = 0$, all workers have equal valuations and the equilibrium when $\beta_f < 1$ described in chapter 6 obtains. As $\phi \to 1$, there is a mix of type A and B workers, with an increasing share of those who fully value social security. When $\phi = 1$, the equilibrium with $\beta_f = 1$ obtains. It is then natural to let $\phi^* = L_f^*/L$. The equilibrium in the labor market is efficient or inefficient depending on whether $\phi \gtrless \phi^*$, with the associated implications for social security coverage. Alternatively, one can think of the average worker's valuation of social security as the weighted mean of type A and B workers' valuation with weights $\phi$ and $(1 - \phi)$, so that $\beta_f = \phi \beta_f^A + (1 - \phi) \beta_f^B$ provides a measure of the average valuation.[3]

Rather than pursue these alternative technical representations, I highlight two points. The first is methodological and can be stated simply: *the assumption of uniform workers' valuation of social security is not essential.* If one allows for differences

---

3. One can also think of a continuum of workers: type A, B, C . . . , and so forth, ordered along an interval from the worker with the highest to the worker with the lowest valuation of social security, of which there are $L^A$, $L^B$, $L^C$ of each type, generating a similar weighted valuation. The discussion in terms of two types of workers simplifies the exposition, however.

in workers' valuations of social security, the numerical solution to the system of simultaneous equations shown in footnote 9 of chapter 6 changes depending on the distribution of workers' valuations, but the qualitative nature of the solution does not differ from the case in which all workers have the same valuations. As usual, a sharp assumption produces sharper and simpler results, but what matters is that the same line of reasoning holds when this sharp assumption is dropped.

The second point relates more to policy. Differences in workers' valuation of social security might reflect inherent differences in workers' preferences (with or without bundling), or they may result from the fact that the quality of social security services differs for different workers because of, for example, their place of residence. Differences in workers' inherent preferences need no explanation and there is little that policymakers can do about them. But there is much that they can do about differences in quality differentials. For example, assume that a worker's social security benefits consist only of a retirement pension and health insurance, and consider two unskilled workers, one a construction worker living in a large urban area (type A) and the other a *jornalero agrícola* living in a rural area (type B). Following the discussion in chapter 3, assume that both workers have the same preferences in terms of their discount rate, trust of the Afores, and need for health services (both are either married or single, healthy or unhealthy, with children of day care age or not, trustworthy or not, and myopic about the future or not). Assume, however, that there is an IMSS health clinic where the urban worker lives but not where the rural worker lives. Then, even though "inherent" preferences suggest that $\beta_f^A = \beta_f^B$, in fact $\beta_f^A > \beta_f^B$, if only because for the rural worker, who has no access to health services, affiliation with IMSS is not worth as much as for the urban worker. Since by law $T_f$ is the same for both, the rural worker will prefer informal employment and the urban worker formal employment, all else being equal. Needs are the same for both, but social security services, in practice, are not. *Quality differentials make some workers with identical abilities and identical preferences self-select into the informal sector and others into the formal sector.*

These results have implications for the discussion of evasion in chapter 7. All else being equal, there will be more evasion in geographical areas where services are of lower quality or nonexistent. If services are better in urban areas, there will be more evasion in rural areas. *Regional differences in social security services will make evasion more likely in some regions than others, even if workers have identical abilities and preferences in all regions.*

## The Labor Market with Social Security and Social Protection

Consider the same situation described above in which two sets of workers have different social security valuations, $L^A$ and $L^B$, but allow for the effects of social protection so that $T_i > 0$. An immediate question arises about workers' valuations of $T_i$, $\beta_i^A$, and $\beta_i^B$. The discussion in chapter 3 suggests that the relevant case for

Figure A6-2. *Different Valuations of Social Security and Social Protection*

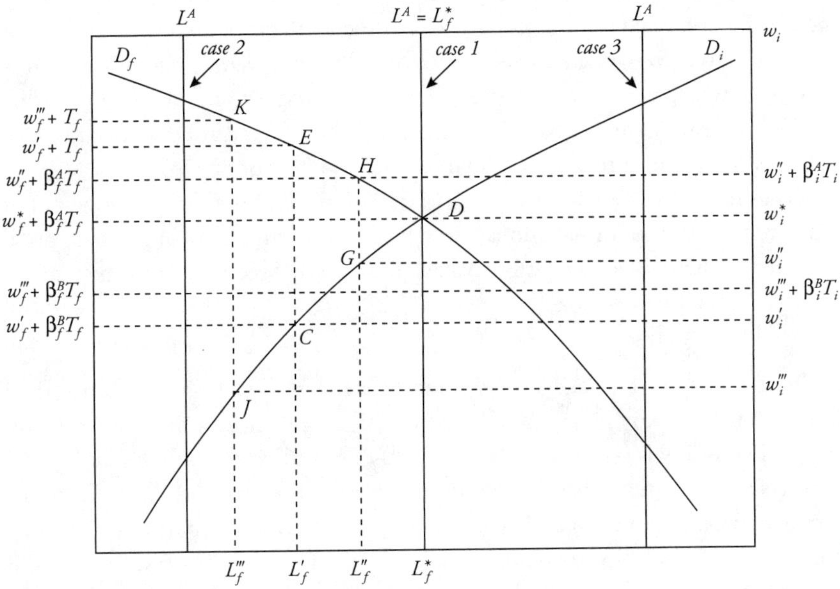

Source: Author's analysis.

Mexico is one in which social protection services are better in regions where social security services are more deficient. If workers' preferences are evenly distributed across regions—and it is hard to imagine that they are not—then it is useful to explore an ordering opposite to that in equation A6-1:

$$\text{(A6-5)} \qquad\qquad 1 = \beta_i^B > \beta_i^A \geq 0.$$

From a formal standpoint, the model is the same as before except that equations A6-2e and A6-2f are replaced by

$$\text{(A6-2g)} \qquad\qquad w_f + \beta_f^A T_f = w_i + \beta_i^A T_i$$

$$\text{(A6-2h)} \qquad\qquad w_f + \beta_f^B T_f = w_i + \beta_i^B T_i.$$

Figure A6-2 illustrates a particular solution in which I assume that the ordering of valuations is given by equations A6-1 and A6-5. The figure builds on figure A6-1 and explores the same three cases, depending on the size of $L^A$.

Consider case 1, in which $L^A = L_f^*$. I pointed out before that in this case differences in workers' valuation of social security do not matter, because those workers who fully value social security are employed in the formal sector and those who do not value it fully are employed in the informal sector. Equilibrium is at point D, and the wage structure is $(w_f^* + T_f) = w_i^*$. Assume now social protection benefits are offered. At least some workers find the informal sector, at the margin, relatively more attractive. In particular, some type A workers will move to the informal sector (because all type B workers already are informally employed). That reduces informal sector wages to $w_i''$ and increases formal sector wages to $w_f''$. At $(w_f'' + T_f)$, formal firms are at H and formal employment is $L_f'' < L_f^*$. And at $w_i'' < w_i^*$, informal firms are at G with informal employment at $L_i'' > L_i'$ (not drawn).

What happens to equations A6-2g and A6-2h? Because there are now type A workers in both the formal and the informal sector, equation A6-2g must hold. And because there are no type B workers in the formal sector, it must be that

$$(A6-6) \qquad w_f'' + \beta_f^A T_f = w_i'' + \beta_i^A T_i > w_f'' + \beta_f^B T_f.$$

In other words, type A workers are indifferent to the choice between formal and informal employment, and all type B workers prefer informal employment, where their utility is $(w_i'' + \beta_i^B T_i) > (w_f'' + \beta_f^B T_f)$. Note that that implies that type B workers get some rents, because all of them were willing to work in the informal sector for $w_i^*$ but are now receiving $(w_i'' + \beta_i^B T_i) > w_i^*$. However, note that, as before, there are no rents from the point of view of type A workers because only type B workers perceive any additional benefits.

The case just described tells us that even if $L^A = L_f^*$, when $T_i > 0$ the equilibrium is no longer efficient. Without social protection, workers had self-selected into the formal or the informal sector, and because it happened that $L^A = L_f^*$, that self-selection process distributed the labor force exactly between formal and informal employment, to match $L^A = L_f^*$. But social protection alters that equilibrium by making informal employment more profitable. Consequently, the result mentioned before, when $T_i = 0$, no longer holds, and social policy reduces the productivity of the economy even if all workers employed in the formal sector (type A) fully value social security.[4]

Consider now the second case, when $L^A < L_f^*$. Without social protection the initial equilibrium is at E and C, formal employment is at $L_f'$, and the wage structure is given by equation A6-4, reproduced here for convenience:

$$(A6-4) \qquad w_f' + \beta_f^A T_f > w_i' = w_f' + \beta_f^B T_f \quad \left( \text{with } L^A < L_f' \text{ and } L^B > L_i' \right),$$

because some type B workers are employed in the formal sector (this is the same equilibrium as in figure A6-1). When $T_i > 0$, informal employment becomes more attractive, and those who move to the informal sector first are those who value social protection benefits more—type B workers, given the assumption in equation A6-5.

---

4. Note that this inefficiency also would occur if there were no differences in workers' valuations. If one started from the equilibrium with $\beta_f = 1$ and no social protection and then set $T_i > 0$, the same result would follow (although this particular case was not explored in chapter 6).

The new equilibrium depends on the size of $T_i$; it could be to the right or left of $L^A$. As drawn in figure A6-2, it is to the right at points J and K, with higher formal sector wages and lower informal sector wages, at $w_f'''$ and $w_i'''$. That implies that even though there are fewer type B workers in the formal sector, the benefits of social protection were not large enough to make all of them move to the informal sector. At $L_f'''$, there are still some type B workers in formal employment, so wages need to satisfy

$$(A6-2h) \qquad w_f''' + \beta_f^B T_f = w_i''' + \beta_i^B T_i < w_f''' + \beta_f^A T_f$$

to make type B workers indifferent to the choice between formal and informal employment (while all type A workers are in formal employment receiving, from their point of view only, some rents).

Consider finally the third case, with $L^A > L_f^*$. Without social protection, the initial equilibrium is, for the reasons explored before, the same as with $L^A = L_f^*$ (although there are some type A workers in the informal sector), so that $w_f + \beta_f^A T_f = w_i$ (not drawn in figure A6-2). But with $T_i > 0$, informal employment becomes more attractive and more workers move to the informal sector. These must be type A workers because all type B workers already are in the informal sector. So equation A6-6 holds, there are some rents for type B workers (from their perspective), and formal employment is somewhere to the left of $L_f^*$.

In summary: for a given ratio $L^A/L$ that captures the distribution of workers' valuations of social security benefits, there is an equilibrium in the labor market with a wage structure depending on whether $L^A/L > \leq L_f^*/L$. When social protection is introduced, there also is a distribution of workers' valuations over $T_i$. Differences in workers' valuation of social benefits affect the distribution of formal and informal sector employment and the coverage of social security and social protection programs across the labor force. Those differences also impact efficiency, productivity, profits, and the fiscal accounts along the lines described in chapters 6, 7, 8, and 9. But in all cases, however, the qualitative nature of the solution is similar to the situation in which workers' valuations do not differ. The key point is this: *for a given distribution of workers' valuations of social security and social protection benefits, the introduction (or strengthening) of social protection at the margin alters the profitability of formal relative to informal sector employment in favor of the latter.* As a result, the equilibrium with social protection exhibits a larger informal sector than the one without, although with social protection all workers receive social benefits, under one form or the other. Therefore, even with $T_i > 0$, the assumption that all workers value social protection benefits equally is not essential and, mutatis mutandis, the discussion in chapters 6 to 8 follows through.

I close with one additional remark on the implications for policy. Self-selection of workers into formal and informal employment when workers have different $\beta_i$'s has an impact on evasion. Evasion is more likely for workers having higher $\beta_i$'s, just as it is for workers having lower $\beta_f$'s. *Furthermore, the interaction of low $\beta_f$'s and high $\beta_i$'s reinforces the incentives to evade,* an important observation when reinforcement results from public policies. Assume that social security services are nonexistent or of low quality in rural areas and that there is a great deal of evasion and little formal employment. Assume that the government responds to the low coverage of social security by expanding the coverage of social protection. As it does, it strengthens the incentives to evade and promotes informal employment. On the other hand, if the government responds to evasion by expanding services through social security, it reduces the incentives to evade and promotes formal employment. If the quality of social security and of social protection services are similar, rural workers obtain the same social services. But their productivity is not the same, and the fiscal implications are not the same.

As discussed in chapter 3, given statutory benefits, valuations of social security and social protection are influenced by the extent to which those benefits are or not bundled and by workers' inherent preferences. But they also are influenced by the quality of services. Significant asymmetries in service provision (urban-rural, north-south, large cities–small cities) may produce differences in valuations that otherwise would not exist, inadvertently promoting or reinforcing the process of self-selection of workers into informal employment. *Two points: first, provision of more and better social services is clearly an objective for social policy, but the form of provision matters greatly for wages, productivity, and growth. Second, the form of provision is especially important for poor workers, because the more that services are provided through social protection programs, the more that poor workers are induced into low-productivity informal jobs.*

# 7

# Equilibrium in the Labor Market with Evasion of Social Security

The model of the labor market with evasion of social security is

(A7-1a) $p^w \partial Q_f \left( L_f + L_{if} \right)/\partial L_f - \left( w_f + T_f \right) = 0$

(A7-1b) $p^w \partial Q_f \left( L_f + L_{if} \right)/\partial L_{if} - \left[ w_{if} + \lambda F + \left( \partial \lambda \left( L_{if} \right)/\partial L_{if} \right).F.L_{if} \right] = 0$

(Firms hiring salaried workers maximize profits, equating the marginal cost of illegal and legal workers.)

(A7-1c) $p^w \partial Q_i/\partial L_i - w_i = 0$ (Firms hiring nonsalaried labor maximize profits.)

(A7-1d) $\left( w_i + \beta_i T_i \right) = \left( w_{if} + \beta_i T_i \right)$

} (Workers maximize utility.)

(A7-1e) $\left( w_{if} + \beta_i T_i \right) = \left( w_f + \beta_f T_f \right)$

(A7-1f) $\lambda = \lambda \left( L_{if} \right); \lambda' > 0 ; \lambda(0) = 0$ (The probability of detection increases with evasion.)

(A7-1g) $L_i + L_{if} + L_f = L$ (All workers are employed, legally or illegally.)

Let the solutions to equations A7-1a through A7-1g be $w_i'''$, $w_f'''$, $w_{if}'''$, $L_i'''$, $L_f'''$, $L_{if}'''$ and $\lambda'''$ $(L_{if}''')$. For some parameter values, one will observe $L_{if}''' > 0$. Intuitively that happens when $\beta_f$ is "low," so that workers and firms hiring salaried workers have large rents to share and strong incentives to cheat. Of course, as elaborated on in chapter 7, it also depends on the production technology, the value of F, and the shape of $\lambda(.)$, so some equilibriums could have $L_{if}''' = 0$, even with low $\beta_f$'s. High fines or a very strict IMSS auditing policy could rule out evasion even if workers and firms were tempted to try it. But as table 5-1 shows, that is not the case in Mexico.

# 8

## *Profit Maximization under Informality*

This appendix has two parts. In the first, it elaborates on the analysis of the demand for labor by firms when there are incentives to evade the law. In the second, it calculates the profits made by formal and informal firms when capital investments are made.

### Demand for Labor

Consider a firm hiring a mix of legal and illegal salaried workers. The average cost of a legal worker is $(w_f + T_f)$, and the expected average cost of an illegal one is $(w_{if} + \lambda F)$. Given its capital stock, the firm's problem is to

$$(A8\text{-}1) \qquad \text{Max } \Pi(L_f, L_{if}) = p^w Q[K_f, (L_f + L_{if})]$$

$$- (w_f + T_f)L_f - [w_{if} + \lambda(L_f, L_{if})F]L_{if}.$$

The key aspect of the problem is the firm's decision with regard to the legal-illegal composition of its workforce. A critical input in the firm's decision is the probability of being fined, which, following the discussion in chapter 7, is given by

$$= 0 \text{ for } (L_f + L_{if}) \in \left[0, \underline{L}\right]$$

$$(A8\text{-}2) \qquad \lambda(L_f, L_{if}) = \lambda_1(L_f, L_{if}) + \lambda_2(L_f, L_{if}) \text{ for } (L_f + L_{if}) \in \left[\underline{L}, \overline{L}\right]$$

$$= 1 \text{ for } (L_f + L_{if}) \in \left[\overline{L}, \infty\right].$$

Note that in the interval $[\underline{L}, \overline{L}]$, $\lambda$ depends on $L_f$ and $L_{if}$, reflecting the effect of the interaction of firm size and the legal-illegal composition of the firm's workforce on the probability of being fined. The first term captures what can be called the size effect and the second the composition effect. It follows that

(A8-3a)             $\partial\lambda_1/\partial L_f = \partial\lambda_1/\partial L_{if} > 0$    (size effect)

(A8-3b)             $\partial\lambda_2/\partial L_f < 0; \partial\lambda_2/\partial L_{if} > 0$    (composition effect).

In other words, legal and illegal workers have the same weight in terms of increasing the size and visibility of the firm and thus in terms of the probability of being fined. However, they act in opposite directions in terms of the impact of the composition of employment on the same probability. The higher the proportion of legal to illegal workers for any given level of employment, the lower the probability of being fined.

Note also that the marginal productivity of legal and illegal workers is the same because I assume that they are perfect substitutes in terms of the production function—that is, $\partial Q/\partial L_f = \partial Q/\partial QL_{if}$. As a result, in the $(L_f, L_{if})$ space, the isoquants are linear. That, in turn, implies that

(A8-4)
$$
\begin{array}{lll}
L_f = 0 \text{ and } L_{if} > 0 & & \left[w_{if} + \lambda\left(L_f, L_{if}\right)F\right] < \left(w_f + T_f\right) \\
L_f > 0 \text{ and } L_{if} > 0 & \text{as} & \left[w_{if} + \lambda\left(L_f, L_{if}\right)F\right] = \left(w_f + T_f\right) \\
L_f > 0 \text{ and } L_{if} = 0 & & \left[w_{if} + \lambda\left(L_f, L_{if}\right)F\right] > \left(w_f + T_f\right).
\end{array}
$$

The first-order conditions for the firm are obtained by maximizing equation A8-1 with respect to $L_f$ and $L_{if}$, which in turn provides the demand functions for legal and illegal workers, $L_f^D$ and $L_{if}^D$. Those functions are given by the simultaneous solution to

(A8-5)
$$
L_f^D \rightarrow p^w \partial Q/\partial QL_f \geq \left[\left(w_f + T_f\right) + \left(\partial\lambda_1/\partial L_f + \partial\lambda_2/\partial L_f\right).F.L_{if}\right]
$$
$$
L_{if}^D \rightarrow p^w \partial Q/\partial QL_{if} \geq \left[w_{if} + \lambda\left(L_f, L_{if}\right)F + \left(\partial\lambda_1/\partial L_{if} + \partial\lambda_2/\partial L_{if}\right).F.L_{if}\right].
$$

Inspection of equations A8-2 and A8-5 shows that it is not possible to obtain a closed form solution in which labor demands are just a function of exogenously given wage rates, output prices, and the capital stock. The problem has two parts: one, because the isoquants are linear, one can get corner solutions in which only legal or illegal labor is used in the firm; two, the price of legal relative to illegal workers depends on the level and composition of employment; expected input prices are not exogenous.

To provide a qualitative solution to the firm's maximization exercise given the two parts to the problem, I proceeded in three steps, following equation A8-2. First, it is clear that the size of the fines is irrelevant if the firm believes that it will not be fined. So in the interval $[0, \underline{L}]$, the firm disregards the fines and hires only illegal workers because $w_{if} < (w_f + T_f)$. Second, it also is clear that if the firm believes that it will be fined regardless of the number of illegal workers that it hires, it will not hire any (as long as $(w_{if} + F) > (w_f + T_f)$, which I assume is the case).[1] Those two statements imply that if total employment is in the interval $[0, \underline{L}]$, then it consists of illegal workers only, and that if total employment is greater than $\overline{L}$, it consists of legal workers only. That in turn implies that the demand for illegal labor is initially positive and coincides with the firm's total demand for labor, but at some point it is zero and the firm demands only legal workers.

The third step consisted of analyzing the range in which there is a mix of legal and illegal workers. For that mix to occur, the intermediate option in expression A8-4 must be observed. That implies that

$$(A8\text{-}6) \qquad \begin{aligned} (w_f + T_f) + (\partial\lambda_2/\partial L_f).L_{if}.F &= w_{if} + \lambda(L_f L_{if}).F \\ &\quad + (\partial\lambda_2/\partial L_{if}).L_{if}.F, \end{aligned}$$

where I have made use of expression A8-3a.

This expression is useful in understanding the conditions under which firms decide to mix legal and illegal workers. For some insight, recall that $\partial\lambda_2/\partial L_f < 0$ because, all things being equal, one more legal worker reduces the probability of being fined. That effect may or may not, on a one-to-one basis, compensate for the increase in the probability of being fined for hiring one more illegal worker, $\partial\lambda_2/\partial L_{if} > 0$. But the point is that from the standpoint of the exposure of the firm to risk and thus its expected labor costs, when the firm mixes legal and illegal workers it is because a legal worker costs the firm less than $(w_f + T_f)$. Why? When a firm hires a legal worker it has to pay $(w_f + T_f)$, but at the same time the firm lowers its risk of being caught and having to pay fines on all the illegal workers that it hired because the legal-illegal composition of its workforce tilts in the direction of legality. As a result, that legal worker contributes to reducing the firm's overall labor costs (the second term on the left side of equation A8-6, which is negative, captures that). However, as the firm increases its size, measured by the total number of workers (legal and illegal), it increases its probability of being fined; therefore the marginal cost of the optimal combination of legal and illegal workers must be increasing because the average risk is increasing. Consequently, as the firm expands, the average cost of illegal workers cannot be compensated for by replacing those workers one for one with legal workers. The absolute number of illegal workers must diminish as employment expands until all workers are legal. That occurs at the point where $(w_f + T_f) = (w_{if} + \lambda F)$, which most likely is to the

---

1. As stated in chapter 7, in Mexico $F \approx 1.4T_f$. That does not guarantee the condition mentioned in the text because $w_{if}$ could be very low if $\beta_f$ is very low and $\beta_i T_i$ is very high. But that is very unlikely, and therefore I assume that $(F - T_f) > (w_f - w_{if})$.

left of $\bar{L}$ (unless, as noted, $w_{if}$ is very low). That describes the behavior of $L_{if}^D$ and $L_f^D$ in the intermediate range.

Recall from chapter 7 that when a firm is said to fire an illegal worker and hire a legal worker, it need not refer to two different individuals. It may refer to the same individual, whom the firm initially decided not to register with IMSS but after some point did register. The issue is how much risk the firm perceives and is willing to bear. The worker from Nuevo Leon discussed in the beginning of chapter 5 is an example.

Figure A8-1 pulls together the three steps described above. The upper panel graphs total employment $L$ $(= L_{if} + L_f)$ on the horizontal axes and graphs the marginal cost of labor to the firm on the vertical axes. On the vertical axes I marked three exogenous values: $w_{if} < (w_f + T_f) < (w_{if} + F)$, as assumed. The lower panel also graphs $L$ $(= L_{if} + L_f)$ on the horizontal axes and $L_{if}$ and $L_f$ separately on the vertical axes. To ensure that $(L_f + L_{if}) = L$, use is made of a 45 degree line. In the lower panel the demand for informal labor, $L_{if}^D$, is the inverted U-shaped curve, and the demand for formal labor, $L_f^D$, is the difference between the 45 degree line and $L_{if}^D$.

The endogeneity of the firm's expected labor costs to the size and composition of the demand for labor can now be described, along with the firm's behavior depending on where the demand for labor falls. Given the firm's production function, the world price of the good produced by the firm ($p^w$), and the capital stock installed in the firm ($K_f$), the total demand for labor is determined, labeled $L^D$ in the upper panel. Doing so is easy because total demand for labor does not depend on input prices; it is just the value of the marginal product of labor given the production function. The troublesome element is the marginal cost of labor. Clearly, up to $\underline{L}$, it is $w_{if}$. As a result, in the lower panel $L_{if}^D$ coincides with the 45 degree line; all workers in that range are illegal. To the right of $\underline{L}$, the marginal cost of labor increases because the probability of being fined turns positive; that increases the price of illegal relative to legal workers, and as a result the firm mixes the two types of workers. Note the critical point that at $(\underline{L} + \varepsilon)$, the firm does not fire all illegal workers, given that $[w_{if} + \lambda(\underline{L} + \varepsilon)F] < (w_f + T_f)$, so there is no discontinuity in the demand for illegal workers at that point. In other words, close to $\underline{L}$ it still pays to cheat a little and hire illegal workers. For larger levels of total employment $L$, the mix of legal and illegal workers changes as the former increases and the latter falls.

(One could draw the demand for legal workers in the lower panel, beginning on the horizontal axes at point A, increasing up to point B on the 45 degree line, and then overlapping with the 45 degree line to the right of that point. In the intermediate range between A and B, demand is equal to the 45 degree line minus $L_{if}^D$; that is not drawn so as not to clutter the diagram.)

When $[w_{if} + \lambda(L_f + L_{if})F] = (w_f + T_f)$ in the upper panel, the firm ceases to hire any illegal workers. All its workers are legal, and the firm's marginal cost

Figure A8-1. *Marginal Cost of Labor and Demand for Legal and Illegal Workers*

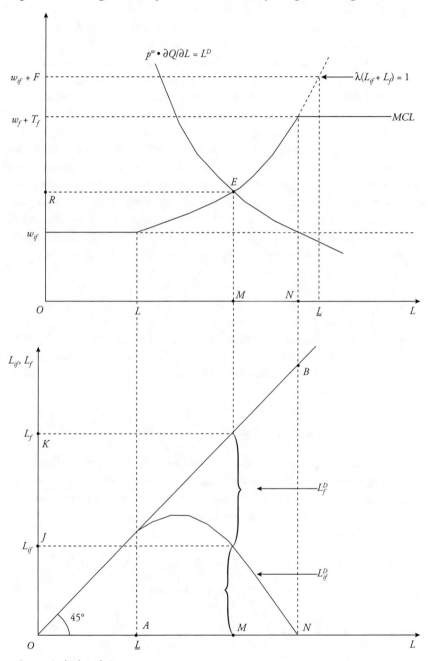

Source: Author's analysis.

of labor equals $(w_f + T_f)$. Note that depending on the size of the fines, F, that might occur before $\bar{L}$ at a point like N in both horizontal axes. Given the probability of being fined, high fines deter illegal behavior. *That explains why even firms that do not cheat still lobby to have fines reduced; as F falls, some firms that currently do not cheat could do so.* That highlights that the marginal cost of labor curve is drawn for a given F, and that increasing (reducing) that parameter makes the curve steeper (flatter), with fewer (more) workers hired for a given demand function for labor, $L^D$, and a smaller (larger) proportion of illegal workers in the firm's workforce.

Figure A8-1 depicts a demand function for labor that falls in the range in which the firm hires legal and illegal workers. Equilibrium is at point E in the upper panel. The firm hires a total of M workers, with the marginal cost of the last worker at point R on the vertical axes, given by equation A8-6. *That is the marginal productivity of that level and composition of legal and illegal workers, which is the same for both because $\partial Q/\partial L_f = \partial Q/\partial L_{if}$. On the other hand, although the productivity of legal and illegal workers is the same, the monetary payment that the firm makes for its JK legal workers is $(w_f + T_f)$, and for its OJ illegal workers is $w_{if}$ because the cost of the risk of hiring illegal workers is not reflected in the firm's accounts.* (That is similar to the contingent costs of firing and severance pay regulations, which also are part of the firm's labor costs but are not reflected in its accounts.) Meanwhile, workers are getting utility of $(w_f + \beta_f T_f) = (w_{if} + \beta_i T_i)$ but wages of $w_f$ and $w_{if}$. Finally, on the horizontal axes of the lower panel, the same employment level M is marked, divided between OJ illegal workers and JK legal workers on the vertical axes.

## The Profitability of Investments

The following equations calculate the additional or new profits, $\Delta\Pi$, associated with the investments made in the options discussed in chapter 8. To simplify notation, I did not index wage rates by time periods, it being understood that the relevant wage in each case is the one that clears the labor market along the lines of the discussion in chapter 7.

$$(A8\text{-}7a) \qquad \Delta\Pi^a = \left\{ p^w Q^a_{\tau+1} - \left[ w_{if} + \lambda \left( L^a_\tau + \Delta L^a \right) F \right] \left( L^a_\tau + \Delta L^a \right) \right\}$$
$$- \left\{ p^w Q^a_\tau - \left[ w_{if} + \lambda \left( L^a_\tau \right) F \right] L^a_\tau \right\}$$

$$(A8\text{-}7b) \qquad \Delta\Pi^b = p^w Q^b - \left[ w_{if} + \lambda \left( L^b \right) F \right] L^b$$

$$(A8\text{-}7c) \qquad \Delta\Pi^c = \left\{ p^w Q^c_{\tau+1} - \left[ w_{if} + \lambda \left( L^c_\tau + \Delta L^c \right) F \right] L^c_\tau - \left( w_f + T_f \right) \Delta L^c - C \right\}$$
$$- \left\{ p^w Q^c_\tau - \left[ w_{if} + \lambda \left( L^c_\tau \right) F \right] L^c_\tau \right\}$$

(A8-7d) $\Delta\Pi^d = \left\{ p^w Q_{\tau+1}^d - \left( w_f + T_f \right)\left( L_\tau^d + \Delta L^d \right) \right\}$

$$\left\{ p^w Q_\tau^d - \left[ w_{if} + \lambda\left( L_{f\tau}^d + L_{if\tau}^d \right) F \right] L_{if\tau}^d - \left( w_f + T_f \right) L_{f\tau}^d \right\}$$

(A8-7e) $\Delta\Pi^e = \left\{ p^w Q_{\tau+1}^e - \left( w_f + T_f \right)\left( L_\tau^e + \Delta L^e \right) \right\} - \left\{ p^w Q_\tau^e - \left( w_f + T_f \right) L_\tau^e \right\}$

(A8-7f) $\Delta\Pi^f = p^w Q^f - \left( w_f + T_f \right) L^f - C.$

To provide some insight: equation A8-7a measures the additional profits made by the already existing informal firm; the relevant point to note is that expansion may raise its expected marginal costs of labor due to higher exposure to the risk of detection by IMSS and SAT—that is, that $\lambda(L_\tau^a + \Delta L^a) \geq \lambda(L_\tau^a)$. Equation A8-7b measures the profits of a new informal firm, which, depending on $\lambda$, may face a lower probability of detection by IMSS and lower labor costs than the existing informal firm would face if it expanded. In particular, if the expansion in equation A8-7a still leaves the firm below the threshold level of workers $\underline{L}$ in expression 7-3 in the text, where the probability of detection is practically nil, then the expansion may provide more profits than a new venture; otherwise, a new venture is started. Note that the workers hired by the new informal firm, $L^b$, may or may not be the same as the additional workers that the expanding informal firm would hire, $\Delta L^a$.

Equation A8-7c is interesting because the informal firm minimizes the risk of detection as a result of its expansion by becoming formal, although it has to incur registration costs of C to do so. Nonetheless, it enrolls only some of its workers with IMSS, which are assumed to be the new ones, $\Delta L^c$; the workers previously hired are assumed to remain illegal. In equation A8-7d, the firm already is formal, although it was hiring a mix of legal and illegal workers, $L_{f\tau}^d + L_{f\tau}^{di}$. Its expansion involves no registration costs and is associated with becoming fully legal; because there is no evasion of IMSS, the cost of the previously hired workers and the newly hired workers is $(w_f + T_f)$. Note that in this case IMSS registries overstate the number of jobs created because, as a result of the firm's investments, some are just a conversion of illegal salaried workers already in the firm into legal workers (see figure 7-6). Equations A8-7e and A8-7f, finally, refer to two fully formal firms, one that has expanded and one that is new, but both create new net formal jobs.

# 9

# Further Remarks on Retirement Pensions as a Social Entitlement

This appendix discusses some implications of the proposal for retirement pensions presented in figure 10-1. Under the proposal all workers are forced to save the same amount for retirement: the equivalent of what a worker earning three times the minimum wage is forced to save plus the government subsidy (the *cuota social para el retiro*), or 372 pesos a month in the calculations shown in table 10-4. But because there is a distribution of wages, the ratio of savings in the Afore to the wage is not the same for all workers; in fact, it is a decreasing function of a worker's wage. Savings would be equivalent to 25.3 percent of the wage for workers earning the minimum wage, to 8.5 percent for workers earning three times the minimum wage, and to 2.5 percent for workers earning ten times the minimum wage.

Of course, workers could save more in their Afore accounts voluntarily, and salaried workers in particular could negotiate with firms to increase the contributions to their accounts. But if no such savings occur (or at least not through the Afore system), then replacement rates will be higher for lower-wage than for higher-wage workers. To help determine whether that feature of the proposal should be modified or left as in figure 10-1, it is useful to ask the following question: *should the government force all workers to save the same amount or an amount proportional to their income?*

That question is difficult to answer, and no attempt is made to do so here. I only note that under the status quo, the amount that a formal worker is obligated to save is proportional to his or her wage and that informal workers are not obligated to save at all. The proposal in figure 10-1 requires all workers to save, but the amount is fixed regardless of a worker's wage or other forms of income, because the proposal is based on the premise that in Mexico the imputed wages and, more generally, earnings of nonsalaried workers can be observed only imperfectly and taxed hardly at all. The proposal therefore changes the point of taxation from the place where workers pick up their paycheck to the place where they spend it; by doing so, it taxes nonsalaried workers' earnings without observing them, the implicit assumption being that consumption and earnings are strongly correlated. A critical point, however, is that a worker's individual consumption taxes are not measured; all revenues from VAT are deposited in a single account at the Finance Ministry without anybody knowing who paid how much.

As a result, under the terms of figure 10-1 the same amount is deposited in the Afore accounts of all workers regardless of their wage or earnings and, of course, labor status. That approach has two advantages and one potential disadvantage: on one hand, retirement pensions are redistributive and extend to all workers, salaried or nonsalaried; on the other, replacement rates fall as wage or income levels increase. The fact that forced saving rates *in the Afores* are a decreasing function of workers' wages or earnings does not imply that total individual workers' savings rates also are a decreasing function of wages or earnings because workers can save in other instruments. Depending on the government's objective, the fact that saving rates in the Afores are a decreasing function of wages or earnings may or may not be a problem. The point that I want to highlight is that there is a difference between an entitlement to a universal pension that is the same for all workers and a pension that is proportional to a worker's lifetime earnings. The former can be achieved using the proposal as it stands in figure 10-1; the latter may be *partly* achieved by modifying the proposal.

If there are reasons to force workers to save an additional amount proportional to their wage while they are in salaried employment, figure 10-1 needs to be modified to divide pensions into two parts: a universal entitlement included in $T^{CP}$, which could be called the basic pension, and an additional obligation (entitlement?) specific to salaried workers included in $T_f^{CP}$, which could be called a complementary pension (with due adjustment of the contribution rate to take into account that some forced saving already occurs under $T^{CP}$). In terms of figure 10-1, that implies rewriting $T^{CP}$ and $T_f^{CP}$ as

(A9-1)     $T^{CP} = [\,$health insurance $\oplus$ basic retirement pension $\oplus$ life insurance
$\oplus$ disability insurance$\,]$

(A9-2)     $T_f^{CP} = [\,$work-risk insurance $\oplus$ severance pay (unemployment
insurance?) $\oplus$ complementary retirement pension$\,]$.

Of course, *that implies that for the purposes of retirement pensions, when workers are salaried the way that they are treated is different from the way that they are treated when they are nonsalaried:* when they are nonsalaried, there is no mechanism to force them to save more than what is derived from $T^{CP}$, but when they are salaried the government can conveniently do so by directly taxing their paychecks.

Figure 10-1, together with equations A9-1 and A9-2, defines a system of universal social entitlements that has a *two-pillar pension system:* one pillar is the basic retirement pension; the second is the complementary pension that workers accumulate during the time that they spend as salaried employees. Of course, to the extent that workers do not fully value the forced-savings component of $T_f^{CP}$ (the second pillar), they and the firms that hire them will react to the tax implicit in $(1 - \beta_f^{CP}) T_f^{CP}$ and, at the margin, will choose nonsalaried contractual relationships to avoid it. The trade-offs to the government follow from the discussion in chapters 6 to 9 of the main text. As stated above, one can evaluate them only by making explicit the reasons why salaried workers should be forced to save more than other workers and why the amount saved needs to be proportional to income. In any event, I highlight here that under the terms of the proposal both pillars would be paid for with current taxes or contributions, with no contingent obligations for the future, and in both cases resources always would be owned by the worker as they always would be deposited in her or his Afore.

The effects of the proposal on individual savings need to be separated from the effects on aggregate savings. According to the IMSS registries, the average wage under which 14.1 million workers contributed to the Afores in 2006 was 4.26 times the minimum wage. Assuming that the proposal is adopted with only the first pillar—that is, without adding any retirement saving component to $T_f^{CP}$—implies that 41.4 million workers would contribute to the Afore on the basis of a wage of three times the minimum wage. Clearly, the potential loss of contributions from high-wage workers is more than offset by the increase in the number of workers contributing. As shown in chapter 10, the net impact of the proposal is this: *the flow of resources to the Afores would more than double.*

In any case, a potential by-product of the proposal in figure 10-1 could well be an increase in domestic savings, which, given the long-term nature of saving for retirement in the Afores, would expand the supply of credit for long-term investments. (As an aside, the market for annuities to provide workers with retirement income also would gradually deepen because eventually the number of workers purchasing annuities would almost triple.) It is beyond the scope of this book to assess the impact of such a change on the rate of growth of GDP, but it could be, as pointed out in chapter 8, *another channel through which economic growth would accelerate,* in addition to the lower incremental capital-output ratio resulting from a more efficient portfolio of firms' investments.

Under the terms of the proposal, *individual workers also would save for retirement during their entire working life,* regardless of shifts between salaried and nonsalaried employment. To illustrate the relevance of that change, table A9-1 shows the distribution of contribution densities observed in all the Afore accounts

Table A9-1. *Distribution of Contribution Densities to Afore Accounts, 1997–2007*

| Density range[a] | Number of accounts | Percent of | | Percent of total |
|---|---|---|---|---|
| | | High wage workers | Low wage workers | |
| 1–10 | 8,930,258 | 0.7 | 22.9 | 23.6 |
| 10–20 | 4,756,809 | 1.0 | 11.6 | 12.6 |
| 20–30 | 3,288,344 | 0.7 | 8.0 | 8.7 |
| 30–40 | 2,815,576 | 1.1 | 6.3 | 7.4 |
| 40–50 | 2,695,070 | 1.3 | 5.8 | 7.1 |
| 50–60 | 1,919,150 | 1.2 | 3.9 | 5.1 |
| 60–70 | 2,220,267 | 1.6 | 4.3 | 5.9 |
| 70–80 | 2,361,074 | 1.8 | 4.4 | 6.2 |
| 80–90 | 2,599,103 | 2.5 | 4.4 | 6.9 |
| 90–100 | 6,262,826 | 9.2 | 7.3 | 16.5 |
| Total | 37,848,477 | 21.1 | 78.9 | 100.00 |

Source: Author's analysis based on data from Consar registries.

a. Share of time elapsed since the account was created that it received contributions.

created between the time that the system began in July 1997 and February 2007. The table shows the share of the time that an account was active—that is, was receiving contributions—since it was first created or, more precisely, the share of bimesters in which contributions were made in total bimesters elapsed since the date of first registration of each account (or first entry of each worker into formal employment). I identify high- and low-wage workers separately, by the usual cut-off point of three times the minimum wage.

Almost one-fourth of all accounts received contributions only up to 10 percent of the time since they were opened, and almost 60 percent received contributions 50 percent of the time at most. In accordance with the results in chapter 5, low-wage workers had lower contribution densities than high-wage workers (that is, a lower average stay in formal employment); that is why under present trends few will qualify for the minimum pension guarantee.[1] Assuming a one-to-one mapping between workers and accounts (that is, ignoring duplicate accounts), the table indicates that since the Afore system began in 1997, almost 60 percent of all "formal" workers in Mexico contributed to their accounts at most half of the time that they could have done so. In fact, the observed average contribution density over the last decade was 45 percent.

1. Casal and Hoyo (2007) estimates that only about 30,000 workers who entered IMSS since 1997 will qualify for the pension guarantee; *that implies that most low-wage and poor workers—who according to the results in chapter 5 entered formality at some point in their working lives—will not.* Note from table 8-4 that at least 1.8 million beneficiaries of Progresa-Oportunidades were sixty years of age or older in 2005. That implies that the vast majority of poor workers will retire with less than the minimum pension.

Those results serve to illustrate two points: one, how problematic it is to base retirement pensions on the characteristics of "formal" workers in Mexico; two, the importance of the feature of the proposal in figure 10-1 to increase *all* workers' contribution density to 100 percent. The replacement rate for the average worker today, who contributes 45 percent of the time on the basis of a wage of 4.26 times the minimum wage, is 0.33 percent; the replacement rate for the average worker in the proposal, who contributes 100 percent of the time on the basis of a wage of three times the minimum wage, is 0.40 percent.[2] Combining the results of table A9-1 with those presented in chapter 5, in particular the positive relationship between wage level and stay in formality—or, in the context of this appendix, contribution density—it follows that *for the average worker as well as for all low-wage and poor workers, the proposal increases the replacement rate.* On the other hand, the majority of workers earning more than 4.26 times the minimum wage who have a contribution density of more than 45 percent probably would face lower replacement rates under the proposal than at present *from their forced savings in the Afores;* if there are reasons suggesting that that result would be undesirable, the proposal can be modified as suggested in equations A9-1 and A9-2 above.

I close this appendix with a brief mention of a third implication of a system of universal retirement pensions. An implicit assumption of the discussion has been that the supply of total labor, L, is completely exogenous. But an individual may make many moves in and out of the labor force during his or her adult life, aside from shifts between formal and informal employment. Individuals may leave the labor force temporarily to migrate elsewhere, to pursue their education, to care for children, and so on; furthermore, participation rates can change in response to the system of social entitlements. That raises the question of whether the entitlement to a basic retirement pension should be associated with the *condition of work or the condition of citizenship.*

The first condition requires extending the right to a pension from salaried workers to all workers; the second abandons the association of a retirement pension with any type of worker altogether. The first case requires monitoring whether workers are employed or not and increases the difficulty of achieving a contribution density of 100 percent; the second avoids those drawbacks but increases the

---

2. The comparison assumes the same working life of forty years for two workers, A and B, beginning, say, at age twenty-five and ending at age sixty-five. Both workers earn the same constant wage during their working lives of 4.26 times the minimum wage, or 6,246 pesos a month. Under the terms of the proposal, worker A saves 372 pesos a month over forty years; under the status quo, worker B saves 487 pesos a month over eighteen years (40*0.45). Both earn a real annual rate of 3.5 percent and, to make the most favorable assumption possible for the status quo, worker B contributes continuously during the first eighteen years of his forty-year career, accumulating the maximum interest possible in his Afore account. At retirement worker A gets a pension of 2,532 pesos a month; worker B gets a pension of 2,058 pesos a month.

cost of the proposal.[3] Both alternatives have been present in recent practice in Mexico. Programs like Adults over Seventy target all adults, while social security retirement pensions are associated with the condition of previous (salaried) work. This issue deserves further discussion, which I do not undertake here. But clearly it is essential to clarify the exact nature of the beneficiary of the universal pension and design the rest of the system of universal entitlements on that basis, including, if any, the second pillar discussed above.

3. Although that can be countered by increasing the age at which such a pension is paid to, say, seventy years or reducing the size of the basic pension or both.

# References

Angelucci, Manuela. 2005. "Aid Programs' Unintended Effects: The Case of Progresa and Migration." University of Arizona, Department of Economics.

Aterido, Reyes, M. Hallward-Driemer, and C. Pagés. 2007. "Investment Climate and Employment Growth: The Impact of Access to Finance, Corruption, and Regulations across Firms." Washington: Inter-American Development Bank (September).

Azevedo, Joao Pedro. 2006. "An Investigation of the Labor Market Earnings in Deprived Areas: Evaluating the Sources of Earning Differentials in the Slums." In *Informal Labor Markets and Development,* edited by B. Guha-Khasnobis and R. Kanbur. Helsinski, Finland: Palgrave-Macmillan for the United Nations University, World Institute for Development Economics Research.

Banerjee, Abhijit, and E. Dufflo. 2004. "Growth Theory through the Lens of Development Economics." Massachusetts Institute of Technology, Department of Economics.

Basu, Kaishuk, N. H. Chau, and R. Kanbur. 2005. "Turning a Blind Eye: Costly Enforcement, Credible Commitment, and Minimum Wage Laws." Working Paper 2005-13. Cornell University, Department of Applied Economics and Management (June).

Bell, Linda, 1997. "The Impact of Minimum Wages in Mexico and Colombia." *Journal of Labor Economics* 15, no. 3, pp. 103–35.

Blanchard, Olivier. 2004. "Designing Labor Market Institutions." Paper presented at the Seventh Annual Conference on Economic Policy in Chile. Banco Central de Chile, Santiago, November 6–7, 2003.

Bosch, Mariano, and W. Maloney. 2006. "Gross Worker Flows in the Presence of Informal Labor Markets: The Mexican Experience." Washington: World Bank.

Bruhn, Miriam. 2006. "License to Sell: The Effect of Business Registration Reform on Entrepreneurial Activity in Mexico." Massachusetts Institute of Technology, Department of Economics.

Budar-Mejía, Oscar, and R. García-Verdú. 2003. "A Dynamic Model of Formal and Informal Aggregate Labor Force Participation." Mexico City: Banco de México, Research Department.

Calderón, Angel. 2000. "Job Stability and Labor Mobility in Urban Mexico: A Study Based on Duration Models and Transition Analysis." Research Network Working Paper R-419. Washington: Inter-American Development Bank.

————. 2006. "Mobility of Workers between Formal and Informal Job Status: An Empirical Assessment of Earnings Variations and Exit Hazards in Mexico's Urban Labor Market." Mexico City: El Colegio de México, Department of Economics.

Casal, José Antonio, and C. Hoyo. 2007. "Costo Fiscal de la Reforma a la Ley del Seguro Social" [Fiscal Cost of Reform of the Social Security Law]. Documento de Trabajo 2007-2 [Working Paper 2007-2]. Mexico City: Comisión Nacional del Sistema de Ahorro para el Retiro, Coordinación General de Estudios Económicos [National Commission of the System of Retirement Saving, General Coordinating Agency for Economic Studies].

Coase, Ronald H. 1988. *The Firm, the Market, and the Law.* University of Chicago Press.

Chen, Martha. 2006. "Rethinking the Informal Economy: Linkages with the Formal Economy and the Formal Regulatory Environment." In *Linking the Formal and Informal Economy: Concepts and Policies,* edited by B. Guha-Khasnobis, R. Kanbur, and E. Ostrom. Oxford University Press.

Chiquiar, Daniel, N. Quella, and M. Ramos Francia. 2006. "Determinantes de la Ventaja Comparativa y el Desempeño de las Exportaciones Mexicanas en el Período 1996–2004" [Determinants of the Comparative Advantage and Performance of Mexican Exports over the 1996–2004 Period]. Documento de Investigación 2006-XX [Research Report 2006-XX]. México City: Banco de México.

Dávila, Enrique. 1994. "Regulaciones Laborales y Mercado de Trabajo en México" [Labor Regulations and the Job Market in Latin America]. In *Regulación del Mercado de Trabajo en América Latina* [Regulation of the Job Market in Latin America], edited by G. Márquez. San Francisco: Centro Internacional para el Desarrollo Económico [International Center for Economic Development].

Dávila, Enrique, G. Kessel, and S. Levy, S. 2002. "El Sur También Existe: Un Ensayo sobre el Desarrollo Regional de México" [The South Also Exists: An Essay on the Regional Development of Mexico], in *Economía Mexicana* [Mexican Economy] 11, no. 1, pp. 202–60.

Dávila, Enrique, and S. Levy. 2003. "Taxing for Equity: A Proposal to Reform Mexico's Value-Added Tax." In *Latin American Economic Reform: The Second Stage,* edited by J. A. González and others. University of Chicago Press, pp. 357–92.

De Soto, Hernando. 2000. *The Mystery of Capital: Why Capitalism Triumphs in the West and Fails Everywhere Else.* New York: Basic Books.

Duryea, Susan, and others. 2006. "For Better or for Worse: Job and Earnings Mobility in Nine Middle- and Low-Income Countries." Washington: Inter-American Development Bank.

Duval, Robert. 2006. "La Evolución Salarial en México" [The Evolution of Wages in Mexico]. Washington: Inter-American Development Bank.

Fajnzylber, Pablo, W. Maloney, and G. Montes Rojas. 2006. "Releasing Constraints to Growth or Pushing on a String? The Impact of Credit, Training, Business Associations, and Taxes on the Performance of Mexican Micro-Firms." Washington: World Bank.

Gertler, Paul, S. Martinez, and M. Rubio. 2005. "The Effects of Oportunidades on Raising Household Consumption through Productive Investments in Micro-Enterprise and Agricultural Production." Oportunidades Technical Evaluation Paper 19. Mexico City: Coordinacion Nacional del Programa de Desarrollo Humano Oportundidades, Secretaria de Desarrollo Social [National Coordinating Agency of the Human Development Program Oportunidades, Secretary of Social Development].

Gong, Xiadong, A. Soest, and E. Villagomez. 2004. "Mobility in the Urban Labor Market: A Panel Data Analysis for Mexico." *Economic Development and Cultural Change* 53, no. 1, pp. 1–36.

González de la Rocha, Mercedes. 2006. "Nuevas Facetas del Aislamiento Social: Un Acercamiento Etnográfico" [New Facets of Social Isolation: An Ethnographic Approach]. In *Desmitificación y Nuevos Mitos sobre la Pobreza* [Demystification and New Myths about Poverty], edited by M. Székely. Mexico City: Miguel Angel Porrúa.

Guha-Khasnobis, Basudeb, R. Kanbur, and E. Ostrom. 2006a. "Beyond Formality and Informality." In *Linking the Formal and Informal Economy: Concepts and Policies,* edited by B. Guha-Khasnobis, R. Kanbur, and E. Ostrom. Oxford University Press.

———. 2006b. *Linking the Formal and Informal Economy: Concepts and Policies.* Oxford University Press.

Haber, Stephen. 2007. "Why Banks Don't Lend: The Mexican Financial System." Stanford University, Department of Political Science.

Harris, John, and M. Todaro. 1970. "Migration, Unemployment, and Development: A Two-Sector Analysis." *American Economic Review* 60, pp. 126–42.

Hart, Keith. 2006. "Bureaucratic Form and the Informal Economy." In *Linking the Formal and Informal Economy: Concepts and Policies,* edited by B. Guha-Khasnobis, R. Kanbur, and E. Ostrom. Oxford University Press.

Heckman, James, and C. Pagés. 2004. *Law and Employment: Lessons form Latin America and the Caribbean.* University of Chicago Press for the National Bureau of Economic Research.

Hsieh, Chang-Tai, and P. Klenow. 2006. "Misallocation and Manufacturing TFP in China and India." Standford University, Department of Economics.

Instituto del Fondo Nacional de la Vivienda para los Trabajadores (Infonavit) [Institute of the National Housing Fund for Workers]. 2007. "Reglas para el Otorgamiento de Créditos a los Trabajadores Derechohabientes del Instituto del Fondo Nacional de la Vivienda para los Trabajadores" [Rules for Granting Home Credits to Beneficairy Workers]. Mexico City.

Instituto Mexicano del Seguro Social (IMSS) [Mexican Institute of Social Security]. 2003a. *Informe al Ejecutivo Federal y al Congreso de la Unión sobre la Situación Financiera y los Riesgos del IMSS 2002–2003* [Report to the Federal Executive and the National Congress on the Financial Situation and the Risks of IMSS 2002–2003]. México (June).

———. 2003b. *Informe de los Servicios Personales 2002-2003* [Report on Personal Services 2002–2003]. México (June).

———. 2004. *Informe al Ejecutivo Federal y al Congreso de la Unión sobre la Situación Financiera y los Riesgos del IMSS 2003–2004* [Report to the Federal Executive and the National Congress on the Financial Situation and the Risks of IMSS 2003–2004]. México (June).

———. 2005. *Informe al Ejecutivo Federal y al Congreso de la Unión sobre la Situación Financiera y los Riesgos del IMSS 2004–2005.* [Report to the Federal Executive and the National Congress on the Financial Situation and the Risks of IMSS 2004–2005]. México (June).

———. 2006. *Informe al Ejecutivo Federal y al Congreso de la Unión sobre la Situación Financiera y los Riesgos del IMSS 2005–2006* [Report to the Federal Executive and the National Congress on the Financial Situation and the Risks of IMSS 2005–2006]. México (June).

———. 2007. *Informe al Ejecutivo Federal y al Congreso de la Unión sobre la Situación Financiera y los Riesgos del IMSS 2006–2007* [Report to the Federal Executive and the National Congress on the Financial Situation and the Risks of IMSS 2006–2007]. México (June).

Instituto Nacional de Estadística, Geografía, e Informática (Inegi) [National Institute of Statistics, Geography, and Information Sciences]. 2004. *Metodología de los Censos Económicos de 2004* [Methodology of the 2004 Economic Census]. México City.

Inter-American Development Bank. 2004. "Good Jobs Wanted: Labor Markets in Latin America." Economic and Social Progress Report. Washington.

International Labor Office. 1972. *Incomes, Employment, and Equality in Kenya.* Geneva.

———. 2005. *Key Indicators of the Labour Market,* 4th ed. Geneva.

Kaplan, David, G. Martínez, and R. Robertson. 2005. "Worker and Job Flows in Mexico." Mexico City: Instituto Tecnológico Autónomo de México [Autonomous Technological Institute of Mexico], Department of Economics (June).

Kaplan, David, E. Piedra, and E. Seira. 2006. "Are Burdensome Registration Procedures an Important Barrier on Firm Creation? Evidence from Mexico." Mexico City: Instituto Tecnológico Autónomo de México [Autonomous Technological Institute of Mexico], Department of Economics.

Levenson, Alec, and W. Maloney. 1988. "The Informal Sector, Firm Dynamics, and Institutional Participation." World Bank Policy Research Working Paper. Washington: World Bank.

Levy, Santiago. 2006a. *Progress against Poverty: Sustaining Mexico's Progresa-Oportunidades Program.* Brookings.

———. 2006b. "Productividad, Crecimiento, y Pobreza en México: Qué Sigue después de Progresa-Oportunidades?" [Productivity, Growth, and Poverty in Mexico: What Follows after Progresa-Oportunidades?] Washington: Inter-American Development Bank, Research Department.

———. 2006c. "Social Policy, Productivity, and Growth." Washington: Inter-American Development Bank, Research Department.

———. 2006d. "Social Security Reform in Mexico: For Whom?" Paper presented at the World Bank conference "Equity and Competition in Mexico." Mexico City, November 27–28.

Levy, Santiago, and M. Walton. 2007. "Equity and Growth in Mexico." Washington: World Bank, Latin American and Caribbean Region.

Lewis, William. 2004. *The Power of Productivity: Wealth, Poverty and the Threat to Global Stability.* University of Chicago Press.

Lopez-Acevedo, Gladys. 2006. "Determinants of Technology Adoption in Mexico." Washington: World Bank, Latin American and Caribbean Division.

Lopez-Acevedo, Gladys, and H. Tan. 2006. "Mexico: In-Firm Training for the Knowledge Economy." Washington: World Bank, Latin American and Caribbean Division.

Madero, David, and A. Mora. 2006. "Fomento a la Competencia entre las Administradoras de Fondos para el Retiro: Acciones y Resultados en México" [Promotion of Competition among Administrators of Retirement Funds: Actions and Results in Mexico], Documento de Trabajo 2006-1 [Working Paper 2006-1]. México: Comisión Nacional del Sistema de Ahorro para el Retiro, Coordinación General de Estudios Económicos [National Commission of the System of Retirement Saving, General Coordinating Agency for Economic Studies].

Maloney, William. 1999. "Does Informality Imply Segmentation in Urban Labor Markets? Evidence from Sectoral Transitions in Mexico." *World Bank Economic Review* 13, pp. 275–302.

———. 2004. "Informality Revisited." *World Development* 20, pp. 1–20.

Maloney, William, and J. Nuñez Mendez. 2004. "Measuring the Impact of Minimum Wages: Evidence from Latin America." In *Law and Employment: Lessons from Latin America and the Caribbean,* edited by J. Heckman and C. Pages. University of Chicago Press.

McKenzie, David, and C. Woodruff. 2003. "Do Entry Costs Provide an Empirical Basis for Poverty Traps? Evidence from Mexican Microenterprises." Bureau for Research in Economic Analysis and Development. University of California at San Diego, Department of Economics.

Navarro, Samuel, and P. Schrimpf. 2004. "The Importance of Being Formal: Testing for Segmentation in the Mexican Labor Market." University of Chicago, Department of Economics.

Roberts, Brian. 1991. "Employment Structure, Life Cycle, and Life Chances: Formal and Informal Sectors in Guadalajara." In *The Informal Economy,* edited by A. Portes, M. Castells, and L. A. Benton. John Hopkins University Press.

Rosenbaum, Paul R., and D. B. Rubin. 1983. "The Central Role of the Propensity Score in Observational Studies for Causal Effects." *Biometrika* 70, no. 1, pp. 41–55.

Secretaria de Salud [Ministry of Health]. 2006. *Anuario Estadistico 2005.* Mexico City: Secretaria de Salud y Servicios de Salud en los Estados [Ministry of Health and Health Services in the States].

Skoufias, Emmanuel, and V. di Maro. 2006. "Conditional Cash Transfers, Adult Work Incentives, and Poverty." World Bank Policy Research Working Paper 3973. Washington: World Bank.

Tokman, Victor. 1978. "An Exploration into the Nature of the Informal-Formal Sector Relationships." *World Development* 6, no. 9/10, pp. 1065–75.

World Bank. 2004. "How Well Do SME Programs Work? Evaluating Mexico's SME Programs Using Panel Firm Data." Research Report. Latin American and Caribbean Region. Washington.

———. 2005a. *Income Generation and Social Protection for the Poor.* Latin American and Caribbean Region. México.

———. 2005b. *World Development Report 2006: Equity and Development.* Washington.

———. 2007. *Informality: Exit and Exclusion.* Latin American and Caribbean Region. Washington.

World Bank–International Finance Corporation. 2006. *Doing Business in Mexico 2007.* Mexico City.

Young, Mary Eming, and L. Richardson. 2007. "Early Child Development: From Measurement to Action." Washington: World Bank.

# Index

Access to capital: intangible capital, 13; international flows, 217 n.8; recent economic growth patterns and, 2; self-employment and, 13; worker mobility and, 95

Adults over Seventy, 21, 27, 279, 280, 283

Afores, 218; aggregate savings, 217; commissions, 54–55; costs and benefits structure, 54–57; purpose, 18; rates of return, 218, 221; universal social entitlement program and, 268, 278; wage-based contributions, 278 n.30

Age demographics: frequency of formal employment entries and exits and, 103; future of pension system, 280; length of stay in formal employment and, 99; poor worker population, 78; Progresa-Oportunidades population, 225; social security enrollment, 97 n.13

Agricultural sector: land ownership among poor, 72–76; salaried and nonsalaried workers, 76–77; social policy–productivity linkage, 2; social security evasion in, 190–191. *See also* Urban-rural economies

Bosch, M., 35, 40, 113
Brazil, 90, 232
Budar-Mejía, O., 114

Calderón, A., 114
Chile, 90
Coase, R., 37–38
*Comisionistas,* 115, 206; definition and characteristics, 13, 14, 15; demand, 139–140; labor market composition, 33–34, 36, 86, 139, 201–204; possible mobility patterns of workers, 92–93, 95, 96

Comisión Nacional del Sistema del Ahorro par el Retiro (Consar), 18; worker mobility data, 108–111

Consumption taxes, to finance social entitlements, 5, 260, 261–262, 264, 265–267, 268–269, 272–273

Contractual nonsalaried labor, 13–14

Dávila, E., 40, 265, 266
Day care: access, 81, 82; current system, 271 n.15; poor workers' valuation of social programs, 81, 82; social program resources, 29–30; social protection benefits, 20, 21; social security benefits, 48; supply and demand, 54; universal social entitlement program, 271

Desarrollo Integral de la Familia, 21 n.16
De Soto, H., 37, 41, 198
Domestic servants, 206 n.35

Economic dimension: of formal *vs.* informal employment, 36–37; integration with social dimension in social policy reform, 285; of social programs, 3

Economic growth: causes of slow growth, 2; efficiency losses from informality and, 223–224; forced domestic saving and, 216–217; impact of social programs on firm investment behavior and, 213; informal employment and, 4, 5, 208, 215, 219–223, 288–289; jobless growth, 223; labor force composition and, 221–223; recent patterns, 1; significance of formal-informal segmentation, 45–46, 288; significance of Mexico's policies and experiences, 9–10; social policy rationale, 219; social policy reform rationale, 289–290; social program linkage, 1–3, 5–6, 43, 208, 220, 221; social program outcomes, 253; universal social entitlement and, 258

Educational attainment: current labor force, 226; labor wage rate and mobility patterns, 117; poor worker population, 78; rates of return, 231

Educational system: causes of slow economic growth, 2; Progresa-Oportunidades outcomes, 225–226; Progresa-Oportunidades subsidies, 22

Efficiency costs: informality and, 223–224; social programs, 157–163, 253, 259–260; social security evasion, 173–174; tax policy and, 155–156; universal social entitlement, 259–260

Elderly population: Progresa-Oportunidades benefits, 23. *See also* Adults over Seventy; Age demographics

Employment patterns and trends: causes of slow growth, 2; international comparison, 88–90; recent experience, 1; social policy linkage, 2, 43. *See also* Labor market

Employment relationship, 11–12

Encuesta Nacional de Empleo Urbano, 111–114

Energy costs: oil rents, 251; Progresa-Oportunidades benefits, 23; recent economic growth patterns and, 2

Entrepreneurship, 215–216, 218. *See also* Self-employed workers

Fajnzylber, P., 214

Federal Labor Law, 67

Firing and severance pay regulation. *See* Severance regulation

First Job program, 234–235, 239–240

Formal employment: average length of stay, 98–100; barriers to, 40, 42, 94, 107, 113–114, 130; cost to firms, 177–178; definition and characteristics, 33–34, 36–37; effects of fully valued social security, 144–147; effects of incompletely valued social security, 147–150; effects of social protection programs, 151–155; evolution of employment status distribution, 90; firm investment behavior, 208–211; frequency of entry and exit, 100–107; government subsidy of labor costs, 236–237, 238–239; implications for social policy design, 43–44, 135; inadequacy of formal-informal model, 253; labor costs, 40, 129; labor market composition, 85–88; labor mobility and, 8, 42; mixed formal-informal firms, 38–39; new job creation and labor force evolution, 220–223; outcomes of poverty reduction programs, 228–233; poor workers in, 71; possible mobility patterns of workers, 91–96; productivity, 37–38, 43, 156–157; productivity in absence of social programs, 142–143; recent mobility patterns of workers, 96–114; significance of labor market segmentation, 45–46; social policy effects, 4, 23–24, 175; social program efficiency costs, 160–163; tax policy, 7; under universal social entitlement, 259; wage rates, mobility and, 114–129; worker choices in absence of social programs, 143–144. *See also* Informal employment

García-Verdú, R., 114

Gender differences: labor wage rates and mobility, 126–127; length of stay in formal employment and, 99–100

Global economy: labor mobility and, 130–131; nonwage costs of labor, 176–177; productivity comparisons, 205

Gong, X., 113–114

Government subsidy: First Job program, 239–240; patterns, 248–250; productivity effects, 238; redistributive effects, 246–248, 255; social contribution for retirement, 54; social programs, 8, 27–32, 45; social protection, 20, 26; social security, 18, 26, 51–52, 234–240

Gross domestic product: costs of universal social entitlements program, 276, 278; efficiency costs of social programs, 160–163, 255; government subsidy to social programs, 238–239, 248; growth patterns, 221; per capita growth, 1; productivity differences between labor sectors and, 156–157; recent history, 248–251; redistributive effects of social programs, 245, 255; social program spending, 30–32, 154, 244; social protection health programs, 279; tax revenues, 266 n.10; worker mobility patterns and, 112–113, 114. *See also* Economic growth

Guha-Khasnobis, B., 34

Harris, J., 40

Health services and insurance: levels of care, 53 n.10; for poor workers, 20, 21; poor workers' valuation of social programs, 81; service delivery infrastructure, 53; social program resources, 29; social protection benefits, 20–21; social security coverage, 48; universal social entitlement, 270, 272, 277; workers' valuation of social protection, 61–63; workers' valuation of social security, 52–53

Heckman, J., 40

High-wage workers: frequency of formal employment entries and exits, 103–106, 114; labor market composition, 85–86; length of stay in formal employment, 98–100; valuation of social programs, 127–129. *See also* Wages

Housing: poor workers' valuation of social programs, 79–80; social program resources, 29; social protection benefits, 19, 21; social security benefits, 18–19, 48; universal social entitlement program, 270–273; workers' valuation of social protection benefits, 63; workers' valuation of social security benefits, 57–59

Hungary, 90

Illegal employment: composition of firm output and, 9, 199–207; cost of social programs and, 167–168; cost to firms, 7, 168–169, 178, 186, 187; demand for total labor within firms and, 193–196; determinants of firm behavior, 168–169, 173, 174, 177–179, 183–184, 193; determinants of worker behavior, 169–170; differences among firms, 167; economic efficiency, 173–174; economic significance, 175–176; effects on wages, 172–173, 175; enforcement, 191–192; enforcement costs, 181–183; extent, 107, 167, 168, 237–238, 255; firm investment decisions in informal and formal sectors and, 209–211; implications for government social objectives, 174; international comparison of employment status, 89–90; labor market composition, 86, 87–88, 170–172; motivation, 166–167; poor workers in, 172, 191; productivity effects, 37, 167, 173, 192, 196; punishment, 168, 174, 178 nn.12–14, 183, 184; reduced cost of governance, 167–168; registration costs for firms and, 197–198; size distribution of firms and, 9, 179–193; social norms, 181–184, 190–192; social policy linkage, 41, 175–176; social program and firm size interaction with, 190–194, 205–206; social protection policy coverage, 169, 171–172, 190–192; tradable goods sector and, 206–207

IMSS. *See* Instituto Mexicano del Seguro Social

Income redistribution: goals of Progresa-Oportunidades, 3–4; government subsidy of social programs and, 8, 255; housing loan effects, 59; illegal employment and, 192–193; incomplete valuation of social security and, 150; social policy and, 4, 243–252; social protection effects, 154; social security effects, 146–147; strategies for improving social policy, 5, 6; universal social entitlement program, 260–263, 272–273

Income tax law, 275 n.24

Infonavit. *See* Instituto del Fondo Nacionale de la Vivienda para los Trabajadores

Informal employment: conceptual economic models, 40–41; definition and characteristics, 33, 34–37, 38–40, 41–42; domestic savings behavior, 216–219; economic growth and, 4, 5, 208, 215, 219–223, 288–289; economic significance of segmentation, 45–46; effects of fully valued social security, 144–147; effects of incompletely valued social security, 147–150; effects of social protection, 151–55; efficiency losses, 223–224; evolution of employment status distribution, 90; firm investment behavior, 208–211, 220; fiscal implications, 242–243; future prospects, 256; government subsidy of labor costs, 236–237, 238–239; high status in, 39; impact of social programs on firm investment behavior and, 211, 213–214; implications for social policy design, 43–44, 135; inadequacy of formal-informal model, 253; labor costs, 40, 129; labor market composition, 85–88; labor mobility and, 8, 39, 42; legal institutions and, 44–45; legality, 34, 35; mixed formal-informal firms, 38–39; new job creation and labor force evolution, 220–223; outcomes of poverty reduction programs, 228–233; poor workers in, 7–8, 163–164, 172; possible mobility patterns of workers, 91–96; productivity, 4, 7, 8, 37–38, 43, 149, 156–157; productivity in absence of social programs, 142–143; property rights regime and, 41; recent mobility patterns of workers, 96–114; size of firm and, 34, 214; social policy outcomes, 4, 23–24, 44, 175; social program efficiency costs, 160–163; transaction costs, 37–38; under universal social entitlement, 259; voluntary affiliation with social security plan, 61; wage rates and mobility patterns, 114–129; worker choices in absence of social programs, 143–144. See also Formal employment; Mobility of labor; Social protection
Instituto del Fondo Nacionale de la Vivienda para los Trabajadores (Infonavit): function, 18; loan allocation patterns, 58, 59, 80, 82, 221; rate of return, 221; resources, 29–30; universal social entitlement program and, 268, 286; workers' valuation of benefits, 57–59
Instituto de Seguridad y Servicios Sociales de los Trabajadores del Estado, 86
Instituto Mexicano del Seguro Social (IMSS): day care services, 271 n.15; employees of, 42; enforcement, 181–183, 184; enrollment patterns, 1 n.1, 96–111; job creation statistics, 195 n.27; purpose, 18; statutory versus actual benefits, 51–54; universal social entitlement program and, 268, 287
Intangible capital assets, 13
International Labor Office, 40
Investment behavior by firms: deterrents to worker training, 232; formal-informal segmentation, 208–211; impact of social programs, 208, 211–214, 220; poverty reduction strategies, 231–232

Labor market: classification in universal social entitlement program, 257–258; composition and structure, 11–16, 33, 85–88, 139, 163, 175, 200, 201, 221; demand, 136–142, 193–196, 222; determinants of employers' hiring choices, 134; determinants of workers' employment choices, 134; effects of fully valued social security, 144–147; effects of incompletely valued social security, 147–150; effects of Progresa-Oportunidades, 228; effects of social protection programs, 151–155; effects of social security evasion, 170–172, 175–176; employment relationship, 11–12; evolution of employment status distribution, 90; formal-informal segmentation, 4, 6–7, 8, 42–43, 129, 132; international comparison of employment status, 88–90; new job creation, 110, 195 n.27, 220–221; possible mobility patterns of workers, 91–96; productivity in absence of social programs, 142–143; Progresa-Oportunidades outcomes, 225–226; social benefit eligibility, 17; social program distortions, 45, 175, 176; urban-rural distinctions, 15–16; workers' employment choices in absence of social programs, 143–144; workers without remuneration, 14

Labor regulation: costs of salaried labor, 24–26; definition of informal employment, 34–35; legality of informal employment, 34, 35; recent economic growth patterns and, 2; as social policy, 3 n.4; as social program, 24; workers' valuation of, 59–61. *See also* Severance regulation

Land ownership: access to profitable investment projects and, 75; among poor workers, 72–76; future prospects, 75; irrigated land, 73–74; tenure system, 72

Legal institutions: formal-informal segmentation and, 44–45; universal social entitlement program and, 291

Levy, S., 265, 266

Life insurance: social protection benefits, 20; universal social entitlements, 272, 277

López-Acevedo, G., 214–215

Low-wage workers: frequency of formal employment entries and exits, 103–106, 114; labor market composition, 85–86; length of stay in formal employment, 98, 99–100; valuation of social programs, 127–129. *See also* Wages

Maloney, W., 35, 40, 113, 214

Manufacturing sector, 201

Marginal cost of labor, 178, 197–198

Marginal product of labor, 156, 196, 238

McKinsey Global Institute, 205, 232

Microenterprises: informality, 214; investment project design, 215–216; poverty reduction programs, 230; worker investment in, 217–218; worker training in, 214–215

Migration: employment patterns and, 95; labor mobility data, 129–130; patterns, 72; workers' valuation of social programs and, 51

Minimum wages: informal employment and, 41, 42; minimum pension guarantees, 57, 83 n.10; patterns, 94 n.10

Mobility of labor: barriers to formal employment, 40, 42, 94, 107, 113–114, 130; current Mexican economy, 42, 130; data sources, 129–130; definition, 39; determinants, 96, 120, 131, 134–135; evidence from employee surveys, 111–114; evidence from social security registries,

96–111; frequency of entry and exit, 100–107; implications for social policy, 131–133; informality and, 39, 42; length of stay in formal employment, 98–100; for low-wage workers, 42; possible patterns, 91–96; recent patterns, 96–97; relevant incidence analysis, 244–245; retirement savings and, 132–133; salaried and nonsalaried work, 129; self-employed persons, 139; short-term influences, 130–131; significance of, in Mexico, 8; social security evasion, 107; transition to and from salaried work, 15, 42; wages and, 82, 98, 99–100, 103–106, 114–129

Montes Rojas, G., 214

National Council for Social Protection, 21–22

National Survey of Urban Employment, 111–114

Navarro, S., 114

New job creation, 110, 195 n.27, 220–222

Nonsalaried labor: in absence of formal-informal dichotomy, 161; costs, 133, 166–167; definition and scope, 12–14, 15; demand, 140; inefficiencies, 14; labor market composition, 87; poor worker population, 77, 82; transition to and from salaried work, 15; in universal social entitlement program, 257–258; valuation of social programs, 63–66, 68–69; voluntary affiliation with social security plan, 61; wage rates and mobility patterns, 129. *See also* Informal employment; Social protection

North American Free Trade Agreement, 130

Pagés, C., 40

Peso crisis (1994-95), 4 n.5, 130, 222–223

Poland, 90

Poor workers: barriers to formal employment, 208; cost of forced savings for, 79–81; cost of social protection programs, 20–21; formal-informal employment, 71, 82, 228–229; housing loan access, 80; labor market composition, 88, 163, 172; land ownership, 72–76; migration patterns, 72; nonsalaried workers, 77; population statistics, 4 n.5, 72, 76, 78; productivity, 164, 231; social benefit eligibility, 17; social programs in perpetuation of poverty, 84, 164; social security coverage, 77; social security evasion, 77–78, 88, 191; training for labor status advancement, 78–79; under universal social entitlement program, 259, 273; valuation of social programs, 7, 79–84, 163–165. *See also* Poverty reduction programs; Progresa-Oportunidades

Poverty reduction programs: challenges, 226–227; opportunities for improvement, 5, 164–165, 227–229, 231–232, 233; social policy effects, 4, 6, 7–8, 164, 225, 228–229, 255–256; universal social entitlement model, 259, 273. *See also* Progresa-Oportunidades

Productivity: causes of slow growth, 2; cost disadvantage of salaried labor, 25–26; firm size and, 196–197, 204; formal-informal segmentation of labor market and, 4, 7, 8, 37–38, 42, 43, 45, 141–142, 156–157, 158; government subsidy of social security and, 238; illegal employment and, 37, 167, 173, 192, 196; impact of social programs on capital investment and, 211–214; international comparison, 205; outcomes of current poverty reduction programs, 229–230; poor workers in informal employment, 164, 231; recent patterns, 1; social policy linkage, 2–3, 4, 70, 135; social policy outcomes, 253, 255; social policy reform rationale, 289–290; in universal social entitlement program, 258, 259–260, 262; workers' valuation of social protection and, 151–152, 154; workers' valuation of social security and, 146, 148–149; worker training and, 232. *See also* Efficiency costs

Profit sharing, 25

Programa de Atención a Adultos Mayores de Setenta Años, 21

Progresa-Oportunidades: age distribution of beneficiaries, 225; beneficiaries, 17, 71, 78, 88; benefits for elderly, 23; distinctive features, 22; educational subsidies, 22; effectiveness, 225–226; energy cost subsidies, 23; funding, 26, 27; health insurance access, 20, 22; incentive

incompatibility with social programs, 4, 23–24, 255–256; labor status eligibility, 23; population characteristics, 71–72, 78; purpose, 3–4, 17, 22; retirement account, 22–23; shortcomings, 229–230, 233; strategies for improving, 5, 164–165, 227–228, 232–233; universal social entitlement and, 259, 286

Property rights regime, 208–209; bank lending behavior and, 2; informality and, 44; models of informality, 41

Public sector workers, 86–87

Redistributive effects. *See* Income redistribution

Registration of firms: costs, 198; illegal employment and, 197–198; patterns, 180–181, 252 n.11; transition to universal social entitlements, 287

Relevant incidence analysis, 244–245

Retirement: Afore system, 54–57; demographic trends and, 280; funding, 26–27; government subsidy, 54; implications of worker mobility, 132–133; market competitiveness, 54 n.12; minimum pension, 57; noncontributory pensions, 218–219, 280–283; poor workers' savings patterns, 79–80; social protection benefits, 19; social security benefits, 18–19, 48; social security costs, 51–52; universal social entitlement, 270, 271–272, 280–283; voluntary contributions to savings account, 57; worker mobility patterns and, 108–111; workers' valuation of social protection programs, 63; workers' valuation of social security benefits, 51

Salaried labor: in absence of formal-informal dichotomy, 161; costs, 25–26, 133, 166–167, 185–190, 235; definition, 11–12, 14, 15; demand, 140–142; health insurance access, 20–21; international comparison of employment status, 88–90; labor market composition, 12, 87; labor regulation burden, 24–26; poor worker population, 76–77, 82; transition to and from nonsalaried work, 15; in universal social entitlement program, 257–258; valuation of social programs,

63–66, 68–69; wage rates and mobility patterns, 129. *See also* Formal employment; Illegal employment; Social security

Savings behavior: informal employment and, 216–219; noncontributory pensions and, 219

Schimpf, P., 114

Seguro Popular, 20, 21, 23, 61, 279

Seguro Universal de Primera Generación, 21, 61

Self-employed workers: definition and scope, 12–14; demand, 136–139; high status, 39; intangible capital assets, 13; investment project design, 215–216; labor market composition, 12, 86, 88, 139, 201–204; savings investment behavior, 217–218; transition to and from salaried work, 15, 139; under universal social entitlement program, 259; wages, 115, 136–138

Severance regulation: costs of, 24–25, 45; economic significance of, 175; regulatory framework, 24; universal social entitlement program, 273–274; workers' valuation of, 59–61

Share croppers, 13–14

Size of firm: cost of salaried labor, 185–190; expected outcomes of universal social entitlement model, 258; illegal employment and, 179–193; informal sector characteristics, 34, 214; investment project design, 215–216; labor wage rate and mobility patterns, 117; large firms, 187, 188; patterns, 38, 181, 200, 201; productivity, 196–197, 204; technology adoption and, 214; transaction costs, 38; worker training and, 214–215

Social dimension of social programs, 3; integration with economic dimension in social policy reform, 285

Social enterprises, 230 n.17

Social programs: current deficiencies, 3, 68, 69, 82, 131–132, 255–256; definition and scope, 3, 11, 255; economic behavior in response to, 9; economic dimension, 3, 255; economic growth linkage, 1–3, 5–6, 208, 220, 221, 253; effects on wages, 175, 176, 211; efficiency costs, 160–163, 223–224, 253, 255, 259–260; employees of, 279 n.31; entitlement pro-

grams, 20 n.12; firm investment behavior and, 208, 211–214; firm size and illegal employment interactions with, 190–194; fiscal implications, 234, 240–243; funding, 8, 26–32, 160, 245; government objectives, 68–69, 135, 245–248, 253–255; government spending, 244, 248–251; implications of labor mobility, 131–133; importance of goal setting for, 47; inequitable delivery, 82; informal employment and, 288–289; interactions among, 10; international comparison, 176–177; labor force composition and, 16–17, 175, 176; labor market productivity without, 142–144; labor market segmentation and, 4, 6–7, 8, 17, 23–24, 43–44, 175; labor regulations as, 24; opportunities for improvement, 3, 5, 6, 160; origins and growth, 1, 66–68; policy design challenges, 224; poor workers' access, 82; poverty reduction and, 4, 6, 84, 164, 228–229, 255–256; productivity linkage, 4, 70, 135, 156; productivity outcomes, 253, 255; purpose, 2–3, 255; redistributive effects, 243–252; reform rationale, 253–256, 289–290; relevant incidence analysis, 244–245; self-employment market wages and, 138; significance of, in Mexican economy, 289–290; significance of labor status distribution, 135; significance of Mexico's policies and experiences, 9–10; social dimension, 3, 253–255; sustainability, 253; transition to and from salaried work and, 139; transition to universal social entitlements, 283–288; workers' valuation, 61–66, 68. *See also* Social protection; Social security; Universal social entitlements

Social protection: administrative structure, 21–22; aggregate domestic savings and, 216–217; cost to beneficiaries, 20–21; coverage for illegal salaried workers, 169, 171–172; definition and scope, 3, 11, 16, 19–20, 255; effects on labor market, 151–155; efficiency costs, 157–160; fiscal implications, 241, 242; formal-informal segmentation of labor and, 6–7; funding, 20, 26, 27–32, 154, 221, 238–239; government social objectives for, 154–155; health programs, 61–63; housing program, 63; poverty reduction and, 7–8, 227–229; productivity and, 151–152, 154; rationale, 219; recent growth, 21–22; redistributive effects, 154; retirement savings program, 63; self-reinforcing nature of Mexican policy, 240; social security evasion and, 190–192; as subsidy to nonsalaried labor, 45; valuation by worker, 7, 43, 82; wages and, 152–154. *See also* Social programs

Social security: account structure and administration, 18–19; aggregate domestic savings and, 216–217; benefit design, 17–18, 47–48; definition and scope, 3, 11; design problems, 50–51; evasion incentive, 166–167, 168–169, 221; fiscal implications, 240–241, 242; formal-informal segmentation of labor and, 6–7; frequency of evasion, 107, 167, 168, 237–238, 255; funding, 19, 26, 27–32, 51–52, 146, 147; government subsidy, 8, 18, 234–240, 242; legal entitlement, 16; obligation to enroll, 48–49; poor workers' coverage, 77; poor workers' evasion, 77–78; population coverage, 87–88, 255; poverty reduction and, 227–229; public sector workers, 86–87; purpose, 48; redistributive effects, 146–147; retirement savings system, 54–57; strategies for improving, 5; voluntary affiliation from nonsalaried workers, 61. *See also* Illegal employment; Social programs; Workers' valuation of social security

Social Security Law, 67, 97

Soest, A., 113–114

Support for Older Adults, 23, 280

Sustainability of social programs, 253

Tax policy: causes of slow economic growth, 2; current percent of GDP, 266 n.10; efficiency costs, 155–156, 158; financing universal social entitlements, 260, 261–262, 264, 265–267, 268–269, 271, 272–273, 275, 278, 287; fines for social security evasion, 168; formal-informal segmentation of labor and, 7, 88; government subsidy of social programs, 8; labor

taxes, 25; revenue patterns, 248–251; strategies for improving social policy, 5; tax on firm's profits, 177–178

Technology adoption, firm size and, 214

Telecommunications cost, 2

Todaro, M., 40

Trade, illegal employment and, 206–207

Transaction costs of informal employment, 37–38

Transportation sector, 201

Unemployment insurance, 24 n.23, 94 n.8; universal social entitlement program, 274, 277, 287

Unemployment rate, 87, 90, 93–94

Unions, educational system performance and, 2

Universal social entitlements: administrative feasibility, 267–269; aggregate productivity in, 258, 262; benefits package, 269–276; conceptual basis, 256; core proposal, 256–259; cost of labor, 258–259; costs, 276–280; economic growth outcomes, 258; efficiency costs, 259–260; financing, 260–269, 271, 275; firing and severance pay regulation and, 273–274; formal-informal dichotomy under, 259; implementation strategy, 283–288; implications for size of firms, 258; labor force classification, 257–258; noncontributory pensions and, 280–283; objectives, 256, 274, 290–291; poverty reduction under, 259, 273; program designs, 256; redistribution objectives, 256, 263; redistributive outcomes, 263–267, 272–273; rule of law and, 291; salary-specific entitlements, 273–274; wage outcomes, 258, 259; without income redistribution, 260–263

Unpaid workers, 14

Urban-rural economies: labor mobility data, 129–130; labor wage rate and mobility patterns, 117; land ownership patterns, 72–76; significance of, 15–16; social program infrastructure, 61–63, 82; social security evasion, 77–78. *See also* Agricultural employment

Value-added taxes, 265–267

Vertical integration, 38, 189

Villagomez, E., 113–114

Wages: *comisionista* rates, 139–140; cost of illegal salaried labor, 168–169, 170–171; costs of firing and severance pay regulations, 25; effects of incompletely valued social security, 147–148, 149; effects of social programs, 175, 211; effects of social protection, 152–154; effects of social security evasions, 172–173, 175; formal employment, 117–121, 128, 149; government subsidy, 235; housing loan access and, 58, 59, 80; informal employment, 39, 117–121, 128; new job creation and, 222; non-wage costs of labor, 235; Progresa-Oportunidades goals, 226; rates of return to education, 231; for self-employed workers, 136–138; social security contributions, 19; universal social entitlement program outcomes, 258, 259; worker mobility patterns and, 114–129; workers' employment choices, 134. *See also* High-wage workers; Low-wage workers; Minimum wages

Workers' valuation of labor regulation, 59–61

Workers' valuation of social protection, 61–66; patterns of formal and informal employment and, 83; poor workers, 79, 82, 163–165; wage rates and, 127–129; worker's employment choice, 134–135

Workers' valuation of social security: accumulated time in formal employment and, 82–84; bundling of benefits and, 50, 51; determinants, 61, 79; effects of incompletely valued benefits, 147–150; effects of with fully valued benefits, 144–147; evasion rationale, 167, 169–170, 172; formal-informal sector differences, 63–66; government objectives and, 48–50, 68; household composition and, 50–51; housing benefits, 57–59; at less than its cost, 50; patterns of formal and informal employment and, 83; poor workers, 7, 79, 82, 83–84, 163–165; productivity and, 146, 148–149, 156–157; retirement savings accounts, 56–57; service delivery infrastructure and, 79; significance of, 43, 47; statutory versus actual benefits, 51–61, 79; wage rates and, 127–129; workers' employment choices, 134–135

Worker training: deterrents to, 232; poor workers, 78–79; productivity and, 232; size of firm and, 214–215

World Bank, 197